TEACHING CHILDREN SCIENCE

A PROJECT-BASED APPROACH

TEACHING CHILDREN SCIENCE

A PROJECT-BASED APPROACH

Joseph S. Krajcik
The University of Michigan

Charlene M. Czerniak
The University of Toledo

Carl Berger
The University of Michigan

McGraw-Hill College

Boston   Burr Ridge, IL   Dubuque, IA   Madison, WI   New York   San Francisco   St. Louis
Bangkok   Bogotá   Caracas   Lisbon   London   Madrid
Mexico City   Milan   New Delhi   Seoul   Singapore   Sydney   Taipei   Toronto

McGraw-Hill College

A Division of The **McGraw·Hill** *Companies*

TEACHING CHILDREN SCIENCE: A PROJECT-BASED APPROACH

Copyright © 1999 by The McGraw-Hill Companies, Inc. All rights reserved. Printed in the United States of America. Except as permitted under the United States Copyright Act of 1976, no part of this publication may be reproduced or distributed in any form or by any means, or stored in a data base or retrieval system, without the prior written permission of the publisher.

 This book is printed on recycled, acid-free paper containing 10% postconsumer waste.

3 4 5 6 7 8 9 0 QPD/QPD 9 3 2 1

ISBN 0–07–036007–3

Editorial director: *Jane E. Vaicunas*
Sponsoring editor: *Beth Kaufman*
Developmental editor: *Cara Harvey*
Senior marketing manager: *Daniel M. Loch*
Project manager: *Cathy Ford Smith*
Production supervisor: *Deborah Donner*
Freelance design coordinator: *Mary L. Christianson*
Senior photo research coordinator: *Lori Hancock*
Supplement coordinator: *Sandra M. Schnee*
Compositor: *Shepherd, Inc.*
Typeface: *10/12 Veljovic Book*
Printer: *Quebecor Printing Book Group/Dubuque, IA*

Freelance cover designer: *Jamie O'Neal*
Cover photographs: © *David Young-Wolff/PhotoEdit*

The credits section for this book begins on page 334 and is considered an extension of the copyright page.

Library of Congress Cataloging-in-Publication Data

Krajcik, Joseph.
   Teaching children science : a project-based approach / Joseph Krajcik, Charlene Czerniak, Carl Berger. — 1st ed.
     p.   cm.
   Includes index.
   ISBN 0–07–036007–3
   1. Science—Study and teaching—Methodology. I. Czerniak, Charlene. II. Berger, Carl. III. Title.
Q181.K73 1999
507.1—dc21   98–39798
                                      CIP

www.mhhe.com

ABOUT THE AUTHORS

Joseph S. Krajcik, a Professor of Science Education in the School of Education at the University of Michigan, focuses his research on designing science classrooms so that students engage in finding solutions to meaningful, real world questions through collaboration and the use of learning technologies. His working philosophy is that such learning environments will help students develop deep understanding of content as well as strategies for generating new comprehension. Professor Krajcik has authored and co-authored over 60 articles or chapters in books. His publications have appeared in *The Journal of Research in Science Teaching, Elementary School Journal,* the *Journal of Computers in Mathematics and Science Education,* the *Educational Researcher,* and the *Journal of Learning Sciences.* Professor Krajcik makes frequent presentations at national and regional conferences that focus on his research as well as presentations that translate research findings into classroom practice. His principal teaching responsibilities include graduate science education and science education methods. He is an active member of the National Association of Research in Science Teaching and reviews manuscripts for a number of journals. His colleagues have recognized his leadership abilities by recently selecting him to be President of NARST, the National Association for Research on Science Teaching. Prior to his work at the collegiate level, he taught high school chemistry.

Charlene M. Czerniak is currently a professor at The University of Toledo. She received her Ph.D. in education from The Ohio State University. A former elementary teacher, she has authored and co-authored over 35 articles. She has also published two chapters in books and illustrated 12 children's science education books. Her publications have appeared in *The Journal of Research in Science Teaching, Journal of Science Teacher Education, School Science and Mathematics, Science Scope,* and *Science and Children.* Professor Czerniak has been the author and director of numerous grant-funded projects that targeted professional development of science teachers. She has made frequent presentations at national and regional conferences focusing on her research interest concerning teachers' beliefs about teaching science. Professor Czerniak's areas of specialty also include professional development for elementary and middle grade teachers, science education reform, and school improvement. She is an active member in the National Association of Research in Science Teaching, the Association for Education of Teachers of Science, the School Science and Mathematics Association, and the National Science Teachers Association and reviews manuscripts for a number of journals associated with these organizations. Her colleagues have recognized her leadership ability by recently electing her to be President of the School Science and Mathematics Association.

Carl Berger is a Professor of Science and Technology Education at the University of Michigan. A former public school teacher, he is a co-author of the *Science Curriculum Improvement Study*, the *Modular Program in Science*, and *Science*, all elementary school science series. His research focuses on understanding how students use technology with concepts and processes to develop deep understanding. He has authored and co-authored over 150 books, chapters in books, and articles. His work has appeared in *The Journal of Research in Science Teaching, Science Education, Science and Children, The Grade Teacher, Magazine for Elementary Teachers, Science Activities, Journal of Educational Computing and Educational Technology*. He is a lifetime member of the National Science Teachers Association, and a member of the National Association for Research in Science Teaching. He has been recognized for his work by election as Science Educator of the Year in Michigan, President of the National Association for Research in Science Teaching, and most recently, he was bestowed the award for Distinguished Contributions to Science Education through Research by the National Association for Research in Science Teaching.

PREFACE

This book presents an approach to teaching science to all children. We believe that all children should develop an indepth and meaningful understanding of unifying concepts, principles, and themes of science as well as the processes of science. We define understanding as helping students to see relationships among ideas, to find underlying reasons for these relationships, to use these ideas to explain and predict phenomena, and to apply their understandings to new situations. Such a focus on science learning emphasizes less the coverage of content, but more the indepth exploration of major ideas. Moreover, we strongly believe that all students should understand and know how to apply the process of scientific inquiry. Finally, we firmly believe that all students should have equitable opportunities to learn science. In this book, *Teaching Children Science: A Project-Based Approach,* we focus on helping both the novice and experienced teacher learn how to teach science to elementary and middle school children.

To accomplish the goal of helping both the new and experienced teacher learn how to teach science, we present an exciting teaching method referred to as project-based science. A central tenet of this approach is that it engages young learners in exploring important and meaningful questions through a process of investigation and collaboration. Project-based science engages children in asking and refining questions; seeking background information; making predictions; designing investigations; collecting, analyzing, and interpreting data; making explanations; and making products to share ideas. Project-based science stresses that science teaching should emphasize students actively engaging in science rather than teachers giving science information to students. The teaching of science should de-emphasize the simple recall of facts and focus on students using evidence and strategies for developing and revising explanations of phenomena. As a result, students learn fundamental science concepts and principles that they apply to their daily lives. As stated in the *National Science Education Standards,* inquiry should be the preferred mode of instruction at all grade levels and for all students. "Learning science is something students do, not something that is done to them" (NRC, 1996). The approach we take helps meet these National Standards.

Although intended primarily for university students studying to become elementary and middle school teachers, this book is also very suitable for practicing teachers striving to find new, exciting approaches to science teaching. Throughout this book, we strive to answer important questions about teaching science to children. We have included numerous strategies to support students in inquiry learning that will help both new and experienced teachers. We also pay attention to the important role collaboration plays in inquiry and in developing an understanding of science. Although teaching science to elementary and middle grades students is complex, it is also very rewarding.

The various chapters in the book focus on helping students learn science through inquiry as well as providing support in planning and managing science teaching. In Chapter 1, Why and How Should I Teach Science to Children?, we introduce you to project-based science. Chapter 2, How Do Children Construct Understanding in Science?, focuses on the special characteristics of children and the role of development on learning science. Chapter 3, What Is a Driving Question?, is an important chapter because driving questions are critical to initiating, implementing, and sustaining inquiry. In Chapter 4, How Are Scientific Investigations Developed?, we explore how to help students engage in investigations and find solutions to questions that are of interest to them. In Chapter 5, How Do I Develop Collaboration in the Science Classroom?, we discuss types of collaboration between students, teachers, and members of the community. Chapter 6, How Do I Develop and Use Benchmark Lessons?, focuses on methods and procedures a teacher can use to help students learn fundamental science concepts. In Chapter 7, How Is Student Understanding Assessed?, we discuss the purpose of assessment in a science classroom. Characteristics of assessment are presented and benefits are discussed. In Chapter 8, How Do I Manage the Project-Based Science Classroom?, we discuss classroom climate, classroom organization, and management skills. Chapter 9, How Do I Plan a Project-Based Curriculum?, explains ways that teachers can plan projects that meet school district's curricular objectives and frameworks. In Chapter 10, What Are the Next Steps?, we summarize features of project-based science, and we discuss benefits and challenges associated with a project environment.

ACKNOWLEDGEMENTS

The ideas in the book would not have been possible without the innovative thinking of colleagues at the University of Michigan and The University of Toledo. We owe much of the theoretical work to Phyllis Blumenfeld, Ron Marx, and Elliot Soloway at The University of Michigan. These educational researchers have worked with Joe to help identify, explore, and expand the ideas of project-based learning. Much of their work in developing the ideas of project-based learning was supported by funding from the National Science Foundation. Colleagues at the University of Toledo inspired Charlene's writing and ideas.

We would also like to acknowledge the many teachers who have expanded our ideas on teaching project-based science. Appreciated are the teachers at Greenhills Middle School—Ann Novak and Chris Gleason—who helped expand Joe's views of supporting students in inquiry within and across projects. We are also appreciative of the teachers of Community High School in Ann Arbor—Mike Mouradian, Liz Stern, Madeline Drake, and Kathy Hette—for allowing us to try out new technology ideas to support project learning. Finally, we appreciate teachers Conney Harvey and Betty Hopkins from Willow Run Public Schools District and Karen Amatia and Deborah Peek-Brown from Detroit Public Schools who pioneered using project-based science in urban settings. The contributions of Jon Singer, a post-doctorate fellow at the University of Michigan, helped expand Joe's thinking about assessment in a project-based environment and ideas to contextualize projects. Our thanks are also extended to the following reviewers for their comments on this text: Nancy W. Brickhouse, University of Delaware; James A. Shymansky, University of Iowa; Andrew Anderson, Michigan State University; Larry E. Schafer, Syracuse University; Meghan Twiest, Indiana University of Pennsylvania; John T. Norman, Wayne State University; William W. Cohen, Western Michigan University; William J. Boone, Indiana University at Bloomington; and Norman E. Dee, Lesley College.

We want to acknowledge the many graduate students who have worked with us and who have expanded our thinking about teaching and learning. In particular we would like to acknowledge from The University of Michigan Barbara Crawford, Margaret Roy, Michele Wisnudel-Spitulnik, and Barbara Ladewski.

Finally, we would like to thank the many undergraduate and graduate students in elementary and middle grades education at The University of Toledo who field tested and used chapters of this book as it was being written. These students provided many suggestions for describing classroom scenarios, improving ideas in the book, and revising activities. They also conducted their own project-based investigations and helped shape ideas presented in the book.

We also want to acknowledge Lane Akers' involvement. Lane initially approached and convinced us that this book could make an important contribution to the teaching and learning of science. His involvement helped shape the structure of this book at the beginning of this project. We also want to thank our current editors and project managers, Cathy Smith, Cara Harvey, and Beth Kaufman, for encouraging us to complete this work. Finally, we want to thank our families who encouraged us in this effort by allowing us to spend numerous extra hours on the writing of the book when we could have been with them. Thanks go to Joe's family—wife, Ann and children Michael, Paul, and Ellen; Charlene's husband, David; and Carl's wife, Shari.

BRIEF CONTENTS

CONTENTS

TEACHING CHILDREN SCIENCE

A PROJECT-BASED APPROACH

Chapter 1

WHY AND HOW SHOULD I TEACH SCIENCE TO CHILDREN?

OVERVIEW OF THE BOOK

When you think about the prospect of teaching science to children, many questions probably come to your mind. What characterizes science in elementary and middle grades? How should science be taught to young learners? How can I motivate children to become interested in science? How can I help them learn about science in their everyday world?

Helping children learn about their world is one of the primary goals of science education in schools today. Helping you learn how to teach science to elementary and middle school children is the goal of this book. Throughout this book, we will attempt to answer questions that you might have about teaching science to children. Although teaching science to young students is complex, it is also very rewarding.

To accomplish this goal of helping you learn how to teach science, we present an exciting science teaching method that we refer to as *project-based science*. A central tenet of this approach is that it engages young learners in exploring important and meaningful questions through a process of investigation and collaboration. Throughout this dynamic process, students ask questions, make predictions, design investigations, collect and analyze data, make products, and share ideas. As a result, students learn fundamental science concepts and principles that they apply to their daily lives. Moreover, project-based science is an approach that helps all students—regardless of culture, race, or gender—engage in science learning.

The roots of project-based learning are found in the writings of many distinguished educators including John Dewey, Jerome Bruner, and Robert Karplus.[1] Elements of this approach also can be found in other forms of science teaching: inquiry-based learning, which focuses instruction on students using science process skills such as observing and interpreting data; science, technology, society (STS), which focuses instruction on issues related to societal problems; and problem-driven science, which focuses on science issues. Project-based science stands apart from these other forms of science teaching, however, in that it situates the learning of science in questions that children find meaningful, and, as a result, it shifts the responsibility of learning to the child. With this approach, the learner asks questions, makes decisions, designs plans, and creates products.

Support for this approach can be found in the works of contemporary educators including Ann Brown and colleagues (1994), Wolff-Michael Roth (1995), Phyllis Blumenfeld and colleagues (1991), and Richard Roup and colleagues (1992). This approach requires dynamic teaching methods that match the guidelines of today's major science education reports including *The National Science Education Standards* (National Research Council, 1996), *Project 2061: Science for All Americans* (Rutherford & Ahlgren, 1989), *Benchmarks for Science Literacy* (AAAS, 1993), and the National Science Teachers Association recommendations for elementary science (NSTA, 1991). At the end of this chapter, we will discuss more thoroughly how project-based science works with these national efforts.

Although it has a solid foundation in educational theory, project-based science represents a fundamental shift from how science is taught and learned in most classrooms today. While this approach already is being used successfully in many schools—such as in Detroit; Bellingham, Washington; Chicago; and Concord, Massachusetts—you may find this kind of science instruction quite different from what you have experienced in the past. Learning to teach in a way that is different from what you have experienced can be very difficult. As you work through this book, most likely you will be changing the way you think about science and science teaching. More importantly, you'll be changing the way you help students learn science. We will help you with these changes by providing strategies for helping children engage in inquiry involving important and worthwhile questions. Although this book does not provide teaching activities to help you learn science content, we do believe that content understanding is critical to effective sci-

---

1. John Dewey was the founder of the progressive education movement that encouraged students to be active learners. In the 1930s, the Lincoln School of Teachers College and other schools used real situations to help students ground their learning. Jerome Bruner, an education theorist, helped establish curriculum reform during the 1960s. His book *Toward a Theory of Instruction* set the stage for much of the modern direction of curricula today. Robert Karplus was a physicist who co-founded The Science Curriculum Improvement Study, a pioneer elementary science program of the 1960s. The program exists today in a third incarnation of the "hands-on, minds-on" movement of that era.

ence teaching. When appropriate throughout the chapters, we will refer to other references that cover science content or children's science activities.

Chapter 1, Why and How Should I Teach Science to Children? introduces you to project-based science. It also answers the question, "What is science?" and discusses why it is important for young children to learn fundamental concepts and principles as well as processes of science. This chapter also presents important information about current national goals in science education and illustrates how project-based science matches these initiatives.

Chapter 2, How Do Children Construct Understanding in Science? focuses on the characteristics of children and the connection with learning science. It pays close attention to factors that influence students' construction of understanding, including prior experiences, social interactions, and teachers. In addition, it discusses how technology can enhance learning.

Chapter 3, What Is a Driving Question? is an important chapter because driving questions are critical to initiating, implementing, and sustaining inquiry. This chapter explores characteristics and issues of driving questions. It provides answers to the questions "What are driving questions?," "Where do they come from?," and "What makes a good driving question?"

Investigation is an essential element of project-based science. Chapter 4, How Are Scientific Investigations Developed? explores how to help students engage in investigations and find solutions to questions that are of interest to them. It examines the various components of investigations, such as asking and refining questions, designing experiments, analyzing data, and presenting findings. It also discusses ways that a teacher can support inquiry and overcome the challenges of implementing investigations.

Collaboration in science teaching is frequently much more effective than individual learning. Chapter 5, How Do I Develop Collaboration in the Science Classroom? discusses types of collaboration among students, teachers, and members of the community. It presents ways that a teacher can create a collaborative environment, build students' social skills needed to sustain collaboration, hold students accountable during collaboration, and overcome challenges

that might arise while implementing collaborative groups.

Chapter 6, How Do I Develop and Use Benchmark Lessons? focuses on methods and procedures to help students learn fundamental science concepts. Benchmark lessons are teacher-directed classroom activities that help students develop understandings essential to project work. Topics covered include questioning strategies, instructional strategies (such as demonstrations and discrepant events), activities, and concept mapping.

Assessment is a critical step in the educational process. Chapter 7, How Is Student Understanding Assessed? discusses the purpose of assessment in a science classroom. It presents characteristics of assessment and discusses benefits. The chapter also presents numerous ideas about how to assess students' understanding, skills, and attitudes in science. Finally, it discusses the advantages for teachers, students, and parents of using various assessment strategies.

Managing an elementary and middle grades classroom is a challenging task. This is particularly true when teachers try out new ideas. For this reason, Chapter 8, How Do I Manage the Project-Based Science Classroom? discusses classroom climate, classroom organization, and management skills. It presents many practical strategies that teachers can use to manage students successfully as they engage in science learning.

Chapter 9, How Do I Plan a Project-Based Curriculum? explains ways that teachers can plan projects that meet school districts' curricular objectives and frameworks. It also shows how existing curriculum materials can be modified to fit in a project environment. Attention is given to integrating science across the curriculum. Finally, it discusses how teachers can find and manage resources.

Finally, Chapter 10, What Are the Next Steps? summarizes features of project-based science and discusses benefits and challenges associated with a project environment. The book concludes with self-reflection of principles and ideas explored throughout this book about teaching science to children.

Each of these chapters includes activities to help you engage in learning this exciting way to teach science. First, each chapter starts with several scenarios that are designed to help you envision various classroom scenes that we will discuss. Throughout the text, questions encourage you to stop and think about ideas before you continue to read. Other questions ask you to think about your own experiences as a student to help you construct an understanding of how to teach science. There are activities throughout each chapter that are designed to help you construct meaning from what you're reading. When you complete these activities, you will have portfolio products (or artifacts). You will look more closely at artifacts in Chapter 7, which concerns assessment, and you will re-examine these artifacts in Chapter 10.

Throughout the book, we discuss how technology can be used to teach science. For example, Chapter 2 discusses how technology enhances learning. Chapter 5 explores how technology can be used to enhance collaboration among members of a community. Chapter 7 introduces you to ways that technology can be used in assessment procedures.

INTRODUCTION TO THE CHAPTER

In this chapter, we introduce you to project-based science teaching. Later, we answer the question, "What is science?" We explore why it is important for young children to learn science, and we review the goals of science education. Finally, we discuss how project-based science matches today's science education goals.

First, however, to challenge your thinking about science and science teaching, we start this chapter by encouraging you to reflect on your own past experiences as a student of science. This reflection will help you examine your personal views of science teaching and learning. In Activity 1.1, you begin the portfolio that you will use throughout this book. Take time now to complete Activity 1.1.

As you reflected about your own experiences in Activity 1.1, you may have found that you did not have many memories of learning science, or you may have had good memories of science class. Maybe you did hands-on activities. Perhaps your teacher was very excited about teaching science. By studying science, you may have learned about important questions related to your world. Your memories may not have been

positive ones; science may have been presented as dull, boring, or difficult to learn. Perhaps your out-of-school memories about science learning, such as that second grade field trip to the zoo, were the strongest and most positive. The literature shows that many of us did not experience learning science in a dynamic and active manner that includes asking questions, collaborating with others to find solutions, and designing investigations (NRC, 1996; Stake & Easley, 1978). As a result, many of us don't have good models of a project-based approach to use in our own classrooms.

Let's examine several models of science teaching. As you read these scenarios, contrast them with your memories of elementary and middle school science.

Scenario 1: Reading About Science[2]

Maybe your class was like this. "Okay, boys and girls, let's turn to page thirty-seven in the science book. Don't forget to write down the bold print science words for your spelling list for the quiz on Friday. Al, would you please read the first paragraph?"

Al sat in the middle of the classroom. You all had figured out the order of reading and who would read next, and you sighed a little relief as you counted the paragraphs and found that yours was beyond the last page of assigned text. At the end of each paragraph, Mrs. Patterson wrote new words on the board. If it was after Wednesday, they would be on next week's spelling list. After looking at the colored pictures in the book and daydreaming a little, you heard Mrs. Patterson say, "Now turn to page forty-one and answer the first four questions. Make sure to use complete sentences and check your spelling!"

Sound familiar? We call this **read about science,** and we sometimes use the expression in upcoming chapters. In classes in which students only read about science, teachers often focus primarily on vocabulary words and facts in the textbook. Although reading about science is one important strategy to help students learn, it is

2. All scenarios and names of people in scenarios throughout this book are fictitious. Any similarity to actual teachers, students, or schools is coincidental.

ACTIVITY 1.1

What Are Your Elementary and Middle School Science Experiences?

MATERIALS NEEDED:
- something to write with
- folder or binder to start a portfolio

A. Think back to your elementary and middle school days. Do you recall your teachers teaching science? What do you remember about learning science in early elementary grades? Middle grades? What kinds of topics did your teachers cover? How did they teach science? Did you take field trips to planetariums, zoos, or science museums? Did you conduct "experiments"? Were you required to complete a science fair project? Take notes in your portfolio about what you remember.

B. What science learning experiences are most vivid in your mind? Do you remember stories such as about Newton "discovering" gravity when an apple fell on his head? Write a short paragraph in your portfolio about your most vivid memories of science learning experiences.

---

too often done in a passive manner as illustrated in this scenario.

Scenario 2: Direct Instruction

Perhaps your class was like this. Mr. Velasquez stood in front of your class by the hot plate he kept near his desk. Normally, he had his coffee on the plate, but today there was a soda can resting on it. "This pop was empty, but I rinsed it out; and I added about 2 centimeters of water in the bottom of it. You can see the steam coming out of the top of the can, and some of you can hear the water boiling on the inside. I'm going to take the can off the hot plate with these hot pads and quickly turn it over into this icy pan of water. I want you to watch what happens and try to figure out what is going on." You thought it might explode; after all, it was boiling inside and very hot. As you watched, Mr. Velasquez set the can in the icy water, almost instantly the sides of the can crumpled inward as though it had been crushed by a giant force. "Well, what do you think?" As usual, Bobby Wilson's hand shot up. "Yes," said Mr. Velasquez. He didn't wait for anybody else to think. You had some ideas but they had not quite formed in your mind. Bobby Wilson blurted out, "It's the suction; when the can cools down, something on the inside is sucking the can in!" "Well," said Mr. Velasquez, "it does have to do with the can cooling, but you see, as the can cools, the steam turns back to water and that takes up less space. Actually, it is the air on the

outside of the can that is pressing in. It is the air pressure that does it." To this day, you remember this dramatic demonstration.

We call this kind of teaching **direct instruction**. It occurs when a teacher provides the direct answers, sometimes after a demonstration. Although demonstrations can be powerful benchmark lessons, the teacher in this scenario told the students what they had seen. Students were expected to understand the concept told to them only because they had witnessed the demonstration.

Scenario 3: Process Science Teaching

Maybe your class was like this. "Today we're going to find out how high a ball bounces when it is dropped and if the kind of ball makes a difference. This is part of the science process of prediction, and you will be graphing your results. Each pair of you has a ball with a letter on it, a meter stick, and a sheet of graph paper. First, drop the ball from a height of 100 centimeters onto the floor and record the height of the bounce. After you have done this four times, drop it from a different height four times and record your results. Then answer the questions on the board."

You look up at the board and the questions are as follows:

1. Did the ball bounce back to the same height for each height it was dropped?

2. Graph the height of the bounce on the Y axis and the height from which it was dropped on the X axis. What is the pattern?

3. What would the graph look like if you dropped the ball onto a carpeted floor?

You and your partner didn't quite understand the teacher's question, but you had a meter stick and a rubber ball so there would be a lot of things you could try. Anyway, if it got too bad, the teacher would come around and show you what to do. Graphing always presented two difficulties. One, the last point you would try to plot would always fall just outside the edge of the graph paper and, two, you would always do the whole thing in ink and then when you'd make a mistake, you'd have to start all over. By the time you finished graphing the thing you had forgotten what you were supposed to find out. Oh well, science was fun and you did some interesting activities.

This kind of science teaching we label **process science teaching.** The primary purpose of the lesson is for students to use science process skills such as observing, predicting, and graphing. Process science lessons can be used as benchmark lessons, but processes should not be presented as separate stand-alone lessons. Rather, processes need to be connected with important concepts. For example, in the lesson described, the processes could have been connected to learning about forces and motion. Then, students would have understood why they were doing the activity.

Scenario 4: Project-Based Science

Maybe your class was like this. You and a couple of friends were looking at the pet rabbit in the cage in your classroom. Normally, the rabbit was eager to eat the carrots you gave him. Maybe he's sick, you thought. You and your friends *questioned* why the rabbit wasn't eating. With your teacher's encouragement, you and classmates formed teams to *investigate* the sudden change. You had other pets in your classroom (including hamsters, gerbils, a snake, and fish), and your teacher encouraged you to investigate the question, "What do pets need to stay healthy?"

Each day, *teams of students* from your class visited one of the classroom pets and provided them with several different foods. You gave the rabbit foods such as carrots, celery, oats, alfalfa, and rabbit pellets purchased from the pet food store. Some teams used computer *technology* to obtain information from the World Wide Web about the needs of various pets. When you heard that one of the members of another team had called the local pet store, and the manager was interested in your class investigation and would come to talk about the needs of pets, you were surprised that members of the *community* would *collaborate* with you in your investigation. You knew you had to come up with some great questions.

After *several weeks* of investigating what pets need to stay healthy, you and your classmates *shared results* in graphic form. A couple of teams included photographs of animals and models of healthy environments in their presentations. You found that different pets need different habitats, special kinds of food, a clean environment, and veterinary care to fight against diseases or infections. In fact, you were able to change a few things in the rabbit's diet to entice him to eat. You still had a question about the needs of your pet iguana at home, but you knew that the classroom rabbit was happy and healthy.

This last scenario is an example of what we call **project-based science.** The primary purpose of the project is for students to collaborate for a substantial length of time in the investigation of an important question that is interesting to them. In the process, students learn science concepts, use technology, and develop products. Take time to complete Activity 1.2 now.

The scenarios you just read are, in some respects, stereotyped. Throughout this book, we will reflect on these techniques; you shouldn't completely dismiss any one kind of science teaching based solely on these scenarios. There is no one best way to teach, but there are ways that can produce more student understanding, better motivation, and do more to develop lifelong interest in science. Some of the techniques just described are appropriate for **benchmark lessons,** lessons that teach basic skills or concepts (to learn more about benchmark lessons, see Chapter 6). Although project-based science is, for many reasons that will be elaborated on throughout this book, a more appropriate overall approach to teaching science, you will find times when teacher directed activities are not only ac-

---

ACTIVITY 1.2

What Are the Characteristics and Challenges of Each of the Scenarios?

MATERIALS NEEDED:
- ◆ something to write with

A. Respond in your portfolio to the following questions about each scenario:
 1. What are the characteristics of the scenario?
 2. What are students doing to help them learn science?
 3. What is the teacher doing to help students learn science?
 4. Who is responsible for the learning?
 5. How would the teacher evaluate what the students learned?

B. What are the challenges you see in teaching science in each of the scenarios? List them in your portfolio.

C. In your portfolio, write about which scenario seems to provide the most meaningful science experiences for elementary students? Middle grade students? Why?

---

ceptable but preferred. For instance, as part of answering a question about water pressure in the school's drinking fountains, you might want to investigate how powerful the air pressure is in the water lines. For safety purposes, you wouldn't want an elementary student boiling water in a soda pop can to demonstrate how air pressure can crush the can. Instead, you might decide to demonstrate the activity yourself so that students could develop an understanding of air pressure and apply it to their investigation of pressure in the water pipes. Demonstrations like this serve as benchmark lessons that provide important information needed by students.

As you thought about your own science learning experiences, you may have found that you had more than one kind of experience. Indeed, science teaching has gone through several revolutions or evolutions in the last thirty years. So, amid all this change, why has project-based science emerged as such an important way to teach science? In the next section, you'll explore the features of this approach and learn why it is so important.

AN OVERVIEW OF PROJECT-BASED SCIENCE

Project-based science can be used to answer students' and teachers' questions about the world around them. Investigating real-world questions that are meaningful to students has long been touted as a viable educational structure; the roots of the idea go back to John Dewey who is often described as the father of progressive education. Because it is focused on students and their interests, project-based science is sensitive to the varied needs of diverse students with respect to culture, race, and gender (Haberman, 1991; Atwater, 1994).

Project-based science has several fundamental features. The fourth scenario is a brief introduction to some of these features, which we will discuss thoroughly throughout the book. However, to provide you with an initial framework, let's examine some of them briefly now. First, driving questions or problems serve to organize and guide instructional tasks and activities. Second, students engage in investigations to answer their questions. Third, communities of students, teachers, and members of society collaborate on the question or problem. Fourth, students use technology to investigate, develop artifacts or products, collaborate, and access information. Finally, the result is a series of artifacts or products that address the question or problem.

Driving Questions

Science classes should have children explore solutions to questions (NRC, 1996). Project-based science calls for a question or problem that is meaningful and important to learners (Blumenfeld et al., 1991; Krajcik et al., 1993). We refer to such a question as a **driving question**. An example is, "What is the pH of rainwater in our city?" The driving question is the first step in meeting all of the other key components of project-based science. It sets the stage for planning and carrying out investigations to measure the acidity of rainwater and test the impact acid rain has on living and nonliving things. Once the stage has been set, students might use technology to investigate the question: They might use electronic pH meters and find out information about acids and bases from the World Wide Web. As students collaboratively pursue solutions to the driving question, they develop meaningful understanding of key scientific concepts such as acids and bases, pH, and concentration. Hence, instruction is anchored in real-world situations that students find meaningful and from which questions emerge, and it leads to students developing deep understandings. Finally, students can develop concrete representations, such as posters, of the results of their investigations of the driving question.

The source of the questions being asked and investigated is an important feature of project-based science that distinguishes it from other methods of teaching science. In the fourth scenario, how did the question about the health needs of pets emerge? Often, but not always, the question comes from the student. Sometimes it is possible to set up a learning situation that will lead to a natural question from the students. In one science curriculum, for example, second and third grade students set up a series of aquaria with clear plastic shoe boxes, water, sand, fish, and water plants but no water pumps or filters. As you can imagine, a layer of "black stuff" settles on the bottom in a week or so and always one or more students asks, "Where does the black stuff on the sand come from?" The teacher can then build with the children a clear set of investigations/experiences to find the answers to this question.

In other situations, teachers may have to present the driving question themselves but in a context of the real world, one with which the students can identify and about which they can ask subquestions. For instance, if a teacher starts a project with the question, "Is our water safe?" students have the potential to ask a number of subquestions, such as "Is our water safe to swim in?" "Is our water safe to drink?" or "What can live in our water?" Another example comes from consumer products. For instance, the

teacher might set up this question for the class: "Are our products environmentally friendly?" Students' subquestions might include, "Is my ink pen environmentally friendly?" "Are my batteries environmentally friendly?" or "Is my chewing gum environmentally friendly?"

All driving questions should be meaningful and important to students. We will discuss the features and benefits of driving questions more thoroughly in Chapter 3.

Students Engaged in Investigations

One of the hallmarks of science is that of sustained inquiry based on important and meaningful questions. In project-based science, students investigate a question over a long period of time rather than engage in short-term activities or investigations that are out of the context of real life. Questions such as "What do pets need to stay healthy?" and "Where did the black stuff come from in the bottom of the aquarium?" can provide the basis for long-term investigation. These investigations are meaningful to students and therefore keep the students' attention for long periods of time—sometimes over the course of the entire school year.

In project-based science classrooms, students find solutions to questions by messing about with ideas, asking and refining other questions, finding information, planning and designing, building apparatus, collecting data, analyzing data, making conclusions, and communicating findings. We refer to the process of carrying out an investigation as the **investigation web,** and we will discuss this more thoroughly in Chapter 4, but to briefly illustrate how students investigate questions, let's look at how they might find answers to the question, "Where does the black stuff on the sand come from?" Students might refine this question by asking additional questions such as, "Did the fish leave the black stuff?" "Is the black stuff alive?" "Does it grow?" "Did the black stuff grow because the aquarium was in the sun near the window?" "Would we still have the black stuff if we added a filter to the aquarium?" Students can look for and find information about aquarium maintenance in books and magazines in the school library, on the World Wide Web, or from pet stores. One group of students might decide to test the idea of

FIGURE 1.1
Students collect data to help answer questions important to them.

whether the black stuff is caused by placing the aquarium in the sun. They might set up several different aquariums in different locations in the room, collect data about the growth of the black stuff, analyze the data, and make a conclusion. These students might communicate their findings by creating a newsletter that tells owners of aquariums what to do to limit the growth of the black stuff in the bottom of their aquariums.

Communities of Learners Collaborating Together

As we discuss in Chapter 2, learning occurs in a social context. Project-based science involves students, teachers, and members of society collaborating together to investigate questions. In Chapter 5, we discuss in detail how teachers can develop and implement collaboration in the classroom. In this manner, the classroom becomes a community of learners. Students collaborate with others in their classroom and with their teacher to form conclusions, make sense of information and present findings. The use of telecommunication helps create a collaborative environment by allowing students access to a wider community in which they can communicate with knowledgeable individuals, take advantage of resources others have to offer, communicate with other students in different parts of the world, and share data with other student scientists and professional scientists.

For instance, students investigating the black stuff in the bottom of the aquarium might call a local pet store owner to discuss the question. Students investigating the needs of pets might collaborate with experts from a local pet store or veterinary hospital to find answers to their problem. In each situation, students can use the World Wide Web to obtain additional information, and they can use electronic communications to describe their projects to others.

Use of Technology

Technology can help transform the science classroom into an environment in which learners actively construct knowledge (Tinker & Papert, 1989; Linn, 1997; White & Fredrickson, 1995). Using technology in project-based science makes the environment more authentic to students, because students can use the computer to access real data on the Internet, expand interaction and collaboration with others via networks (such as e-mail), use tools to gather data (such as light and heat probes that are plugged into computer ports to conduct experiments), employ graphing and visualization tools to analyze data, and produce multimedia artifacts. Finally, the multimodal and multimedia capabilities of technology make information more accessible not only physically (easy access for obtaining and gathering information), but intellectually (incorporate new information into your understanding) as well (Blumenfeld et al., 1991).

For example, students actively "construct" knowledge when they use technology such as a computer-based temperature probe to gather data about the temperature of the aquarium with the black stuff at the bottom. Real-time graphing (simultaneous graphing with the temperature probe) makes information intellectually accessible because it allows students to make immediate interpretations of their data. Another example involves the study of weather. Students can study how temperature fluctuates during the day and night by taking continuous temperature readings with an electronic temperature probe. They can download satellite weather maps off the World Wide Web and then predict the weather just like meteorologists do. In these ways, technology makes weather information physically accessible. When children use simple draw programs to create pictures to represent their ideas, technology has helped make their ideas intellectually accessible. By sharing data with others, they make their information physically accessible to others.

Technology should be used as a tool to support science teaching. Rather than have a separate chapter on technology, we have integrated discussion of its importance throughout all of the chapters of this book.

Creation of Artifacts

Because artifacts show what students have learned, they can be used as forms of assessment of students' understanding of science (Marx, Blumenfeld, Krajcik, & Soloway, 1997). Project-based science results in a series of artifacts, or products, that address the driving question and show what children have learned. Often, teachers have students share their artifacts with other class members and with teachers, parents, and members of the community.

The creation and sharing of artifacts serves several purposes. First, artifacts are real and motivating. For example, making a display of appropriate habitats for classroom pets is more enjoyable and, therefore, more motivating than taking a test about animal habitats. The creation and sharing of artifacts also makes science class more like doing real science. Scientists frequently expose their ideas to public scrutiny through the process of publishing and presenting their work at conferences. Presenting an artifact to an audience of peers, professionals, and community members provides an outcome for the investigation and lets students talk with others about their work.

Second, artifacts help students develop and represent understanding. Because artifacts

(such as physical models, reports, videotapes, and computer programs) are concrete and explicit, they can be shared and critiqued. Feedback permits learners to reflect, extend their understanding, and revise their artifacts.

Third, artifacts allow students to show what they have learned throughout an investigation, and they document broad learning—sometimes over an entire school year. Because artifacts show learning over time, they show how student understanding develops. For these reasons, artifacts are excellent forms of assessment.

While studying the question, "What kind of insects live on our playground?" students could construct maps of where on the playground they found various insects. Students could then compare their maps with the maps of other students in the class (making the investigation real and motivating). By comparing and contrasting their maps, students might construct new knowledge: They might discover that the playground provides several different types of habitats for insects (sandy area, grassy area, wooded area), and that different insects live in different habitats. Finally, students in the class could study these habitats throughout the school year to document changes in insect populations during different seasons, thereby providing a measure of learning over time. We discuss artifacts more thoroughly in Chapter 7.

WHAT IS SCIENCE?

What do you think science is all about? Don't be surprised if you have difficulty answering this question. It is never easy to explain what science is. However, to teach science to children, it is important to develop some understanding of this question. More thorough descriptions of science can be found in the works of Kuhn (1962), Phillips (1987), and others, but we will spend some time exploring the question "What is science?" here.

Science was created by humans to predict and explain events and phenomena. These explanations are dependent upon the ideas or, more formally, the theories that scientists have developed that are consistent with observations. Theories represent detailed explanations of how the world works. For instance, the theory of plate tectonics gives us a detailed explanation of

---

ACTIVITY 1.3

Where's the Other Film Canister?

MATERIALS NEEDED:
- an assortment of 35 mm film canisters
- a variety of small objects that can be placed inside 35 mm film canisters (there must be two of each item; for example, two paper clips or two marbles)
- duct tape or packing tape

A. In this activity, each team of students should get a 35 mm film canister and objects to place inside it. Each team should have the same assortment of small objects. The team should place one, two, or three objects but only one of each item in its canister and then permanently seal it with duct tape or packing tape.

B. Each team's task is to find a film canister from another team that when shaken makes sounds similar to its own canister. NOTE: This can become challenging if teams put more than one small object in each canister.

C. Try to construct a model about what is in each of the other teams' canister by using an empty film canister and shaking it with the different objects inside to test the theory.

D. What are the various activities or processes that you went through to develop a theory of what is in the film canister? Without opening the cans and looking inside, how sure can you be that your theory is correct?

E. How does this activity resemble the construction of scientific theories to explain real-world phenomena? How do the methods you used resemble the scientific methods you use in your daily life?

---

the origin of the continents. The fact that this theory has also helped us explain other related phenomena like earthquakes and volcanic activity enhances its strength.

Theories are useful for their predictive and explanatory power, but when theories can no longer explain and make predictions, humans create new theories to replace the old ones. The new theory explains everything the old theory does but also accounts for observations that the old theories could not explain. For instance, chemists once thought that atoms were small indivisible spheres. However, this model of the atom could not explain all observable data related to how atoms behaved nor could it help us explain how various atoms reacted with different atoms. Chemists replaced the indivisible atom with an atom that had various components. Theory construction and the replacement of old theories with new ones also illustrates the tentative nature and the dynamic, recursive process of science. Activity 1.3 helps illustrate this point.

In Activity 1.3, your theories helped you explain what objects you thought were in the film canisters. Theories influence how we see and interpret (or make sense) of data and the world around us. To illustrate how our world views influence what we see and how we interpret data, let's examine a theory that influenced interpretations for many years. In 1817, William Bucklund found a giant pointed tooth that resembled the smaller tooth of a modern-day lizard. He built a theory that the tooth came from a giant lizard. Later, other researchers found giant teeth that were flat. In 1841, Richard Owen put together a theory that the pointed and flat teeth came from giant animals that were extinct, and he named these extinct animals *dinosaurs*, which means "terrible lizards." Because theories shape the way we see the world, for many years scientists believed dinosaurs were giant lizards or cold-blooded reptiles. Scientists believed that dinosaurs buried their eggs and left them to hatch much like many reptiles today lay eggs in the sand and leave them to hatch. Recently, Bob Bakker, a paleontologist, developed a theory that dinosaurs, because of their large rib cages and huge chest area, had very large hearts—and most modern animals with large hearts are warm blooded. Further, he suggested that the large hip sockets and thighs were characteristic of fast-moving animals and similar to the hips and thighs of modern chickens or turkeys. Jack Horner, another paleontologist, found evidence that dinosaurs did not lay eggs and leave them to hatch like reptiles. Instead, they tended to their eggs and reared their young in families (Czerniak, 1995a; Czerniak, 1995b). As you can see, as humans gained more evidence about dinosaurs, our theories changed. Our current theories about dinosaurs are also tentative, and it is quite likely that these too will change some day.

Science is also about finding solutions to real-world problems by forming hypotheses (best guesses) informed by theories. Scientists test these hypotheses by collecting data, analyzing data, making conclusions, and communicating findings. To be classified as scientific, the observations, measurements, and conclusions made by one group of scientists must be verified by others. The understanding that results from science is tentative and changes with new observations, and it is dependent upon the agreement of other scientists. Science allows us to revise ideas, gather more data, or change predictions and test again. In this sense, science is a dynamic, recursive process that results in tentative findings that help explain the way the world works.

In some respects, we use ideas about the nature of science in our daily lives. Trying a variation of a recipe, for example, is an experiment. We might change the ratio of whole wheat to white flour to experiment with making the bread heavier. We might add more sugar to make it sweeter, or we might add more yeast to make if fluffier. How many times have we groaned at the results when we realized we changed two or more ingredients (variables) at the same time and couldn't figure out which one (or ones) caused the different results, either bad or good? Inevitably, the confounding results taught us to be more careful and use more scientific ways of testing the recipe so that it could be replicated the next time we made bread.

The Nature of Science in Project-Based Science Teaching

Why have we introduced these ideas about the nature of science? Like scientists, students in science classes ask questions and try to find answers that will help them explain their world. Students use investigative processes just as scientists do. Students create artifacts and share these with members of a learning community; likewise, scientists share their research findings with others. Students and scientists alike generate new ideas and questions as a result of their investigations and communication with others. Finally, students develop creativity, open-mindedness, and imagination, qualities essential for successful scientists. Project-based science is a teaching approach that develops learning environments that reflect the nature of science.

WHY SHOULD YOUNG LEARNERS STUDY SCIENCE?

As we watch children play, we realize that they are imaginative tool designers and theory builders. For example, children turn cardboard boxes or sets of kitchen utensils into other things as they play. Just like scientists construct theories, children construct their view of reality. For example, a child watching a tree's leaves blowing in the wind might construct his or her own belief that trees make wind. Although this is not a scientifically accepted explanation of the phenomenon, the process used to generate the theory is not that far from the processes used by scientists.

Helping young children learn science can be one of the most enjoyable experiences in teaching. Watching them develop skills and learn the concepts and facilitating that development and learning can be empowering experiences. Students have a natural inquisitiveness that generates many questions such as "Why do pumpkins decompose?" "What happens to all the garbage?" "How does my electrical train work?" "Why does Sally run faster than Sue?" This is what project-based science is all about: helping students investigate answers to questions like these.

Science is in every elementary and middle school curriculum, and over the last several decades much more attention has been given to elementary and middle level science education. People have written position statements (for example, The National Science Teachers Association 1991 position statement stresses that science instruction should be a regular part of the school day), developed state models or frameworks for science, created new science curriculum materials, and, in many states, written science proficiency tests that are taken as early as the first grade. Science teaching also receives a great deal of attention in the national media. For example, it is not uncommon to read about

ACTIVITY 1.4

Why Should Children Learn Science?

MATERIALS NEEDED:
- a sheet of paper
- something to write with

A. On a sheet of paper, make three columns. Label the first column "Things I Did Today," label the second column "Related Science Concept," and label the third column "Related Questions." Take about five minutes to reconstruct what you did since you got up this morning. List as many things as you can remember in the first column.

B. In the second column, identify as many related science concepts as you can. For example, you may have used a curling iron and hair spray to style your hair. The curling iron is heated with electricity, and the hair spray is a chemical, so the related concepts are electricity and chemistry.

C. In the third column, write down related questions for each situation, such as "How can I make hair spray work better?" "Where does electricity come from?"

D. Reflect upon the list you have constructed. How does it help answer the question, "Why should children learn science?" Record your thoughts and your lists in your portfolio.

how this generation's science achievement compares with that of a previous generation or with those of other international countries. The media continually review and examine state proficiency scores and goals for science education. Why has the teaching of science in elementary and middle schools received such substantial attention? Why is it important for children to learn science? In Activity 1.4, you will think about this question.

Like you, a child may awake to the sound of an alarm clock. The clock is operated by electricity, and the sound reaches her ears through vibrating air molecules. She showers using water heated by gas and uses soap and shampoo which are chemicals. She eats cereal or bread that is processed from plants, fortified with vitamins, packaged with technology and delivered to stores through other technology. Her clothes are made from cotton (a plant) and acrylic (a synthetic fabric). The morning newspaper is made from trees. The headphones bring radio waves to her ears. The music is created by vibrations. The school bus runs on gasoline burned in a combustion engine. The brakes on the school bus cause it to stop through friction. At school, she uses computers, laser discs, and CD-ROMs, and at home she plays with computer toys, she watches videos, and she listens to CDs—all inventions and technology that resulted from basic scientific discoveries about electricity, light, and magnetism. Her day, like yours, con-

tains hundreds of events that are related to science. Each of these situations give rise to questions that students could ask and investigate: "What chemicals are in our homes?" "What kinds of foods promote better health?" "How does technology improve our lives?"

Because science clearly affects every aspect of our lives, we need a basic understanding of science in order to understand our lives. There are also many other reasons for students to learn science: It helps them acquire knowledge and skills that will be useful throughout their lives; it teaches them to think critically, solve problems, and make decisions that can improve the quality of their lives; it develops attitudes, such as curiosity or sensitivity to environmental concerns, that foster students taking responsibility for their actions; and it guides students in understanding real life issues and participating in a global society— the hallmark of scientifically literate citizens. Finally, some students will be encouraged by their studies in the elementary and middle level to pursue science studies in high school grades when the study of science is often optional and in postsecondary education.

Science Affects Every Aspect of Our Lives

As you saw in Activity 1.4, science (or technology that results from the efforts of science) affects every aspect of our lives, in the workplace, at home, at school, in transportation, and in entertainment. Young children are especially curious and interested in understanding phenomena in their lives. They ask a lot of "Why?" and "What if?" questions. Much of what they are curious about is related to science.

Students Acquire Useful Knowledge, Skills, and Attitudes

By studying science, children acquire knowledge, skills, and attitudes that will be useful to them throughout their lives as they engage in such things as choosing lifestyle habits related to food and exercise, conducting everyday activities that affect the environment, making informed voting decisions, and solving everyday problems. For example, knowledge about the systems of the human body and nutrition provides the basis for making informed decisions about the food one eats. Skills such as comparing and contrasting are involved in selecting one food over another. Attitudes, such as curiosity, lead one to seek more information about nutrition and exercise in journals or on the World Wide Web.

Science Teaches Critical Thinking, Problem Solving, and Decision Making

In science, students learn to think critically, solve problems, and make decisions. For example, students investigating the black stuff at the bottom of the aquarium must critically analyze and review possible causes of the growth. They learn to solve the problem by investigating different variables such as the amount of light reaching the aquarium, the pH of the water, the filtration systems, and the types of gravel. Finally, they make decisions regarding the best procedures to be used to maintain the aquarium. This science investigation, of course, is related to real life, because some students also have aquariums in their homes and many students are interested in animals. More importantly, however, students learned skills they can apply to other situations. For example, the next time they encounter an everyday problem such as trying to figure out why certain plants are not growing well in the garden or why a toy doesn't work properly any more, they will have the skills of analysis, review, investigation, and making conclusions.

Science Helps Students Take Responsibility for Their Actions

As students investigate many scientific questions, they acquire knowledge and develop attitudes that encourage them to take responsibility for their own actions. For example, if students learn in an investigation that motor oil kills plants, their future behavior regarding the disposal of motor oil will be affected.

Science Develops Scientifically Literate Citizens

Science guides students in understanding real-life issues and helps them participate in local, national, and world issues—the hallmark of a scientifically literate citizen. As we enter the next millennium, we find that now more than at any other time in our history, students face crucial decisions about global issues. These include environmental pollution, AIDS, overpopulation, world hunger, nuclear power, and genetic engineering. Science and engineering have generated solutions to some of these issues: cars with better fuel mileage, more fuel-efficient homes, and great quantities of more nutritious foods. Scientific investigation, invention, and technology have also resulted in discoveries that make life easier for humans, provide cures for diseases, and inspire exploration of new frontiers such as the ocean or space. We need professional scientists to investigate these matters, but we also need a scientifically literate citizenry who can participate in making informed decisions about them. Today's students, more than those of any previous generation, will need to understand basic scientific principles.

Students in project-based science classrooms learn to investigate, understand, and interpret information and interface with people in their own communities. As a result, they are better prepared to deal with the scientific, technological, and social issues that will face them in the future.

Positive Science Experiences Are Important in Elementary and Middle School Grades

Educators agree that science is an essential and crucial subject for all students. The elementary and middle school grades are especially impor-

FIGURE 1.2
Children explore their environment.

tant years for constructing understanding about the world and developing interest in science so that students will pursue scientific studies as they continue into upper grades where science may become optional (NRC, 1996).

Poor instruction and shallow development of science concepts in elementary and middle school grades are often at fault for persistent, inaccurate beliefs about scientific phenomena. Students come to school with their own ideas about how things in the natural world work, ideas that are not always consistent with the conceptions of experts in the field. For instance, children often believe that a force is needed to keep an object in motion or that mass is lost when substances are burned. Both these ideas make intuitive sense and are consistent with casual observations and life experiences. For instance, when driving a car, the car doesn't keep moving unless we keep our foot on the gas pedal. Typically, we need to apply a force to keep it moving because of the opposing force friction. When we burn a log in a fireplace, we see ashes that remain and it appears that other mass is gone. Therefore, we find that many adults, in

spite of school instruction in science, still hold ideas that differ from that of scientists (Harvard Private Universe Tapes, 1995).

The elementary and middle grades are also important years for developing curiosity and interest in science. Research by Yager and Yager (1985) has shown that negative attitudes toward science increase by grade level, and students, especially girls, as early as grade three exhibit dislike of and anxiety toward science. The Third International Mathematics and Science Study (TIMSS, 1997, 1998) found similar patterns in students' attitudes toward science. Eighty-five percent of fourth graders indicated that they liked science. However, by the time students reached the twelfth grade, their favorable attitudes toward science had decreased. The percentage of students who liked science ranged from 49 percent to 68 percent, depending upon the discipline, with chemistry on the low end and biology on the high end. The reason students gradually come to dislike science frequently lies in the way science is taught (passively) and the type of curriculum used (not relevant to students' lives). As a teacher, you will be in the position to stimulate student interest in science or extinguish it. Project-based science will help you develop students' interests in science because it involves active investigation of important and meaningful questions.

GOALS OF SCIENCE EDUCATION

In the next two sections of this chapter, we examine the goals of science education in the United States and we consider why this approach enables you to teach in a way that meets those goals. This is an exciting and challenging time in science education history. Many parents, educators, scientists, and public officials are concerned that students be able to cope with the massive explosion of knowledge and the tremendous changes that science and technology will bring about in our future. More and more, we're concerned about the ability of our students to develop an understanding of science that they can apply to real life. We all realize that the understanding students develop in school will impact what they are able to do throughout their lives, regardless of their chosen careers. It's not surprising that one fundamental

---

ACTIVITY 1.5

What Are Your Personal Goals for Science Education?

MATERIALS NEEDED:
- ◆ a sheet of paper
- ◆ something to write with

A. Before reading the section on goals of science education, brainstorm in small groups the goals that you think are important for science education. Try to reach group consensus. Share your group's goals with the rest of the class.

B. How do the goals of science education differ among your groups? What are the similarities?
C. Think about one national goal already mentioned—the development of scientifically literate citizens. What do you think characterizes a scientifically literate citizen? What does a scientifically literate citizen need to know? What skills does this person need to have? What attitudes should this person possess? How does this goal compare with your group's goals?
D. Record your thoughts in your portfolio.

---

national goal of science education today is to develop a scientifically literate society.

This goal like our other science education goals has been affected by a number of forces—history, social changes, governmental concerns about economic competitiveness, research findings, and the powerful influence of science and technology on modern society. Our science education goals have changed dramatically during this century, and as we head into the twenty-first century, educators continue to grapple with the appropriate goals for science education. The success of our national goals strongly depends on the individual goals we set in our classes. Tying national goals to our own classroom goals can be helpful in guiding our students to become scientifically literate citizens. In this section, we examine several reform documents, national policies, and position statements that have established the goals for science education in our country today. Specifically, we summarize the *National Science Education Standards* (National Research Council, 1996), *Project 2061: Science for All Americans* (Rutherford & Ahlgren, 1989), *Benchmarks for Science Literacy* (AAAS, 1993), and *An NSTA Position Statement: Elementary School Science* (NSTA, 1991). Before we do this, however, take a moment to complete Activity 1.5 and think about the goals you believe are important for science education.

National Science Education Standards

The National Research Council, with the assistance of the National Academy of Sciences, recently developed the *National Science Education*

Standards (National Research Council, 1996). These goals are to "educate students who are able to experience the richness and excitement of knowing about and understanding the natural world; use appropriate scientific processes and principles in making personal decisions; engage intelligently in public discourse and debate about matters of scientific and technological concern; and increase their economic productivity through the use of the knowledge, understanding, and skills of the scientifically literate person in their careers" (p. 13). To accomplish these goals, the *National Science Education Standards* addresses simultaneously standards for teaching science, the professional development of teachers of science, assessment in science education, K–12 science content, science education programs, and the science education system. These standards represent a consensus of teachers, science educators, scientists, and the public.

The *National Science Education Standards* stresses that science should be inquiry based and adapted to meet the interests, abilities, and experiences of students. It emphasizes that science teachers should use strategies that develop science understanding through a community of learners, use resources outside the school that support inquiry, guide and facilitate learning by promoting collaboration and discourse among students, help students become responsible for their own learning, and work with colleagues within science (biology, chemistry, geology, and physical science) and across disciplines (mathematics, language arts, social studies, art, music, and physical education).

Teachers should engage in ongoing assessment of their teaching and of student learning to help themselves, parents, the general public, and policy makers improve instruction. Assessment standards are designed to change the focus of assessment to include what we value most in science education. This means that we need to assess, "rich, well-structured knowledge," "scientific understanding and reasoning," and deep understanding of what students know.

The content standards are based on unifying concepts and processes in science, science as inquiry, physical science, life science, earth and space science, science and technology, science in personal and social perspectives, and history and nature of science. These unifying concepts are described as the powerful, overarching ideas in science such as systems, order, change, constancy, and equilibrium.

The *National Science Education Standards* demand that science be taught through processes (such as observing, classifying, measuring, experimenting, and making conclusions) and require students to use knowledge to reason and think critically. The standards for physical, life, earth, and space science focus on subject matter and list facts, concepts, principles, theories, and models that all students should know in grades K–4, 5–8, and 9–12. The standards for science and technology focus on the connections between science and invention and are designed to help students make decisions. The personal and social perspectives science standards emphasize the fact that students need to understand the world around them so as to be able to make decisions about personal and societal issues. Finally, the history and nature of science standards challenge teachers to teach students about the historical nature of science, that it is an ongoing, changing process.

Project 2061: Science for All Americans

Project 2061: Science for All Americans was published by the American Association for the Advancement of Science (Rutherford & Ahlgren, 1989). The overall purpose of Project 2061 is to achieve science literacy nationwide. *Project 2061: Science for All Americans* was the synthesis of five panel reports on biology and health science, mathematics, technology, physical science

and information sciences and engineering, and social and behavioral sciences. Project 2061 is intended to focus on the meaningful learning of science rather than on sheer coverage of numerous science topics. Project 2061 plans to transform K–12 science while paying attention to all parts of the educational system (goals, curriculum testing, teacher education, and instruction).

Project 2061 is a large-scale, long-term project with several broad goals. First, in order to ensure scientific literacy for students of diverse cultures, the amount of material covered throughout the academic year needs to be reduced. Instead of reading about vast amounts of material, students need to think deeply about central concepts, themes, and principles of science. Second, because the boundaries of science are much grayer than they are portrayed in the science textbooks, emphasis must be placed on showing the integration of and connections among the various science fields as well as with social science, mathematics, language arts, and technology. Third, because philosophers and historians of science now view science as human enterprise, the influence of human thought and action on scientific endeavor and the influence of scientific endeavor on human thought must be illustrated by the curriculum and through science instruction. Fourth, because science is more than a culmination of facts, science education must foster scientific ways of thinking, including skepticism, open-mindedness, and creativity. Science teaching for scientific literacy needs to be consistent with the spirit and character of scientific inquiry and with scientific values. Science teaching needs to portray science as a dynamic, recursive enterprise that focuses on explanation of observed phenomena and generation of new questions. Fifth, educational reform must be comprehensive, focusing on the learning needs of all children, covering all grades and subjects, and dealing with all components and aspects of the educational system.

Benchmarks for Science Literacy

The American Association for the Advancement of Science also developed *Benchmarks for Science Literacy* (1993). *Benchmarks* is designed to serve as a curriculum model for curriculum developers, state departments of education, and school

---

TABLE 1.1   The Scientific World View Benchmark

Grades K–2	Grades 3–5	Grades 6–8
When a science investigation is done the way it was done before, we expect to get very similar results.	Results of similar investigations seldom turn out exactly the same.	When similar investigations give different results, the challenge is to judge whether the differences are trivial or significant.
Science investigations generally work the same way in different places.		Scientific knowledge is subject to modification as new information is found.
		Some scientific knowledge is very old but still applicable today.
		Some matters may not be examined usefully in a scientific way.

---

systems developing science curriculum. The benchmarks are not instructions on how to teach; they are statements about what *all* students should know or be able to do in science, mathematics, and technology at grades 2, 5, 8, and 12. There are twelve benchmarks: (1) the nature of science, (2) the nature of mathematics, (3) the nature of technology, (4) the physical setting, (5) the living environment, (6) the human organism, (7) human society, (8) the designed world, (9) the mathematical world, (10) historical perspectives, (11) common themes, and (12) habits of mind.

Let's take one benchmark and look at what is expected of students at the end of second grade, fifth grade, and eighth grade. We'll use the benchmark the Scientific World View (AAAS, 1993, pp. 5–8). We'll paraphrase the benchmark for brevity. You should look at the entire report to see all the thinking of the contributing teachers and researchers. A good way to compare how the benchmarks change from one grade level to the next is to examine Table 1.1.

As you can see, the benchmarks become more complex as the grades progress, but the most important feature is how the idea becomes elaborated throughout the grades. That means that it is as important for first and second graders to achieve this understanding as it is for sixth graders. You should see that this benchmark, like the others in *Benchmarks for Science Literacy*, can be used to provide direction for what students should know and be able to do in science at specific grade levels.

The National Science Teachers Association Position Statement

The National Science Teachers Association (NSTA) publishes position statements on a variety of topics in science education. One position statement provides educators with basic guidelines for elementary science (NSTA, 1991). *An NSTA Position Statement: Elementary School Science* advocates daily science instruction for every elementary child at every grade level. This statement emphasizes the need to involve children in science at an early age to develop interests in science and prepare children for living in an increasingly scientific and technologically oriented society. The NSTA position statement stresses problem-solving skills; firsthand investigation and inquiry; broad conceptual themes integrated across the curriculum; and assessment aligned with problem solving, inquiry, process skills, instructional modes, and curriculum objectives.

Summary of National Goals

In the previous section, we explored four major reform efforts. Impacts from the *National Science Education Standards*, *Project 2061*, *Benchmarks for Science Literacy*, and NSTA's position statement will influence the character of science education in schools for years to come. These efforts have resulted from the work of some of the best thinkers in science, science education, teaching, and learning. What they have advocated is consistent with how children learn. There have been other reports as well, reports that match closely the recommendations of the four major reform efforts we described. Next we summarize the common themes that are advocated in each as ways to develop science literacy for *all* students. We can cluster these recommendations under three broad categories: learning, curriculum, and teaching.

Learning   With respect to learning, six major themes are apparent. First, students should explore broad concepts or "big ideas" instead of isolated facts or skills. A quote from Alvin Toffler's 1970 book *Future Shock* illustrates the need to cover large, conceptual ideas rather than facts:

> At the rate at which knowledge is growing, by the time the child born today graduates from college, the amount of knowledge in the world will be four times as great. By the time that child is fifty years old, it will be thirty-two times as great, and 97 percent of everything known in the world will have been learned since the time he was born. (p. 157)

Because of the rate of knowledge growth, no individual knows all there is to know and never will. For this reason, teachers should focus on broad topics. For instance, students should explore ecosystems instead of isolated topics such as rivers, plants, animals, and other environmental elements. In this way students learn the connections between concepts and principles and are able to apply their understanding to new as yet unencountered situations.

Second, *all* students should learn to think critically, solve problems, and make decisions. Science is for all students and not just those going into scientific careers. We live in a world that is scientifically and technologically based. As our children develop into adults, the world will continue to change as a result of scientific and technological decisions. To make informed decisions regarding their own lives and society, our children need to have a firm understanding of both the content and process of science. For example, when our children become adults, they might be called upon to make informed decisions regarding the management of natural resources.

Third, children should construct meaning from experiences with concrete materials rather than through passive means. Literature on child development is clear about the fact that children develop understanding by cognitively engaging in the exploration of phenomena. While some children learn about plants simply by reading about them, most children also need to grow plants and observe their development to construct deep understandings.

Fourth, students should learn how to apply science and technology to everyday life. Science should be relevant to students and not consist solely of learning concepts but also of their application. For example, if students study decomposition of matter, they might also create school and home composting systems.

Fifth, science should foster the development of students' natural curiosity, creativity, and interest. For example, if students are interested in magnets but their textbook only covers matter and energy, the teacher should take advantage of the students' interest in magnetism and set the textbook aside.

Sixth, science instruction should foster the development of scientific attitudes. Students should learn to seek out knowledge, be skeptical, rely on data, accept ambiguity, be willing to modify explanations, cooperate in answering questions and solving problems, respect reason, and be honest. For instance, students typically believe that what they read in a book, hear on television, or read in the newspaper is true. Science instruction can teach students to question what they read and see. Additionally, elementary and middle grades science should aim to promote positive attitudes about science.

Curriculum   With respect to curriculum, three major themes come to the forefront. First, less content should be covered. Students should be allowed to discover and learn in depth a few major concepts and principles. Instead of covering weather, the human body, magnetism, electricity, chemical change, and the solar system in one year, students might explore only three or four major areas.

Second, science should be portrayed to students as interdisciplinary, connected to other fields of study. In actual practice, science areas are interwoven. Paul DeHart Hurd, in an article entitled "Why We Must Transform Science" (1991, p. 33), wrote,

> Science today is characterized by some 25,000 to 30,000 research fields. Findings from these fields are reported in 70,000 journals, 29,000 of which are new since 1978. Traditional disciplines have been

hybridized into such new research areas as bio-chemistry, biophysics, geochemistry, and genetic engineering. . . . These changes in the way modern science is organized have yet to be reflected in science courses. There is little recognition that in recent years the boundaries between the various natural sciences have become more and more blurred and major concepts more unified.

Topics should be connected. For example, in exploring a question such as "What is in our stream?" students study basic chemical concepts such as concentration and equilibrium as well as perform basic chemical tests for various substances. They explore biology concepts by examining living organisms found in the water. They study earth science concepts such as the water cycle and the watershed. All of these areas are studied in an integrated and unified manner rather than as isolated facts.

Third, students should explore the interrelationships among science, technology, and society. The study of science should highlight the integration of technology and societal issues. For example, in investigating "What is in our lake?" students could explore how our waterways get polluted. They might also explore how we as a society make decisions and pass laws that govern many of the actions taken by individuals and industries.

Teaching   With respect to teaching, five major themes are apparent. First, the teacher serves as a guide in the classroom, encouraging student exploration and learning, rather than as an authoritative presenter of knowledge. For instance, instead of lecturing about decomposition and bacteria, a teacher might have students explore why pumpkins decompose by setting up various conditions to investigate decomposition. Students might set up a compost pile at the school, they might build a worm bin for their classroom, or they might create a decomposition column. In these situations, the teacher would serve as a facilitator, setting up the situations, but the students would conduct the actual investigations.

Second, the content of science should be taught as a process, involving investigation and answering questions. For example, in the process of exploring why pumpkins decompose, students would ask questions, design plans, collect and analyze data, and make decisions. Assessment should be consistent with this process

of inquiry and investigation. In other words, assessment should measure what is taught. Assessment is also typically embedded into instruction rather than becoming something done at the end of a chapter or unit.

Third, science instruction needs to be integrated with instruction in the other discipline areas. Teachers should focus on the relationships between science, language arts, social studies, and mathematics. For instance, a class exploring air pollution might write letters to legislators, create posters expressing their opinions, or make graphs.

Fourth, science instruction should encourage students to challenge conceptions and debate ideas. In this process, they form communities of learners who collaborate together. For example, students might work together to challenge each others' ideas about which factors contribute most to the decomposition of leaves.

Fifth, science instruction should build upon children's prior experiences and knowledge. For instance, if a child believes that air doesn't have mass or take up space, instruction should be designed to foster new understanding. Many of the ideas that children come to school with results from their experiences in play. For instance, a student might develop the idea that gases don't have mass from playing with helium balloons.

HOW DO THE CURRENT NATIONAL GOALS COMPARE WITH PROJECT-BASED SCIENCE?

Now that you have been introduced to the major national goals, you might wonder how they match the goals of project-based science. This approach to science learning is congruent with current goals as represented in projects such as the *National Science Education Standards* (National Research Council, 1996), *Project 2061: Science for All Americans* (Rutherford & Ahlgren, 1989), *Benchmarks for Science Literacy* (AAAS, 1993), and *An NSTA Position Statement: Elementary School Science* (NSTA, 1991).

First, all of the national goals stress teaching less content at each grade level. Project-based science is consistent with this emphasis, because the focus is on covering less in greater depth. Students *investigate authentic questions* that encompass central concepts over an *ex-*

tended period of time. The process of *asking and modifying questions, performing investigations,* and *building artifacts* to answer questions might take place over weeks or months. For instance, in order for students to discover what bugs they have in their school yard and when the bugs disappear and reappear, they will have to conduct investigations throughout the entire school year. By covering broader, "big ideas" instead of isolated facts, students in project-based classrooms develop richer, fundamental understandings of major themes or issues.

Second, all of the major national goals stress that science should be relevant to students' daily lives and that students should apply understanding to the real world. Project-based science's driving questions are important, meaningful, and worthwhile. The questions are followed by students' applying of answers to their own life situations. For example, students learning about the black stuff in the bottom of the aquarium learn how to set up and maintain aquariums at home. They learn to make informed decisions regarding pollution in an aquarium.

Third, all of the national goals call for the integration of science throughout the curriculum, within the sciences and across all disciplines. Project-based science promotes this interdisciplinary approach to instruction because in the investigation of real-world questions science cannot be separated from other subject areas. For instance, when students explore a question such as the quality of water, they combine a number of science disciplines including chemistry (chemicals in the water), biology (effect on plant and animal life), and earth science (polluted water seeping into groundwater supplies below rock layers). Opportunities to connect with other curricular areas also exist. For instance, students might explore public policy governing the pollution of waterways by private industry (social studies). They might create three-dimensional models of their local watersheds (art).

Fourth, it is stressed in the national goals that the teacher should serve as a guide to instruction that takes place in the classroom. In project-based science, the teacher's role is not to impart knowledge to passive learners but to guide students through the processes of modifying driving questions, developing investigations, engaging in explorations, collaborating with others, and creating artifacts. The teacher *facilitates* learning by teaching benchmark lessons, helping students find resources, putting students in touch with members of the community, fostering collaboration, and asking questions that lead to new investigations.

Fifth, national recommendations call for classrooms composed of communities of learners. In project-based science classrooms, students are encouraged to collaborate with students and members of the community, debate ideas, challenge the thinking of peers, share ideas, and communicate with people around the world. Teachers in project-based science classrooms see themselves and their students as members of a learning environment.

Sixth, a major focus of the national goals is on the way students learn: Prior experiences should be taken into account and hands-on materials should be used. In project-based science classrooms, teachers identify students' prior knowledge about a concept and use this information to guide lessons and assess learning. Students in project-based science classrooms construct meaning by exploring phenomena: They don't just read about water pollution; they use materials such as secchi disks, pH meters, and water test kits to investigate water quality.

Seventh, all of the national goals argue that science should be learned through investigation. Investigation is the core of project-based science. Investigations provide students with the opportunity to ask questions, explore and initiate ideas, plan, seek information, construct designs, collect and interpret data, make inferences, reevaluate their understandings, and construct useful connections among real-life ideas. For example, students investigating the cause of the black stuff at the bottom of the aquarium ask and refine questions about variables related to the growth of the black stuff, design experiments to identify what causes the growth, collect and analyze data about the amount of black stuff in the bottom of aquariums, and make decisions about aquarium maintenance.

Eighth, an essential element of the national goals is building interest in science. Meaningful questions are a fundamental part of project-based science and they capitalize upon students' natural curiosity. Students' questions drive the curriculum, and they investigate topics that are meaningful and interesting to them. Because project-based science builds off of students' interests, it helps meet the needs of diverse students.

ACTIVITY 1.6

Case Study of an Elementary or Middle Grade Classroom

MATERIALS NEEDED:

♦ an elementary or middle school to study

A. Obtain permission from the appropriate officials (usually a school district superintendent, curriculum director, or principal and a classroom teacher) at an elementary or middle school to conduct a small case study.

B. Research how the school's course of study, curriculum, instructional practices, and assessment techniques compare with the guidelines proposed by national organizations (such as AAAS, NRC, and NSTA).

C. In your opinion, how well are schools meeting suggested goals? In what ways are they falling short?

D. How well are the schools implementing the features of project-based science? In what ways are they failing to implement project-based science ideas?

E. What obstacles might you face trying to implement project-based science in this environment?

F. Record all of these ideas in your portfolio.

Ninth, national goals stress fostering scientific attitudes and habits of mind such as accepting ambiguity, being skeptical, and respecting reason. Project-based science supports the development of habits of mind through the processes of investigation (asking questions, developing experiments, collaborating with others, making conclusions, and constructing artifacts).

Tenth, each of the national reports calls for new methods of assessing student understanding in science that are fair, are reliable, and match instructional goals. Project-based science stresses assessment methods that are embedded in the instructional process. Student-developed artifacts, for example, represent students' understandings of the topic they have investigated. For instance, while investigating what insects live on the playground, students might make drawings of insect life cycles. Such activity is developed during the process of investigation, but it also serves as a tool of assessment because it can tell the teacher whether students understand the concept of the investigation.

In Activity 1.6, you will conduct a case study of an elementary or middle grade classroom to see for yourself whether classrooms in your region are meeting the fundamental national goals for science and how many of the elements of project-based science are evident in these classrooms.

We hope you have seen how project-based science serves to implement suggested national goals for teaching science. Throughout this book we will explore in greater depth many of the ideas that were introduced in this chapter. You probably have many questions at this point about teaching in a project-based science environment. Just as this approach is driven by questions, this book should also be driven by questions. Practice asking yourself questions as you work through each section of a chapter. Questions like "Does this work as well for early elementary grades?" and "What would I have to do to make it work?" are driving questions that are important to teaching. Now that you have been introduced to project-based science, use your questioning ability to become one of the best science teachers in the country. Begin by asking questions about science teaching in Activity 1.7.

SUMMARY OF CHAPTER

Project-based science is an exciting way to teach science. In project-based science classrooms, students investigate and collaborate with others to seek answers to real-world questions. Using technology, students investigate, develop artifacts, collaborate, and make products to show what they have learned. This method of teaching science is motivating and fun. It parallels what scientists do, and it meets the national goals for and standards of science education. Throughout the remaining chapters of this book, you will encounter more in-depth information about the fundamental features of project-based science and strategies for implementing the approach. In the process, we hope you see how enjoyable teaching science can be.

ACTIVITY 1.7

Questions About Science Teaching

MATERIALS NEEDED:
- paper to write on
- something to write with

A. Think about the questions you now have about teaching project-based science that you believe you should have the answers to by the time you finish this book.

B. What are your top three or four driving questions about learning to teach elementary or middle school science? Include questions on the goals of science education, why young students should learn science, how science should or should not be emphasized in elementary and middle education, and project-based science.

C. Use your portfolio to record these questions.

REFERENCES

American Association for the Advancement of Science. 1993. *Benchmarks for science literacy.* New York: Oxford University Press.

Atwater, M. M. 1994. Research on cultural diversity in the classroom. In *Handbook of research on science teaching and learning,* ed. D. L. Gabel. New York: Macmillan.

Blumenfeld, P., E. Soloway, R. Marx, J. Krajcik, M. Guzdial, and A. Palincsar. 1991. Motivating project-based learning: Sustaining the doing, supporting the learning. *Educational Psychologist* 26: 369–98.

Brown, A. L., and J. C. Campione. 1994. Guided discovery in a community of learners. In *Classroom lessons: Integrating cognitive theory and classroom practice,* ed. K. McGilly, 229–70. Cambridge, Mass.: MIT Press/Bradford Books.

Czerniak, C. M. 1995a. Dinosaur! *School Science and Mathematics* 95(3): 160–61.

Czerniak, C. M. 1995b. Dinosaurs: Fantastic creatures that ruled the earth. *School Science and Mathematics* 95(3): 161–62.

Haberman, M. 1991. The pedagogy of poverty versus good teaching. *Phi Delta Kappa,* 73(4): 290–94.

Hurd, P. D. 1991, October. Why we must transform science education. *Educational Leadership* 33–35.

Krajcik, J. S. 1993. Learning science by doing science. In *What research says to the science teacher: Science, society and technology,* ed. R. Yager. Washington, D.C.: National Science Teachers Association.

Kuhn, T. S. 1962. *The structure of scientific revolutions.* Chicago, Ill.: The University of Chicago Press.

Linn, M. C. 1997. Learning and instruction in science education: Taking advantage of technology. In *International handbook of science education,* ed. D. Tobin and B. J. Fraser. The Netherlands: Kluwer.

Marx, R. W., P. C. Blumenfeld, J. S. Krajcik, and E. Soloway. 1997. Enacting project-based science: Challenges for practice and policy. *Elementary School Journal,* 97: 341–58.

National Research Council. 1996. *National science education standards.* Washington, D.C.: National Academy Press.

National Science Teachers Association. 1991. *An NSTA position statement: Elementary school science.* Washington, D.C.: NSTA. See also http://www.nsta.org/.

Phillips, D. C. 1987. *Philosophy, science, and social inquiry.* Oxford: Permagon Press.

Presidents and Fellows of Harvard College. 1995. *The private universe project.* South Burlington, Vt.: Annenburg/Corporation of Public Broadcasting Mathematics and Science Collection.

Roth, W. M. 1995. *Authentic school science.* Netherlands: Kluwer Publishers.

Roup, R. R., S. Gal, B. Drayton, and M. Pfister, ed. 1992. *LabNet: Toward a community of practice.* Hillsdale, N.J.: Erlbaum.

Rutherford, J., and A. Ahlgren. 1989. *Science for all Americans: Project 2061.* New York: Oxford University Press.

Stake, R. E., and J. A. Easley et al. 1978. *Case studies in science education.* Urbana, Ill.: Center for Instructional Research and Curriculum Evaluation, University of Illinois.

Third International Mathematics and Science Study (TIMSS). 1997. http://nces.ed.gov/TIMSS/.

Third International Mathematics and Science Study (TIMSS). 1998. http://nces.ed.gov/TIMSS/.

Tinker, R. F. and S. Papert. 1989. Tools for science education. In *1988 AETS Yearbook: Information technology and science education,* J. Ellis, ed. Columbus, Ohio: Association for the Education of Teachers in Science.

Toffler, Alvin. 1970. *Future shock.* New York: Bantam Books.

White, B. Y., and J. R. Fredrickson. April 1995. *The Thinker Tools Inquiry Project: Making scientific inquiry accessible to students and teachers. Causal Models Research Group Report 95-02.* Berkeley, Calif.: School of Education, University of California.

Yager, R. E., and S. O Yager. 1985. Changes in perceptions of science for third, seventh, and eleventh grade students. *Journal of Research in Science Teaching* 22(4): 347–58.

Chapter 2

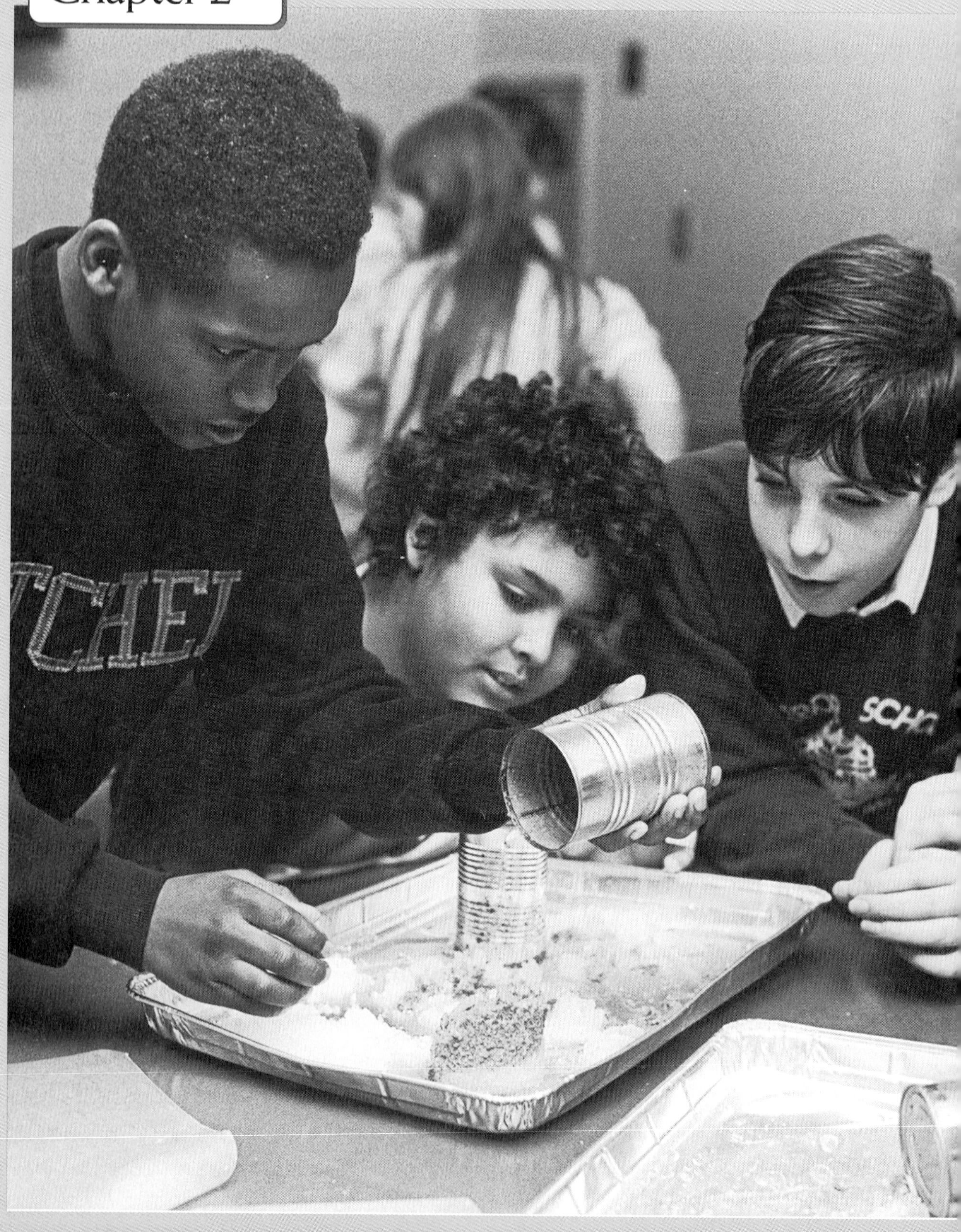

HOW DO CHILDREN CONSTRUCT UNDERSTANDING IN SCIENCE?

INTRODUCTION

The world children face is an increasingly scientific and technological one. Information and access to information are growing at an exponential rate. Schools need to prepare our youth to learn and apply scientific knowledge to solve real world problems. Do students in our schools develop understandings to use science? What does a useable understanding of science mean? How can teachers help students develop useable science understanding? This chapter examines the educational literature that anchors project-based science in the social constructivist theory of learning. We'll consider a social constructivist model of teaching that focuses on active engagement with phenomena, using and applying knowledge, multiple representations, use of learning communities, and the role of authentic tasks. This chapter presents types of knowledge and ways to help students develop integrated understandings through the construction of knowledge in social situations. Practical techniques are presented to help teachers scaffold students' learning in science. Finally, we'll consider the role of technology in constructing science understanding. First, however, let's develop a working definition of *understanding.*

STUDENT UNDERSTANDING

What kinds of science understandings do students develop in school? Does school help them develop understandings that are useful for their lives? Unfortunately, a number of research studies (Osborne & Freyberg, 1986; Rutherford & Ahlgren, 1989; AAAS, 1993; and Linn, 1998) indicate that students at the elementary, middle, and high school levels do not develop an understanding of science that is useful for their everyday lives. Most students memorize science terms without understanding, and they memorize how to solve problems (Eylon & Linn, 1988; Osborne & Freyberg, 1986). Students learn bits of factual information and how to solve problems at the end of chapters by using formulas. Scientific facts and algorithmic problem solving are the essence of much of the science curriculum taught in U.S. schools. Most children do not develop rich understanding and cannot apply

what they learn to give explanations of scientific phenomena. This kind of knowledge has been defined as *inert knowledge.* Inert knowledge is understanding that is stored in the mind but that cannot be retrieved or used in appropriate situations (Perkins, 1986). The learner lacks connections and relationships between ideas. A fifth grader might be able to define "atom," but not know how to use the definition to explain properties of matter.

Moreover, although most elementary children start school with an interest in the physical world, they soon lose interest in learning about science. As students transition to middle school, they develop negative attitudes toward science and lose the motivation to continue their learning of science. Yager and Penick (1986) summarized the data from various national studies and concluded that "the more years our students enroll in science courses, the less they like it." This conclusion is also supported by the Third International Mathematics and Science Study (TIMSS, 1998), which indicates that interest in science decreases from elementary grades to high school. This lack of motivation stems largely from the fact that students are not being engaged in the process of learning science and that the curriculum frequently focuses on students memorizing facts and formulas.

Three Scenarios of Student Understanding

Let's examine three scenarios that illustrate the variety of understandings students have of scientific ideas.

Scenario 1: What Is Alive?   The first scenario comes from a common biology phenomena: "What is alive?" Mr. Ramirez asked his second graders if a seed, such as that from an apple, is alive. Most of his students responded, "No." When Mr. Ramirez probed them to explain their answers, many said that a seed does not move and so cannot be alive. Young children tend to categorize *alive* and *not alive* according to superficial physical characteristics and to the presence or absence of locomotion (Carey, 1985; Ladewski, Krajcik, Levy, & Hall, 1992). Older students and students more knowledgeable of biology retain aspects of this categorization scheme but seem to broaden their criteria for *life* to include more carefully differentiated ideas of function (autonomous movement is distinguished from simple movement) and ideas about additional functions (growth, metabolism, and reproduction). If we ask older children (seventh or eighth grade) if an apple seed is alive, many will say that it has the "potential" to grow but that it is not alive. This example shows how students do not develop rich ideas about basic biological phenomena.

Scenario 2: Boiling Water The second scenario centers on common physical phenomena: the boiling and condensing of water. Ms. Beacher asked two of her fourth grade students, Kristen and Shawn, to make observations and explain a laboratory setup in which water was boiling in a beaker and condensing on a cool glass surface held above the beaker. Figure 2.1

shows the experimental setup. Kristen said that the water was boiling. Ms. Beacher asked how she knew, and Kristen answered, "Because of the bubbles in the water." Shawn added that water was condensing on the glass surface. Ms. Beacher probed them further to elicit more in-depth responses. She asked, "What is inside the bubbles?" Kristen responded, "Air," and Shawn agreed. When Ms. Beacher asked, "Well, if there is air in the bubbles, where does the air in the bubbles come from?" Both Kristen and Shawn looked at Ms. Beacher with blank faces. She then asked them, "Shawn, you mentioned that water was condensing on the glass surface. Where does that water come from?" Shawn responded, "It evaporated from the beaker." Ms. Beacher probed further: "Can you tell me what it means to evaporate from the beaker?" Shawn replied, "You know; it came from the beaker."

This example shows that the children were able to use scientific terms, but they could not use the terms to explain some everyday phenomena. Children might use terms such as *evaporate, condense,* and *boil*. However, if we use probing questions to elicit from them more in-depth descriptions and explanation of the phenomena, we find that many of them don't have a very rich understanding of the terms they use. As the example illustrates, many of them cannot go beyond just using terms (Osborne & Cosgrove, 1983). Interestingly enough, the responses of eighth graders are not very different. In their explanation of boiling, some eighth grade students say that the bubbles in the water are made of air or hydrogen and oxygen gas instead of saying "the bubbles are filled with water molecules in the gaseous phase."

Scenario 3: Burning Steel Wool The third scenario centers on a common chemical phenomenon. Ms. Jackson's sixth graders observed a piece of steel wool burning in air. Many of the students explained that a chemical reaction was occurring. However, when Ms. Jackson asked them to predict how the original mass of the steel wool would compare to the mass of material remaining after burning, almost all of the students predicted that the mass of the material remaining after burning would be less than the original mass of the steel wool. Ms. Jackson then asked the students to explain why they

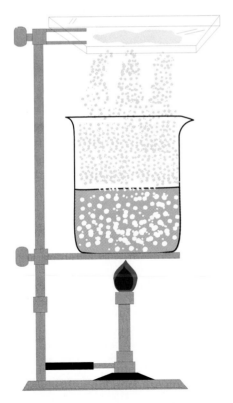

FIGURE 2.1
Children cannot frequently explain simple phenomena such as the boiling and condensing of water.

thought the mass decreased. Many of them said that it turned to ash, like paper or wood, when it burned. Once the students measured a new mass of steel wool before burning and then measured it again after burning, they noticed that the mass had not decreased but increased. Most children, and adults too, would be surprised at these results. When Ms. Jackson asked the students to explain the increase in mass, some said that the steel wool turned into carbon, which is heavier than steel wool (Anderson, 1986). Once again, the responses of eighth graders do not differ substantially. The example illustrates that students

lack understanding of combustion, in which a substance chemically combines with oxygen to form a new substance, iron oxide.

These examples illustrate that when we ask students to qualitatively explain scientific phenomena, students typically use the "correct" words such as *evaporation, condensation,* or *reaction,* but they lack understanding of the underlying scientific concepts (Ben-Avi et al., 1982, 1987; Eichinger & Lee, 1988; Osborne & Cosgrove, 1983).

How would you have answered the questions in the three scenarios? Qualitative explanations

FIGURE 2.2
Children believe that the residue that remains after steel wool is burned will weigh less than the steel wool.

ACTIVITY 2.1

Thinking About Your Own Understanding

MATERIALS NEEDED:
- something to write with
- if available, the *Private Universe Project* tapes (Presidents and Fellows of Harvard College, 1995)

A. Picture a tree seed. Next, picture an entire tree. How did the tree get its mass? Where did it come from? Answer these questions in your portfolio.

B. Contrast your answers with those of a few classmates. What ideas do you and your classmates have about where the mass came from? Try to come to a consensus.

C. Look up the word *photosynthesis* in a science book and read about it. What are your thoughts now about how a tree gets its mass? How do these differ from your initial thoughts? How are they alike?

D. If available, watch some of the episodes of the Harvard *Private Universe Project* series. What are your reactions to students' understandings of science concepts?

E. Think about the types of understandings you have developed about science concepts. How often have you used your science ideas to explain phenomena in your daily life? List as many examples as you can in your portfolio.

of scientific phenomena are a challenge, not only for many elementary and middle school students, but also for many high school, undergraduate, and even graduate students. When the three scenarios were replicated in science methods classes and in graduate courses, even students with backgrounds in science had a difficult time giving solid, qualitative explanations of the observed phenomena. Many college students were surprised that the residue after burning the steel wool had more mass than the steel wool, even though they had successfully completed introductory college chemistry. Take time now to complete Activity 2.1.

What is *your* reaction to the fact that the mass of a tree comes primarily from carbon dioxide found in the air and water taken from the environment? Many students, even biology majors, seem surprised by this information. Yet this is the basic premise of photosynthesis—a concept that is found in every elementary book and covered in every basic biology class in high school and college.

To learn more about scientific understandings, talk with some children about common physical, chemical, or biological phenomena. Having conversations with children of different ages and comparing their responses can help you discover some surprising things about what they know. Activity 2.2 is designed to help you begin talking to children about their science ideas.

ACTIVITY 2.2

Investigate Young Learners' Ideas Regarding Physical and Chemical Change

MATERIALS NEEDED:
- something to write with
- baking soda
- a 250 ml beaker
- vinegar
- water
- two students of different ages to talk with

A. Set up a conversation with two students of different ages to learn about how they understand some science concepts. You might want to tape your interview. Make sure to find out the following information:
- age of student
- current grade
- what science topics they remember studying in school or at home

   NOTE: Probing a child to determine his or her conceptual understanding is a difficult process. It is a good idea to practice with a classmate or a friend before you conduct these interviews with students. Tape these practice sessions and study the way you asked questions. In general, observe the following guidelines when interviewing your learners

1. Avoid using leading questions that suggest responses. For example, don't say, "How do you think this will react?" By saying *react,* you lead the students to think something is going to happen.

2. Avoid praise or negative comments. For example, don't say, "good." Rather, say, "I see."

3. Use phrases that allow a learner to clarify and expand on his or her ideas. Be sure to probe when scientific or technical terminology is used. For example, if the student says, "It will evaporate," ask, "What do you mean by 'it will evaporate'?" To clarify ideas, say things like, "Could you tell me more about what you mean? Other phrases include
   - "Please describe that further."
   - "What do you mean by . . . ?"
   - "Tell me more about . . . ?"
   - "Is this what you mean . . . ?"
   - "Please explain that further."
   - "Hmm. That's interesting. Tell me more about that."
   - "What else would you like to tell me about what you observed?"

4. Listen to the learner—use active listening techniques. For example, look at the child when he or she is speaking. Paraphrase what the student says. For example, if the child says, "I think it will disappear," you might say, "Do you mean you wouldn't be able to see it?" Ask for explanations. Summarize what you think the student said.

5. Use the learner's language to rephrase and further probe the learner's response. For example, if a student says, "I won't be
—continued

ACTIVITY 2.2 *Continued*

able to see it," say, "Why can't you *see* it?" Don't say, "Do you mean it will dissolve?"

6. Provide the learner with ample time to construct a response. Wait at least three to five seconds after asking a question before you say anything more.

7. Establish a calm and accepting atmosphere. Don't rush the conversation by talking hurriedly or being judgmental about responses.

8. If a learner cannot answer a question, try rephrasing the question. For example, if you first ask, "What do you think will happen?" and the child doesn't respond, rephrase the question to say, "What do you think will happen when I put this baking soda into this water and stir it?" However, be careful; don't add more than what the student said.

B. Complete the following tasks with the two students:

Physical Change Task

In this task, you will mix a teaspoon of baking soda in 100 ml of water. This is a physical change; the baking soda will dissolve in the water.

◆ Show students a teaspoon of baking soda and a 250 ml beaker with 100 ml water. Ask students to predict what will happen if you mix the baking soda in the water.

◆ Place the baking soda in the beaker of water and stir. Ask the students to describe what they see. Ask the students to explain what they observe. Find out what the students mean by the words

they use. For instance, if they say, "It dissolved," ask them what they mean by *dissolved.*

◆ Ask the students what they might see if they could magnify the contents of the beaker 100 million times. Ask the students to draw what they think they would see.

Chemical Change Task

In this task, you will mix a teaspoon of baking soda in vinegar. This is a chemical change; the baking soda will react with the vinegar to form new products.

◆ Show students a teaspoon of baking soda and a 250 ml beaker with 100 ml of vinegar. Ask students to predict what will happen if you mix the baking soda in the vinegar.

◆ Place the baking soda in the beaker of vinegar. Ask the students to describe what they see. Ask the students to explain what they observe. Find out what the students mean by the words they use. For instance, if they say, "It reacted," ask them what they meant by *reacted.*

◆ Ask what they might see if they could magnify the contents of the beaker 100 million times. Ask the students to draw what they think they would see.

C. Process what you found. Combine your data with the data from other students in your class. Summarize your data. What conclusions can you draw? What educational implications do your conclusions indicate? Record these in your portfolio.

Integrated Understandings

Instead of developing the inert knowledge we have been examining, project-based science is designed to help students develop integrated understandings. *Integrated understanding* results from the learner building meaningful relationships and connections between ideas and blending personal experiences with more formal scientific knowledge (Anderson, 1987; Anderson & Roth, 1988; Pines & West, 1986). Imagine a child who understands from a prior lesson the relationship between molecules in gaseous, liquid, and solid states. The child learns a new concept about sound vibrations traveling through different substances. The child notices during some activities that sound travels best through solids, next best through liquids, and least well through air. The teacher asks, "Why do you think sound travels best through the solid and least well through the air?" The child answers, "Well, it probably has something to do with what it is made of." The teacher replies, "What did we learn about what all matter is made of?" The child says, "Molecules." The teacher prompts the student by saying, "What do you know about the molecules in different states of matter?" The

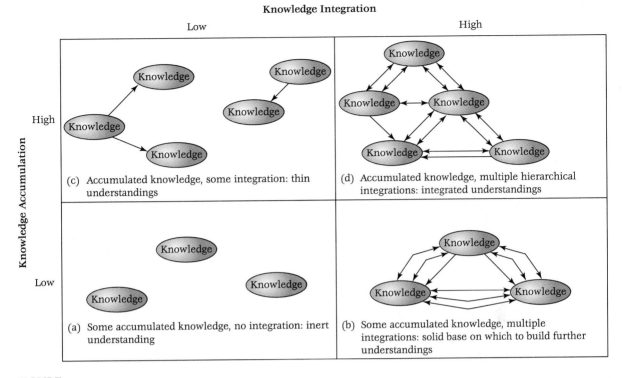

FIGURE 2.3

Understanding is a function of knowledge accumulation and knowledge integration. Theoretically, it is possible to accumulate a large number of discrete bits of knowledge without creating relationships between those pieces of knowledge or with only a few weak relationships (Cells A and C). It is also possible to have a limited amount of knowledge of which each piece is well integrated or linked to other knowledge, perhaps in multiple ways (Cell B). Rich, integrated understandings are achieved as knowledge becomes both structured and integrated (Cell D) (Talsma, 1998).

child answers, "Well, the molecules are close together in solids and far apart in gases." The teacher questions, "And what might this tell you about sound travel?" The child says, "Oh, I get it. If the molecules are close, the vibrations can move faster because they are close together to be able to move quickly from molecule to molecule. And that's not true in gases, so they can't move as fast!" This student has integrated understandings: she used her understanding of molecules in different states of matter to come up with a new explanation of the effect of states of matter on sound travel.

Integrated understanding is useable knowledge that can be applied to solve a problem and that can be applied in a variety of different situations and contexts. Another term for integrated understandings is *meaningful understandings*. Meaningful understanding is enabling: It en-

ables students to use what they know. For instance, a child who uses Newton's laws of motion to explain why a person needs to wear a seat belt when riding in a car is showing meaningful understandings. Newton's first law of motion states that an object will stay at rest or continue in motion unless acted upon by a force. Therefore, we wear a seat belt so that our bodies don't continue in motion (hit the windshield or get thrown out of the car) if the car comes to a sudden stop. Integrated understanding means learners can build relationships between ideas, explain these relationships, and use their ideas to explain and predict phenomena.

Figure 2.3, created by Valerie Talsma of the University of Michigan (Talsma, 1998), is an excellent way of illustrating the difference between inert and integrated understanding. The cell in the lower left corner, Cell A, represents a learner who has very little understanding and whose understandings are not connected to each other. This is inert knowledge—disconnected, unusable, fragments of facts. The cell in the lower right corner, Cell B, represents a learner with some understanding that is tightly integrated. This is the type of understanding we want a student to develop at the third or fourth grade level. Upper elementary students can't understand everything, but their understandings should be integrated. The cell in the upper left corner, Cell C, represents a learner who has accumulated knowledge but has not integrated the knowledge. This is the type of understanding that often emerges in schools. The cell in the upper right corner, Cell D, represents a learner who has accumulated knowledge and meaningful understandings. This is the rich, integrated understanding that we are trying to achieve in project-based science.

Types of Knowledge   One way to think about integrated and meaningful knowledge is to think about three types of knowledge: content, inquiry and problem solving, and epistemic (Perkins, 1992, Perkins et al., 1995). All three types of knowledge are needed in order for understandings to become integrated and meaningful. *Content knowledge* refers to the central concepts and principles in a domain. In science, one example of a central concept or principle is force. Integrated understanding depends on the learner understanding essential content of a discipline. Knowing content is essential. For example, a learner who understands why an object stops moving once it is given a push understands some central concepts and principles of physics. These include force, acceleration, velocity, inertia, and Newton's three laws of motion.

However, content knowledge is only one type of knowledge that is essential for student understanding (Perkins, 1992; Perkins, Crismond, Simmons, & Unger, 1995; Spitulnik, Stratford, Krajcik, & Soloway, 1997). Understanding also depends upon supporting knowledge that helps the learner know how to learn. This supporting knowledge includes inquiry and problem-solving knowledge and epistemic

knowledge. *Inquiry and problem-solving knowledge* is essential in helping a learner find solutions to questions, in being able to design an experiment, and in being able to find and evaluate background information related to a question. This classification of knowledge also includes metacognitive strategies (strategies that learners use to think about their own thinking) that helps monitor a learner's progress or knowing when to seek help. A student with strong metacognitive strategies will be able to track how well he is completing a task such as following through on procedures that are part of an investigation that extends over time.

Epistemic knowledge is knowledge about the "rules of the game" (Perkins, 1992; Perkins et al., 1995). For example, students should know that science is a theory that is cohesive. For this reason, there are "rules" in science that help us understand what is acceptable as evidence. Imagine a third grade child who grew one sample of mold in the sun and one in the shade and concluded that darkness was necessary for mold to grow best. The child would understand the "rules of the game" if she understood that one experiment does not provide sufficient evidence to make a valid conclusion and that other factors, such as moisture, might also affect mold growth.

We present this summary of the types of knowledge because all three are essential for students to develop integrated and meaningful understanding needed for learning to continue. Just having content knowledge robs a learner from learning more. In fact, the *National Science Education Standards* (NRC, 1996) stress that content knowledge must be taught in the context of effective teaching and assessment standards: "Using the [content] standards with traditional teaching and assessment strategies defeats the intentions of the National Science Education Standards" (p. 112). Meaningful understandings will occur only if content knowledge is taught in the process of doing inquiry. To illustrate, if a child knows only definitions about molecular states, she will not be able to use the understandings and apply them to a new situation related to sound travel. Table 2.1 summarizes the three types of knowledge.

TABLE 2.1   Three Types of Knowledge

Type of knowledge	Definition	Examples
Content	Knowing the central concepts and principles in a domain	◆ Biology: understanding predator and prey relationships ◆ Chemistry: understanding physical and chemical change ◆ Physics: understanding inertia
Inquiry and problem-solving	Knowing how to problem solve, design, and carry out investigations and metacognitive strategies	Knowing how to design an experiment; knowledge of how to analyze data; strategies for monitoring one's progress
Epistemic	Knowing the "rules of the game"	Knowing what counts for evidence; knowing when to collect more evidence to support a position

CONSTRUCTION OF KNOWLEDGE

What can be done to help children develop integrated and meaningful understanding of science? How can we help children apply scientific concepts and principles to solve real world problems that are of interest to them? What can be done to help children develop content, inquiry and problem solving, and epistemic knowledge? Research findings from the last two decades have shown growing support for the notion that integrated and meaningful types of knowledge are best learned when what occurs in schools is less receptional and more transformational.

Receptional approaches are those in which teachers transmit information, and students receive the information. Receptional approaches to teaching and learning have long dominated our school systems. Armstrong (1994) writes, "For most Americans, the word *classroom* conjures up an image of students sitting in neat rows of desks facing the front of the room, where a teacher either sits at a large desk correcting papers or stands near a blackboard lecturing students" (p. 86). *Transformational approaches* to teaching and learning are those in which students make sense of the material themselves rather than receive information to memorize. Project-based science is one example of a transformational approach to teaching and learning.

How do students come to make sense of material rather than only memorize it? Brown,

Collins, and Deguid (1989) argue that "knowledge is . . . in part a product of the activity, context, and culture in which it is developed and used" (p. 32). These researchers see knowledge as contextualized. By *contextualized* they mean that knowledge cannot easily be separated from the situation in which it is developed. Blumenfeld and colleagues (1998) reiterate this notion: "knowing and doing are not separated; knowledge is not an abstract phenomenon that readily can be transferred from how it is learned in the classroom for use in other situations." The *National Science Education Standards* (NRC, 1996) state, "Student understanding is actively constructed through individual and social processes. In the same way that scientists develop their knowledge and understanding as they seek answers to questions about the natural world, students develop an understanding of the natural world when they are actively engaged in scientific inquiry—alone and with others" (p. 29). This learning model that suggests that learning cannot be separated from the social context in which it takes place is often referred to as *social constructivism.*[1]

---

1. This book adopts a social constructivist perspective. Other forms of constructivism are radical constructivism and contextual constructivism. For more information on other variants of constructivism, see Tobin, K., ed. 1993. *The practice of constructivism in science education*, Washington, D.C.: American Association for the Advancement of Science, or consult Shapiro, B. 1994. *What children bring to light: A constructivist perspective on children's learning in science.* New York: Teachers College Press.

SOCIAL CONSTRUCTION OF KNOWLEDGE

Social constructivist theories in education developed primarily from the works of Lev Vygotsky, a Russian psychologist, who concluded that children construct knowledge or understanding as the result of thinking and doing in social contexts (Vygotsky, 1986). He believed that development depends on biological factors (such as brain growth and maturation) and on social and cultural forces (such as interactions with others at home, in school, or on the playground). He also believed that learning takes place in social contexts (such as during playtime with peers, in conversations with classmates, or while parents or teachers are speaking), and children internalize the information to form understanding. Children gradually become more independent and autonomous through social interactions with others such as teachers and other adults. Researchers in science education have found evidence to support the social constructivist viewpoint about how children learn science (Brown & Campione, 1994; Driver, 1989; Roth, 1995).

Social constructivism holds that children learn concepts or construct meaning about ideas through their interactions with and interpretations of their world, including essential interactions with others. From the moment a child is born, he (supported through interactions with others) is constructing knowledge of his environment. Knowledge is not something that is simply memorized; it is constructed by the learner based upon his experiences in the world. For example, a child may learn that leaves fall from trees when they turn colors during the autumn after she has observed this happen several years in a row. Discussions with family members or peers may influence her understanding. For example, a parent might explain that leaves fall when the weather becomes cold. Knowledge is the result of individual interpretations (the child notices they fall after they turn color) and constructions of reality as it occurs in a social context (a parent says this happens when it gets cold).

Children receive information, interpret it, and relate it to other preexisting knowledge and experiences. As a result, they come to school already holding concepts that teachers will be expecting to help them learn. These prior experiences and conceptions will influence any new

FIGURE 2.4
Children learn about their environment by interacting with others.

knowledge they attempt to acquire. For example, a teacher who attempts to teach a class about why trees drop leaves will encounter any number of prior ideas about this phenomenon in the minds of her students. Some might think the leaves drop because they are dead. Some might think the tree runs out of food. Others might think that the color of the leaves causes them to fall. Some might think the tree sleeps in the winter. Still others might think that the cold winter winds blow the leaves off. These prior beliefs will affect the teaching and learning going on in the classroom. Because prior experiences influence the learning of new knowledge, it is important to reflect frequently on prior experiences. You probably have already noticed that the chapter titles in this book are questions, that each chapter begins with reflective questions, and that many activities ask you to think about your own experiences. These questions help you reflect on your ideas.

Because children come to school with prior understandings about their world, their concepts and theories are not always the same as those developed over the years by scientists. As a teacher, you might try, for example, to teach elementary students that air is matter and that matter is something that takes up space and has mass. A typical activity in many elementary textbooks demonstrates to children that two deflated balloons will be balanced on a balance scale but that one deflated and one inflated balloon will result in the tilt of the inflated balloon toward the ground. This activity is designed to "prove" to students that air has mass and takes up space—the balloon filled with air has more mass than the one without air.

What if, before showing children the result of this activity, a teacher asked them to predict the event? What do you think young children would predict? Think about some of the prior experiences elementary children may have had with air. Air (helium) in a balloon causes it to float away. Air in a raft or beach ball causes it to float on water. Air cannot be seen. These prior experiences may have convinced students that air is nothing or that air has no mass. They may predict, therefore, that nothing will happen—air is a nonentity, so the inflated and deflated balloons should still balance. Perhaps they will predict that the inflated balloon will float upward and the empty balloon will sink. Young students will probably not be convinced otherwise by a teacher's demonstration.

It is the job of the teacher to create a learning environment that encourages students to revise their own concepts to accept these new formulations. This is not an easy task. Learning is a continuous process that requires many new experiences in which students can construct and reconstruct knowledge by interacting with others. Children need many opportunities to express and explore their ideas. These ideas about social constructivism have a number of implications for teaching science and are the foundations for project-based science.

A Social Constructivist Model of Teaching

The social constructivist theory asserts that children take an active role in constructing meaning; they cannot construct meaning by passively taking in knowledge transmitted from a teacher. An ancient Chinese Proverb captures this idea in three simple lines:

Tell me, and I forget.
Show me, and I remember.
Involve me, and I understand.

Accordingly, a model of teaching that utilizes social constructivist theory is one that focuses on the child as an active builder of knowledge in a community of learners. Social constructivist

theory has implications for the way a teacher creates the learning environment, sets up lessons, asks questions, reacts to students' ideas, and carries out lessons. Lorsbach and Tobin (1992) suggest that teaching science using a constructivist approach means that teachers do *not* teach science as "the search for the truth." Instead, they teach science more as scientists really do science—by actively engaging children in the "social process of making sense of experiences." This approach differs greatly from much of what can be seen in "school science" today, where science teaching is only viewed as finding correct answers.

A social constructivist model of teaching is characterized by the following features:

Active engagement with phenomena

- ◆ Students ask and refine questions related to phenomena. For example, students might ask, "Why do worms help the materials in our pop bottles to decompose faster?"

- ◆ Students predict and explain phenomena. For instance, students are asked to predict what happens to the banana peel after it is in the bottle for a week. Or students are asked to explain why the worms helped materials decompose.

- ◆ Students mindfully interact with concrete materials. For example, students set up decomposition columns—miniature composts in 2-liter pop bottles filled with leaves, dirt, banana peels, and worms— rather than only read about decomposition.

Use and application of knowledge

- ◆ Teachers and students use prior knowledge. For example, the teacher might ask students what they know about decomposition, or the teacher might ask if any have compost piles at home.

- ◆ Students identify and use multiple resources. For example, the students might identify the need to consult books, the World Wide Web, and naturalists to answer questions about composts.

- ◆ Students plan and carry out investigations. For instance, students plan what variables they will investigate in the decomposition column, such as temperature, moisture, sunlight, rate of decomposition, and number of worms. Then students carry out their investigations.

- Concepts and skills are applied to new situations. For instance, students apply understanding of decomposition to a discussion about landfill problems.
- Students are given time for reflection. For example, students have time to talk with others in class and record their thoughts in journals.
- Students take action to improve their own world. For example, students decide to start a school paper recycling program as a result of learning that paper doesn't decompose quickly in a landfill.

Multiple representations

- Teachers use varied evaluation techniques. For example, students might be evaluated on journal entries, artifacts created to explain results from their investigations on decomposition columns, and peer evaluations of students' contributions to the project.
- Students create products or artifacts to represent understanding. For example, students might create posters or multimedia products to depict the factors that aid decomposition.
- Students revise products and artifacts. For example, students might revise their posters to include photographs after classmates suggest that photos might show results better than drawings.

Use of learning communities

- Students use language as a tool to express knowledge. For example, students debate, share, and explain ideas about the problem of decomposition as it relates to landfills.
- Students express, debate, and come to a resolution regarding ideas, concepts, and theories. For example, students discuss whether worms affect decomposition, and they come to a consensus on this idea.
- Students debate the viability of evidence. For instance, students discuss whether numbers of worms are ample evidence for determining their effect on decomposition.

- Learning is situated in a social context. For example, students learn about decomposition by participating in discussions with teachers and peers and interactions with community members such as naturalists from local agencies.
- Knowledgeable others help students learn new ideas and skills that they couldn't learn on their own. For example, the teacher helps students understand that rate of decomposition is influenced by presence of oxygen. Next, the teacher helps students make the connection to landfills that are covered up, preventing oxygen from reaching the garbage.

Authentic tasks

- Driving questions focus and sustain activities. For example, students might investigate the question, "Where does all our garbage go?"
- The topic or question is relevant to the student. For example, students might explore why they are charged 10 cents on every soft drink can or bottle they buy.
- Learning is connected to students' lives outside school. For example, students visit a local recycling plant in their community to see where the glass, aluminum, and paper their families recycle are processed.
- Science concepts and principles emerge as needed to answer a driving question. For example, students learn how to read a thermometer because they need to have this skill to measure the temperature changes in their decomposition column. Or students learn about chemical processes to understand decomposition.

Using these features, let us compare two lessons.

A Receptional Approach to Teaching   Marie, a sixth grade teacher, believes that children need to be quiet and in their seats to learn the information she is telling them. In a recent lesson in which she taught about sound, she first had the students read from the textbook the chapter on sound. Students read out loud one paragraph at a time. Marie pointed out to students what the important concepts were as they were read by writing them on the board. Students wrote definitions of the important vocabulary words—frequency, pitch, amplitude, waves, rarefaction, and compression—in their science journals. Marie attempted to prove to the students that sound is produced by waves by demonstrating the waves that are created by striking a tuning fork and placing it in water. Next, Marie showed the children the different frequencies produced by various pitched tuning forks. Finally, Marie reinforced the important concepts by showing a videotape covering the same ideas. Students received a homework assignment in which they had to answer three questions at the end of the chapter. Marie evaluated the students with a quiz at the end of the week. On this quiz, students chose the correct definitions for words including pitch, amplitude, and frequency.

A Transformational Approach to Teaching

Roberta, another sixth grade teacher, introduced the same sound lesson as Marie in a very different manner. Roberta is investigating with her class the driving question "What Makes Music?" She introduced a benchmark lesson to help students understand basic concepts of sound. First, she handed each child in the class a balloon, a rubber band, and a ruler. The students were instructed to spend the next ten minutes exploring ways to make sounds with each of the objects to see what they could discover about sound. At the end of the exploration time, students were asked to discuss their findings with each other in small groups and later share with the whole class what they discovered. Roberta did not evaluate these ideas but listed all of them on the board. One child said that the balloon was louder than the rubber band. Another said that the ruler changed sound as it was hung off the table at different lengths. A third student said that a loud sound was created when she snapped Randy, her neighbor, with the rubber band. (Oops—the teacher forgot to set some basic ground rules for behavior! See Chapter 8 for more information about classroom management.) Yet another child said that all the objects were moving when the sounds were produced. Roberta wrote the word *vibration* on the board and told the children that scientists call such movement *vibrations*. She asked the class to stop and compare each object again. She asked, "Is it true that all the ob-

jects need to be moving to produce sound?" The students debated about the evidence supporting this conjecture. One student asked how the sounds made by a thick rubber band would differ from those made by a thin one, just like the strings on his guitar made different sounds. Roberta encouraged the students to explore this idea. Through questioning, she guided the students through a comparison of the lengths, thicknesses, and stretched widths of the various objects and a comparison of the pitches. She asked students to think about why the pitch would be different—was there anything different about the vibrations? Using materials, students explored the question in small groups. By analyzing evidence collected, the students explained that the differences in pitch seemed to be caused by variations in how fast the rubber bands were moving. Roberta introduced the class to the term *frequency* and helped students see how their findings matched the definition of this term. Students were encouraged to think about instances at home when they experienced something to support the concept that sound is caused by vibrations and that pitch is caused by variations in the frequency of the vibrations. A student mentioned the digital monitors on her stereo system that visually displayed the frequency of vibrations. Another told about a time that he dropped salt on the top of the TV; the salt "danced" up and down and vibrated while the TV was turned on but was still when the TV was turned off. A third student discussed how she would place her fingers and move her lips to play her clarinet. Yet another talked about watching the pictures on her brother's wall vibrate when he turned up his rock music. Roberta consistently asked students to elaborate on their examples and to explain how the examples supported the question asked. Students were frequently asked to confirm or refute comments made by others in the class. Finally, to evaluate what students learned, Roberta asked them to write down in their journals what they had learned in the lesson.

Unlike the receptional approach to teaching, the transformational approach is consistent with social constructivist theory and project-based science. Can you identify a constructivist lesson? Activity 2.3 will help you explore this idea on your own.

ACTIVITY 2.3

Recognizing and Evaluating
a Social Constructivist Lesson

MATERIALS NEEDED:
- something to write with
- a classroom to visit or a videotape of a lesson
- a videotape of yourself teaching a lesson

A. Read the following classroom descriptions.
1. Marquette, a kindergarten teacher, asks her students to tell her what they want to know about pets. Three students want to know more about dinosaurs, two students want to know how they can get pet rabbits, one inquires about a lizard, and two want to learn more about kittens. As students suggest these animals, she writes the words *dinosaur, rabbit, lizard,* and *kitten* on the board. Marquette does not tell the three students that dinosaurs are not pets; instead, she asks the students what they think about the pets suggested. Quickly a number of students point out that dinosaurs are not pets. Marquette asks the students to elaborate on their reasons for this belief, and then she asks the students who originally suggested dinosaurs what they think. Two agree that they are not pets, but one, Tyrone, says that he has a whole collection of them. Marquette asks this student to explain what he thinks it means to have a pet; he says that a pet is an animal you collect. She asks him if he has ever been to a pet store. He has. She asks whether he has ever seen dinosaurs for sale at the pet store. He agrees that he hasn't. Another student quickly quips that they must be alive and fed and cared for. Tyrone agrees and says that he would like to learn more about lizards that look like the dinosaurs in his collection.

   Marquette leads the class in a discussion about what students would like to know about each animal, and she asks them to suggest how they might learn these things. From this discussion comes the idea that veterinarians and pet store

owners would be able to answer a number of their questions. Carlos, a boy in the class, says that his mother is a veterinarian and that he will ask her to come to school to talk. Marquette agrees, and the mother calls the teacher to make arrangements. Mrs. Hernandez comes to school the next week and teaches the students about the nutrition necessary for various types of pets—articularly the lizard, rabbit, and kitten suggested by the students. She also discusses dogs, guinea pigs, hamsters, and gerbils, as instructed by Marquette. The next day, Marquette passes out a worksheet with pictures of animals and the foods they eat. The children are evaluated on their ability to match the proper food with the animal that eats it.

2. Ron, a third grade teacher, is very interested in space flight and astronomy. He has shared with the students in his class many artifacts including photographs taken on vacations and trips to the Kennedy Space Center at Cape Canaveral in Florida and the Neil Armstrong Center in Wapokoneta, Ohio. He has shown many movies and videos on space travel, and he has even brought his telescope to school for the students to look through. His students have become quite interested in astronomy and space travel. During science class, a student in the class shares with the others that his parents took him to a planetarium at a nearby university over the weekend. Ron decides this would be a great trip for his class and schedules it. On the trip, students learn about the constellations and apparent movement of stars in the sky throughout the year. Ron finds an activity in a teacher book with a star locating device in it. He has his students make the star finder and assigns the students to look for certain constellations in the sky over the next month. Daily, he has students share information they have discovered about

the stars and various constellations. At the end of the month, he gives the students a quiz in which they match the constellations with their names. He also quizzes students on the definitions of *star, constellation, sun, orbit, revolution, rotation,* and other important words that are in the textbook.

B. Using the following chart, evaluate the two lessons in terms of how well they meet the criteria for social constructivist lessons.

Record the results in your portfolio. Then meet with teammates to discuss your evaluations. Come to a consensus.

C. Neither of these two lessons has all the features of a social constructivist classroom. How could they be revised to contain more of the features?

D. Meet with your classmates to come to a consensus on improving the lessons.

E. Record the results of your meetings and thoughts in your portfolio.

Scale for Evaluating Degree of Constructivist Learning

Active Engagement with Phenomena

Students ask and refine questions related to phenomena.
often _____ _____ _____ _____ _____ _____ _____ seldom

Students predict and explain phenomena.
often _____ _____ _____ _____ _____ _____ _____ seldom

Students mindfully interact with concrete materials.
often _____ _____ _____ _____ _____ _____ _____ seldom

Use and Application of Knowledge

Teachers and students use prior knowledge.
often _____ _____ _____ _____ _____ _____ _____ seldom

Students identify and use multiple resources.
often _____ _____ _____ _____ _____ _____ _____ seldom

Students plan and carry out investigations.
often _____ _____ _____ _____ _____ _____ _____ seldom

Students apply concepts and skills to new situations.
often _____ _____ _____ _____ _____ _____ _____ seldom

Students are given time for reflection.
often _____ _____ _____ _____ _____ _____ _____ seldom

Students take action to improve their own world.
often _____ _____ _____ _____ _____ _____ _____ seldom

Multiple Representations

Students use varied evaluation techniques.
often _____ _____ _____ _____ _____ _____ _____ seldom

Students create products or artifacts to represent understanding.
often _____ _____ _____ _____ _____ _____ _____ seldom

Students revise products and artifacts.
often _____ _____ _____ _____ _____ _____ _____ seldom

Use of Learning Communities

Students use language as a tool to express knowledge.
often _____ _____ _____ _____ _____ _____ _____ seldom

Students express, debate, and come to a resolution regarding ideas, concepts, and theories.
often _____ _____ _____ _____ _____ _____ _____ seldom

Students debate the viability of evidence.
often _____ _____ _____ _____ _____ _____ _____ seldom

Learning is situated in a social context.
often _____ _____ _____ _____ _____ _____ _____ seldom

Knowledgeable others help students learn new ideas and skills that they couldn't learn on their own.
often _____ _____ _____ _____ _____ _____ _____ seldom

Role of Authentic Tasks

Driving questions focus and sustain activities.
often _____ _____ _____ _____ _____ _____ _____ seldom

The topic or question is relevant to the student.
often _____ _____ _____ _____ _____ _____ _____ seldom

Learning is connected to students' lives outside school.
often _____ _____ _____ _____ _____ _____ _____ seldom

Science concepts and principles emerge as needed to answer a driving question.
often _____ _____ _____ _____ _____ _____ _____ seldom

FEATURES OF SOCIAL CONSTRUCTIVIST LESSONS

Now that we have explored a few general ideas about social constructivist theory and teaching strategies consistent with this theory, we will discuss in more detail some of the features of social constructivist lessons.

Active Engagement with Phenomena

Children construct understanding in science by actively engaging with phenomena. *Active engagement* describes several experiences: Students ask and refine questions related to phenomena. They predict and explain phenomena; and they mindfully interact with concrete materials. Active engagement, then, is both mental and physical.

Students Ask and Refine Questions and Predict and Explain Phenomena
To actively engage students intellectually, teachers must create a learning environment in which students can *ask questions* freely, *dialogue* with classmates and more knowledgeable others *to refine questions,* and *predict and explain phenomena.* Such cognitive activities help students make connections and develop in-depth understandings (Brooks & Brooks, 1993). The *National Science Education Standards* (NRC, 1996) state, "An important stage of inquiry and of student science learning is the oral and written discourse that focuses the attention of the student on how they [sic] know what they know and how their knowledge connects to larger ideas, domains, and the world beyond the classroom" (p. 36). It is through this discourse (asking questions, having discussions about important questions, making predictions, and providing explanations) that students come to understand what they know. (The role of questioning and ways to set up project-based learning environments that support questioning in greater detail are covered later in several chapters. Chapter 4 explores the role of predicting and explaining phenomena.)

Imagine a second grade teacher asks, "How could we find out if the apple seed is alive?" She is stimulating the students to ask questions. Students might ask, "Could we plant it?" "Can we cut it open to see if something is growing inside?" "Could we ask a farmer?" The teacher has

the students work in groups to discuss and refine these questions. They might debate the fact that cutting open the seed could kill it and, therefore, defeat the purpose of their investigation. This thought might lead them to settle on planting the seed to see if it is alive. If the students planted the apple seed, they could predict what would happen. This could lead to more refined questions like, "Why isn't it sprouting yet?" and "Do we need to water it more?" If the apple seed began to sprout, students could explain that the seed was alive. However, a lively debate could still take place about whether the seed was alive before being planted. It is through the process of asking and refining questions, making predictions, and providing explanations about the apple seed that students will begin to understand whether the seed is alive.

Students Mindfully Interact with Concrete Materials
One hallmark of social constructivist teaching is that students mindfully interact with concrete materials. Some teaching strategies tend to use concrete materials more than do others. Dale's Cone of Experience (Dale, 1969), provides teachers with a tool for thinking about teaching strategies. This categorization is not a prescription for determining how actively students are engaged cognitively, because, for example, even active reading strategies[2] can make reading about science far less passive. Rather, it provides a framework for thinking about how a particular strategy might use concrete materials.

Children retain more of what they are taught if they engage in more active, concrete types of learning. In fact, it is estimated that the more active and concrete their learning, the more they retain (Bruner, 1977). Notice where demonstrations fall on the scale of Dale's Cone of Experience[3] in Figure 2.5. A demonstration is visually oriented; students do not work directly with materials but rather watch the teacher work with materials. Demonstrations, thus, are moderately abstract compared with activities in which students work with concrete materials themselves. Some instructional tools, such as computers,

2. See, for example, Carr, E. M., and L. E. Aldinger. 1994. *Thinking works: Using cognitive processes in the language arts classroom.* Ann Arbor, Mich.: Exceptional Innovations.

3. Edgar Dale's Cone of Experience pictured in Figure 2.5 was modified by a personal friend, Rolinda LeMay, to include comments pertaining to level of involvement and percentage of retention.

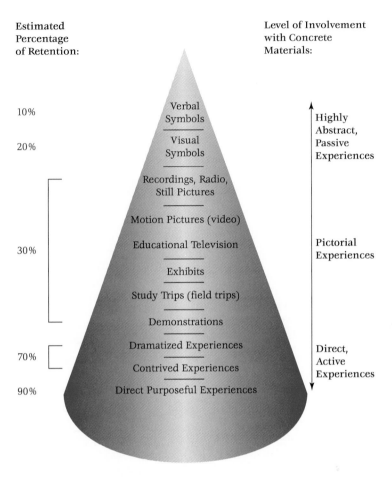

Estimated
Percentage
of Retention:

Level of Involvement
with Concrete
Materials:

10%   Verbal Symbols

20%   Visual Symbols

Recordings, Radio, Still Pictures

Motion Pictures (video)

30%   Educational Television

Exhibits

Study Trips (field trips)

Demonstrations

70%   Dramatized Experiences

Contrived Experiences

90%   Direct Purposeful Experiences

Highly
Abstract,
Passive
Experiences

Pictorial
Experiences

Direct,
Active
Experiences

FIGURE 2.5
Dale's cone of experience.

videodisks, and CD-ROMS can provide different levels of direct student interaction. For example, computers (which were not yet widely used in schools at the time Dale proposed this hierarchy) can fall into several categories. Some computer programs are very abstract—requiring mostly reading or symbol interpretation. Computer simulations fit into the Contrived Experiences category. Programs with interface devices permitting students to investigate with temperature and light probes provide Direct Experiences. Take time to complete Activity 2.4.

Use and Application of Knowledge

To develop integrated understandings, students need to use and apply their knowledge. This use and application of knowledge is supported by several strategies: First, teachers must consider students' prior knowledge. Second, activities must encourage students to identify and use multiple resources. Third, activities must involve students in planning and carrying out investigations. Fourth, learned concepts and skills must to be applied to new situations. Fifth, students should be allowed time for reflection. Sixth, teachers must help students to take action to improve their own world.

Teachers and Students Use Prior Knowledge   In order for a teacher to help students use and apply their knowledge, she or he must consider what it is that students already know. The following paragraph serves as an illustration of this point:

It is really actually simple. First, you arrange things into different groups depending upon their makeup. Of course, one pile may be enough depending on how much there is to do. If you have

---

ACTIVITY 2.4

Determining Levels of Concreteness
and Abstractness

MATERIALS NEEDED:
- a copy of Dale's Cone of Experience (Figure 2.5)

A. What follows is a list of a number of strategies for teaching about recycling. Rank each strategy's level of abstraction on a scale of 1 to 5 (1 being very concrete and 5 being very abstract).

1. watching a television documentary about landfill problems
2. watching the teacher sort aluminum, glass, and plastic into three recycling bins
3. visiting a recycling center
4. burying a piece of plastic, a glass cup, a banana skin, a piece of bread, and an aluminum can; watering the items weekly; and periodically uncovering the items to see if they are decomposing
5. painting a poster to promote recycling
6. writing a rap song about recycling
7. coloring a picture about the ways to limit litter (reuse, recycle, reduce)
8. starting a compost in the school playground
9. arranging in sequence pictures about how long it takes some items to biodegrade
10. reading a newspaper article about recycling
11. listening to a guest speaker from the local recycling center
12. writing a story about the future if people fail to solve landfill problems
13. creating a poem about recycling
14. sorting items from the school lunch into aluminum, glass, and plastic bins
15. starting a school paper recycling program
16. keeping track of the amount of waste produced in the classroom for the week and estimating how much would be produced in a year
17. role playing what to do if a friend drops a candy wrapper on the ground
18. looking at photographs of landfills

B. Convene with some of your classmates to share your rankings of the teaching strategies. Try to come to a consensus about the rankings.

C. Obtain a variety of teacher resources and activity books. Look in them for lessons to teach about plant growth. In your portfolio, make a list of lessons, activity ideas, or investigations that would be more concrete than the ones in the books. How could you make any abstract strategies more concrete?

---

to go somewhere else due to a lack of equipment, that is the next step; otherwise, you are pretty well set. It is important not to overdo any particular part of the job. That is, it is better to do too few things at once than too many. In the short run, this may not seem important, but trouble from doing too many can easily arise. A mistake can be expensive as well. Working the equipment should be self-explanatory, and we need not dwell on it here. Soon, however, it will become just another facet of life. It is difficult to see an end to the necessity for this task in the immediate future, but then one can never tell (Bransford, 1979).

What is this paragraph about? You probably had difficulty understanding it because you were not given any clue about its topic. If you had known from the start that it was about washing clothes, you would have instantly understood it. Reread the paragraph now that you know what it is about. Doesn't it make more sense? In this case, activating your prior knowledge clearly would have enhanced your ability to understand new material.

Constructivist teaching approaches focus on the learner's prior knowledge, because it is the learner who must integrate new ideas into his or her current understandings. Shapiro (1994) writes,

> The role of the teacher [in a constructivist view] is not to simply present new information, correct students' "misconceptions," and demonstrate skills. It is to guide the learner to consider new ways of thinking about phenomena and events. In order to do so, the teacher must have some understanding of what the learner brings to the learning experience, that is, his or her prior ideas, and thoughts" (p. 8).

To help students integrate their understandings, teachers must know about their prior understandings. Recall the examples earlier in this chapter of the role played by prior knowledge and experience in learning. Children have had years of experience with leaves falling or with air (blowing, in balloons, in balls) before they come to school to receive formal instruction about these concepts. When teachers attempt to teach students that air has mass, for example, prior experiences may conflict with the new ideas as students try to integrate the new understandings into their conceptual framework of "air." With some awareness of students' past experiences, teachers can help students reconcile what seem to be conflicts between those experiences and new learning. Without this awareness, teachers will still be able to ensure that teaching takes place but not that learning does.

There are many ways to probe for students' prior knowledge. For example, in the washing clothes scenario, a teacher could provide students with a mental organizer (such as telling them they are about to read about washing clothes) and discuss what they know about washing clothes before students read the paragraph. Another strategy is to remind students of an activity or investigation done earlier in the year that has some connection to new learning.

Students Identify and Use Multiple Resources
An important strategy in helping children construct understandings in science is having them identify and use multiple resources. *Multiple resources* might be used in the course of answering a driving question. They include books, journals, science equipment, supplies, and computers. Multiple resources reinforce student understanding through different presentation and through emphasis of different information. While a book might explain how a landfill works via text and photographs, a Web page might present a slightly different explanation through different illustrations and through interactive charts of statistics on landfill usage and cleanup efforts. When students analyze and synthesize this different information presented in these different ways, they create more solid, integrated understandings.

Students Plan and Carry Out Investigations
The cycle of asking a question, designing an investigation, analyzing results, and asking new questions, which is a key feature of project-based science, requires children to use and apply their understandings. (The investigation web is further explored in Chapter 4.) Assume a class is exploring the question "Where does all our garbage go?" To explore this driving question, students might set up a decomposition column, which is a small composter in a 2-liter pop bottle filled with leaves, dirt, banana peels, and worms. Students ask questions such as, "Why do worms help the materials in our pop bottles to decompose faster?" or "How does moisture affect how fast decomposition occurs?" Students gather information from multiple resources such as books, journals, and the World Wide Web to gather background information related to their questions. Students plan investigations to answer these questions, considering the materials they will need, how they will collect and analyze the data, and how they will present their findings to the class. They make predictions about what will happen to the items in the bottle. Then students carry out their investigations. They debate whether two pop bottles can provide ample evidence for whether moisture affects the rate of decomposition. Students create artifacts such as posters or multimedia products to represent their understanding of decomposition. Finally, students share and explain ideas about the problem of decomposition as it relates to landfills. This process of asking and refining questions, debating ideas, making predictions, designing experiments, gathering information, collecting and analyzing data, drawing conclusions, and communicating ideas and findings to others helps students construct a solid, integrated understanding of the topic and related concepts.

Students Apply Concepts and Skills to New Situations Students develop rich, integrated understandings when they apply their knowledge to new situations. This phenomenon is illustrated as the change in understanding from Cell C to Cell D in Figure 2.3. By applying concepts and skills to new situations, students elaborate on their understandings, form new connections with old ideas, and build connections between new ideas and old ideas. For instance, in the decomposition example, students can apply their knowledge of how oxygen affects decomposition to real world situations such as landfills. Through discussions with others, students can make connections between the understanding that oxygen is needed for decomposition and the awareness that materials don't decompose quickly in a landfill.

Students Are Given Time for Reflection   In science, *reflection* involves thinking about alternative questions, considering possible hypotheses, contemplating a variety of answers, speculating on outcomes, deliberating on steps that can be taken, and meditating on conclusions found. Reflection takes *time.* Teachers cannot rush through topics, lessons, and examples and expect students to learn new material thoroughly. For this reason, constructivist teachers present fewer topics in the curriculum and spend more time on them. During discussions teachers use the technique wait-time: They wait three to five seconds after asking a question before calling on a student. Teachers ask probing questions, which are questions designed to elicit more details. (Wait-time and probing questions are discussed in more detail in Chapter 6.) Brooks and Brooks (1993) write,

> Classroom environments that require immediate responses prevent these students from thinking through issues and concepts thoroughly, forcing them, in effect, to become spectators as their quicker peers react. They learn over time that there's no point in mentally engaging in teacher-posed questions because the questions will have been answered before they have had the opportunity to develop hypotheses (p. 115).

Teachers provide students with time in class to discuss ideas with others, write about experiences, and revise ideas and products. For an example, recall the teacher who has students discuss whether the apple seed is alive.

Students Take Action to Improve Their Own World   The idea of taking action to improve the world has become popular in science education in the last few decades. The Science-Technology-Society (STS) movement that was popularized in the 1980s is one example. STS incudes topics such as health, population, resources, pollution, and environment—topics that people must understand in order to become a active citizens making personal decisions and taking actions related to society or for improving their lives. The *National Science Education*

Standards (NRC, 1996) include the following content standards for grades K–4:

> As a result of activities in grades K–4, all students should develop understanding of
> - personal health
> - characteristics and changes in population
> - types of resources
> - changes in environments
> - science and technology in local challenges (p. 138)

Similarly, the *National Science Education Standards* (NRC, 1996) include the following content standards for grades 5–8:

> As a result of activities in grades 5–8, all students should develop
> - abilities of technological design
> - understandings about science and technology (p. 161)

Children are particularly interested in studying questions that can be applied to their own lives and improve their own world. Adolescents see themselves as emerging adults and feel a particular urgency about the future. Many adolescents are interested in ecological topics and environmental issues (Barnes, Shaw, & Spector, 1989). Adolescents see exploring these topics as a way of taking action to improve their world. Young elementary students have less global concerns. They are interested in concerns such as improving the living conditions and nutrition of their pets at home. Middle grade students may be interested in more far-reaching local issues, such as the heath of a local stream. They may be interested in monitoring the quality of the stream and reporting it to a local governmental agency. Children of all ages care about improving the school environment. They can put up bird feeders, plant wildflowers, and organize a litter pickup day. When learning includes taking action to improve their world, children see the importance of it, and the action solidifies their knowledge.

Multiple Representations

Constructivist theory asserts that learning involves developing multiple representations of ideas that integrate understanding. Writing, building a poster, and manipulating materials are three different representations. For instance, in the decomposition activity described earlier, students constructed a decomposition column, wrote about their investigation, and built a poster to express their ideas. These three activities include the translation of their understandings in three different formats—in concrete, textual, and graphical representations. When students make connections between these representations, they develop integrated understandings that can be applied to new situations.

Teachers Use Varied Evaluation Techniques

There are two reasons for varied evaluation techniques. First, different types of evaluation techniques can better assess different types of understanding formed through a variety of intellectual activities. Second, multiple forms of assessment help learners show their understandings in ways that enable different learners to succeed at showing what they know.

In project-based science, students are developing different types of understandings, which must be assessed. This assessment requires various assessment techniques. (Assessment and evaluation are covered in detail in Chapter 7.) Students can demonstrate understanding about water quality in a stream, for example, by writing reports, presenting artifacts to classmates, taking photographs, and creating multimedia products that document a stream cleanup effort.

Because different learners will respond to different assessment techniques in different ways, a variety of assessment techniques will help ensure that all students are evaluated appropriately. Whereas one child might flourish on a written exam, another might present her ideas more effectively with a poster or three-dimensional model, and yet another might express his ideas better through written journals. By using a variety of forms of assessment, teachers let students express their understandings in ways consistent with their individual strengths.

Because constructivist theories seek students' ideas and use their prior experiences to frame teaching and learning, multiple paths (from different students' ideas) emerge during learning. Therefore, assessment also needs to include students' interpretations of their learning. Students' interpretations can be captured with self-evaluation techniques. Teachers can interview

students about how they think they have progressed in learning about a topic or skill. Students can also keep journals to track their own progress throughout a project.

Students Create and Revise Products or Artifacts to Represent Understanding

Another approach to helping students create understanding is through the building and revision of artifacts. Artifacts are tangible representations of student understanding related to answering a driving question such as models, reports, videotapes or computer programs. They can be thought of as external, intellectual products. Papert (1980, 1993) refers to artifacts as "objects-to-think-with," because they are concrete and explicit and serve as tools of learning. Students build understanding by constructing artifacts and explaining to each other the meaning of their artifacts. Artifacts and products can be critiqued by others—students, teachers, parents, and community members. As a result, learners have many opportunities to reflect on and revise their artifacts, and so they have many opportunities to further enrich their knowledge.

Imagine that students decide to make a poster presentation to explain how they will explore the influence of fertilizer on plant growth. In the process of developing this artifact, students need to select plants and explain their selections, and they need to determine the amount of fertilizer. The students need to provide answers to questions such as, "How many plants?" "How much fertilizer?" and "How often?" All of these decisions focus the students' thinking and helps develop deeper understanding. Students again have an opportunity for enhanced understanding when their teacher and classmates give them feedback on their poster.

Use of Learning Communities

Social constructivism emphasizes language, community, and context. In this section, we explore five aspects of learning communities: students using language as a tool to express knowledge, students using language to come to a resolution about science ideas and theories, students debating the viability of evidence, students learning in a social context, and students learning from knowledgeable others. We will also discuss ways that knowledgeable others can use scaffolding to help students learn.

Students Use Language as a Tool to Express Knowledge Children (and adults) learn best when they can talk about and share their ideas with their peers and with concerned adults. Hence, meaningful learning develops as an interplay between the child thinking about ideas (an *intrapersonal* use of language) and talking with others (an *interpersonal* use of language or discourse). This interplay helps the child build connections between ideas, making understanding integrated. By using examples of a push or pull to describe force to another child, a learner demonstrates his or her understanding of the concept.

Teachers can help students use language in a variety of ways. One, students can debate ideas. For example, they can debate whether temperature affects the growth of seeds. Two, students can share information both orally and in written form. For example, students can share the results of their investigations with others. They can also exchange journals so that members of their class can read about their investigations. Many teachers have students explain their investigations to classmates using artifacts or products.

Students Express, Debate, and Come to a Resolution Regarding Ideas, Concepts, and Theories Healthy debates are a critical aspect of developing understanding in science. Constructivists define science as knowledge that has been publicly debated and accepted by scientists (Shapiro, 1994). Scientists continually obtain new information from investigations, and they debate ideas based on this information. Similarly, in science classrooms, teachers want students to debate ideas, concepts, and theories and come to resolutions about them. Recall the example given earlier in this chapter of a student who believed dinosaurs are pets because he collected them. Other classmates debated this idea, giving reasons that dinosaurs are not pets. Finally, all students came to the resolution that dinosaurs are not pets.

Students Debate the Viability of Evidence Scientists constantly debate the viability of evidence. One group of scientists may speculate that mutations being found in frogs around the world are the result of depleted ozone. Another group of scientists argues that the deformations are a result of pollutants in the environment. The viability of evidence is debated until one supposition or another is supported by most in the scientific community. Just as scientists debate the viability of evidence, students need to do this in science classrooms. The *National Science Education Standards* (NRC, 1996) state, "Thinking critically about evidence includes deciding what evidence should be used and accounting for anomalous data" (p. 145). An example of this type of thinking in a classroom is students debating whether the height of a plant is a good indicator of growth. Some students might argue that number of leaves and color are more important indicators than is height, because height might only indicate that the plant is stretching to reach sunlight (a tropism).

Learning Is Situated in a Social Context Understanding is not constructed in isolation but in a social context. Parents, friends, teachers, peers, community members, books, television, movies, and cultural customs all affect the construction of student understanding. For example, students learning about decomposition share with classmates their findings from various experiments performed on decomposition columns. They visit local landfills or recycling plants and talk with the managers. They connect to the World Wide Web to talk with other students around the country about the problem of landfills in their region. They talk with peers to see if any use composts at home. Each of these social interactions helps students build integrated understandings. In isolation, these understandings might not be connected, but through social construction of ideas, students link new understandings with old ones.

Knowledgeable Others Help Students Learn New Ideas and Skills That They Couldn't Learn on Their Own A basic idea that follows from these ideas about language, culture, and community is that more competent others can assist learners in accomplishing a more difficult task than they otherwise could on their own. The development of understanding occurs as a result of social interaction with more knowledgeable others and with peers. Even second graders are able to carry out sophisticated investigations under the guidance of a classroom teacher. Vygotsky (1978) developed the construct of the *zone of proximal development* to represent the hypothetical space between assisted and unassisted performance of a learner. He studied the difference between concepts learned *spontaneously,* or out of school, with those learned in school, and he concluded that students learned more when they were assisted by the teacher or more knowledgeable adults because they discussed, thought about, and debated ideas. Vygotsky defined the zone of proximal development as the distance between the actual developmental level as determined by independent problem solving and the level of potential development as determined through problem solving under adult guidance or in collaboration with more capable peers (1978, pp. 85–86). He believed that the social interaction between students and teachers or other adults is an important aspect of intellectual development, because the zone of proximal development allows learners to take part in more cognitively challenging tasks and problem solving than they could on their own.

Others have expanded Vygotsky's ideas to include collaborative interactions with peers. Researchers have found that students learn more effectively when working in collaborative groups with advanced or knowledgeable peers than they do working alone. Forman (1989) coined the term *bi-directional zone of proximal development* to describe the expertise levels in collaborative groups. The bi-directional zone of proximal development describes the fluctuations among group members—sometimes members are the teacher and sometimes they are the learner. Using Vygotsky's ideas, a collaborative classroom becomes an environment that comprises "multiple zones of proximal development." Students are exposed to overlapping zones as they learn by interacting with many different people—the teacher, peers, and community members. Each person with whom the student interacts can become a support that will enable the student to climb to the next level of learning.

By identifying the learners' zones of proximal development, a teacher can provide the assistance that is needed to move a learner to a higher level of understanding than would be possible without the support. Good teachers have always provided this support by doing things such as modeling ideas for students. The *zone of proximal development* simply serves to name these types of support so we can talk about them.

Scaffolding Scaffolding stems from Vygotsky's notion of the zone of proximal development. *Scaffolding* (Bruner, 1977; Wood, Bruner, & Ross, 1976) is a process in which a more knowledgeable individual provides support to another learner to help him or her understand or solve a problem. In scaffolding, the more knowledgeable other directs those aspects of the intellectual task that are initially beyond the capacity of the learner. This allows the learner to take part in intellectual activities that otherwise would be unwelcoming, activities that he or she doesn't completely understand. Imagine a parent helping her child put together a Lego structure. The parent might say, "Let's find all the pieces that are blue." Next the parent might suggest snapping all the blue pieces together. Although the child might not see how the individual steps fit together to build a castle, because the parent has structured the activity, the child can participate in building the structure.

Scaffolds used by knowledgeable others (parents, teachers, other adults, or peers) include modeling, coaching, sequencing, reducing complexity, marking critical features, and using visual tools. In the Lego example, the parent has provided a very important aspect of instruction that is known as *sequencing.* Sequencing is just one of the many types of scaffolds that can be used in a classroom. Sequencing breaks a difficult task into much smaller, manageable, step-by-step subtasks. What follows is a summary of scaffolding strategies that teachers can use to support learning.

> **Modeling.** Modeling is the process through which a more knowledgeable person illustrates to the learner how to complete a task. For example, a teacher could demonstrate how to use the concept of "average" to analyze data or how to read a balance scale. Many science processes can be modeled for students. Some of these are

asking questions, planning and designing investigations, and forming conclusions.

Coaching. Coaching involves providing suggestions to help the student develop knowledge or skills. For example, a teacher might make suggestions to a student about how to make more precise measurements when reading a spring scale. The teacher might suggest, for instance, that the student make sure the scale is calibrated to start at zero before beginning to use the scale. Other forms of coaching include asking thought-provoking questions (such as "How do your data support your conclusion?"), giving students sentence stems (such as "My data support my conclusion because . . .), and supplying intellectual or cognitive prompts (such as asking students to write down predictions, give reasons, and elaborate answers).

Sequencing. Sequencing is breaking down a larger task into step-by-step subtasks so a child can focus on completing just one subtask at a time rather than worry about the entire task at once. A teacher might break down the process of investigations into various components, not allowing the learner to proceed to the next step until completing a step. For example, the teacher could require the learner to complete a rough blueprint plan before moving on to building an apparatus.

Reducing complexity. Reducing complexity involves withholding complex understandings or tasks until the learner has mastered simpler understandings or subtasks. The classical example is helping a child learn to ride a bicycle by using training wheels. In science classrooms, a teacher might use an analogy to reduce the complexity of a concept. For instance, a teacher might compare DNA to the instructions for building a model airplane.

Marking critical features. One way that a knowledgeable other can support the learning of another is to mark or highlight the critical (key) features of a concept or task. For instance, a teacher might point out to young students that animals called *mammals* all have hair. In teaching a student how to focus a microscope, a teacher might point out that it is important to always start with the lowest-power lens first.

Using visual tools. Sometimes teachers use visual tools (pictorial prompts that help students understand their own thinking processes) to help students understand concepts or tasks (Hyerle, 1996; Parks & Black, 1992). Visual tools make abstract ideas more concrete by organizing them or illustrating relationships among them. Although there are many kinds of visual tools, we illustrate two: one designed to help students understand a concept (Figure 2.6) and another designed to help students understand a task (Figure 2.7). Compare and contrast diagrams (Parks & Black, 1992) are visual tools that illustrate the relationships among the characteristics of two different objects. Learning the classifications of various animals, for example, requires students to understand similarities or differences among animals. Figure 2.6 is a sample compare and contrast diagram that depicts the similarities and differences between mollusks and arthropods. Steps provide a simple pictorial representation of a task, and help students visualize a task. Figure 2.7 is a simple pictorial representation of the steps to focus a microscope.

Using Scaffolds   Often, the teacher provides the scaffolds during instruction. Other vehicles for scaffolding, however, are peers (same age or older), community members, parent volunteers, and technology. Many teachers find that, at first, they (or knowledgeable others) must provide much support and structure in the classroom. However, gradually, the learner can take more and more responsibility for structuring his or her own learning.

For example, at the beginning of year, a teacher might model for students how to ask good questions and demonstrate why they are appropriate questions. However, as the year progresses, students are expected to ask their own questions and give justifications for why they are good questions. When students have reached this point, it is still critical that the teacher provide feedback.

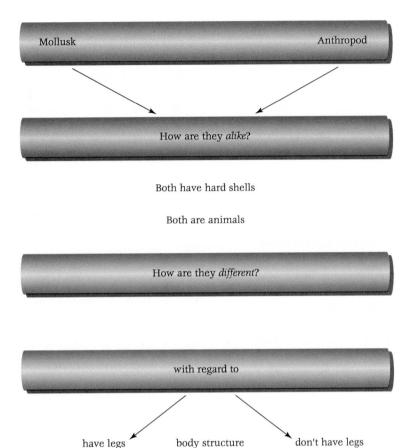

FIGURE 2.6
Compare and contrast diagram to represent a concept.

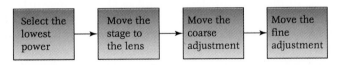

FIGURE 2.7
Visual tool to represent steps in a task.

For scaffolding to be beneficial to the learner, the following must be true.

◆ Support must be relevant to the student and the student's task. To be relevant, the support must be related to a task a student needs to complete. For instance, the teacher can reduce the complexity of data analysis by providing a chart for collecting data.)

◆ Support must correspond to the level of help needed by the student. If the support is geared too high for students, it will not match their understanding. If it is too low, it will not be useful. The analogy that DNA is like a set of instructions for putting together a model airplane might be appropriate for a fifth grader who has put together an airplane. Comparing DNA to the instructions in a computer program would be beyond most fifth graders' experience.

◆ The support must be given in close proximity in time to the student's request for help. Delaying support might mean that an educational opportunity is lost and that support is given when a student no longer needs it.

◆ The student must take action on the opportunity (or apply what he or she has learned). For example, a student needs to apply their understanding of finding averages from their own data.

◆ Scaffolds need to be *faded:* This means that the support must decrease over time. A child first learning to ride a bike uses training wheels. The training wheels are gradually raised up. Next, the training wheels are removed, and the child tries to ride the bike with an adult running alongside the bike. Finally, the child rides the bike on his or her own. In science class, a teacher might start by showing students how to create a bar graph. Next, the class and the teacher co-construct bar charts. After that, students working in groups construct bar graphs with the teacher giving them feedback.

Authentic Tasks

Constructivism also points to the need for students to learn by addressing problems that they see as authentic (Brown, Collins, & Duguid, 1989; Newman, Griffin, & Cole, 1989; Resnick, 1987). To develop integrated understandings, students must develop knowledge related to real situations. Because deep learning occurs only when a task is situated, tasks must take on meaning beyond what occurs in the school. We'll explore four aspects of authentic tasks: the driving question, the relevance of a question or topic to students, the connection of learning to students' lives outside of school, and the emergence of science concepts and principles when they are needed.

Driving Questions Focus and Sustain Activities
Driving questions are a vehicle for bringing authentic problems into classrooms. (Chapter 3 ex-

plores the driving question in greater detail.) In project-based science, the driving question contexualizes the learning experiences in the lives of learners, organizes concepts, and drives activities. As students pursue solutions to a question, they develop meaningful understanding of key scientific concepts. For instance, the question "What is the pH of rainwater in our city?" allows students to explore concepts such as acids and bases, pH, and concentration. The question also organizes the activities involved in planning and carrying out investigations of the acidity of rainwater and the impact acid rain has on living and nonliving things. A question such as "How do you light a structure?" allows students to explore principles such as parallel and series circuits, voltage, resistance, current, and power. Activities might be organized around students designing and building structures that they can light.

The Topic or Question Is Relevant to the Student   A guiding principle of constructivism is that problems, questions, and topics must be relevant to children; that is, they must be pertinent to students. Greenberg (1990) suggests that relevant questions are testable by children, involve the use of equipment in testing ideas, are complex enough to elicit problem-solving approaches, and can be solved through group efforts. Similarly, Blumenfeld and colleagues (1991), in a summary of the literature, argues that student interest is enhanced when (a) tasks are varied and include novel elements, (b) the problem is authentic and has value, (c) the problem is challenging, (d) there is closure through the creation of an artifact or product, (e) there is choice about what and/or how work is done, and (f) there are opportunities to work with others (Malone & Lepper, 1987).

Some people criticize the idea of relevance, arguing that certain curriculum, whether pertinent to students or not, must be covered in schools. Brooks and Brooks (1993) write that, "relevance does not have to be preexisting for the student. . . . Relevance can emerge through teacher mediation" (p. 35). (For this reason, the book discusses ways teachers can stimulate curiosity and develop relevant investigations in Chapter 3, Chapter 4, and Chapter 8.) Few children will come to school interested in the topics of force, momentum, and acceleration. However, a teacher can help make these

---

ACTIVITY 2.5

Why Should Children Use Learning Technology?

MATERIALS NEEDED:
- paper/pencil or computer

A. Take several minutes to brainstorm the reason(s) children should use learning technologies in science. List as many ideas as you can. Don't let any disadvantages, such as cost, get in the way of your thinking.

B. Pair with one of your classmates and compare your lists.

C. Explain the rationale for each item you listed. For example, does it improve learning concepts, improve attitudes, increase skill ability, provide a more interactive instructional strategy?

D. Record in your portfolio your conclusions about the use of technology.

E. After reading the next section on the role of technology, return to this activity and record in your portfolio any new thoughts you have.

---

topics relevant to students by turning the topics into driving questions like, "How do we stay on a skateboard?" or "Why do I have to wear a helmet, knee pads, and wrist protectors when I'm rollerblading?"

Learning Is Connected to Students' Lives Outside School Children (and adults) usually exert greater effort to study questions that relate to their own lives outside of school. If a lesson being presented to students is not connected to their lives, it is not uncommon for an upper elementary or middle school student to ask, "Why do we need to know this?" Unfortunately, teachers sometimes reply, "Because it is in the book" or "You will need it when you get older." Few children have the patience to study something simply because it is in the book, and most children do not have the cognitive capacity to accept that they will need something far in their future.

Most topics in the elementary curriculum can be situated in students' lives. For example, teachers can connect the concept of insulation to students' lives by emphasizing the role of insulation in coats and gloves, Thermos bottles that keep drinks hot or cold, and coolers that keep food from spoiling.

Science Concepts and Principles Emerge as Needed to Answer a Driving Question In constructivist classrooms, the concepts and skills presented are used to answer a driving question rather than presented for their own sake. When concepts and principles emerge on an as-needed basis, students can more easily integrate them

into their understandings. For example, students learn to read a thermometer so that they can measure the temperature in their decomposition column. They learn about oxygen so that they can understand why worms help the decomposition process. In each of these examples, students aren't learning something for the sake of learning it; they are learning it so that they can solve a problem or apply it to a particular situation. Before continuing, complete Activity 2.5.

THE ROLE OF TECHNOLOGY IN CONSTRUCTING SCIENCE UNDERSTANDINGS

One of the major global changes that has occurred since the early 1980s is the explosion in technology. While the capability of technology has increased, the cost of technology has decreased. These two factors have made it more feasible for schools to purchase technology and to use it for instructional purposes. Technology, in particular the use of computers, software, and various peripherals that support students' learning, are known as *learning technologies*. Learning technologies can support teachers and students in project-based science, because they can help students and teachers communicate, carry out investigations, and develop products. Technology can play a powerful role in enhancing student and teacher motivation and in helping students and teachers implement projects.

Dwyer (1994) found that technology transformed the way teachers taught. With technology, the classroom changed from one in which the teacher was the center of attention and used mostly lecture to one in which children became the center of learning and children interacted with each other, the teacher, and the computer. The teacher's role changed from "expert" to "collaborator." These changes in a classroom can contribute to student learning in science.

Learning Technologies to Support Active Engagement with Phenomena

Microcomputer-Based Laboratories Learning technologies can help students actively engage with phenomena. *Microcomputer-based laboratories* (*MBLs*) allow students to use microcomputers as laboratory tools. Interfaced electronic probes can detect temperature, voltage, light intensity, sound, distance, dissolved oxygen, or pH while the microcomputer digitally records and graphs the data. Using MBLs, students can observe graphs being produced as an experiment is being conducted and thus obtain immediate graphical results of their data. Immediate graphical results allow students to see trends in their data that allow them to focus on the concepts they are exploring and ask new questions related to the experiment.

Microcomputer-based laboratories have many applications for elementary and middle school science. In a pond project students can use temperature probes to monitor the temperature, use a pH probe to measure the pH, or use a dissolved oxygen probe to test how dissolved oxygen varies at different locations. Although many of these measurements can be taken with traditional laboratory equipment, using MBLs has a number of advantages. Probes are often time-efficient. They are also more reliable instruments. Because they can display the results both graphically and numerically, children can more easily interpret the results. One of the two biggest advantages is simultaneous collecting and graphing of data. Research (Brasell, 1986; Morkos & Tinker, 1987) supports the importance of simultaneous data gathering and graphing to help students form understanding. The other big advantage is that probes allow students to do explorations not typically possible in the science classroom.

Simulation and Microworld Sometimes it is difficult for learners to experience phenomena first-

FIGURE 2.8
Learning technologies help students develop science understandings.

hand. Computer simulations and microworlds, such as those developed by White (1998), allow students to explore and manipulate ideas actively in artificial environments that minimize extraneous details and make it easier to note interactions among variables. For instance, students can explore what motion would be like in a frictionless environment. Appropriate simulations also permit students to see and interact with underlying scientific models that are not readily observed firsthand. For instance, simulations can help students explore the galaxies or the structure of the atom. We consider simulations the next best thing to direct purposeful experiences with phenomena. For this reason, we encourage teachers to use computer software programs that simulate phenomena that cannot be seen or done in the regular classroom. There are software programs that simulate trips through the human body, voyages through outer space, and adventures into the ocean. Chariot Corporation has two programs entitled *Eco-Adventures in the Oceans* and *Eco-Adventures in the Rainforest* that simulate life in the ocean and the rain forest. Similarly, Sunburst/WINGS for Learning sells programs called *Earthquest Explores Ecology, The Voyage of the Mimi, A Field Trip to the Sea,* and *A Field Trip to the Rainforest* that simulate ecological issues, a whale research expedition, ocean life, and a visit to the rain forest. All of these programs take students on an electronic adventure, complete with full color pictures and authentic sounds, to places they may not visit in person.

Interactive Video Technology Interactive video technology (compact disks or videodisks) combines video pictures, microcomputer graphics, and text to present to students phenomena that otherwise would be inaccessible. Such technology allows students to visualize chemical reactions or natural disasters like tornadoes that would otherwise be too hazardous, time-consuming, or expensive for students to observe. For instance, using interactive video technology, students can observe the colorful but violent and noxious reaction between liquid bromine and aluminum foil or the inside of the eye of a hurricane. The technology might go further and ask students to record their observations or explain what they see. Linking the concrete phenomena with writing about the phenomena can help students develop deep understandings.

Learning Technologies to Support Using and Applying Knowledge

Some learning technologies help students apply their knowledge by supporting them in planning, explaining, and reflecting. For instance, *Model-It* (Cogito, 1998; Jackson, Stratford, Krajcik, & Soloway, 1996) guides students through the process of building qualitative models. *Model-It* helps students plan their models, supports students in building dynamic models using qualitative relationships, and helps students test and evaluate their models. To create a model of a specific phenomenon, students select or create Objects, which are real world entities related to the phenomenon. For example, to create a model of pollution, students might create a stream and a golf course. Then the students define quantifiable Factors, characteristics related to the Objects. In the pollution example, one Factor might be the amount of pollution given off by a factory. Students connect related factors with Relationships, which they create with qualitative rather than quantitative or formulaic representations. For example, a direct causal relationship represented mathematically by the function $y = x$ may be expressed qualitatively in *Model-It* with the phrase "as x increases, y increases by about the same." These verbal representations are visually linked with graphical representations. The model as a whole may be viewed as an

abstract representation similar to a concept map. Finally, *Model-It* provides graphs, meters, and sliders for interactive testing of the model.

Figure 2.9 shows a screen shot from the *Model-It* relationship editor window. In this example, students were building a model of water quality. The screen shows the tools available for students to build Relationships among the various Objects and Factors they identified. Across the top, the students selected the Relationship "The factory's pollution affects the stream's water quality" using pull-down menus. The students defined the Relationship this way: "As the factory's pollution increases, the stream's water quality decreases by about the same." Notice how the students' qualitative expression is graphed on the right.

Marcia Linns' *Knowledge Integration Environment* also supports students in explaining and reflecting on a range of scientific phenomena including light and temperature. Linn and her colleagues (Linn, 1992; Linn, Songer, Lewis, & Stern, 1993) have also used built-in questions in a microcomputer-based laboratory (MBL) environment to encourage students to make predictions and then, after the experiment, to compare their results to their predictions.

Technology, especially the expansion of the World Wide Web, has made information so accessible that students can easily obtain information about key ideas, concepts, and subject matter topics that arise as they explore solutions to questions. The Web is an excellent source of background information and data to support students in finding solutions to their questions. For example, when investigating the water quality of a local stream, students might search the Web for additional information regarding water quality. Simply providing access to information, however, does not guarantee that it will be useful to learners. Unlike a library, the Web contains many documents that have not been screened for content and validity of information. Efforts like the University of Michigan's Digital Library and the Middle Years Digital Library Project (Wallace, Krajcik, & Soloway, 1996) screen documents available on the Web for content, validity, and development level of the learner. The Middle Years Digital Library Project used an interface and searching device that were designed for learners. When using this interface and searching

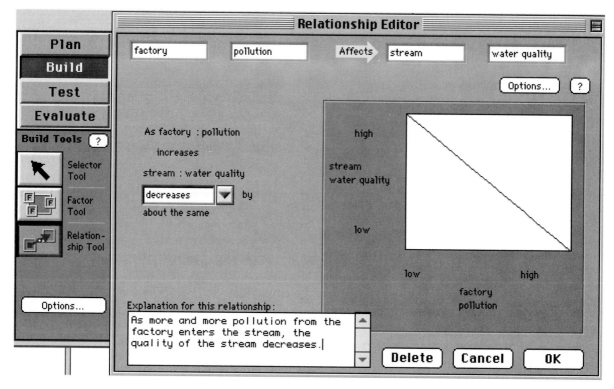

FIGURE 2.9
Screen shot from **Model-It** *relationship editor window.*

device, students receive in response to search requests only a small number (ten or twenty) of documents that are related to their search, rather than the large lists that include many unrelated documents that other search engines produce.

Using Learning Technologies to Support the Creation of Multiple Representations

There has been an explosive growth in the use of media (sound, graphs, color pictures, and video) in technology. The variety of media provides for representation of concepts in multiple, simultaneous ways. For example, when studying tornadoes, students can use media to observe various tornadoes, examine graphs of wind speed, read text explaining how a tornado works, and interpret graphical illustrations of tornadoes. Exploring these linked multiple representations can enhance student understanding.

Technology also allows students to manipulate and construct their own representations in several media. Software tools such as Roger Wagner Publishing's *HyperStudio* allow students to create hypermedia documents of their investigations. For instance, students can take pictures of plants germinating and growing, scan them, and import them into *HyperStudio*. They can also record their observations around their picture and include graphical information such as how the heights of their plants change over time. The incorporation of multiple representations of concepts within documents is especially important in helping students develop conceptual understanding of scientific concepts (Lemke, 1990; Kozma, 1991). Moreover, by building thoughtful connections and constructing meaningful relationships among representations, students form more integrated understandings (Novak & Gowin, 1984; Linn, 1998). For instance, Hare and Papert (1990) have noted substantial gains in mathematics learning among their students who devised various graphical and textual representations of fractions in Logo programs.

Learning technologies and application software minimize the physical work that students need to do to create products, freeing them to learn more and develop deeper understandings. Application software such as word processors, spreadsheets, desktop publishing programs, and drawing programs help students create a variety of products to represent what they know in a variety of forms. New learning technologies (such as *HyperStudio,* Microsoft's *Powerpoint,* and Claris *Homepage*) allow students to manipulate video, text, and graphics to develop multimedia products and presentations. Using these new tools, upper elementary students can easily incorporate diagrams, drawings, graphs, and video in computer-generated products. Moreover, students can link products together in unique ways to represent their understandings.

Using technology tools to create products also allows students the opportunity to more readily revise their work and develop understanding over time (Hare, 1991; Wisnudel-Spitulnik, 1995). Because of the digital nature of multimedia documents, students can revisit their productions over time. Students can save their work in a current version and continue constructing new versions as they gather more information and develop their ideas further. For instance, a student could continue to add digital shots of plant growth over time to a hypermedia document. The student could also link these shots to observations of plant growth and to background information.

Finally, with technology tools that support the creation of multiple representations, students can increase the quantity and quality of their writing. Word processing and hypermedia programs help students expand and elaborate on what they have already written.

Using Learning Technologies to Support the Creation of Learning Communities

Telecommunication, including e-mail and chat rooms, allows students access to a wider community in other parts of the world. Students can use e-mail to communicate with other schools, community members, and even members of the scientific community. One advantage of this technology is the rapid rate of response that the medium encourages.

Chat rooms allow a number of individuals from a variety of locations to communicate in real time. Through chat room technology, live conferences can be set up involving students from one school, scientists, and students from other schools. These conferences encourage and support students in finding solutions to questions of interest and debating ideas and evidence.

Technical Education Research Center (TERC) and the National Geographic Society have published a variety of science projects that stress students communicating with each other. The project *Acid Rain* (National Geographic Kids Network, 1989) teaches students about pH, acids, bases, neutralization, and the effects of acid rain on the environment. Students predict the pH of their local rainfall by collecting information about factors that affect the pH of rain, including the numbers of acid gas-producing factories, of cars, and of people in their communities and surrounding areas. They also predict the pH of other regions throughout the country using information they receive through telecommunications with other classes on their research team. After gathering and measuring the pH of rainwater for three weeks students analyze the data by looking for patterns. They draw conclusions from the data they collect and the data telecommunicated from participating classrooms. Then, students share their findings via telecommunications with research team members in other schools and a unit scientist.

Using Learning Technologies to Support the Creation of Authentic Tasks

Because students see technology in use all around them, they will perceive that the tasks they are asked to perform are more authentic if technology is involved. Technology is used to check out groceries. Technology monitors and measures all sorts of physiological functions in hospitals. It is used to measure the speed of pitches during baseball games and to tabulate

---

ACTIVITY 2.6

Developing a Social Constructivist Lesson

MATERIALS NEEDED:
- a videotape of an elementary or middle grade science lesson or a classroom that you can observe in person
- materials to develop and teach a lesson
- videotaping equipment and videotape
- rating scale from Activity 2.3

A. Obtain a videotape of an elementary or middle grades science lesson or observe a teacher teaching a science lesson. Use the rating scale from Activity 2.3 to evaluate the teaching. What could the teacher do to make the lesson more consistent with the social constructivist view?

B. Prepare your own lesson to teach a new concept to a child or to a group of peers. Videotape yourself teaching the lesson. Use the rating scale found in Activity 2.3 to analyze how well you teach the concept through constructivist approaches.

C. How would you improve upon your lesson if you were to reteach it? Record your ideas in your portfolio.

Olympic skaters' scores. It detects moisture in dryers and records seismic events. It is even used to monitor some playgrounds. Why shouldn't students also use technology in school? Technology that helps students collect real data, that gives students access to numerous sources of current information, and that expand interaction and communication with others makes tasks more authentic. Now is a good time to complete Activity 2.6.

SUMMARY OF CHAPTER

In this chapter, we discussed student understanding and examined several scenarios of student understanding. Project-based science strives to create integrated understandings. To support this importance of integrated understanding, the chapter next presented information about how students construct knowledge.

Then the chapter outlined a social constructivist model of teaching that included several key characteristics. The first characteristic is active engagement with phenomena. In a constructivist classroom, students ask and refine questions, predict and explain phenomena, and engage with concrete materials. The second characteristic is using and applying knowledge. In constructivist teaching, teacher and students consciously address prior knowledge, and students identify and use multiple resources, plan and carry out investigations, apply concepts and skills to new situations, have time for reflection,

and take action to improve their own world. The third characteristic is multiple representations. Multiple representations include varied evaluation techniques and student products or artifacts to represent understanding. The fourth characteristic is the use of learning communities. Learning communities are created when students use language to express knowledge; express, debate, and come to a resolution regarding ideas, concepts, and theories; debate the viability of evidence; learn in a social context; and obtain help from knowledgeable others in learning new ideas and skills that they couldn't learn on their own. The chapter included an overview of the types of scaffolds teachers can use to help students learn science. The fifth characteristic is authentic tasks. What makes learning authentic are driving questions that focus and sustain activities, topics or questions that are relevant to the student, learning that is connected to students' lives outside school, and science concepts and principles that emerge as needed to answer a driving question. These five characteristics differentiate between receptional and transformational approaches to teaching.

The chapter concluded with a summary of the role of technology in constructing science understanding, including an overview of learning technologies to support active engagement with phenomena, using and applying knowledge, the creation of multiple representations, the creation of learning communities, and the creation of authentic tasks.

REFERENCES

American Association for the Advancement of Science. 1993. *Benchmarks for science literacy.* New York: Oxford University Press.

Anderson, B. 1986. Pupils' explanations of some aspects of chemical reactions. *Science Education* 70 (5):549–63.

Anderson, C. W. 1987. *Incorporating recent research on learning into the process of science curriculum development.* Unpublished manuscript, Biological Science Curriculum Study, Colorado Springs, Colo.

Anderson, C. W., and K. J. Roth. 1988. *Teaching for meaningful and self-regulated learning of science.* Unpublished manuscript, Michigan State University, Institute for Research on Teaching, East Lansing, Mich.

Armstrong, T. 1994. *Multiple intelligence in the classroom.* Alexandria, Va.: Association for Supervision and Curriculum Development.

Barnes, M. B., T. J. Shaw, and B. S. Spector. 1989. *How science is learned by adolescents and young adults.* Dubuque, Iowa: Kendall-Hunt Publishing Company.

Ben-Zvi, R., B. Eylon, and J. Silberstein. 1987, July. Students' visualization of a chemical reaction. *Education in Chemistry* 24 (4):117–20.

Ben-Zvi, R., B. Eylon, and J. Silberstein. 1982. *Students vs. Chemistry: A study of student conceptions of structure and process.* Unpublished manuscript, The Weizmann Institute of Science, Department of Science Education, Rehovot, Israel.

Blumenfeld, P., E. Soloway, R. Marx, J. S. Krajcik, M. Guzdial, and A. Palincsar. 1991. Motivating project-based learning: Sustaining the doing, supporting the learning. *Education Psychologist* 26(3 & 4): 369–98.

Blumenfeld, P. C., R. W. Marx, H. Patrick, and J. S. Krajcik. 1998, in press. Teaching for understanding. In *International handbook of teachers and teaching,* ed. B. J. Biddle, T. L. Good, and I. F. Goodson. Dordrecht, Netherlands: Kluwer.

Bransford, J. D. 1979. *Human Cognition: learning, understanding and remembering.* Belmont, Calif.: Wadsworth Publishing Company.

Brasell, H. 1987. The effect of real time laboratory graphing on learning graphic representation of distance and velocity. *Journal of Research and Science Teaching* 24(4):385–95.

Brooks, J. G., and M. B. Brooks. 1993. *In search of understanding: The case for constructivist classrooms.* Alexandria, Va.: ASCD.

Brown, A. L., and J. C. Campione. 1994. Guided discovery in a community of learners. pp. 229–70 in *Classroom lessons: Integrating cognitive theory and classroom practice,* ed. K. McGilly. Cambridge, Mass.: MIT Press, Bradford Books.

Brown, J. S., A. Collins, and P. Duguid. 1989. Situated cognition of learning. *Educational Researcher* 18:32–42.

Bruner, J. 1977. *The process of education.* Cambridge, Mass.: Harvard University Press.

Carey, S. 1985. *Conceptual change in childhood.* Cambridge, Mass.: Harvard University Press.

Cognito Learning Media. 1998. *Model-It.* New York: Cognito Learning Media, Inc.

Dale, E. 1969. *Audiovisual methods in teaching.* New York: Dryden Press.

Driver, R. 1989. The construction of scientific knowledge in school classrooms. pp. 83–106 in *Doing science: Images of science in science education,* ed. R. Millar. Lewes, East Sussex: Falmar Press.

Dwyer, D. C. 1994. Apple classrooms of tomorrow: What we've learned. *Educational Leadership* 51:4–10.

Eichinger, D. C., and O. Lee. 1988, April. *Alternative student conceptions of the kinetic molecular theory.* Paper presented at the annual meeting of the National Association for Research in Science Teaching, Lake Ozark, Mo.

Eylon, B., and M. C. Linn. 1988. Learning and instruction: An examination of four research perspectives in science education. *Review of Educational Research* 58(3):251–302.

Forman, E. A. 1989. The role of peer interaction in the social construction of mathematical knowledge. *International Journal of Educational Research* 13:55–70.

Greenberg, J. 1990. *Problem-solving situations. Volume I.* Grapevine Publications, Inc. Corvallis, OR.

Harel, I. 1991. *Children designers.* Norwood, N.J.: Ablex Publishing Corporation.

Harel, I., and S. Papert. 1990. Software design as a learning environment. *Interactive Learning Environments* 1:1–32.

Hyerle, D. 1996. *Visual tools for constructing knowledge.* Alexandria, Va.: Association for Supervision and Curriculum Development.

Jackson, S., S. J. Stratford, J. S. Krajcik, and E. Soloway. 1996. Making system dynamics modeling accessible to pre-college science students. *Interactive Learning Environments* 4(3):233–57.

Kozma, R. 1991. Learning with media. *Review of Educational Research* 61(2):179–211.

Lemke, J. 1990. *Talking science: Language, learning, and values.* Norwood, N.J.: Ablex Publishing.

Ladewski, B., J. S. Krajcik, J. S. Levy, and R. Hall. 1992, March. *The development of elementary school students' ideas related to the categorization of living things.* Paper presented at the 65th Annual Meeting of the National Association for Research in Science Teaching, Cambridge, Mass.

Linn, M. C. 1998. The impact of technology on science instruction: Historical trends and current opportunities. *International handbook of science education,* ed. M. C. Linn. Netherlands: Kluwer Publishers.

Linn, M. C. 1992. The computer as a learning partner: Can computer tools teach science? pp. 31–69 in *This year in school science 1991: Technology for teaching and learning,* ed. K. Sheingold, L. G. Roberts, and S. M. Malcolm. Washington, D.C.: American Association for the Advancement of Science.

Linn, M. C., N. B. Songer, E. L. Lewis, and J. Stern. 1993. Using technology to teach thermodynamics: Achieving integrated understandings. pp. 5–60 in *Advanced educational technology for mathematics and science, Volume 107,* ed. D. L. Ferguson. Berlin, Germany: Springer-Verlag.

Lorsbach, A., and K. Tobin. Sept. 1992. *Research matters to the science teacher: Constructivism as a referent for science teaching.* NARST, Columbus, Ohio.

Malone, T. W., and M. R. Lepper. 1987. Making learning fun: A taxonomy of intrinsic motivation for learning. In *Aptitudes, learning, and instruction: Conative and affective process analyses, Volume 3,* ed. R. Snow and M. Farr. Hillsdale, N.J.: Erlbaum.

Mokros, J. R., and R. F. Tinker. 1987. The impact of microcomputer-based labs on children's ability to interpret graphs. *Journal of Research in Science Teaching* 24(4):369–83

National Geographic Kids Network. 1989. *Acid rain.* Washington, D.C.: National Geographic Society.

National Research Council. 1996 *National science education standards.* Washington, D.C.: National Academy Press.

Newman, D., P. Griffin, and M. Cole. 1989. *The construction zone: Working for cognitive change in school.* Cambridge, Mass.: Cambridge University Press.

Novak, J. D., and B. D. Gowin. 1984. *Learning how to learn.* Cambridge, England: Cambridge University Press.

Osborne, R., and P. Freyberg. 1986. *Learning in science: The implications of children's science.* London: Heinemann.

Osborne, R. J., and M. M. Cosgrove. 1983. Children's conceptions of the changes of states of water. *Journal of Research in Science Teaching* 20(9):825–38.

Parks, S., and H. Black. 1992. *Organizing thinking: Graphic organizers.* Pacific Grove, Calif.: Critical Thinking Press and Software.

Papert, S. 1993. *The children's machine: Rethinking school in the age of the computer.* New York: Basic-Books.

Papert, S. 1980. *Mindstorms: Children, computers, and powerful ideas.* New York: BasicBooks.

Perkins, D. 1992. *Smart schools: Better thinking and learning for every child.* New York: The Free Press.

Perkins, D., D. Crismond, R. Simmons, and C. Unger. 1995. Inside understanding. In *Software goes to school: Teaching for understanding with new technologies,* ed. D. Perkins, J. Schwartz, M. West, and M. Wiske. New York: Oxford University Press.

Perkins, D. N. 1986. *Knowledge as design.* Hillsdale, N.J.: Lawrence Erlbaum Associates, Inc.

Pines, A. L., and L. H. T. West. 1986. Conceptual understanding and science learning: An interpretation of research within a sources-of-knowledge framework. *Science Education* 70(5):583–604.

Presidents and Fellows of Harvard College. 1995. *The private universe project.* South Burlington, Vt.: Annenburg/Corporation of Public Broadcasting Mathematics and Science Collection. See also http://www.learner.org/content/k12/acpbtv/schedule/universe/

Resnick, L. B. 1987. Learning in school and out. *Educational Researcher* 16:13–20.

Roth, W. M. 1995. *Authentic school science.* Netherlands: Kluwer Publishers.

Rutherford, J., and A. Ahlgren. 1989. *Science for all Americans: Project 2061.* New York: Oxford University Press.

Shapiro, B. 1994. *What children bring to light: A constructivist perspective on children's learning in science.* New York: Teachers College Press.

Spitulnik, M. W., S. Stratford, J. Krajcik, and E. Soloway. 1997. Using technology to support student's artifact construction in science. In *International handbook of science education,* ed. K. Tobin. Netherlands: Kluwer Publishers.

Talsma, V. 1998. *Student scientific understandings in a ninth grade project-based science classroom: A river runs through it.* Unpublished dissertation, University of Michigan, Ann Arbor, Mich.

Third International Mathematics and Science Study (TIMSS). 1998. See also http://nces.ed.gov/TIMSS/.

Vygotsky, L. 1986. *Thought and language.* Translated by A. Kozulin. Cambridge, Mass.: MIT Press. (Original English translation published 1962.)

Vygotsky, L. S. 1978. *Mind in society: The development of higher psychological processes.* Cambridge, Mass.: Harvard University Press.

Wallace, R., J. S. Krajcik, and E. Soloway. Sept. 1996. Digital libraries in the science classroom: An opportunity for inquiry. *D-Lib Magazine* at http://www.dlib.org/dlib/september96/umdl/09 wallace.html.

White, B. Y. 1998. Computer microworlds and scientific inquiry: An alternative approach to science education. In *International handbook of science education,* ed. M. C. Linn. Netherlands: Kluwer Publishers.

Wisnudel-Spitulnik, M. 1995. Construction of technological artifacts and the teaching strategies used to promote flexible scientific understanding. Unpublished dissertation, University of Michigan, Ann Arbor, Mich.

Wood, D., J. S. Bruner, and G. Ross. 1976. The role of tutoring in problem solving. *Journal of Child Psychology and Psychiatry* 17:89–100.

Yager, R. E., and J. E. Penick. 1986. Perceptions of four age groups toward science classes, teachers, and the value of science. *Science Education* 70(4):355–64.

Chapter 3

WHAT IS A DRIVING QUESTION?

INTRODUCTION

Project-based science has several features, one of which is the driving question. This chapter will explore the nature of the driving question and attempt to answer a variety of questions about the driving question itself: What is a driving question? What makes a good driving question? What is the value of a driving question? How do I develop driving questions? And how do I use them to teach science?

The **driving question** organizes and drives the diverse activities of a project. Examples of some driving questions are "Will it rain tomorrow?" "Why do I look the way I do?" "What care do our classroom pets need?" "What type of trees grow in our neighborhood?" "How healthy is our stream?" and "Does my community have acid rain?" In the fall of the school year, a good question for many early elementary students might be, "Do pumpkins all have the same number of seeds?" This question would give students many opportunities to explore characteristics of pumpkins and the growth of plants.

What characteristics do these example driving questions have in common? Usable driving questions are

1. **Feasible:** Students can design and perform investigations to answer the questions.
2. **Worthwhile:** They contain rich science content, relate to what scientists really do, and can be broken down into smaller questions.
3. **Contextualized:** They are pertinent to the world, nontrivial, and important.
4. **Meaningful:** They are interesting and exciting to learners.
5. **Sustainable:** They lead to the pursuit of detailed answers over time.[1]

These characteristics also meet the learning and motivational needs of *all* students (Atwater, 1994; Haberman, 1991) and, therefore, are critical for creating learning environments for both boys and girls as well as for children from different cultures and races.

This chapter provides many examples of driving questions that meet these criteria. The chapter also explores how teachers and students can develop driving questions. The chapter ends with a discussion of the value of using a driving question throughout a project. Before we begin our discussion of the driving question, let's examine three scenarios that describe ways in which teachers might organize science instruction. These scenarios will illustrate the importance of using driving questions to teach children science.

Scenario 1: Reading About Force and Motion

Think about your own elementary and middle school science experiences. Perhaps your science class was like this. Mr. Simmons, your fifth grade science teacher, started class by saying, "Today we're going to find out about force and motion. Open your books and read pages 121 to 123, which focus on motion and force. Pay attention to the photographs and diagrams." You scanned the pages and read carefully the captions under the graphs and photographs. After about fifteen minutes, Mr. Simmons directed the class to work in groups at their tables to answer several questions at the end of the chapter. After another fifteen minutes, Mr. Simmons called on several students to give their responses to the questions.

You followed most of the reading, but occasionally you drifted off, thinking about the conversation you had with Liz on the phone last night. You weren't sure why you were learning about force and motion. It was fun working with the students at your table to answer the questions. You were pleased that Mr. Simmons said, "Very good," when you responded, "You need a force," to the question, "Why does an object stop moving?" You had picked up the answer from your reading. It was confusing to you because it seemed from your everyday experiences that force must be applied to *keep* something moving. You kept thinking about pedaling your bike and how you needed to keep pedaling to keep moving.[2]

Sound familiar? In Chapter 1, we referred to this method of science instruction as *read about*

---

1. Blumenfeld, Soloway, Marx, Krajcik, Guzdial, & Palinscar, 1991; Krajcik, Blumenfeld, Marx, & Soloway, 1994.

2. This is a classic misconception. The appropriate scientific concept is Newton's First Law of Motion which states that every object continues at rest or in motion, unless acted upon by a force.

science. Although students were introduced to new ideas, they experienced science as a reading activity. The concepts of science were not shown to be linked to the children's everyday lives. Although reading is an important part of science learning, when reading about science is not tied to a larger picture that has meaning for students, it can become a routine and uninteresting way of learning.

Scenario 2: Learning About Force and Motion Via an Activity

Maybe your class was like this. Mrs. Wilson, your fifth grade teacher, always had you doing activities in science. Mrs. Wilson directed the class to work in groups to test if the mass of a block at the bottom of a ramp influenced how far it would move when hit by a moving toy car. Previously we concluded that the number of washers in a toy car influenced how far it could push a wood block at the bottom of an inclined plane (a ramp supported by two books). Mrs. Wilson wrote on the board, "Does mass influence how far the block will move?" She handed out a sheet with directions on how you should set up and carry out the activity. She also handed out a sheet of paper with two columns on it. The columns were labeled "Number of Blocks (Mass)" and "Distance the Blocks Moved."

You were pretty sure that the more blocks you had, the shorter the distance they would move, so you were not sure why you were doing the activity. It was pretty easy, except for measuring the distance the blocks moved. Sometimes you and your partners disagreed about how far the blocks moved. Overall, the time went by pretty fast. You always looked forward to doing the activities, although you weren't always sure why you were doing them.

Once the class completed the testing, Mrs. Wilson had different groups summarize what they found. Overall, the class results supported what you had expected and your own group's findings. Mrs. Wilson wrote on the board, "The more blocks, the less distance they moved when hit by the toy car." You were pretty pleased because this seemed to support your ideas. It made sense. In the class discussion, however, Mrs. Wilson also said and then wrote on the board, "The more mass an object has, the more

force that is needed to change its motion." This was confusing. You still didn't really understand "force." You wrote down both of the statements Mrs. Wilson had written. You knew that any sentence Mrs. Wilson wrote on the board would probably be on a test.

As described in Chapter 1, this kind of science teaching is called *process science teaching.* The students performing this activity did learn some new ideas, and they enjoyed themselves, but the students' observations were not connected to other ideas they were learning. Although Mrs. Wilson used the activity to answer a question, "Does mass influence how far the block will move?" the question was tied directly to learning a topic (motion and force). Students did not see how the question was tied to their lives, except that it might appear on a test.

Scenario 3: Learning About Motion and Force Through a Driving Question

Perhaps your class was more like this. Your class was exploring the question, "Why do I have to wear a helmet and knee and elbow pads when I'm roller blading?" As part of this exploration, your class performed a number of activities. Mrs. Brink started each of the activities by saying, "If we are going to explore the question, 'Why do I have to wear a helmet and knee and elbow pads when I'm roller blading?' then we should know something about the laws of motion and about what causes injuries." Mrs. Brink selected the driving question because she knew that it would let the class explore a number of ideas related to force and motion as well as some ideas in biology related to human anatomy. She also knew that it would allow her students to do a number of related activities and also plan some investigations. Finally, she knew that a number of students in her class liked to roller blade.

Here is how Mrs. Brink used the driving question. Mrs. Brink directed the class to work in groups to test whether mass influences how far an object will move when pushed by another object. Mrs. Brink handed out a sheet of directions on how to set up and carry out the activity. She directed you to set up an incline plane (a ramp raised on one end by two books). Mrs. Brink had the class relate this activity to the previous day's

---

ACTIVITY 3.1

Comparing the Three Scenarios

MATERIALS NEEDED:
- paper and pencil or computer
- *National Science Education Standards* (National Research Council, 1996)

A. Write a paragraph describing the differences among the three instructional approaches presented in Scenarios 1, 2, and 3. What are the advantages and disadvantages of each approach?

B. Obtain a copy of *National Science Education Standards* (National Research Council, 1996). How does Scenario 3 compare with recommendations found in *National Science Education Standards*?

C. Record your responses in your portfolio.

---

activity which consisted of defining *force*. She asked the class why it was important to have the ramp at the same height each time. On the board in big letters she had written, "A Force Is a Push." Because of the previous day's work, your class was able to come up with the idea that it is important to have the same push on the blocks each time. She also handed out a sheet of paper with two columns on it. The columns were labeled "Number of Blocks (Mass)" and "Distance the Blocks Moved."

Once the class finished its testing, Mrs. Brink had various groups compare their findings and come to an agreement. All the groups posted their results on the board. Then Mrs. Brink asked, "How should we analyze the data?" The class had a debate on whether it was more useful to just look at it or create bar graphs. In the end, the class developed bar graphs. Mrs. Brink directed each group to write a conclusion based on the graphs. Your group wrote, "The more blocks (mass), the less the blocks moved when pushed by the same thing." Another group wrote, "The fewer the blocks, the farther they moved when hit by the car." Mrs. Brink recorded these various conclusions on the board. From the various conclusions, the class developed a consensus conclusion: "The greater the mass (more blocks), the less it will move when the same force (push) hits it; and the smaller the mass (fewer blocks), the farther it will move when the same force (push) hits it." At the end of class, Mrs. Brink asked, "How is this activity related to the driving question of the project: Why do I have to wear a helmet and knee and elbow pads when I'm roller blading?" Mrs. Brink first had each student write his or

her own response. You wrote in your notebook, "I wear knee pads when I roller bade because when I fall, my body isn't heavy enough to move the sidewalk and my knees will take the full blow. The knee pads soften the hit." Next you shared and compared responses with students at your table. The science lesson ended with various groups sharing their responses.

This third scenario illustrates what is called *project-based science*. The main activity is very similar to what occurred in the second scenario. However, this lesson goes far beyond that one. Rather than teaching an isolated lesson, the teacher tied all lessons to the driving question of the project. The students learned an important idea related to the motion of objects, but this important idea was connected to the driving question. The scenario illustrates how the driving question can be used to link activities in an overall project. The activity of testing whether mass influences how far an object will move was not done in isolation, but rather was an essential component in the process of answering the driving question. Activity 3.1 will give you the opportunity to think about the value of driving questions.

WHAT IS A DRIVING QUESTION?

What is a driving question? A **driving question** is a well-designed question used in project-based science that is elaborated, explored, and answered by students and the teacher. As seen in Scenario 3, the driving question is the central organizing feature of project-based science. In fact, the driving question is the first step in meeting all of the other key features of project-based science, because the question sets the stage for all activities and investigations. Project-based science requires a question that is meaningful and important to children and serves to organize and drive activities (Blumenfeld et al., 1991; Krajcik, 1993; Krajcik et al., 1996). As students collaboratively pursue answers to this question, they develop understanding of key scientific concepts associated with the project.

To learn more about driving questions, let's explore further the example driving question, "Why do I have to wear a helmet and knee and elbow pads when I'm roller blading?" presented in Scenario 3. How is this question useful? First, the question serves the purpose of organizing and driving activities that take place in a science class. Second, the teacher can use the question to introduce the students to a number of important science concepts and principles—motion, force, inertia, and Newton's laws of motion—that are needed to answer the driving question. Third, the question can be used to link these various concepts together. Fourth, the question can inspire applied use of technology—students might want to use motion probes[3] in their investigations, for example. The question might also prompt exploration of the World Wide Web as students try to find out about the different types of materials used to make helmets and pads, for example. Fifth, the question is motivating because it is meaningful to the children in the class; many children enjoy roller blading. Sixth, the question can lead to the creation of products, such as posters or videos, that show what students have learned about why they need to wear helmets and pads and that can thus be used as assessment tools. Hence, the driving question, "Why do I have to wear a helmet and knee and elbow pads when I'm roller blading?" ties together activities, skills, concepts, and educational objectives.

Let's now look at the key features of driving questions.

3. Motion probes are sonic range detectors (like those found in Polaroid cameras), electronic instruments attached to a computer's serial port through an interfacing box. The probe sends out sound waves that cannot be heard by humans. The sound waves bounce off objects in front of them and are deflected back to the probe. The probe can then calculate the distance the object is from the probe. Accompanying software plots the data on a computer monitor, allowing learners to view real-time, distance-time, or velocity-time graphs.

Features of Driving Questions

A good driving question has several key features:

- *Feasibility:* Students should be able to design and perform investigations to answer the question.
- *Worth:* Questions should deal with rich science content and process that match district curriculum standards.
- *Contextualization:* Questions should be anchored in the lives of learners and deal with important, real-world questions.
- *Meaning:* Questions should be interesting and exciting to learners.
- *Sustainability:* Questions should sustain students' interest for weeks.

Feasibility A key feature of a good driving question is feasibility. Feasibility has several components. A driving question is feasible if (1) students can design and perform investigations to answer it, (2) resources and materials are available for teacher and students to perform the investigations necessary to answer it, and (3) it is developmentally appropriate for students. We will now explore each of these components.

Good questions allow students to design and perform investigations to help find solutions to them. For instance, in the project with the driving question "What birds live in our neighborhood?" students can conduct bird watching inquiries. They can track bird types throughout the seasons. They might try to attract different birds to their playground or nature area by erecting birdhouses and using different types of bird seeds. A question like, "How can you cure a sick animal?" although meaningful for children, doesn't lend itself to students doing investigations because students don't have the knowledge or materials needed to cure a sick animal. Also, such a project has the potential to be harmful to animals. Finally, any project involving sick animals is potentially harmful to students as well (see Chapter 8 for more information about safety in the classroom).

Another component of feasibility is the availability of materials. Teacher and students should be able to find resources and materials to perform a variety of investigations related to the driving question. For instance, in the project with the driving question "Does our community have acid rain?" students can readily collect and measure the pH of rainwater using a variety of techniques, including pH paper, a pH meter, and a pH probe attached to a computer. Because pH paper is inexpensive, all students in the class can measure the pH of rainwater several times during the school year. Students can also take pH paper home to measure the pH of rainwater near their homes. Some questions, however, involve materials that are much more difficult to obtain. For instance, the question "How clean is my air?" does not readily allow students to design investigations. Testing for pollutants in the air often requires sophisticated pumps and filters that are too expensive and advanced for most school systems.

Good driving questions are also developmentally appropriate for students. For instance, the project with the driving question "What birds live in our neighborhood?" is developmentally appropriate for children of various ages. The investigations might differ among age groups, but children of many ages can investigate what birds live in their neighborhood. However, a question such as "What is the quality of my air?" although potentially very meaningful for most children, is probably not developmentally feasible for students in grades 3 and lower. The content and the investigations for this question, which involve understanding the particulate nature of matter, are more suitable for students in middle and high school.

Even the most interesting driving question will fail to generate a successful learning experience if appropriate investigations cannot be done, there is a lack of resources, or students are not developmentally ready for it.

Worth   Another key feature of the driving question is its worth. Like feasibility, worth has several components. A question that is worthwhile contains rich science content that students can explore and that helps meet district, state, or national standards and can be broken down into smaller questions that students can ask and answer.

Perhaps the most important feature of a worthwhile driving question is the quality of science content and process that it can encompass. The most worthwhile driving questions are di-

rectly linked to science content in such a way that they cannot be answered without students gaining an understanding of the intended science content. Students should be able to see how the science content relates to the driving question, and the driving question should be used to help place all the science content into a real-world setting. For instance, in Scenario 3, students explore a number of important science concepts related to force, motion, and the human body. Students cannot answer the question "Why do I have to wear a helmet and knee and elbow pads when I'm roller blading?" without understanding these science concepts. Also, the concepts of force, motion, and human anatomy are situated in a real-world setting with such a question because roller blading is something students do.

Another way of looking at this component of worth is to consider that the driving question must subsume important science content that helps teachers meet district, state, or national curriculum standards. If a question cannot help a teacher meet curriculum requirements, then it lacks worth. A question such as, "Does our community have acid rain?" provides students with the opportunity to explore numerous concepts related to chemistry, ecology, and geology. In exploring the question, students are exposed to much science content: They learn about acids and bases, they learn about weather, they study the effect of acid rain on the environment, and they learn about how experiments are designed. However, these outcomes might not be included in the objectives of a school's curriculum for that year, if so it should not be pursued.

A worthwhile driving question will also allow students to ask and answer their own subquestions. When a driving question is broad enough and is meaningful to students, students should be able to think of many related questions they would like to pursue. For instance, in the project with the driving question "How healthy is our stream or lake?" students might ask, "Does our stream quality change with the seasons?" or they might ask, "What are some biological indicators of our stream's health?" In the project with the driving question "What happens to all our garbage?" students might ask, "What materials decompose the fastest?" and "Does the presence of worms speed up the process of decomposition?"

Other questions don't lend themselves to students generating their own questions and pursuing solutions to those questions. For instance, it would be difficult for students to ask questions related to the driving question "Can we travel to Mars?" It's not that the curriculum content contained in the question is not important. It's that the question won't allow students to explore through investigations the questions they ask.

Allowing students to ask their own questions has several benefits. First, student motivation increases with student ownership of a project. Second, by designing their own experiments, investigations, or presentations, students learn design and process skills and increase their knowledge of a topic. Finally, asking questions and pursuing solutions to these questions is essential to students experiencing and "doing science." A worthwhile driving question helps students realize that they can learn about the natural world by setting up and conducting their own investigations. We explore further the idea of students "doing science" through investigations in Chapter 4: How Are Scientific Investigations Developed?

Contextualization   Contextualization is a key feature of good driving questions. A contextualized question is anchored in an important real-world situation and has important consequences. Students may not see immediately how a question relates to the real world or perceive its consequence. However, a good driving question presents the opportunity to draw students in and teaches them to see how it is related to their lives. A number of various instructional strategies can enhance contextualization of driving questions. Teachers can use investigations, observations, readings, and discussions to help students appreciate how a driving question relates to their lives. For instance, let's explore the question "What happens to all of our garbage?" Many upper elementary and middle school students will not immediately perceive the importance of this question. Most children are not interested in what happens to their trash. Imagine that a teacher asks students to bring to class a number of items that typically get thrown out at home. Children will bring in paper cups, plastic cups, newspaper, and orange peels, among other things. Students are asked to put these items in some "mess stockings" (nets

to hold the items) and bury them in a fenced-off area of the playground and then make predictions about what will happen to the various items they buried. As students pursue this investigation, they come to realize that materials like Styrofoam do not decompose and that some materials decompose more slowly than others. From this activity, students can make the leap to a larger context and begin to think about large landfills and the cumulative effect of garbage on the environment. At this point, the driving question, thanks to the contextualizing activity, assumes importance for the students.

In contrast, think about a question that is not contextualized such as "What are the names of rocks in my environment?" Although identification of elements of the natural world is important scientific content, unless the identification of rocks is tied to something that the children value, the question lacks the potential to motivate students and generate a successful, meaningful learning experience.

Meaning   Students should find driving questions meaningful to their lives. Usually, meaningful questions are those that students see as important and as interesting to them. Meaningful questions intersect with their lives, reality, and culture. For instance, students might see the question, "Why do I have to wear a helmet and knee and elbow pads when I'm roller blading?" as meaningful because they (or others they know) roller blade. The question is directly related to their lives and what they do. It is important to point out, however, that learners might not see the real-world issue involved in this question, which is the prevention of serious head injuries.

Students might not see all the ways that a driving question is related to their lives. For instance, many students might not initially care about the quality of their stream. However, through finding out about water quality and the effects on humans, students come to care about the driving question "What is the quality of our stream?"

Driving questions can also be meaningful just because they refer to phenomena that are inherently interesting to students. For instance, many early elementary students are fascinated with magnets. A good driving question for early elementary school children could be "How are magnets used around my home?" Although many upper elementary students would not find this question of interest, most early elementary students would be captivated by it. A number of phenomena have this potential to attract students' interests. Young learners are frequently interested in sinking and floating things in water, how toys work, rainbows, and animals. Such phenomena can be turned into driving questions, such as "Why does a rainbow form?" that early learners can pursue. Many children also love to find out how to light a bulb with one battery, one bulb, and one wire (Elementary School Science Program, 1970). Once they learn this, they are on to new challenges like lighting a model house or finding out how their battery-operated toys work.

Sustainability   A final feature of a good driving question is that it sustains student engagement over time. Teachers and students can work on a good question for weeks or even months. For instance, to develop a full understanding of the driving question "How healthy is my stream?" students not only must learn content in a variety of disciplines but also explore the content several times during the school year as the changing seasons contribute to variations in temperature, water levels, and animal life in the stream.

In addition to holding student engagement over time, a sustainable driving question encourages students to study information in great detail. For instance, in pursuing solutions to the question "What birds come to my bird feeder?" students can identify, count, and keep track of various birds. The bird feeder question also encourages students to learn about the behavior of the different birds, their eating and nesting habits, and their migrations patterns.

Driving questions have the capability to sustain inquiry, to push us to find answers, and to take interesting side trips that make the interconnectedness of all science so interesting. "How much water can different paper towels hold?" and "Do plants grow better in the shade or light?" are examples of questions that teach important scientific concepts and skills but are not sustainable. In one class period, students can answer the question about paper towels, and in as little as two weeks students can answer the question about the growth of plants. Both of these investigations could make worthwhile components of a project if they were subsumed under a larger

driving question. For instance, the question about whether plants grow better in the shade or light could be subsumed under the broader driving question "What do plants in my environment need in order to grow?" In this case, students could plan and carry-out a number of other experiments to explore the influence of fertilizer, temperature, moisture, light, soil type, and plant type that would keep the project going over time.

Table 3.1 summarizes key features of driving questions. Now that you have learned more about the driving question, revisit your ideas about the three scenarios by completing Activity 3.2.

TABLE 3.1   Key Features of Driving Questions

Feasibility
- Students can design an investigation to answer the question.
- Students can perform an investigation to answer the question.
- Materials for the investigations are readily available.
- The question is developmentally appropriate for the students.

Worth
- The question is related to what scientists really do.
- The question is rich in science content/concepts.
- The question helps students link science concepts.
- The question is complex enough to be broken down into smaller questions.
- The question leads to further questions.
- The question meets district, state, or national curriculum standards.

Contextualization
- The question is anchored in real world issues.
- The question has real world consequences.

Meaning
- The question is interesting and important to learners.
- The question intersects with learners' lives, reality, and culture.
- The phenomena covered by the question are of interest to students.

Sustainability
- The question allows students to pursue solutions over time.
- Students can pursue answers to the question in great detail.

ACTIVITY 3.2

Comparing the Three Scenarios Again

MATERIALS NEEDED:
* paper and pencil or computer

A. Now that you know more about the features of a driving question, reanalyze the first three scenarios. Write a paragraph

describing the differences among the instructional approaches presented in the scenarios. What are the advantages and disadvantages of each approach?

B. How does your analysis compare to what you wrote in Activity 3.1?

C. Record your responses in your portfolio.

Examples of Driving Questions

In this section, we will use the key features of driving questions to explore three examples. The summary of the features of driving questions presented in Table 3.1 will structure the examples.

Example 1: What Kind of Insects Live on Our Playground? Imagine that the district you are working in has a curriculum objective related to students learning about insects. Rather than covering insects as a topic, you decide to ask the driving question "What kinds of insects live on our playground?" Does this question meet the features of a good driving question? Let's explore.

The question is feasible because it gives children opportunities to investigate and ask new questions of their own. They might ask, "When do the various insects first appear on the playground?" "When do the insects disappear?" "What kind of food do they eat?" "Where do they live?" "What type of environment do the insects live in?" and "How do they eat?" Students can design and perform investigations to answer these questions. For example, they can keep journals about when insects appear and disappear. They can collect insects and investigate what they eat or how they react to light. They can take nature walks to investigate where insects live and how they move. Also, there isn't much sophisticated equipment—besides a hand lens, jars, and maybe a net—that is needed for this project.

Second, the question is worthwhile because it enables students to explore rich science content, including insect classification, life cycles, and behaviors. Also, the question enables students to relate to what scientists really do (ask lots of questions and pursue solutions to these

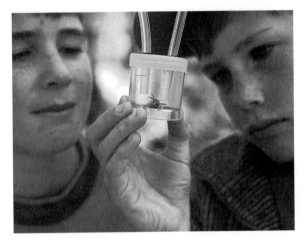

FIGURE 3.1
Children conduct investigations to find solutions to a driving question.

questions). This question matches up with a number of benchmarks for elementary students cited in *Benchmarks for Science Literacy* (AAAS, 1993). For instance, one of the benchmarks for grades 3–5 is that, "Insects and various other organisms depend on dead plant and animal material for food." By exploring the subquestion "What do insects eat?" students can attain this benchmark. The question also helps meet a number of other benchmarks (AAAS, 1993) and standards (National Research Council, 1996) for inquiry and the nature of science. For example, as students observe insect behavior and take notes, they are observing and recording information, two important benchmarks.

Third, the question is contextualized and meaningful. The type of insects found can give an indication of the quality of soil and the local environment. By observing the insects, finding

out information about them, asking subquestions, and conducting investigations to answer
the subquestions, students can come to understand how this is a real world question with
meaning for them: They are not just reading
about insects or exploring them through classroom activities; they are exploring and learning
about insects in their environment, in the back
yard, on the playground, and/or in a local nature area.

Fourth, this question is sustainable: It can
take students an entire year to study all the insects in their environment, given that insects
appear and disappear in different seasons.
Moreover, the question might propel students to
learn more about insects.

*Example 2: What Kind of Land Features Are
in My Environment?*   Often, school districts
have curriculum objectives related to earth science. Imagine that your class is studying the
question "What kind of land features are in my
environment?"

The question is feasible, because it allows students to ask a number of subquestions such as,
"What type of soil do we have?" "What kind of
rocks do we have?" "How was the shape of the
river formed?" and "How were the hills and valleys formed?" However, it is likely that these
questions will not come easily to upper elementary students. Taking walks to help focus students' observations on various geological features would help. Some of these questions allow
students to perform investigations. For instance,
students can collect a variety of rocks from
around the school or at home and then try to
identify what they are. Although students can't
explore how a river was formed, they can do various explorations on a stream table (a long tray
set up with sand and water to simulate erosion)
to duplicate the formation of streams and rivers.
They can also search the library or the World
Wide Web for historical pictures of the river to
see if the shape of the river has changed. Other
questions like, "How were the hills and valleys
formed?" cannot be explored easily through investigations. However, students can read and
discuss how such phenomena occur, and they
can manipulate modeling clay to simulate how a
hill is formed as pressure below the earth
presses up upon it.

Next let's explore whether the question is
worthwhile. The driving question and subquestions provide learners with opportunities to
learn a number of important earth science concepts. For instance, the students can explore
classifications of rocks and soil, compositions of
rock and various soils, types of land formations,
and reasons for various land features. Hence, by
pursuing an answer to the driving question, students have the opportunity to explore important
science content that meets a number of benchmarks cited in *Benchmarks for Science Literacy*
(AAAS, 1993). For instance, one of the benchmarks for grades 3–5 is as follows:

> Rock is composed of different combinations of
> minerals. Smaller rocks come from the breaking
> and weathering of bedrock and larger rocks. Soil is
> made partly from weathered rock, partly from
> plant remains—and also contains many living or-
> ganisms (AAAS, 1993, p. 72).

Taking students on walks to explore various
local phenomena helps show that the driving
question and subquestions are tied to the real
world. Although some children will not see the
question as meaningful to them, allowing them to
bring in different soil samples and various rocks
from their back yards will help them gain ownership of the question. For instance, students can
bring in various sample cores (drillings into the
soil with a tube to show the soil from different
layers) from their back yards and compare them.
They can explore questions like "How are the
samples different?" and "If they are different, why
are they different?"

Finally, as students begin to see the value of
the driving question, the question becomes sustainable because there is much rich content associated with it. Many of the subquestions take
time to explore and investigate. For example,
"What type of soil do we have?" is a question
that can be explored over time as students investigate what plants can grow in the soil type,
whether it can be used for making things (such
as bricks), and if it drains well (such as sand) or
holds water (such as clay).

*Example 3: How Can I Care for the Various
Animals in Our Classroom?*   Let's look at a
third example that focuses on biological objectives. Many children will be interested in the

animals that are in the classroom. Most students, as well as adults, love to watch various animals eat and play. The driving question "How can I care for the various animals in our classroom?" appears to have much potential to engage students in learning about animals.

The question appears to be very feasible. Students can ask a number of related questions and pursue answers to many of these questions through investigations. For instance, students could ask, "How do the eating habits of our animals differ?" "How do the various behaviors of the animals differ?" and "What kind of habitat do the various animals prefer?" All of these questions can be explored through investigations. Students can observe the eating habits of the different animals and find different feeding patterns. Some subquestions like, "What should I do if one of our animals gets sick?" should not be explored via hands-on investigations. Students can explore such questions by finding literature on the topic or talking to experts, such as veterinarians. As mentioned earlier, the care of animals should always be left to the expert.

In pursuing an answer to the driving question and the various subquestions, students will need to explore a variety of different science content areas. For instance, they will study content such as nutrition and environmental needs, habitat, body systems, body function and structure, and behavior. These content areas match *Benchmarks for Science Literacy* (AAAS, 1993) and *National Science Education Standards* (NRC, 1996). Hence, with respect to students exploring important content, the driving question appears to be worthwhile. The question is also worthwhile in that students can perform a number of investigations related to it.

The question also appears to be very motivating. Observing and caring for classroom animals is meaningful. Teachers can enhance interest and ownership by assigning students to care for particular pets. Because the pets are in the classroom and the learners must care for them, the question is contextualized for the learners.

Finally, the scope and the nature of the driving question and subquestions appear to hold students' attention for a long period of time. Caring for and learning about the animals can be done throughout the entire school year.

HOW DOES THE DRIVING QUESTION DIFFER FROM OTHER QUESTIONS?

When you open up a traditional elementary or middle school science textbook, you are likely to see that the book is organized in term of topics: the solar system, phases of the moon, weather, nutrition, plants, the human body, force, and so on. Often, a chapter will also mention reasons for learning the topic. For instance, the study of genetics has led to the development of different hybrids of corn and other vegetables and so is worth study. Although knowing such reasons might increase interest, the reasons are not the driving forces behind learning, and teachers frequently find it difficult to hold students' attention when focusing on topics that a textbook suggests are important.

Traditional science classes, like textbooks, are also organized by topic, rather than by a driving question. Nonproject-based science classes might cover the same science content as project-based science classes, but the material is not connected in the same way. By using driving questions, students can see that everything they learn has a purpose, and when they learn a new skill or concept, they can immediately apply it to help answer their questions.

Contrast the three driving questions just examined with questions like, "What are the six simple machines?" "What are the nine planets of the solar system?" and "What is light?" These questions focus on topics. Although some students might be interested in the structure of the solar system, most children don't have a reason to be. Although these topics might encompass worthwhile content, they are not likely to engage learners. These questions are not directly related to children's lives. These questions lack the ability to help students develop connections between their studies and their own lives.

In addition, traditional science instruction and textbook activities lead to the development of isolated skills and understandings, without context and meaning. Typical activities that students pursue in school science are designed to demonstrate or verify concepts. For example, a traditional science textbook chapter on plants

ACTIVITY 3.3

Evaluating Various Questions

MATERIALS NEEDED:
- ◆ paper and pencil or computer

A. Listed here are several questions. Evaluate whether the questions can serve as driving questions. Are the questions feasible, worthwhile, meaningful, contextualized, and sustainable? Be sure to state your reasons.

B. Contrast your answers with those of another person in your class. Try to come to a consensus.

C. Keep this list in your portfolio.

Question	Can It Serve as a Driving Question?	Reason
What is gravity?		
Why do I need to wear a bicycle helmet?		
Why does my water taste bad?		
What is matter?		
What foods are good for me to eat?		
Do all apples have the same number of seeds?		
How can I run faster?		
How good is the soil in my playground or yard for growing plants?		
Why do only the weeds grow in the cracks of the sidewalk?		
What kind of leaves are these?		
Why is too much junk food bad for me?		
Why is it colder in the winter and warmer in the summer?		

will tell students that plants need sunlight to grow. Then, the textbook activity will likely verify this information by having students grow one plant in the sun and another in a dark closet. (This kind of teaching is similar to that presented in Scenario 2.) Because such activities are tied to topics rather than to driving questions, students fail to make connections between the skills and concepts they learn. Take time now to complete Activity 3.3.

HOW IS A DRIVING QUESTION DEVELOPED?

Coming up with driving questions with the features discussed earlier in this chapter is challenging work. Teachers might make a number of failed attempts before settling on a question for a project. Slowly, however, teachers can develop a repertoire of driving questions and projects.

Teacher-Generated Driving Questions

Driving questions that originate from the teacher or the curriculum have a number of advantages. Perhaps the most important is that such questions can match school district outcomes and standards with a classroom project. Another is that orchestrating a class driven by a teacher's questions is much easier than one driven by students' questions. One risk of teacher-developed questions is that they may not be meaningful to the student or provide opportunities for students to generate subquestions.

There are many ways that a teacher can develop a good driving question. Some teachers like to begin with ideas they come across in their reading. For example, a teacher might use a question found in this book. Others like to begin with ideas they have heard about or experienced in methods classes, at teacher workshops, or in working with students. Some teachers like to develop questions from the school's curriculum. Some great driving questions come from listening to students' questions and ideas. A teacher's hobbies or personal interests can provide the catalyst for driving questions. So can the local newspaper, a news event, or a television program. Finally, other teachers are great sources of ideas for new driving questions and projects. We will discuss each of these sources for developing driving questions. We will also discuss concerns that must be addressed when using teacher-developed questions.

Developing Driving Questions from Personal Experiences

It is possible to glean many driving questions from your reading. This book has presented several questions that can be used to drive projects:

- What care do our classroom pets need?
- What type of trees grow in our neighborhood?
- How healthy is our stream?
- Does my community have acid rain?
- Do apples all have the same number of seeds?
- Why do I have to wear a helmet and knee and elbow pads when I'm roller blading?

- What kind of land features are in my environment?
- What kind of insects live on our playground?

These questions can be used at a variety of grade levels. For instance, the question "Why do I have to wear a helmet and knee and elbow pads when I'm roller blading?" could be used to drive a fourth grade unit on motion or it could be used to drive a seventh grade class on the same topic. We have used the question, "How healthy is my stream?" successfully at both the fifth grade level and at the eighth grade level. Other questions are probably best used only for lower or upper grade levels. For instance, the question "Do apples all have the same number of seeds?" is most appropriately used at the early elementary level (grades K–2).

Other personal experiences besides reading that are good sources of ideas for driving questions include methods classes, teacher workshops, or interactions with students during teaching. A typical science methods class exposes teachers to a variety of physical, life, and earth/space science topics that can be turned into driving questions. For instance, a teacher might have learned about electricity in a methods class by lighting a bulb using a wire and dry cell, constructing series and parallel circuits, and connecting small motors and switches to circuit paths. This experience could be used to develop the driving question "How is electricity used in my environment?" Teaching experience may tell a teacher that students are interested in classroom animals. This knowledge would help the teacher develop the driving question "What care do our classroom pets need?"

There are several advantages to using driving questions with which you have some experience. First, although you cannot possibly anticipate all of the rough spots in a project, knowing what students will be studying helps smooth out the rough spots. Second, with familiar questions, you can map out clearly what curriculum standards a project will meet. Third, teacher-designed familiar questions are often the most effective initial driving questions, because they allow you to start from a familiar basis instead

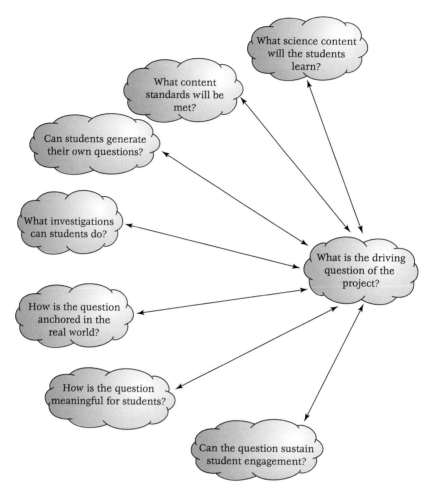

FIGURE 3.2
Prompts for helping to develop driving questions.

of treading into unknown territory. Finally, with a familiar question, you can plan and prepare resources such as equipment, readings, and guest speakers.

Brainstorming Driving Questions Associated with the Curriculum   One of the authors of this book likes to start to develop a driving question by reviewing the curriculum outcomes or standards that need to be met by a project. Next, he likes to brainstorm the investigations that students might conduct. He then considers ways to contextualize the project for students. At the same time, he jots down related questions that might be meaningful to students. Figure 3.2 illustrates this process of brainstorming a driving question to meet curriculum outcomes.

One middle school teacher rejected a number of questions related to her curriculum on forces and motion before she settled on the driving question, "How do I stay on a skateboard?" Science content was the teacher's first consideration in selecting a driving question for the skateboard project. Even before she began thinking about what kind of question would be meaningful and interesting to students, she clearly delineated what science content (force and motion) would need to be covered in order to meet district curriculum standards. Student motivation and interest were also a primary concern for her in the skateboard project. By using "How do I stay on a skateboard?" the teacher helped her students see tangible and interesting connections between abstract physical concepts and their own world.

The strongest advantage to brainstorming driving questions from curriculum is that the teacher can ensure that important curriculum outcomes are met. This is critical in most school districts, because the curricula at different grade levels are interdependent. In addition, in some areas, proficiency tests or graduation requirements are based on particular content.

Developing Driving Questions by Listening to Students Another good way to develop a driving question is to listen to questions that students ask. Some teachers create "test banks" of student ideas. A test bank is a notebook in which teachers record student questions and ideas. For example, a student might ask, "What kind of bird is that pretty red one?" This question might later become the driving question "What birds visit our feeder?"

Another source of student questions is the dialogue journal. This is a journal of correspondence between student and teacher. Science notebooks also provide question possibilities. A teacher might notice that a student writes in her notebook, "My mom was nagging me again last night to wear that stupid helmet when I was roller blading!" This idea might prompt the teacher to develop the driving question "Why do I have to wear a helmet and knee and elbow pads when I'm roller blading?"

Driving questions developed from listening to students are potentially more meaningful to students. This is a powerful reason to use these types of questions. However, because a driving question must meet district curriculum standards and other criteria, use Figure 3.1 as a guide in evaluating these various questions.

Developing Driving Questions from Hobbies and Personal Interests Teachers can come up with ideas for driving questions from their hobbies or personal interests. Rock collecting, fishing, cooking, outdoor activities, traveling, amateur astronomy, and jewelry making can all lead to excellent driving questions.

For example, if a teacher's hobby is outdoor activities, she can take the class on various field trips to set the stage for asking questions related to environmental issues and nature. Driving questions that might arise from this are "What kind of trees and plants are in my neighborhood?" "What kind of animals are in my neighborhood?" and "What kind of land forms are in my neighborhood?"

There are several reasons for developing driving questions from hobbies and personal interests. First, teachers often show a great deal of enthusiasm for questions related to personal interests, and this enthusiasm can be contagious, making the questions meaningful to students. Second, questions related to hobbies and personal interests are frequently sustainable because the hobbies or interests themselves are sustainable. Finally, teachers know a great deal about their personal interests, enabling them to easily make connections with curriculum outcomes and standards.

Developing Driving Questions from the Media Driving questions can also result from reading the newspaper or magazines, listening to the news, or watching documentaries and other shows on television. Newspapers and news shows present ideas that are current, usually less than a day old. Magazines and television documentaries provide information that is only a month or two old. Other ideas presented in magazines or on television shows may be interesting enough to become driving questions.

For instance, imagine that a gasoline tanker overturned a block away from a school in a large urban district. The area had to be evacuated, the sewers were pumped, the air smelled like gasoline, children and adults acquired headaches, and the expressway was closed for hours. A teacher in the district could quickly develop this driving question: "What hazards exist in my environment?" This question might lead to the study of what the hazards were, how chemicals become airborne, why people got headaches, and what breathing problems exist for adults and children.

Questions that result from media sources can be very appealing to students, especially if they are familiar. Familiarity with news items helps contextualize the question for students, making the question interesting and meaningful. However, a major problem with using driving questions that come from media sources is that they are hard to plan for ahead of time. This lack of planning often prevents teachers from reaching the curriculum standards. However, a teacher who is familiar with curriculum standards ahead of time might be able to quickly capitalize on a news story. For this reason, it is a good idea for implementing project-based science to become very familiar with district, state, or national standards before the planning stage.

Developing Driving Questions by Listening to Other Teachers   The personal experiences of others are good sources of driving questions. Your colleagues have probably attended interesting classes and had varied experiences with students. They may participate in novel hobbies or watch different television shows or read different magazines than you do.

In addition to providing fresh ideas for driving questions, colleagues can provide invaluable insight into dealing with the challenges of doing a project. They may have ideas for solving a problem, meeting curriculum standards, or classroom investigations. They may also have connections to community agencies, guest speakers, or resources.

Using Driving Questions That Come from Published Curriculum   A number of projects and driving questions can result from using published curriculum. Published curriculum includes textbook series, computer programs, laser and CD-ROM applications, and kit-based materials. Textbook series and kit-based programs are frequently adopted by school districts to meet their science outcomes and standards. Computer, laser, and CD-ROM applications frequently augment the adopted curriculum. Often these published curriculum materials are a good place to start when doing project-based science for the first time, because they provide a structure for selecting driving questions that meet curriculum standards. In addition, they usually contain some ideas for investigations or activities, resources (such as science supplies, hands-on materials, and student handouts), and background information about the science content for the teacher. Many of these materials provide the structure for benchmark lessons (lessons designed to teach basic knowledge and skills necessary to investigate a driving question).

For example, the National Geographic Society, in conjunction with the Technical Educational Research Center, has developed a number of units that are project-based in flavor. The *National Geographic Kids Network* (1989, 1991) is an innovative computer and telecommunications-based hands-on curriculum in which student-scientists investigate new ideas and exchange information with students around the world. There are seven *Kids Network* units available for students in grades 3–7. These include *Hello!; What's in Our Water?; Weather in Action; Solar Energy; Too Much Trash?; Acid Rain;* and *What Are We Eating?*

Each of the units has a number of features related to projects. For instance, in the unit *What's in Our Water?* students explore the quality of their school's water supply. To answer this question, students investigate a number of sub-questions including "What is the nitrate and chloride concentration of our school's water supply?" and "What are their sources, and how do they enter the water supply?" The unit allows students to deal with important science content. Students learn about watersheds, examine where their water comes from, investigate how local topography influences their watershed, and see how sources of pollution in one component of a watershed can influence water quality in other areas. They study pollution in terms of the context and concentration of various substances, focusing especially on the influence of nitrates in fertilizers on water pollution. Students also engage in teacher-directed investigations. Students measure the nitrate and chloride concentrations of their school's water supply and examine water treatment by investigating the influence of chorine on yeast growth. Class data about nitrate levels are shared with the research team (a team made up of representatives from schools around the world) via an electronic network. Students consider how local environment, commerce, agriculture, and industry might account for the differences reported by various research teams. Students also create a number of products that reflect their understanding. For instance, they debate water policy, design models of sources of pollution, and create posters and videotapes of their debates and panel discussions.

In the *Hello!* unit, children explore if other students throughout the country and world have the same kinds of pets. Although the project does not have a driving question, it is easy to develop one: "Do children throughout the country and world have the same kinds of pets?" or "Do children in different types of geographical regions have the same kinds of pets?" The *Kids Network* unit entitled *Acid Rain* also lacks a driving question, but, again, it is very easy to develop one: "Does our community have acid rain?" Overall, for teachers interested in getting started with projects, the *National Geographic Kids Network* material is a good place to begin.

There are other sources of driving questions in published curriculum materials, such as *The Pillbug Project: A Guide to Investigation,* by Robin Burnett (1992), available through the National Science Teachers Association. Although there is no driving question associated with it, one easily comes to mind: "What are these critters anyway?" Teachers can show students some pillbugs, and the project work can begin. The *Great Explorations in Math and Science (GEMS)* materials, available from the Lawrence Hall of Science, can be used as a base for developing driving questions and projects. There are more than fifty GEMS books, including *Ant Homes, Crime Lab Chemistry, Bubbleology, Acid Rain, Global Warming and the Greenhouse Effect, Mystery Festival,* and *Fingerprinting.* For example, the book *Ant Homes* can be used to develop the driving question "What kinds of insects live on our playground?"

Although topically organized, kit-based curriculum such as the *Full Option Science System (FOSS)* published by Delta (Lawrence Hall of Science, 1993) and *Science and Technology for Children (STC)* published by Carolina Biological (National Science Resource Center, 1991) are excellent project starters because they have a wealth of resources and provide the structure for many benchmark lessons. For example, FOSS's *Trees* kit can be used to develop the driving question "What kinds of trees are in my neighborhood?" The kit entitled *Insects* can be used to study insects that live on the playground. *Earth Materials, Landforms,* or *Pebbles, Sand and Silt* can be used to study the driving question "What kinds of land features are in my environment?" STC's kit, *Food Chemistry,* can be used for benchmark lessons to study the driving question "How do we stay healthy?"

An extensive list of science curriculum materials is published in *NSTA's Science Education Suppliers,* available from the National Science Teachers Association, 1840 Wilson Boulevard, Arlington, Va. 22201-3000. We encourage you to get a copy of this book and write to companies for their catalogues. Another great resource for examining published curriculum materials is the Eisenhower National Clearinghouse for Mathematics and Science Education, available on the World Wide Web at http://www.enc.org.

Using the World Wide Web as a Source of Driving Questions The World Wide Web can also be used by teachers as a source of driving questions and project ideas. A number of research groups are developing projects, and many of these can be found on the Web. The Knowledge Integration Environment (KIE) (http://www.kie.berkeley.edu/KIE.html), the Learning Through Collaborative Visualization Project (http://www.covis.nwu.edu/), and the Center for Highly Interactive Computing in Education (http://hi-ce.eecs.umich.edu/) are three sites that discuss projects.

FIGURE 3.3
Students use technology to find information related to a driving question.

ACTIVITY 3.4

Generating Driving Questions from Topics

MATERIALS NEEDED:
- paper and pencil or a computer
- a variety of curriculum materials (such as from GEMS, AIMS, FOSS, STC, and National Geographic)

A. Use the following topics to create teacher-developed driving questions. Write an explanation of why you think they make good driving questions.

   K–4 Topics from the *National Science Education Standards* (NRC, 1996):
   - changes in the earth and sky
   - light
   - electricity
   - magnetism
   - life cycles
   - organisms and environments
   - properties of earth materials
   - objects in the sky

   Grades 5 through 8 Topics from the *National Science Education Standards* (NRC, 1996):
   - changes and properties of matter
   - motions and forces
   - transfer of energy
   - heredity
   - reproduction
   - structure of the earth
   - solar system
   - environmental hazards
   - personal health

B. Examine a variety of commercially published curriculum materials. Match available materials to the topics listed from the *National Science Education Standards* (NRC, 1996). Write about how the commercially published materials could support the driving question.

C. How could the driving questions you developed provide opportunities for students to ask their own questions and explore solutions to them?

D. Record your responses in your portfolio.

The Knowledge Integration Environment (KIE) curriculum, developed by Marcia Linn from the University of California–Berkeley, involves students in projects in which they work with scientific evidence. Students using KIE reflect on their own scientific ideas while considering new evidence. Although students must find information on the Web to complete a KIE project, they must also analyze evidence and produce scientific explanations for real world phenomena. They learn how to create their own evidence related to a science topic and to design problem solutions based on scientific principles.

The Learning Through Collaborative Visualization Project (CoVis) is a community of thousands of students, over 100 teachers, and dozens of researchers all working together to find new ways to think about and practice science in the classroom. CoVis students study atmospheric and environmental sciences through inquiry-based activities using state-of-the-art scientific visualization software specially modified for a learning environment.

The Center for Highly Interactive Computing in Education (hi-ci) uses a project-based science approach to teaching, the tools of a digital library, and learner-centered software that was created to support students' scientific inquiry into important intellectual problems.

These sources are highly interactive. Their projects meet all of the key features of good driving questions. They are feasible (students can interact with others around the world to design and perform investigations), worthwhile (they contain rich science content that can be broken down into smaller questions), contextualized (they are grounded in the real world), meaningful to students (especially in terms of the interactivity with students around the world), and sustainable (interactions can last the entire school year).

Making Sure Teacher-Generated Driving Questions Work for Students   No matter what the source of a driving question, it should provide opportunities for students to ask their own questions and explore solutions to those questions. Driving questions that are teacher-generated should not be so highly constrained that the outcomes are predetermined, leaving students with little room to develop their own approaches to

---

ACTIVITY 3.5

Analyze Classroom Science and Develop Driving Questions

MATERIALS NEEDED:
- a classroom to visit
- a copy of the school's curriculum framework
- paper and pencil or a computer

A. Obtain permission from appropriate school personnel to visit an elementary or middle grade classroom. Observe the teacher. Look over the classroom materials the teacher is using. Review the district's curriculum framework.

B. Analyze whether the students were exploring the solutions to questions in the science teaching that you observed. Determine if the questions meet the key features of driving questions. If they do not, how might the teacher alter the science instruction to develop questions that meet the key features?

C. Record the information from this activity in your portfolio.

---

them. In Activity 3.4, you will practice generating driving questions and turning curriculum materials into good driving questions.

To contextualize the developing of driving questions in a real elementary classroom, Activity 3.5 provides you with the opportunity to observe a classroom and develop and evaluate driving questions.

Student-Generated Driving Questions

Initially, teachers may feel more comfortable creating the questions and activities themselves. However, driving questions can also arise from students' personal interests. With practice, students can take responsibility for creating both the questions and the investigations. One of the biggest benefits of student-generated questions is that the meaningfulness feature is virtually ensured. However, teachers must still work carefully to determine whether questions are feasible, worthwhile, and contextualized. Sometimes students select topics that have high interest but that cannot be answered through student investigations. Dinosaurs are a common topic of interest among young children, for example, but there aren't many investigations that students can perform related to this topic. For this reason, although dinosaurs might be a good topic to read about, they don't lead to feasible projects. Teachers must also worry about whether content meets district curriculum standards and whether students' questions are real world ques-

tions. For example, students might be interested in spaceships, but spaceships are not a part of students' daily lives and probably don't match any of the district's curriculum standards.

To develop driving questions from students' interests, a teacher must provide students time to develop questions and establish a setting in which questions can emerge. Teachers must develop ways to support students in their asking of questions, select from among the many possible driving questions those that are worth pursuing, and sensitively handle those questions that are not selected. In this section, we explore techniques for helping students ask questions, selecting students' questions, and developing students' ideas into driving questions.

Supporting Students Asking Questions Teachers can use various ways to encourage students to ask questions that might be turned into a driving question for a project or that might be used as subquestions in a project. One of the best ways to accomplish this is to have students make observations of their surroundings. To do this, teachers must build a classroom environment that fosters students asking questions and that exposes students to situations that they can observe. Teachers also can have students brainstorm ideas they know about and help them identify hobbies and personal interests.

An Encouraging Classroom Environment There are a number of ways that a teacher can build an environment that encourages students to ask questions. One technique involves setting up situations in the classroom that allows students to make observations and ask questions. For instance, a teacher might set up an aquarium in the classroom or plant a variety of seeds in a classroom terrarium. Imagine a series of aquariums that are missing pumps and filters but that contain sand, goldfish, snails, and duckweed. Students make careful observations, recording them on a daily basis. After several days, students notice a build up of "black stuff" on the sand at the bottom of the aquariums. Students will likely ask questions such as "What is the black stuff on the bottom of the aquarium?" This situation forms a great learning experience for early elementary students in which they can test theories of where the black stuff comes from. Students might, for example, hypothesize that the black stuff comes from "the snails and the fish going to the bathroom," "the fish vomiting," or from the sand itself being dirty and the dirt rising to the top of the sand as it settles over time.

A second technique involves teachers exposing students to situations in which they can explore their environment. Teachers can take students on walking excursions or on field trips or bring in guest speakers. For instance, teachers can support students asking questions about the quality of the water in a stream near the school by taking the students on a stream walk. Or they can have students explore the types of trees in the neighborhood by walking around the block. By going for a walk around the block, for example, students can make careful observations of the types and locations of trees. By look-ing at the shape of the leaves, the texture of bark, and the color variations in the leaves and the bark, students can begin to ask questions like, "Why do some trees have rough bark and others have smooth bark?" This question can naturally lead to the driving question "What trees are in my neighborhood?"

What Students Already Know   Another strategy that can be used to help students generate their own driving questions is to have them brainstorm about what they know. Students will come up with many ideas about animals, dinosaurs, cars, and toys. Frequently, students will come up with ideas based on interests and hobbies such as their pets, television shows, baseball card collections, doll collections, and musical instruments. Many teachers list these ideas on a chart with three columns labeled, "What we know," "What we want to know," and "What we learned." The ideas that students generate can be listed under the "What we know" column. This method, called *the KWL method* and developed by Debra Ogle (1986), can be used in a variety of contexts.

Next, teachers help students turn these ideas into questions. For example, in the first column students might list, "Animals live outdoors," "Some animals live indoors," "Animals need food to grow," "Animals are big and little," and "Animals can be dangerous." These ideas might lead to an entry in the middle column: "What animals live in our neighborhood." One reason why this is a good driving question is because it can be investigated by students. Future chapters will explore the KWL method in greater detail.

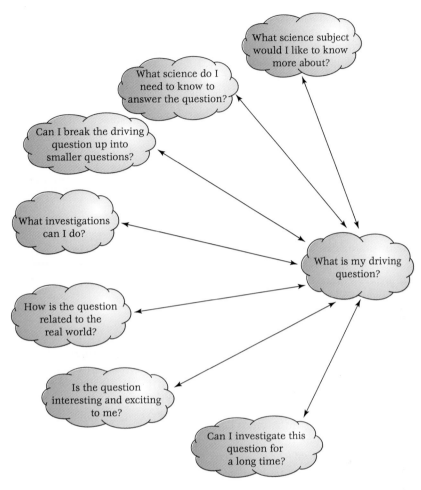

FIGURE 3.4
Students' prompts for developing their own driving questions.

Besides having students brainstorm topics and related questions in a large group, teachers can have the class generate topics and questions in small groups. This method allows students to critique the questions as well since small-group review is much less threatening than having questions exposed to the whole class for review. Some teachers use a "dialogue journal" to accomplish this small group generation of topics and sharing. Dialogue journals are journals that students keep and share with peers or the teacher and that include responses from readers. Now is a good time to complete Activity 3.6.

Selection of Students' Questions After students have generated possible driving questions, teachers must help them select the questions that will be used for projects. This is not an easy task. Many students want their question selected, and their feelings can be hurt and self-esteem damaged if their questions are not selected. Several techniques can be used to select sensitively the driving questions from the pool of questions students generate.

One technique is to have students evaluate and refine their questions. In the process of evaluating and refining questions, they often disregard many of them. Teachers can use the features of a driving question (see Table 3.1) and the questions in Figure 3.4 to support evaluation and refinement of questions. Most students will not know how to evaluate questions, so a critical first step is to model the process of evaluating. For example, imagine the class has generated the question "How do robots work?" The teacher can respond to this question by saying,

My driving question is "How do robots work?" I want to know more about how to make a robot. Let's see . . . I will need to know about electricity and machines. I will also need to know about computers. I could break this question into smaller ones: How is a robot made? How expensive is a robot? Could a robot do my homework? What investigations can I do? Hmmm. I don't know. I don't have money to buy a robot, so we can't experiment on it. I have a toy robot. I could take that apart, but once I took it apart, I'd be done in a few hours. This is interesting, but I guess it's not a good driving question. I can't investigate this very much!

From modeling the process, students can see how the teacher eliminated the robot question because it isn't feasible or sustainable. Once the teacher models the process, students in the class are usually ready to evaluate some of their own questions using the criteria in Figure 3.4.

Another strategy for selecting a driving question from a list of students' questions is to have two groups of students share and critique each other's driving questions. When using this technique, teachers should make sure that the groups who are having their questions critiqued also have the right to defend their questions. It also is critical that students give reasons for their comments. Just claiming that they don't like a question is not a sufficient reason. The criteria in Figure 3.4 can be used to focus and support student evaluation of the questions posed by others. While students are evaluating and refining their questions in small groups, it is vital that the teacher give students feedback on their evaluations. This helps students stay focused before they get too far off track. Active monitoring of group work and encouragement are critical if teachers want students to complete the task with a high level of investment.

Teachers should also help students realize that good driving questions, like most products that have value, don't emerge complete from the first round of revision. Often to arrive at a good product, there must be several revisions. Therefore, modifying questions is a critical step in developing good driving questions. To accomplish this, some teachers like to bring the separate groups back into a large group and have the groups present their questions and give justifications for selecting them. Then, the members of other groups can add their comments to the discussion of a driving question candidate. This

---

TABLE 3.2   Ways to Help Students Generate Driving Questions

- Provide or create an environment in which students can make observations.
- Have students brainstorm what they know.
- Focus on students' hobbies and personal interests.
- Help students modify topics into questions of interest.
- Model the process of evaluating questions using the criteria in Figure 3.4.
- Have students share, evaluate, and refine questions in small groups.
- Have groups share questions and rationales with the whole class.

---

technique helps reinforce the qualities of a good question.

Summary of Strategies to Help Students Develop Questions   Student-generated questions require a little more work on the part of the teacher, because supports need to be used to get students to develop them. Further, a teacher needs to make sure that students work through the process of determining whether all of the key features of driving questions are met in the students' questions. However, most teachers find that, with experience, children will begin to ask, refine, and develop solid projects based upon their own questions. Finally, teachers who are familiar with their school district's curriculum standards are usually able to adapt students' questions to school outcomes. Table 3.2 summarizes ways that students' questions can be developed into driving questions.

WHAT IS THE VALUE OF THE DRIVING QUESTION?

A driving question has value if it (1) is meaningful for students; (2) allows teachers to link together various components of a project; (3) allows students to engage in an intellectual problem over time; (4) links content and process together; (5) helps students see how the science they are learning applies to the real world; and (6) connects various subject areas so that students can develop understandings about the connections.

Often in schools students see what they are learning as separate from their own interests and lives. How many times have students been told, "You will need this for life" or "You will need this for the next class"? Unfortunately, these reasons are not motivating for students of any age. Driving questions, however, help make learning meaningful. Students find the questions and, thus, learning relevant to their lives and their world or culture, and they find the related projects exciting and interesting.

What typically happens in schools is that ideas are taught in isolation from each other. There often is no organizer that can pull together the overall ideas. For example, a common science curriculum might teach students how to classify animals, about habitats needed by animals, and about behaviors of animals. These topics are usually taught as separate ideas—perhaps even through different chapters of a book covered at different times during the year. Driving questions help teachers link the various concepts taught, which helps students develop integrated understandings that are linked together rather than isolated. The questions become anchors for tying together all the new information that students are learning, which results in the information making more sense.

Students frequently fail to see a reason to expend a great deal of energy over an extended period of time when there is no driving question to focus that energy and give them a reason for their efforts. A driving question ties the learning of concepts to the project activities and ties both to a clear, meaningful purpose. With this combination students are engaged throughout the duration of a project.

Sometimes school science is presented as though content and process were separate. For example, in the first scenario in this chapter, the teacher presented content as separate from process. In the second scenario, process was presented as separate from content. A well-written driving question gives coherence and continuity to project-based science, and it links content with process. Deborah Brown, a teacher from Detroit Public Schools, illustrates this in the case report she wrote after doing the "What's in Our Water?" project (Krajcik et al., 1996):

> One of the biggest advantages to using a driving question as the focus was that it gave students a sense of purpose. As we worked together through this first unit, my students began to realize that there was a reason for everything that we did. No more questions like, "Why do we have to learn this?" No matter how different the activities seemed, the end results were the same. We were trying to find out about our tap water.
>
> This sense of purpose did not come about quickly or easily. Many times as I was teaching the first unit ("What's in Our Water?"), I would forget to emphasize our main question. The students may have understood the main concepts of that lesson and still had no idea how it was connected to the unit.
>
> When I did remember to ask the students about our main question, I would many times get blank stares. They were not used to making these kinds of connections. So, when I first asked them to go back to research they had done three weeks ago and apply it to activities they were doing today, they thought I was out of my mind. [But later] students became more adept at making connections. Students were able to draw on previous data to explain new concepts.

This quote also illustrates that a sense of purpose comes about only after the teacher does a lot of active teaching. The teacher must continually help students see how the content and process are linked to the driving question. The teacher is central to the success of project-based science, because the teacher, as an active and supportive leader and guide, orchestrates the educational environment. If the teacher does not play this role, students are not able to focus on the demanding intellectual activities of projects, and they cannot see the purpose of the activities of the project.

A common problem in science classrooms is that students learn only fragmented knowledge without ever relating school science content to the world in which they live. But when science class is centered around an interesting, real world driving question, students can more easily make connections with the content, and they can see firsthand how the study of science relates to issues and problems in their own lives.

Often students don't have experiences in school that help them attach much of what they learn in one subject area to what they learn in other subject areas. For example, students might learn how to use a ruler in mathematics class to solve math problems but not about applications to science. In science class, they might learn about various animal habitats but fail to learn about the connections to history and politics. They may learn how to write a business letter in language arts, but they never learn about the use of writing skills in math and science. As a result of these types of school experiences, students often develop fragmented knowledge that they can't apply in other areas of study.

Through the driving question, project-based science explicitly links different subject areas. For example, through the driving question "How do we care for the pets in our room?" students might learn to use a ruler in mathematics class so that they can measure the amount a pet has grown. They might learn about animal habitats in order to build the best home for their classroom pet. They might learn to write a business letter in language arts so that they can write to companies that test products on animals. When learning is integrated in this way, students develop cognitive structures for processing and linking new information. In this way, learning occurs at a deeper, more permanent level. (See Chapter 2, section on "Integrated Understanding," and Chapter 9 where we discuss integration across the curriculum.)

HOW CAN A DRIVING QUESTION BE USED THROUGHOUT A PROJECT?

Once a teacher has chosen a driving question and begun a project, he or she must keep referring to the driving question. The driving question gives a focus to class activities and to what the students are learning. By keeping the driving question in mind as teachers lead students through different activities, they will help the students contextualize what they are learning and help maintain continuity throughout the project. The driving question can be an excellent vehicle to maintain focus and support integration, but only if the teacher takes an active role in using the driving question throughout a project.

In a project-based science classroom, investigations and activities should play a role in answering the driving question. However, making students aware of these connections can be a challenge. These connections are not always obvious to students until the teacher takes the time to help students understand the reasons behind activities. There are several techniques for applying the driving question throughout a project.

One excellent and simple technique is to refer frequently to the driving question. At the end of every class and activity, before beginning each new activity, and periodically throughout the day, the teacher can ask, "Why are we doing all this?" Soon enough, students will be able to join the teacher in responding, "To learn how to care for the pets in our room," or "To find out what birds visit our feeder." It won't be long before students begin to think about the driving question as they work, even without the teacher's prompts.

Another technique is to develop ways to link activities and investigations in class to the driving question. Teachers need to consider how to introduce a project's driving question so that the connections between the question and classroom activity start out firmly planted in students' minds. Throughout the project, teachers can reinforce this connection by asking periodically, "Why is this investigation important to our project?" and "How does it help us answer our driving question?" Students will come to expect teachers to ask these questions and will develop good responses.

Another way of linking the content and the class activities to the driving question is to have the driving question visible at all times. The teacher can point to the question every time she asks, "Why are we doing this?" Students will soon learn to look at the wall or bulletin board where the question is posted to help them stay on track. One teacher hung a large banner with the driving question on it on the wall outside her classroom. From the banner she hung various student products. The banner with the driving question and products formed a time line of project activities. The banner also generated excitement among other students in the school.*

Another technique is to have students periodically write in their journals about how what they are doing is related to the driving question. Some teachers use this technique in conjunction with class discussion that encourages students to tell how what they do in class on a given day is

---

* Jon Singer, University of Michigan, suggested this idea.

related to their driving question. Because these projects are long term, the potential for losing focus is high, so continual reminders of the driving question can prevent fragmented learning and keep students from getting lost.

SUMMARY OF CHAPTER

A driving question organizes content and drives activities that take place in a science class. The driving question is the first step in meeting all of the other key features of project-based science. The question sets the stage for planning and carrying out investigations. This chapter elaborated on the features of good driving questions: feasibility, worth, contextualization, meaning, and sustainability. It also discussed ways that driving questions can be teacher-generated from the curriculum, the World Wide Web, colleagues, personal interests, and the media and how they can be student-generated. Techniques for encouraging and selecting student questions were explored. The chapter ended with an exploration of the value of a driving question. The question is meaningful for students; it helps teachers link lessons, process and content, and different other subject areas; and it allows students to engage in an intellectual problem over time. Developing driving questions is clearly worth the time and effort because they allow students to learn in a more educationally sound manner, and they make teaching more satisfying and rewarding.

REFERENCES

American Association for the Advancement of Science. 1993. *Benchmarks for science literacy.* New York: Oxford University Press.

Atwater, M. M. 1994. Research on cultural diversity in the classroom. In *Handbook of research on science teaching and learning,* ed. D. L. Gabel. New York: Macmillan.

Blumenfeld, P., E. Soloway, R. Marx, J. Krajcik, M. Guzdial, and A. Palincsar. 1991. Motivating project-based learning: Sustaining the doing, supporting the learning. *Educational Psychologist* 26(3 & 4):369–98.

Burnett, R. 1992. *The pillbug project: A guide to investigation.* Washington, D.C.: National Science Teachers Association.

Elementary Science Study. 1970. *The ESS reader.* Newton, Mass.: Education Development Center.

Haberman, M. 1991. The pedagogy of poverty versus good teaching. *Phi Delta Kappa* 73(4):290–94.

Krajcik, J. S. 1993. Learning science by doing science. In *What research says to the science teacher: Science, society and technology,* ed. R. Yager. Washington, D.C.: National Science Teacher Association.

Krajcik, J., E. Soloway, P. C. Blumenfeld, R. W. Marx, B. L. Ladewski, N. D. Bos, and P. J. Hayes. 1996. The casebook of project practices—an example of an interactive multimedia system for professional development. *Journal of Computers in Mathematics and Science Teaching* 15 (Vols. 1 and 2):119–35.

Krajcik, J., P. Blumenfeld, R. W. Marx, and E. Soloway. 1994. A collaborative model for helping science teachers learn project-based instruction. *Elementary School Journal* 94(5):483–98.

Lawrence Hall of Science. 1993. *Full option science system.* Nashua, N.H.: Delta Education.

National Geographic Kids Network. 1991. *What's in our water?* Washington, D.C.: National Geographic Society.

National Geographic Kids Network. 1989. *Acid rain.* Washington, D.C.: National Geographic Society.

National Research Council. 1996. *National science education standards.* Washington, D.C.: National Academy Press.

National Science Resource Center. 1991. *Science and technology for children.* Washington, D.C.: Smithsonian Institute, National Academy of Sciences.

Ogle, D. 1986. A teaching model that develops active reading of expository text. *The Reading Teacher* 39(2):564–70.

Chapter 4

What Must Farmers Plan For?
Besides planting, what else must
farmers do to grow healthy crops?

HOW ARE SCIENTIFIC INVESTIGATIONS DEVELOPED?

INTRODUCTION

Investigations form the essence of "doing" science. What is an investigation? How are investigations developed? How do I help students plan and design experiments? How can I help students be systematic in analyzing data? In this chapter, we will explore how to help students engage in investigations. We will examine the various components of investigations, including asking and refining questions, planning and designing experiments, assembling and carrying out procedures, analyzing data, and sharing information with others. We will consider the various components as a web of related activities. Throughout the chapter, we will discuss the various instructional supports a teacher can provide to help learners through the various components of investigations, and we will explore answers to numerous questions that might arise about investigations.

First, we will consider several types of school science activities, some of which you may have experienced yourself as a student. As you read each scenario, focus on various features of the instructional setting. What are the students doing and thinking? What is the role of the teacher? What instructional supports does the teacher provide?

Scenario 1: A Step-by-Step Activity

You may have observed a situation similar to this. A fifth grade teacher presents information on the physical and chemical properties of materials. The teacher shows the students some white powders and tells the class they will observe the appearance of each of the powders and what happens when they mix a small amount of each powder with some liquids the teacher calls *solutions*. The teacher hands out a sheet a paper with step-by-step directions about the amounts of powder and liquid to use and about how to mix the materials together. The teacher also passes out a sheet of paper with a carefully labeled table on which the students are to record their observations. The powders are labeled across the top of the table and the solutions are labeled down the side. The teacher directs the class to describe and illustrate their observations in the table.

The teacher allows the students to work in groups of four. Each group has thirty minutes in which to complete the activity. The teacher directs each group to assign one member to gather the required materials—the powders and solutions—from the table at the front of the class. Students from various groups volunteer to gather the materials, but in one group, none of the students wants to go get the materials. After the students return to their tables with the materials, one student grabs some of the powders and begins mixing them with one of the liquids. In some groups, students begin by reading the teacher's directions to decide what they need to do first. In one group, all the students begin working independently of the other students. Some students become involved by reading off the directions and handing materials to the other students. Some students use magnifying glasses to make observations of the powders, and they draw pictures of what they see. The classroom is loud, but everyone appears to be on task. Students make comments like, "Hey, that was cool." A number of the groups really like it when one of the powders bubbles and fizzes after mixing one of the solutions with one of the powders.

In this first scenario, the activity was selected by the teacher, the teacher gave the students directions about how to carry out the activity, and all the students performed the same activity. Although the students manipulated materials and worked in small groups to make and record observations, they spent little, if any, time planning what they were to do and little, if any, time discussing what the observations meant. Moreover, the activity the students performed was not tied to a question that the students asked or that they found meaningful.

Scenario 2: A Trial-and-Error Activity

You may have observed a situation like this. A fifth grade teacher passes out one light bulb, a wire, and a battery. He challenges the students to work in teams of two to find as many ways as possible to light the bulb using just the wire and the battery. The teacher directs the class to work in groups of two and to sketch "all the ways you can to get the bulb to light using the battery and wire." The teacher hands out baggies that contain the various materials.

Almost all of the teams jump into the task with little or no discussion about what to do. A number of the teams try connecting the bulb, wire, and battery in a straight-line configuration, but this method fails to light the bulb. Some students comment that they have a "bad bulb" or a "battery that doesn't work." After several failed attempts, some of the teams discuss ways to get the bulb to light. As some of the groups get their light bulb to light, comments like "cool" or "wow" are made. Some of the teams that fail to light their bulb become frustrated and stop trying, but most of the groups persist, possibly because trying to light the bulb is more fun than answering the questions at the end of the chapter. The excitement in the room grows as various teams light the bulb. After about five minutes, most teams have lit their bulb. The teacher walks around asking each team to demonstrate its strategies.

The teacher challenges the teams to find out how to light the bulb in different ways. Some teams who are having difficulty finding a way to light their bulb ask other teams for help; the successful teams seem happy to share their techniques. The teacher encourages the groups that are having difficulty to think of different ways to light the bulb. The teacher also challenges the teams that had success lighting the bulb in more than one way to "make two light bulbs light so that if you disconnect one light bulb, the other goes out too." Some teams talk about how lighting the bulb is related to switching on the light in the classroom.

In Scenario 2 as in Scenario 1, the teacher selected the activity for the students. Once again, the activity was not tied to a question that the students asked. Unlike Scenario 1, the teacher did not tell the students how to do the activity, so students could have made plans to describe how they would light the bulb, but most just used trial-and-error methods. The activity was fun, but most of the students did not understand why the bulb would or would not light. Little, if any, discussion occurred regarding why the bulb lit in one configuration and not in others. Although some of the students were able to make a connection between lighting the bulb and lighting their school, most students did not understand how lighting the bulb relates to how the lights work in a building.

Scenario 3: An Investigation

Perhaps you experienced a situation like this. In a fifth grade science classroom, one group of four students is sitting in a circle talking with some students writing in notebooks. Another group is standing behind a table putting soil in a pot, and another is gathered around a computer at the back of class. The teacher is talking with a fourth group of students.

The group sitting in a circle is making a list of possible questions to explore: Do worms help decomposition? Will new worms be born in the decomposition column? What will decompose first? One student says that the group can't design an experiment to study whether worms will be born in the decomposition column because it would be hard to count all the worms. Another student responds that it doesn't matter if they count *all* the worms; they just need to see if there are *more*.

The group putting soil in a pot has already made a plan for investigating the effects of compost on the growth of bean plants. The students are planting eight bean plants. They plan to plant two plants with a 75/25 mixture of compost and soil, two plants with a 50/50 mixture, another two with a 25/75 mixture, and two with just soil. Some of the students are still discussing whether they need to plant some plants with 100 percent compost.

The group at the computer is composing a letter to another fifth grade class. The students are explaining to the other class, which is located in another state, their plan for investigating the influence of light on decomposition. They will e-mail their letter to this class when they have finished writing it.

The fourth group is discussing with the teacher how to investigate the effects of air flow on decomposition. This group's plan is to build a decomposition column with numerous holes. The teacher, through a series of questions, is trying to help the group understand the need for a control and a larger sample. The teacher asks, "If you use only one decomposition column, how will that help you understand how air flow influences decomposition?" The students in the group are debating this question. One student says, "You really won't know if you use only one column because there will be nothing to compare it to." Another student argues that they could investigate "how fast the various stuff decomposes" using just one column. Another student responds that "how fast" won't help them answer their question. The group continues to debate. The teacher moves on to work with another group.

This scenario illustrates students engaging in different aspects of the process of investigation: asking and refining questions, planning and designing experiments, assembling materials and apparatus, carrying out procedures, and sharing information with others. The scenario also shows the important role that teachers play in helping students work through the various stages of investigations. Unlike the first and second scenarios, this scenario does not represent an activity that the teacher selected; what the teacher created was an educational environment in which students could learn about decomposition. Then the teacher provided instructional *support* by working with each of the groups, asking probing questions, or providing materials that students could use to investigate their questions.

There are times in the curriculum when step-by-step and trial-and-error activities, like those illustrated in the first two scenarios, are important. (Chapter 6 contains more information on how to develop step-by-step activities.) Such activities, however, are not investigations, because they are determined and set up by the teacher.

INVESTIGATIONS IN ELEMENTARY AND MIDDLE SCHOOL SCIENCE INSTRUCTION

The third scenario illustrates students involved in many aspects of investigating science questions. Students pursue solutions to questions of importance by asking and refining their own questions, debating ideas, making predictions, designing plans and/or experiments, measuring, collecting and analyzing data and/or information, drawing conclusions, making inferences, communicating their ideas and findings

to others, and asking new questions. Research supports the notion that young children are capable of performing all aspects of investigations (Krajcik, Blumenfeld, Marx, Bass, Fredricks, & Soloway, 1998; Metz, 1995; Schauble, Klopfer, & Raghavan, 1991). Metz (1995) presents a strong argument for the investigative ability of young children and for their ability to learn from investigations. Although, because of their limited prior knowledge, their investigations will not be as sophisticated as those of adolescents and adults. The teacher, however, plays the critical role of orchestrating the investigative process and selecting curricular areas that allow students to ask questions that result in developing understanding of important concepts and principles.

Research also suggests that students should be involved throughout their school experience in the process of scientific investigation, and that children should be involved in the business of thinking scientifically:

> From their very first day in school, students should be actively engaged in learning to view the world scientifically. That means encouraging them to ask questions about nature and seek answers, collect things, count and measure things, make qualitative observations, organize collections and observations, discuss findings, etc. Getting into the spirit of science and liking science are what count the most (AAAS, *Benchmarks for Science Literacy*, p. 6).

Asking questions, designing experiments, analyzing data, and sharing what they know should be a routine part of students' science learning. However, students seldom have opportunities to ask their own questions and then define experiments to gather data related to the questions. Science textbooks seldom engage students in the process of investigation. As in Scenario 1, children are often given the purpose of activities, step-by-step directions, and procedures for how to collect data. Carrying out activities of this sort does not engage students in scientific thinking. For activities of this sort, students often are given the outcomes and are not challenged to analyze the purpose or predict outcomes. Students seldom have opportunities during these activities to analyze data, yet it is the process of analysis that leads to deep understanding of a situation or phenomenon. Often-

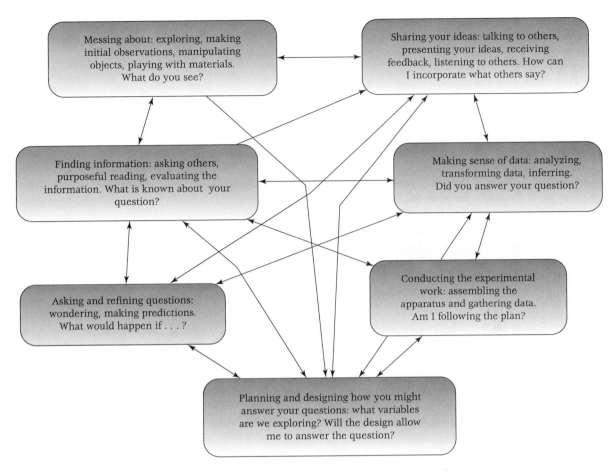

FIGURE 4.1
The investigation web.

times students know the expected outcome to the activity before the activity is conducted.

As clearly stated in the *National Science Education Standards* (National Research Council, 1996), students need to engage in the scientific process: They need to ask their own questions that are important to them, design their own experimental procedures, make sense of their data, analyze their data, share their plans and findings with others for feedback and criticism, and generate new ideas. In fact, congruent with recommendations with AAAS (1993), the *National Science Education Standards* stress that there needs to be less emphasis on didactic instruction that focuses on memorizing decontextualized scientific facts and there needs to be new emphasis placed on inquiry-based learning that focuses on developing a deep understanding of science that is embedded in the everyday world.

THE INVESTIGATION WEB

Engaging in the process of investigation is akin to seeking the answer to a question, for which humans seem to have a deep need. In this section, we will examine the **investigation web,** a process of carrying out an investigation that includes "messing about," asking and refining questions, finding information, planning and designing, building the apparatus and collecting data, analyzing data, making conclusions, and communicating findings.

Figure 4.1 presents one visualization of the process of investigation. The term *web* represents the nonlinear quality of an investigation and illustrates the way that students revisit various components of an investigation. Science is truly a nonlinear endeavor. Each component of an investigation provides feedback for another part. For instance, finding information about a topic might lead students to refine their questions that lead them to the information in the first place. As an example, in Scenario 3 earlier, students might find information about building a compost that causes them to refine their question regarding the impact of air flow on decomposition. Or preliminary data analysis might suggest ways for students to modify their procedures to collect more reliable data. For example, students might notice that their decomposition column feels warm, and this observation suggests that they might collect data on temperature changes. Completing an investigation should lead to other questions. For example, once students find out that oxygen is needed to help materials decompose, new questions might be asked regarding decomposition of materials buried in a landfill. Some investigations might begin with the gathering of data or with the search for a pattern. For example, students might design an investigation of decomposition only after "messing around" with different decomposing materials and noticing that air affects the rate of decomposition. Science is a messy process. Although scientists often have good hunches about important questions based on theories and their own prior knowledge, the questions for investigation and the processes ultimately employed often differ greatly from scientists' original conception.

Imagine that a fourth grade class is making observations of various insects in a nature area. One student group, which is turning over logs and rocks, notices that sow bugs can be found under the logs (messing about). Based on their observations, the students wonder if sow bugs like dark areas (wondering). In their classroom, the teacher has students share their observations and questions with classmates (sharing ideas). The group that has observed the sow bugs asks the question, "Do sow bugs like the dark?" (asking questions). (See Burnett, 1992.) Based on feedback from the class, the students refine their question to "Will sow bugs choose a dark area over a lighted area?" (receiving feedback, refining questions). The students design an experimental procedure to answer their question (designing). They then share their plans with the class (sharing ideas). Students in the class wonder if they are using enough sow bugs (wondering). The students incorporate the class feedback into their de-

sign (incorporating what others say). Next, the students look for information on sow bug habitats (finding information). Then, they gather sow bugs from the nature area, build a habitat so the sow bugs can live, and construct their experimental chamber for testing light and dark habitats (assembling the apparatus). Next, they perform their experiment, carefully recording their data (gathering data). To make sense of their data, they create a bar chart of the number of sow bugs found in dark and light places (transforming data). They draw conclusions based on their findings that sow bugs like dark areas (inferring). After some debate in the group regarding the number of trials needed, they decide to collect more data by carrying out two additional trials to see if their conclusion holds up (gathering data). They analyze their new data by comparing the old and new results and decide that they support their original conclusion (analyzing data). They then present their findings to the class (sharing ideas). Some classmates suggest that they should have ruled out moisture to determine if the sow bugs like dark areas (receiving feedback). The students argue that moisture did not make a difference; however, after some debate they realize that their classmates might have a point (talking to others). The students then redesign their investigation: This time, they keep some of the sow bugs in a dark dry environment, some in a dark moist environment, some in a light dry environment, and some in a light moist environment (planning and designing). The students once again analyze the data and draw a conclusion (making sense of data). The group then presents its findings and reasons to the class (sharing ideas). As students work, they ask a number of new questions about temperature and time. When the students complete their investigations, they return the sow bugs and the habitat materials to the nature area.

This example illustrates the investigative web process in its ideal form; don't expect your classroom investigations to run so smoothly from the start. As the teacher, you will need to provide instructional supports throughout the investigation process. Being good at science, like learning to play tennis, takes practice and experience. You would not expect to be a good tennis player the first time you pick up a tennis racket, and you shouldn't expect a student to be good at carrying out scientific investigations at first either. Good tennis players don't develop even over the course of a season, and so you cannot expect students to develop into good investigators during a single school year.

Let's play out the tennis analogy a little further: Tennis can be broken down into a variety of activities, such as forehand, backhand, serve, and volley, to mention a few. Skill in any one tennis activity doesn't make a good tennis player; neither does skill in all of the activities of tennis without putting them together. Practicing all the components together helps make a person a good tennis player. Similarly, conducting investigations has a number of components, such as planning, sharing, and gathering data. Skill in planning or gathering data alone does not make a good investigator. Students need to practice all of the activities of investigating, not in isolated applications but in concert.

The age of the learner will influence the type of investigations the learner can perform. Children who are in first and second grade are not developmentally ready to plan experiments in which they control variables. Children who are five to seven years old should be observing, measuring, and identifying properties of materials. For example, children in first or second grade could observe the different types of insects or birds found on their playground. Six- to nine-year-old children should be looking for evidence and identifying patterns. For example, fourth grade students could chart throughout the day the length of a shadow cast from a stake placed in the ground to notice the pattern of the sun's "movement" across the sky. As children gain experiences and become more developmentally ready, they can perform more complex investigations. Eight- to twelve-year-old children should begin to design cause and effect experiments and perfect their observations, measurements, and evidence-gathering skills; and eleven to thirteen year olds should design and conduct experiments that involve manipulating variables (AAAS, 1993). For example, middle school students could explore the influence of temperature on seed germination.

Messing About

How do you start students in the process of an investigation? How do you help children ask questions related to a content area? The first step in the investigative cycle is "messing about," or exploring (Hawkins, 1965). Messing about includes exploring, manipulating materials, making initial observations, reading about phenomena, and taking things apart.

Messing about implies having fun and exploring the world. Children can learn much by checking out what is in a pond, taking apart an old flashlight, watching how various gears work in unison, or playing with a stream table. Messing about with natural phenomena creates situations that encourage children to wonder. However, despite the implications of its name, this first step in investigation is not unstructured time. In fact, messing about needs to be carefully orchestrated by the classroom teacher. Although it may look very unplanned, messing about is structured by the teacher, who selects situations that will lead children to ask questions that have important curriculum outcomes.

Students have inadequate background knowledge to ask questions about some science content areas. For example, students may not know enough about physical science concepts such as friction and momentum to ask questions about simple machines. With careful structuring, however, worthwhile investigations of even difficult and unfamiliar content can occur. For example, a teacher can structure a messing about session to help students ask good questions about skateboards (which are a type of simple machine involving wheels and axles). Teachers can use a number of techniques to create learning environments in which children can mess about and ask questions. We will consider two types: initial observations and manipulation of materials.

Initial Observations   One way to structure science lessons so that students can mess about productively and ask worthwhile questions is to encourage **initial observations.** These are introductory observations that students make of physical phenomena that might acquaint them with concepts, pique their curiosity, and motivate them to ask questions. Almost any type of physical object is a great catalyst for initial observations in elementary and middle grade classrooms. You might consider outdoor nature areas, playgrounds, simple machines around the school (for example, a pencil sharpener) terrariums, aquariums, and classroom pets.

FIGURE 4.2
Initial observations of an environment can lead to students asking questions.

Imagine that you want students involved in a biology investigation on insects. To focus early elementary students' observations, have the students map out 8-inch by 8-inch areas of the playground or of a nature area. Figure 4.2 depicts this situation. Some of the areas should be shady, some sunny, some moist, and some dry. Then have the students divide each area into a 2-inch by 2-inch grid. Ask each to select one area, or microbiome, for observation. If possible, supply them with magnifying lenses. While in the field, students might draw what they see onto 8-inch by 8-inch sheets of paper that are also marked off in 2-inch by 2-inch grids. Once in the classroom again, have students compare their grids with one another. Ask them to write down and share questions that emerge from their observations. Students might ask, for example, "Do each of the areas have the same insects?" "What is different about them?" "Why do you suppose they are different?"

Stream or pond walks are also excellent catalysts for initial observations about ecosystems.

FIGURE 4.3
Stream walks catalyze student questions.

ACTIVITY 4.1

Going on a Stream Walk

MATERIALS NEEDED:
- writing materials
- walking shoes

A. Where do questions come from? Questions often arise from exploring our environment. Take a thirty-minute walk around a stream or pond. As you walk, examine the bank. Look closely at the water. What do you see? You might dip a bucket into the water and draw a water sample so that you can make more thorough observations.

B. As you walk and observe your stream or pond, take notes of your observations. What do you find interesting? What catches your eye?

C. Also, note any questions that come to mind. What would you like to find out more about?

D. When you have completed your walk, record your observations and questions on a chart like the following:

Observations	Questions

What other questions come to mind now? You might decide to order your questions from most to least interesting.

E. Compare your observations with those of other students in your class.

F. File your completed chart in your portfolio.

Activity 4.1 will help you experience an initial observation activity; it places you in the role of the learner on a stream or pond walk.

If going to a nature area or a stream isn't possible for your students, you can set up some exciting observation environments for students to explore in your own classroom. For example, you and your students can create chameleon environments so that you can observe the behaviors of chameleons. Craig Berg (1994) developed some excellent techniques for using 2-liter plastic soda bottles as chameleon houses. Building such habitats will allow students numerous opportunities to observe the feeding habitats of chameleons or the life cycles of crickets. *Bottle Biology* (Ingram, 1993) offers a number of ideas on how to use 2-liter pop bottles. You can also use 2-liter plastic soda bottles to create decomposition environments or terrariums. What's wonderful about these environments is that you can easily alter conditions to make noticeable changes. For instance, you can manipulate moisture in the environment to see how it influences plant growth.

Initial observations need not be limited to biological phenomena; students can just as easily focus on physical phenomena. For example, you might have students observe the weather over an extended period. Students might keep weather journals over the course of a school year, which can lead to students asking numerous questions about how weather changes.

Manipulation of Materials Another way to help students become involved in investigations is through the **manipulation of materials.** This may include building apparatus, taking things apart, or handling or playing with objects. For instance, you might have students set up an aquarium, take apart a flashlight, look at different objects through a magnifying glass, or plant some seeds. Many objects are good items for students to manipulate: seeds, toy cars, balls, and magnets as well as scientific equipment like balances, tape measures, magnifying glasses, and measuring cups.

Imagine that you want students to learn about the relationship between streams and streambeds and banks. Have students help you set up sand or stream tables in your classroom. These are long, flat pans filled with sand that can be used to demonstrate the flow of a river or stream. Once the students have set up the tables, have them manipulate the conditions of the stream. They might place clay balls, marbles, and metal objects within the stream of the water and on the banks. Ask students to make observations about what happens with each manipulation. You might want to tie this activity to a stream walk so that students can make connections between what they observed in the stream table and what happens in an actual stream. *River Cutters* (1989), developed by the Lawrence Hall of Science, describes how you can make some inexpensive stream tables for your classroom.

Manipulating materials and making initial observations should not be isolated activities. Manipulation should always be accompanied by observation of the effects of manipulation. Likewise, observations help students make decisions about what variables to manipulate. For example, once students have built something like a stream table or aquarium they make observations of this environment to determine what to manipulate in the stream tables.

The Role of the Teacher   Making initial observations and manipulating materials can motivate students to ask questions, but it is likely that student observations at first will be scattered and nonfocused. It is also likely that children's descriptions will not be detailed. For example, in describing a white powder, a child might say that it "looks like salt," but we want students to go beyond this simple labeling of the material and describe in detail what it looks like. As the classroom teacher, your role is to provide the instructional support to help students focus their observations, write clear descriptions, and become more thorough and complete. With your support, a student might eventually be able to say about the powder, "The stuff is white. Each piece looks like a cube when I look at it with the magnifying glass. Some of the cubes look like they are scratched or chipped."

At the beginning of the school year, you might want to implement a number of benchmark lessons (lessons that teach a necessary concept or skill) to help students improve their observation skills. (Chapter 6 contains more information on benchmark lessons.) You still will need to focus students' observations throughout the school year. One benchmark lesson that many teachers have used successfully is the mystery bag activity. In this activity, a number of different kinds of materials, such as a piece of fur, a piece of a tennis ball, and odd-shaped pieces of wood are placed into opaque bags. Stu-

dents stick their hands into the bags to feel the objects. Without looking, they describe what they feel. Students then can engage in interesting discussions about what they felt, comparing their observations, asking others to explain further what they mean, or disagreeing on what they felt. After discussion, give students a second chance to make observations; this way they may reach a consensus about what is in the bag.

There are a number of spin-offs from this activity. For example, you can build mystery boxes: Glue odd- or regular-shaped objects inside shoe boxes. Then seal the boxes so that students cannot open them. Have students explore what is in the boxes by inserting long wood or metal probes, such as 10-inch wood skewers, through small holes drilled into the box. Students should try to draw to scale the objects that they examine in this way.

You can also create benchmark lessons that focus on observations specific to a project. You might want to begin a project on the behavior of reptiles by having students describe what a chameleon looks like and how it behaves. Record the observations on the board. Then the class can discuss whether the observations contain sufficient detail. After the discussion, the class can create a common description of the chameleon.

Many students have a tendency to make inferences (judgments or conclusions) rather than observations. You need to help your students distinguish between observations and inferences. Imagine that a group of students is recording observations of the insects they find in a nature area. Some students record "Sow bugs eat wood," and others record, "I found sow bugs under a fallen tree branch." "Sow bugs eat wood" is a speculation; "I found sow bugs under a fallen tree branch" is an observation. One way to help students make this distinction is to ask, "Did you see it?"

You should also encourage students to use tools to help them make observations. Elementary students can work with a magnifying glass, a ruler, and a scale. Older students can use a microscope, voltmeter, or light probe. By collaborating with community members, students can have access to more sophisticated equipment such as an electron microscope or telescope.

Students need guidance to become more systematic in recording their observations. Encourage students to keep their observations in a notebook. Their observations should be specific enough and detailed enough so that they can be understood weeks or months later. Imagine that your students are exploring when various insects disappear and reappear. The student who writes, "Insects disappeared when it got cold," and months later writes, "Insects reappeared when it got warm," does not know what temperature was related to the insects' disappearance or appearance. Terms like *cold* and *warm* are relative and tell the student very little.

One technique that you can use to help students improve their recording of observation notes is to have them read their notes out loud in class to receive feedback from other students. You can give them written comments. Gentle reminders can also serve as strong cognitive support in helping students gain clarity and become more systematic.

Asking and Refining Questions

Once students have "messed about" and made initial observations, they need to ask questions based on those observations. The students who are observing insects in a nature area might begin to ask questions like, "Where do different insects live?" "When do the insects first appear?" "When do we stop seeing various insects?" Making observations and asking questions are not necessarily separate activities. Children often begin to ask questions while they are observing. Frequently, students refine these questions as they make more observations and as they find and synthesize information. Figure 4.1 illustrates making observations and asking questions is a back-and-forth process.

Experiences as well as observations may prompt student questions. Reading the newspaper, talking to parents or other family members, or going on a family trip can all lead to questions. As students experience the world around them, questions about the environment can and will arise. For instance, a family might compost lawn clippings. The child might then be interested in why the compost pile doesn't smell. It is the role of the teacher to support students as they move from making observations to asking questions.

The Role of the Teacher   The teacher plays a critical role in helping students develop meaningful and worthwhile questions that will help them learn important curricular content. The teacher is the curriculum leader who guides or selects the driving questions for the project and who supports the selection of the phenomena that students will explore and observe. One technique for helping students generate questions is having them set up their experimental notebooks with two columns: Initial observations and Questions. Table 4.1 shows how a student might set up his or her notebook.

Another technique to help students generate questions is to provide students with question stems. Question stems serve as cognitive support and focus student questions. The following stems are useful in helping students generate questions: "I wonder what would happen if . . . ?" "What if . . . ?" "How does . . . ?" and "What does . . . ?"

It is also likely that students will ask more questions than they can answer; you will need to help students determine which questions are worthwhile and feasible. Students may ask questions that are not related to the curricular goals of the project; you need to help them understand, without discouraging them, that they need to select new questions. Some students will ask questions that are beyond their developmental level or beyond the resources of your classroom; while emphasizing the value of the questions, you need to direct the students in other directions. For example, let's say your class is exploring the driving question, "What lives in our nature area?" One group of students

TABLE 4.1 Observations and Questions	
Observations	**Questions**
Sow bugs under logs	Do sow bugs like dark places?
Green slimy stuff on top of pond	What causes the green slime stuff on top of the pond?
Some leaves with different shapes	I wonder how many different kinds of leaves I can find in my neighborhood?

TABLE 4.2   Types of Questions

Descriptive questions	Relational questions	Cause and effect questions
What materials dissolve in water?	Does salt dissolve faster than sugar?	Does the temperature of water affect the rate at which salt and water dissolve?
What macroinvertebrates are found in a stream?	Are different macroinvertebrates found in different areas of a stream?	Does water quality affect the types of macroinvertebrates found in a stream?
How fast does my heart beat?	Who has a higher heart rate—boys or girls?	If people hear a loud sound, do their heart rates go up?

asks the question, "How do things move?" Although this might be an interesting question to the children, it is not directly related to the current curriculum objectives. As their teacher, you will need to redirect their question to perhaps "How do sow bugs move?"

Types of Questions   There are three types of questions that students might ask as part of an investigation. **Descriptive questions** allow students to find out about observable characteristics of phenomena. **Relational questions** allow students to find out about associations between the characteristics of different phenomena. **Cause and effect questions** allow students to make inferences about how one variable affects another variable. Table 4.2 gives examples of the different question types.

Students in early elementary school will ask many descriptive questions that will lead them to find out information about a phenomenon through making systematic observations. "What kind of foods do meal worms eat?" "How bright can I get a flashlight bulb to shine?" and "How many leaves can a caterpillar eat in one day?" are descriptive questions. Students can answer these questions by making systematic observations either in natural settings or in controlled situations. To illustrate that descriptive questions are answered by making observations, students can answer the question, "What kind of foods do meal worms eat?", by placing different kinds of food in a box that contains meal worms and making observations on which foods the meal worms select.

Students in upper elementary grades should make a transition from descriptive questions to

more complex relational questions. "Which dissolves faster in water—salt or sugar?" "What's a better insulator—paper, Styrofoam, or aluminum foil?" and "What conducts sound better—water, metal, air, or wood?" are relational questions. To answer these types of questions, students need to set up experimental procedures with which they can compare and contrast one or more characteristics. Such experimental situations provide opportunities for students to collect and analyze data and draw conclusions. To answer the question "What's a better insulator—paper, Styrofoam, or aluminum foil?" for example, students would need to compare and contrast the temperature of a substance when wrapped in the different materials. For instance, they could wrap soda cans in the different materials such as aluminum foil, plastic, or newspaper and collect data on the temperature of the soda. To conclude which material is the best insulator, students would need to analyze the data from the different conditions.

Upper elementary and middle grade students need to make the transition to cause and effect questions that provide opportunities to explore the influence of one variable on the outcome of another. "Does water quality influence the type of macroinvertebrates found in a stream or pond?" "How does fertilizer affect the height and size of plants?" and "How does the surface of the ground affect how fast I can move on roller blades?" are cause and effect questions. To answer these questions, students must design experiments in which they manipulate one variable (independent variable) to observe the effect on another variable (dependent variable). Such experimental situations allow students to collect data that they then can analyze to determine the reason for an outcome or result. One way to answer the roller blade question is for students to design simulated environments in which they modify the surface of a 1-foot by 8-foot board (by adding sandpaper, rubber, oil, carpet, and vinyl flooring) and move wheels on axles across the surface. Students might choose to measure the frictional forces with a spring scale or force probe.

Although early elementary students are more likely to ask descriptive questions and middle school students should make a transition to more cause and effect questions, it is not the case that middle school students should never ask descriptive questions or that elementary students should not ask cause and effect questions. Some projects might generate a natural progression through all three types of questions. For example, in a project exploring, "What insects live in our playground?" students might first ask a very descriptive question: "What insects can I find?" Investigating this question may lead to a relational question: "Do I find different insects at different times of the day?" After conducting investigations, with guidance from the teacher, the students might be ready to ask a cause and effect question: "Do certain insects prefer dark or light environments?"

Although young children are unlikely to ask cause and effect questions on their own and then carry out investigations to find answers to them, you can set up an investigation in which the whole class explores the influence of one variable on another. For example, to explore if the amount of sunlight influences how green a plant is, you could set up an experiment in which one plant is kept in the sun and one in the shade. The class could make periodic comparisons between the two plants.

You will need to help students move from asking descriptive questions to asking cause and effect questions. The types of stems that you give students to help generate questions can have an effect on the types of questions they generate. "How does . . . ?" and "What does . . . ?" question stems are more likely to lead to descriptive questions. The "What if . . . ?" stems tend to encourage more cause and effect questions. Another way to facilitate the transition is to list students' questions on the board or overhead, have students specify what each type of question is, and then transpose each question into another type of question. Table 4.2 shows how descriptive questions, relational questions, and cause and effect questions are related and how one type of question can be modified to another type of question. Reading across each of the rows, we see how the various questions are related to each other.

You will also find students asking **basic information questions** (Scardamalia & Bereiter, 1991). Students can find answers to basic information questions in reference source books or on the World Wide Web, but they can't answer them through the design of an investigation. "What is the diameter of the earth?" and "How hot is the sun?" are basic information questions. Although these questions have value and might be intellectually interesting to a student, project-based science stresses students asking questions that they can find answers to by setting up their own investigations. There is, however, a place in project-based science for basic information questions. As part of an investigation, students might need to ask and answer basic information questions to complete the background information for the investigation. For an investigation of the influence of the amount of fertilizer on plant growth, for example, a student might need to find out what fertilizer is made of and if various brands of fertilizer differ in their composition. Benchmark lessons are a good way to answer basic information questions when a whole class needs the information. (Chapter 6 contains more information on benchmark lessons.)

Questions for Investigation and the Driving Question If similar questions arise for a number of students, you might pick one to explore as a class. However, we find it critical that students have their own question on which to work. Working on their own questions leads students to feel ownership of a project and to be more engaged.

Conducting investigations to answer student questions should contribute to answering the driving question of the class, however. For example, students might complete a number of decomposition investigations, such as exploring what causes and promotes decomposition, to answer their own questions: "Do worms cause materials to decompose in soil?" and "Does airflow

---

ACTIVITY 4.2

Identifying Testable Questions

MATERIALS NEEDED:
- the following chart
- writing materials

A. Using the chart below, analyze which statements in the first column of the following chart are testable and which are not.
B. Fill in the missing sections of the chart.
C. File the chart in your portfolio.

Which questions are testable?

Question	Testable?	Testable Revision of Question
Do different types of apples have different numbers of seeds?	Yes	
Why does my bike need to be painted?	No	What happens to metal if it is exposed to air?
How does fertilizer affect plant growth?		
What types of objects fly?		
Do worms like to eat garbage?		

---

speed up decomposition?" Even though such investigations would be designed to answer the student questions, they would be related to the driving question of the project: "Where does all our garbage go?"[1] Maintaining a consistent focus ensures that what happens in the classroom is purposeful and meaningful.

Hypothesizing

Hypotheses are questions stated in testable form. A student can design an experiment to collect data that will either give support for a question or refute a question; such a question becomes a hypothesis. "I wonder if pillbugs like cool places?" is a fine question for fourth grade students, but it is not a testable question. It is not possible to measure if pillbugs *like* cool places. However, the question "Will pillbugs choose cool places over warm places?" can be transformed into the hypothesis "Pillbugs will move to cool places rather than warm places." Students can design an experiment to collect data that will either support or refute this hypothesis. They could count the number of pillbugs that go to the lower-temperature section of the apparatus, for example.

1. Thanks to Ann Novak and Chris Gleason from Greenhills Schools in Ann Arbor for this project idea.

How might you phrase the question "Will wrapping my pop can in newspaper keep it cool?" in terms of a hypothesis? What is missing from this question is a comparison. A testable hypothesis for this question might be, "A pop can wrapped in newspaper will stay cool longer than will a nonwrapped pop can." A thermometer could be used to measure the temperatures of the different cans of pop.

Activity 4.2 helps you learn to identify testable questions. You might want to use this activity with your students to help them learn how to generate hypotheses from their questions.

Activity 4.3 helps you learn how to generate hypotheses from questions. Once again, you might want to use this activity with your students.

Helping your students make hypotheses of their questions should not destroy the excitement students feel about the world around them. Making hypotheses is an intellectual skill that can be developed over time. From a developmental standpoint, you might be more concerned with helping early elementary students ask observable questions. You might want to have upper elementary and middle school students practice formulating hypotheses from their questions. What is most important is that students ask questions that are testable.

One way to help your students change questions into hypotheses is to use a table, like

ACTIVITY 4.3

Making Hypotheses out of Questions

MATERIALS NEEDED:
- ◆ the following chart
- ◆ writing materials

A. Analyze how the first question in the first column of the following chart is changed to a hypothesis in the second column.
B. Fill in the missing sections by changing the questions to hypotheses.
C. File the chart in your portfolio.

Question	Hypothesis
Do meal worms like dry places?	Meal worms will move to dry places rather than moist places.
Do I really need to paint my bike?	
How does fertilizer affect plant growth?	
What types of objects fly?	
Are worms necessary for decomposition?	

TABLE 4.3 Refining Hypotheses

Student questions	Tentative hypotheses	How might you test your hypotheses?	Revised hypotheses

Table 4.3, to show students the transformation. Display the table on the board or on an overhead. First, have students list their questions. Next, have them write tentative hypotheses and decide if these are testable by coming up with ways to test them. Finally, based on classroom feedback, including your own, have students write revised hypotheses.

Remember that the investigation web is not a linear process. As students continue in their investigative work, you should allow them to modify their questions and hypotheses. The questions and hypotheses that are published in research reports are seldom, if ever, the questions and hypotheses with which the researchers started.

Making Predictions

Predictions are students' best guesses about what might happen. These predictions are based on students' previous experiences, knowledge, and observations of the phenomena they are exploring. Having students make initial predictions on questions like "What insects will they see on the playground?" "How many different types of birds will they see?" is important because predictions focus students' thinking. Also, student commitment to work increases when they make predictions. Finally, making predictions helps students become cognitively engaged in the work because it uses their prior knowledge. Making predictions also helps students synthesize their prior knowledge with the new understandings they gain from exploring their topic.

One technique you can use to help children make their own predictions and take ownership for their work is to first have each child in a group make his or her own prediction. Then have group members share their predictions. Next, give group members an opportunity to comment on their predictions, giving reasons for agreeing or disagreeing with the other predictions. Once all group members have shared their predictions, ask a group to generate group predictions, while protecting each student's right to dissent from the group prediction. Table 4.4 is an example of a handout you might distribute to your class to support making predictions.

Another technique for generating student predictions is to expand Table 4.3 to include students' predictions. Table 4.5 shows this expansion.

Finding Information

Seeking information is a vital component of the investigative web. It is through the information-seeking process that students learn the background information so essential to a successful investigation. The term *information* can mean what others have *written* about a topic and it can mean data that others have *collected.*

Students can seek out two types of data: current data and archival data. **Current data** refers to data scientists collected in the recent past; typically, it is anywhere from a few hours old to a month old. Data on today's weather is an example of current data. **Archival data** refers to data that scientists collected in the past and then stored. Data on upper atmospheric ozone readings over the past several years is an example of archival data.

Imagine that students asked the question "Does my community need to worry about lead poisoning from cars?" Students might look for basic information on lead poisoning to help them understand the problem. They might contact the Environmental Protection Agency to find out if others were collecting current data on lead from cars, or they might seek archival data on lead poisoning in their community. Although current data and archival data are very different types of information, both can provide important information for a project.

Numerous resources can help students find information. To find archival data, elementary and middle grade students might consult trade books, magazines, encyclopedias, CD-ROMs, and the World Wide Web. *My Big Back Yard* is an excellent resource magazine for early elementary students and *Ranger Rick, Science World,* and *Scholastic* are excellent magazines for upper elementary and middle school students. To find current information, such as information about a recent news story or a new discovery, students need to use a different set of resources. These include the newspaper, telephone interviews, person-to-person interviews, e-mail, and the World Wide Web. Television specials, like Public Broadcast Station programs and NOVA programs, can provide both archival and current information. Growing access to the World Wide Web and the increasing number of resources available on the Web make it a vital source of both background and current information.

The Role of the Teacher　Within an investigation it is critical for students to explore the related work of professionals. You will need to help your students develop skills in searching out information related to their questions. Young children will need several types of assistance. First, many students will need to learn how to use a va-

---

TABLE 4.4　Making Predictions

My prediction:

Member 1 prediction:	Comment:
Member 2 prediction:	Comment:
Member 3 prediction:	Comment:
Group prediction:	Reason for supporting or not supporting the group prediction:

TABLE 4.5　Refining Hypotheses and Making Predictions

Student questions	Tentative hypotheses	How might you test your hypotheses?	Revised hypotheses	Predictions
_____	_____	_____	_____	_____
_____	_____	_____	_____	_____

riety of resources. You may need to teach benchmark lessons on the card catalog, computerized library search systems, and the Internet.

Second, you will need to help your students learn how to determine which sources to consult for different types of information. Most children will rely on the encyclopedia for much of their information, but encyclopedias do not provide the depth of information many investigations will require. You can use a checklist like the one in Table 4.6 to guide students in their search.

Third, students need assistance in sifting through, abstracting, and outlining the information they find. Imagine a fifth grade science class is studying acid rain. The class could seek basic information related to acid rain or archival data on acid rain to compare to the data they have collected. To help students determine what information is relevant, the teacher could use a chart like the one in Table 4.7 to help students.

Fourth, with the explosion of available information today and the ease of distribution due to electronic networks, you also need to help learners decide if a source of information is valid; that is, if it is propaganda or scientific information. The World Wide Web contains a great deal of information presented by businesses or special interest groups that are trying to advocate certain positions. Such information is often not valid. Students can be taught to think critically about the validity of information by answering questions like those in Table 4.8.

You might want to use tabloid articles to show extreme examples of "information" that is not valid because it cannot be supported, proven, or substantiated by others. Information about a three-headed goat found in the Himalayas by one person who has no photograph of the goat or other evidence is a good example of information that is not valid. Eventually, you can have your students assess the validity of more reputable information from the WWW, local newspapers, and magazines.

TABLE 4.6   Checklist for Finding Information

Information: Data on Car Emissions

Sources of new information (less than several months old)	Sources of old information (more than several months old)
_____ magazine	_____ trade books
_X_ newspaper	_X_ encyclopedia
_____ telephone interview with an expert	_X_ compact disk
_____ person-to-person interviews	_____ laserdisk
_____ e-mail	_X_ books
_X_ World Wide Web	_X_ World Wide Web
_____ television documentaries	_____ television documentaries

---

TABLE 4.7   Evaluating Information

Information found:	Does it add to our knowledge base? How?	Is the information new or different from what we have already found?	Is the information more recent than what we have already found?	Does it help answer our question? How?
Acid rain is thought to be a cause of declining frog populations.	Yes. It provides biological information related to acid rain.	Yes.	Yes. It is a recent discovery.	No. We are looking for information about how acid rain erodes surfaces of buildings.

TABLE 4.8   Assessing the Validity of Information

Information found:	What are the facts to support the claims?	Can a claim be proven? Substantiated by others? If so, how?	Is the source trying to sell something, advocate an opinion, or persuade you to believe something?	How reputable is the source?
What was said?				
Who said this?				
When did they say it?				
Why did they say it?				
Where did this occur?				
How did it occur?				

Planning and Designing

Planning refers to students thinking about and working out how their investigation will take place and answering questions like "Who will measure the data?" and "Who will get the equipment?" *Designing* refers to the structure of the experiment and answers the questions "What data do I need to answer my question?" and "How will I obtain the data?" Planning includes determining who will take which measurements and on which days, whereas designing includes determining what observations will be made (for example, observing the germination of bean plants), how often the data will be collected, what type of observations will be made (drawing or taking photographs of the seeds), and what variables need to be manipulated or controlled (examining the influence of temperature on germination of bean plants).

Many children find planning and designing difficult. This should not be surprising as they require students to engage in difficult cognitive work. Planning and designing makes students think ahead, it requires them to specify materials they need, it makes them create an outline of what they will do, and it makes them create or modify materials. Many elementary and middle grades students don't have such experience, and primary grade students may not be developmentally ready to plan on their own. Don't be surprised if some of their initial designs and plans don't allow them to answer the questions adequately. Frequently, students' initial designs will be flawed, including confounded and ill-defined variables. Students will need to practice designing investigations and receive much support from you.

Although planning and designing are difficult cognitive activities for most children (and adults too), they produce many benefits. First, students become more reflective. Focusing on planning helps students think through issues and become thorough in their thinking. Second, when students make a plan and design, they gain more ownership of an investigation. Because they make the plan and design, they also understand them. This understanding also helps them understand the science involved.

Designing Experimental Procedures   Designing an investigation requires students to develop four important skills. These are the ability to (1) write clear descriptions of the investigations, (2) identify variables, (3) define variables operationally, and (4) control variables.

Writing Clear Procedures   The first thing students need to learn to do when designing an investigation is communicate clearly the procedures they will follow. Activity 4.4 demonstrates just how difficult it is for most people to write clear descriptions.

The Lego activity illustrates just how hard it is to create clear procedures that others can follow. Because writing clear procedures that others can understand is difficult, you might encourage your students to read their plans to one

ACTIVITY 4.4

Writing Procedures

MATERIALS NEEDED:
* Lego building blocks
* writing materials

A. Have your students work in pairs. Give each pair ten types of Lego building blocks in different colors. Ask each pair to construct a structure using all the Lego blocks you gave them. Then ask each pair to write a detailed description of how to make the structure so that someone else, following their instructions, could make the same structure. Instruct the pairs to not look at one another's structures.

B. Have the pairs exchange their written directions. Now ask the pairs to follow the directions they have been given in building a new structure.

C. Ask the pairs to inspect the structures built from their directions. How could the directions be improved?

D. You might also have your students try to explain how to tie a shoe, make a peanut butter sandwich, or make a cube out of paper. Record your notes about this activity in your portfolio.

another and receive feedback. Do other children understand what is intended? How can the procedures be made easier to understand?

Depending on the age and experiences of the learner, designs of investigations will range from descriptions of what observations will be made to descriptions of what variables will be manipulated. Elementary students might design an investigation to observe the life cycle of meal worms. Their data collecting might include drawings of how the meal worms look over time. Middle school students might design an investigation to examine the effects of temperature and moisture on seed germination. Their experimental designs will show more sophistication and describe ways of collecting data systematically.

Designing experimental procedures involves (1) identifying variables, (2) defining variables operationally, and (3) establishing which variables will be controlled and which will be manipulated.

Identifying Variables Students need to identify variables as part of their design effort. **Variables** are the factors that will change in an investigation. For example, if students are studying the influence of the amount of fertilizer on the height of grass seedlings, the amount of fertilizer and the height of the seedlings are variables. The amount of fertilizer is the **independent variable** because it will be changed purposefully by the students. (A good way to help students remember the *independent* variable is to call it the "*you* changed it" variable.)

The height of the plants is the **dependent variable** because it will change as a result of the conditions of the investigation. A good way to remember the dependent variable is to call it the "it changed" variable. This experiment also has a number of other variables involved in it, like sunlight and temperature.

Defining Variables Operationally A critical component of an investigation design is clearly defining variables so that others can understand what is being explored. This clarity helps others replicate the experiment to see if they get the same results. For example, if students were exploring how fast students in their class could run, they would need to operationally define *fast*. They could operationally define *fast* as "the time it takes for a student to run a particular distance" or as "how far a student can run in ten seconds." These definitions are **operational definitions** because they define the operation or process used to measure a variable. Defining variables operationally is a difficult cognitive activity. You will need to work with young learners to help them express variables operationally. One technique is to have students share their operational definitions with their classmates and receive feedback from classmates and from you.

Controlling Variables Controlling variables is holding all variables constant except for the one that is to be tested. In the fertilizer investigation, there were variables other than the dependent variable (the height of the seedlings) and the independent variable (the amount of fertilizer). These other variables, which include amount of sunlight and temperature, will have to be controlled, or held the same, for all the plants, or students will not be able to determine how the amount of fertilizer influenced the height of the seedlings.

Controlling variables is a challenging cognitive activity for students. You should expect children to have difficulty understanding the concept of controlling variables. With younger students, you might use the term *fair* to introduce the idea of controlling variables. Asking, "Is this a fair test?" may help students understand. Students have little trouble understanding that card games in which not all the players have the same number of cards are not fair. It is not a huge leap from that understanding to thinking about making sure that all the plants in an investigation get a "fair" chance. Activity 4.5 is designed to help students understand what is meant by controlling variables.

The paper dragon activity demonstrates why it is critical to control variables during an investigation. Just like adding weights affects how far the paper dragon will move, not controlling variables influences the outcomes of investigations.

The Role of the Teacher   Students will find creating plans and designs of an investigation a challenge. Planning and designing an investigation is hard intellectual work. However, if you support students in their designing, your students will show considerable improvement throughout the school year (Krajcik et al., 1998). Students' designs will become more complex as students include more variables, define variables with greater detail, consider more ways of measuring the variables, and use multiple samples. Students' procedures will also became more clearly defined; they will think of more ways in which to represent their data, identify necessary materials, and divide up responsibilities for conducting the investigation.

Table 4.9 lists questions to prompt and support students in creating their plans and designs. It should be modified to match the age and experiences of the children you are teaching. For example, in first grade, learners are not

TABLE 4.9   Planning and Design Chart
Our question:
Our design:
What variables and terms do we need to define?
What data need to be gathered to answer our question?
What observations should we make?
What will I need to measure?
What variables need to be controlled to answer the question?
What is the independent variable?
What is the dependent variable?
What is my control?
How often should I take measurements?
How often do I need to make observations?
Our plan:
Equipment needed:
What do we need?
How much do we need?
How can we obtain the material?
Procedure:
What is it?
How often do we do it?
How much of each material do we need?
Who will do it?

developmentally ready for controlled experiments and should not be concerned with independent and dependent variables. However, early elementary students are capable of thinking about the observations they will make, how they will record the data, and how data relate to their question.

There are a number of other ways to support students in learning how to plan and design. These include using goal sheets, critiquing plans and designs, modeling planning and designing, creating class plans and designs, and using quicktrials.

Using Goal Sheets   You can help your students learn to be more thoughtful planners and follow through on decision making with goal sheets. Students can use goal sheets to track plans, figure out the division of labor, develop timelines and schedules, and make decisions about resources. A goal sheet is simply a grid in which students record their steps in one column and their plans about who will take responsibility for the steps in a second column. Table 4.10 is an example of a goal sheet. You can have students record in a third column how each step will be accomplished. Table 4.11 illustrates this expanded goal sheet.

Another technique that is valuable in helping students plan is to use a checklist to provoke students' thinking and expand their ideas about possible resources. In an information-based world, making decisions about what information to use is no easy task, and students will need your help. Table 4.12 shows a checklist that can help students select resources. You might even decide to work with students to develop their own checklist.

Critiquing Plans and Designs   One way to help your students learn the initial components of planning and designing is to have them critique some good and poor plans and designs. Activity 4.6 presents the design of an experiment you might use for student critique. Use the questions in Table 4.9 to guide your critique.

Although critiques of made-up plans and designs can make good benchmark lessons, it is important to remember that such critiques are artificial activities akin to practicing a serve in tennis without learning to use a serve in a real game. Within a project-based science classroom, there certainly is a place for these types of benchmark lessons because they *introduce* students to important ideas; however, the real thinking occurs when students develop their own investigations and give and receive feedback on those plans and designs.

A very useful spin-off of critiquing made-up plans and designs is to have students critique a plan and design for an investigation they will conduct in class. Some of the research conducted at the University of Michigan (Krajcik et al., 1998) indicates that initially giving students a plan and design and discussing (critiquing) the important features of the plan with the students is an important first step in helping students create and modify their own plans and designs. Have them ask critical questions like, "Will the data collected help answer the question?" "How and why?" and "What are the independent and dependent variables?" Use other questions found in Table 4.9 as a guide for discussion.

Modeling Planning and Designing   An essential step in helping students learn how to plan and design is to model the process. Model

TABLE 4.10   Goal Sheet

What do we need to do?	Who will do it?
Find information about acid rain.	Bill
Contact the EPA.	Alicia
Make a design for collecting rainwater and measuring the pH of rainwater.	Precious

TABLE 4.11   Expanded Goal Sheet

What do we need to do?	Who will do it?	How will it be done?	When will it be done?
Find information about acid rain.	Bill	Go to the library.	by Friday, May 18th
Contact the EPA.	Alicia	Go to the school office and call.	tomorrow during class
Make a design for collecting rainwater and measuring the pH of rainwater.	Precious	Look for information on collecting rainwater. Ask the teacher and share plans with the class.	today by Friday, May 18th

ACTIVITY 4.5

Controlling Variables: Paper Dragon Races

MATERIALS NEEDED:

- ◆ a large file card and a small file card
- ◆ a rubber band
- ◆ heavy cardboard
- ◆ a stapler
- ◆ scissors
- ◆ a hole punch
- ◆ a paper clip
- ◆ tape
- ◆ metal washers

A. Build a Maxi-Puller/Pusher and paper dragon before doing this activity.

Building the Maxi-Puller/Pusher
The Maxi-Puller/Pusher (Berger et al., 1974) will act as a force gauge. To construct the Maxi-Puller/Pusher, fold a large file card in half lengthwise. Insert heavy cardboard between the folds of the card to add strength. Now staple together the ends of the file card. Punch a hole at one end and attach a rubber band as shown in Figure 4.4. To the free end of the rubber band add a paper clip hook. In one hand, hold the card so that the punched hole is at the top. With the other hand, gently tug down on the hook. Notice that the more you tug, the lower the hook moves along the card.

How can we measure how much an object pushes down on the Maxi-Puller/Pusher? To measure the pushes and pulls of the Maxi-Puller/Pusher, you need a way to calibrate it with equal units. Place a piece of tape down the middle of the folded file card. With nothing hanging from the paper clip hook, mark a zero on the tape beside the top of the hook. This mark shows the zero, or starting point. Next, put one washer on the paper clip hook. Beside the top of the paper clip, mark 1W to stand for "one washer unit." Keep adding washers of the same size one at a time and mark 2W, 3W, and so on, on the tape. You have now built and calibrated your Maxi-Puller/Pusher.

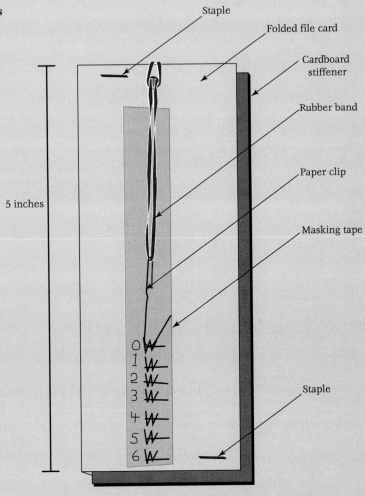

FIGURE 4.4
Building the maxi-puller/pusher.

Building the Paper Dragon
To make a paper dragon, fold a small file card in half and cut the top on a slant so that the shorter edge is near the fold, as shown in Figure 4.5.

B. Now that you have your Maxi-Puller/Pusher and paper dragon, you're ready for some races. First, you need to practice. To use the Maxi-Puller/Pusher as a way of measuring "pushing" force, bend up the end of the paper clip hook to make a trigger. Set the end of the dragon in the cradle formed by the paper clip trigger. See Figure 4.6. Use the Maxi-Puller/Pusher like a slingshot by holding down the Maxi-Puller/Pusher with one hand and pulling the paper clip and paper dragon back with the other hand. Let go of the paper dragon, shooting the dragon forward.

C. Conduct several races.

Race one: Divide the class into two groups. One group should pull the Maxi-Puller/Pusher back to the 5W mark. The other group should pull the Maxi-Puller/Pusher back to the 8W spot. Each group member should have three turns to shoot the dragon. Ask students to keep track of how far the paper dragon moves. Each group should then calculate the average distance the paper dragon moves (the sum of distances divided by the number of "shots" made by the group).

Now have the two groups discuss the results. What were the independent and dependent variables? Was the activity fair? What was wrong with how the contest was set up? How might you make it fair?

Race two: Divide the class into two groups. One group should set three paper clips into the ends of the "wings" of their paper dragon, and the other group should use an unweighted paper dragon. Each group should pull the Maxi-Puller/Pusher back to the 5W mark. Make sure that each group member has three turns to "shoot" the dragon. Ask students to keep track of how far the paper dragon moves. Each group should calculate the average distance the paper dragon moves (the sum of distances divided by the number of "shots" made by the group).

Have the two groups discuss the results. What were the independent and dependent variables? Was the activity fair? What was wrong with how the contest was set up? How might you make it fair?

D. What other variables could you change? With older students you could try a free-throw contest or a race instead of the paper dragon activity.

E. Record your reflections on the activity in your portfolio.

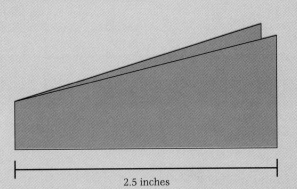

FIGURE 4.5
Building the paper dragon.

2.5 inches

FIGURE 4.6
Racing the paper dragon.

TABLE 4.12   Resources Checklist

What?	Can we use it?	How?
Information		
encyclopedia	yes	Find out more about acid rain.
magazines/journals	yes	Go to library and look for information on acid rain.
CD-ROMs	maybe	The school doesn't have any on acid rain. Need to check the public library.
software	maybe	The school doesn't have any on acid rain. Need to check the public library.
guest speaker	yes	from the EPA
telephone call	yes	to the EPA
e-mail		
interview	yes	someone at the EPA
World Wide Web	yes	Do a search on acid rain.
letter		
Supplies and materials		
writing materials		
computers/probes	yes	
drawing materials	yes	
science equipment	yes	Check with the teacher.
pH paper	yes	
calculator	yes	Check with the teacher.

ACTIVITY 4.6

Sprouting Bean Plants

MATERIALS NEEDED:

♦ the following scenario

A. What follows is a scenario that describes an experiment that a group of students performed to study the influence of temperature on the sprouting of seeds. Read the scenario carefully.

Heather, Michael, and Jackie wonder how temperature influences the sprouting of bean plants. They decide to modify a technique they used earlier in the school year. First, they will soak some kidney beans over night. The next day they will place moistened paper towels into two reclosable baggies. Then they will place five soaked kidney beans and a thermometer in each of the baggies. They will set one of the baggies on top of a heating pad on the window sill and the other baggie just on the window sill. Each day they will observe the beans in each bag, record the temperature of each bag, and moisten the paper toweling.

B. What are the independent and dependent variables in this experiment? What variables are being controlled?

C. Is the procedure complete? What is missing from the procedure? What else, if anything, might influence the sprouting of the bean seeds?

D. What are other pluses and negatives of Heather's, Michael's, and Jackie's plan and design?

E. How might you modify the design to better determine the influence of temperature on bean plants?

F. Record your ideas in your portfolio.

ACTIVITY 4.7

Planning and Designing

MATERIALS NEEDED:
- Table 4.9
- writing materials or a computer

A. Use Table 4.9 to create a plan and a design for an experiment to test how road surface affects the speed at which a skateboard travels. Remember to create a hypothesis and make a prediction. What are your independent and dependent variables? What variables do you need to define operationally? How many trials will you run?

B. Have a classmate critique your plan and design. What suggestions did he or she make? How will you modify your plan and design based on these suggestions?

C. Record your final plan and design in your portfolio.

---

for the students how *you* might go about planning and designing an investigation. This might include thinking aloud about what materials you would need and what procedures you would follow. For example, you could think aloud about how you might explore how shifting gears on your bike influence how fast you can pedal. Say aloud things like, "I wonder if the larger gear will make the pedal go faster or slower." Write down the steps on the board or the overhead projector as you say them. For example, write down, "Shift to the gear to the largest size and determine how fast I can go." Allow students the opportunity to comment on your design and to make their own suggestions. The questions in Table 4.9 can help you think aloud about the various steps you would take.

Creating Class Plans and Designs   The work of Krajcik and colleagues (1998) indicates that another important step in supporting students' planning and design work is to have students work on a plan and design together; this is especially true of early elementary or students new to making their own plans and designs. Again, questions in Table 4.9 can be used to guide discussion of the plans. You should freely add your own comments and suggestions.

Perhaps the best way for students to learn how to plan and design an investigation is to create in small groups a number of designs and plans. Start off your school year with some quick opportunities for planning and designing. For example, you could give students the challenge to plan and design a bridge using plastic straws and pins that could hold the most weight. The *Elementary School Studies* curriculum materials (1970) and Annenberg's *Video Case Studies* (1997) contain a number of ideas for planning and design practice.

While students are creating their plans and designs, provide feedback. Students should also share their plans and designs with the class to receive feedback. Feedback should point out the positive features of plans and designs as well as the features that students need to think about and perhaps revise. You should make sure that students record the comments on their work. Students will learn about the planning and design process not only by listening to what others have to say about their work, but also by listening to others' plans and designs and by contributing comments to others. It is critical for students to have time to revise their plans and designs based on the feedback they receive (Krajcik et al., 1998). After students have revised their designs, it is important that you give them one last round of feedback. Activity 4.7 will give you practice on planning and designing an investigation.

Using Quicktrials   The quicktrial is an experimental technique that should be used more frequently in schools. It involves trying out experimental procedures to see if they work. For example, students might have designs to make a rain collector in order to measure the amount of precipitation. However, before building the final rain collector, students might perform a quicktrial, building a model of the apparatus. Building a model might help them quickly realize that they left out an important design feature, such as a suitable way to anchor the rain collector which could then have been blown over by winds during a storm.

Keeping Track of Ideas   Often as students are conducting their investigation, they will think of new ideas to modify their work. Encourage students to keep track of these ideas and to record them in their notebooks. They might use these ideas to modify a current investigation or in future experiments. For instance, a group of students in second grade might be observing the germination of bean seeds. A student in the group wonders if all seeds germinate in the same amount of time. Students should record these questions in their notebook and use them to plan additional investigations.

One of the difficult decisions you will face as a teacher is when and how to give students the time to incorporate new ideas into their current work. Although this incorporation of new ideas is time consuming, it is a valuable learning experience and it reflects the reality of scientific work. The revision process is an essential component of the investigation web. Remember, good science is not a linear process.

Carrying Out the Procedures

Conducting the procedures of an investigation includes a wide range of activities. It might include students gathering the equipment, assembling the apparatus, following through on procedures, and making observations.

Gathering the Equipment   To perform an investigation, students need to have the necessary equipment. Equipment can be everything from a hands-lens for observing insects outdoors, a thermometer for measuring temperature of a classroom habitat, or a computer-based probe for gathering data over time. Equipment is essential in extending students' abilities to make observations.

Much of this equipment should be a standard component of the elementary and middle school science classroom, but it is often a challenge to obtain the necessary materials and supplies. Students can find many common materi-

als at home, but others will need to be purchased. School budgets sometimes stand in the way. By enlisting the participation of members of the community who might donate needed items you can often obtain the support you need. Chapter 8 discusses how teachers can find and manage equipment and resources.

Assembling the Apparatus   Many investigations involve building an apparatus. If students are doing a project on acid rain, they might need to build a rain collector to collect their rainwater. If students are exploring the effect of a surface on the speed of an object, they might need to build ramps with different surfaces to investigate how different types of surfaces influence the speed at which an object moves. Very often, students' first attempts at building apparatus will need to be modified.

Another challenge you and your students will face is learning how to use the tools needed to build the apparatus. This will be the first time many of your students have ever built something from basic materials. Many students will not know how to hammer, screw, glue, or solder. Often you will need to model these techniques for students, or you will need to solicit support from volunteers in the community who can come into your classroom and supervise construction.

Following Through on Procedures   Don't be surprised if students forget about doing a number of important experimental procedures like watering plants, adjusting temperature, or recording observations. In some circumstances, students might "overdo" their procedures—they might water plants too much or provide too much sunlight. Another common occurrence is "changing procedures on the fly," or modifying of experimental procedures without recording the modification or telling anyone about it. For instance, a student might decide to add twice as much fertilizer to the plants.

To prevent these common experimental errors, you need to monitor investigations carefully. You might need to remind students to make observations—record temperatures, draw diagrams, measure volumes—and to carry out procedures—add fertilizer, water plants, adjust temperature, or feed fish. You might also need to watch students as they carry out procedures to make sure they are doing so correctly, without overdoing anything and without making unplanned modifications.

One useful technique is to pair students. Each member of a pair can help keep the other one on track. Another technique is to have students record their observations on charts, tables, or checklists. These record-keeping systems organize data. They also serve to remind students about what data need to be collected and what procedures need to be completed.

Even though students create a table for recording data, they may not remember to use it. Take the time to discuss the importance of recording data appropriately. Again, having students work together can help them remember to record their data and complete procedures.

Making Observations At first, students will not be very thorough and precise in making either qualitative or quantitative observations. **Qualitative observations** are detailed descriptions of what is seen. Recording qualitative observations might include making diagrams and labeling them, writing a paragraph about observations, or taking a photograph of observable results. **Quantitative observations** are those that can be counted or recorded in a numerical format. Students can use instruments such as thermometers, rulers, and electronic pH probes to make quantitative measurements. Your students will need support collecting both qualitative and quantitative data. At first students' descriptions will be very incomplete and measurements might not be precise.

One way to support students in becoming more precise and detailed in their observations is to have all students in the class observe the same phenomenon. Then have the students in the class compare the observations they made. Typically, there will be a great deal of variation among observations. You might, for example, have all of the students in the class make observations of the sprouting of grass seeds. This is a particularly nice activity for a number of reasons. First, it can be used at a variety of grade levels. Second, both qualitative and quantitative measurements can be collected. Third, grass is easy to sprout and grows rapidly. Each group should grow its own grass, and each student should make his or her own observations. Students may make qualitative observations about the color and texture of the sprouting grass. They may make quantitative observations of the temperature and pH of the soil as well as of the height of grass seedlings. Have each member of a group share each of his or her observations with others in the group. Students should discuss how their observations are similar or different. You need to provide feedback regarding the level of detail and precision of the observations. Whole class feedback is also very valuable. Ask each group to report its observations to the class. Then let class members comment on the thoroughness and precision of the observations. Once the class has given its comments, you can give some feedback, too.

Making Sense of Data

Students make sense of their data by analyzing and interpreting them. The ability or skill to analyze data is an essential aspect of scientific literacy and of doing science. Unfortunately, not many children ever take part in analysis. Frequently, what is expected of children is to answer a series of questions regarding the data they collected. Even many adults don't have good experiences with this aspect of investigative work. Observations in the classroom have demonstrated that this is perhaps the most difficult component of the investigative web (Krajcik, et al., 1998). Often students think that an investigation is complete when they are finished with collecting the data, yet it is only through analysis that students can learn about the phenomena they are exploring. Making sense of the data is an intellectual challenge. How can teachers support students in analyzing data? How can they find trends and patterns in their work?

A number of techniques can be used to support students in making sense of their data. One technique is to transform the data into a different form. This allows students to see their data in new ways and gives them more opportunities to understand it. Children can transform their data by creating tables, graphs, diagrams, or other visualizations. As students become older, they might use more descriptive statistics in the process such as means or averages. Creating models helps students combine the disparate aspects of their work. Helping students think of different ways to represent their data helps them see patterns and trends in their data.

Transforming Data   Perhaps one of the best ways to help students make sense of their data is to have them transform, or change it, into some other form or representation. Scientists have used tables, graphs, diagrams, and maps to transform their data into other forms that might help them understand and see patterns in their data.

Using Tables   In early elementary grades, students can create tables from tallies or counts they have made. For example, perhaps students made a record of the different types of insects they observed on the playground. They could "transform" this data into a large table on newsprint. The table might include a column with the name of each insect, another column with a drawing of each insect, and a third column with the number of sightings. Table 4.13 is an example of a table early elementary students might create.

Students will need practice making tables. One good way to help students learn how to make tables is to model it for them. As you model how to develop a table, allow students the opportunity to contribute their own ideas to the process. You can also help students develop a sense of how to make tables by letting students design their own tables and by giving them feedback on their tables. Another useful technique is to have students share their tables with classmates. Allow classmates to give comments on the tables.

Once students have constructed their tables, they should write summaries of what their tables show. Such summaries are just another example of transforming the data. Once again, feedback from you and classmates will be helpful.

The tables students create will vary according to grade level. Imagine that a first grade class is carrying out a weather project. The teacher has students use a number of pictures to represent the weather. Figure 4.7 illustrates how students might do this.

Older students should record more quantitative measurements. Students might observe and record such measurements as the temperature, barometric pressure, wind speed, and precipitation. Table 4.14 illustrates a table a sixth grade

TABLE 4.13 A Data Table		
Insect	**Drawing**	**Number**
Ant		20
Bee		3

FIGURE 4.7
Chart created by early elementary students.

TABLE 4.14	Weather Data Chart							
		Monday	Tuesday	Wednesday	Thursday	Friday	Saturday	Sunday
Week 1	Temp	_____	_____	_____	_____	_____	_____	_____
	Pressure	_____	_____	_____	_____	_____	_____	_____
	Precipitation	_____	_____	_____	_____	_____	_____	_____
Week 2	Temp	_____	_____	_____	_____	_____	_____	_____
	Pressure	_____	_____	_____	_____	_____	_____	_____
	Precipitation	_____	_____	_____	_____	_____	_____	_____

student might create to record various weather-related measurements.

Using Graphs Graphs communicate visually the data that is collected in an investigation. Graphs show how dependent variables change with the independent variable. By convention, the dependent variables are usually depicted along the y-axis (the vertical axis of a graph), and the independent variables are depicted along the x-axis (the horizontal axis of the graph).

In elementary and middle school, students can transform their data into pie charts, bar graphs, histograms, and line graphs. Software programs, such as spreadsheets, make this relatively easy for children to accomplish. Rather than a simple count, graphs show a different visual representation of the data. Figure 4.8 shows a bar graph created by elementary students who explored the number of insects they found on their playground one afternoon. Figure 4.9 is an example of a line graph created by seventh graders to show the differences in height over time of grass seedlings growing in different soil types.

It isn't always easy to determine when to use bar graphs and when to use line graphs. Bar graphs are typically used when the data are discrete—that is, when they can be divided into categories and when the intervals between the data have no meaning. Types of insects, types of trees, and color of flowers are examples of discrete data. Line graphs are best used when the data are continuous; that is, when the intervals between the data have meaning. The concentration of fertilizer, the heights of plants, and the speed of a ball rolling down a hill are all continuous data. You should give your students practice in using the various kinds of graphs.

Once students have drawn a graph, you should have them come up with statements that

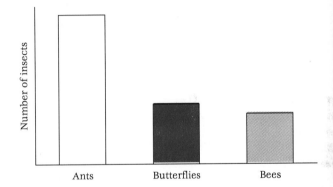

FIGURE 4.8
Insects on the playground.

describe what the graph means. A good technique to use is to have each student in the group make his or her own statements first and then have members of the groups share and compare the statements. Next, have the group construct a group response and share the group statement with the class to receive additional feedback.

Classroom teachers need to support students in making graphs; this is true at both the elementary and middle school levels. Making graphs and their interpretations are cognitively challenging for children, as well as adults. Modeling, sharing of each other's graphs, and feedback are three techniques that you should use frequently.

Young children who do not have an understanding of number concepts should be encouraged to make concrete, physical graphs. For example, if early elementary students are counting the number of seeds in different fruits and vegetables, they can line up the number of seeds in a pumpkin, a watermelon, and a cantaloupe. Then you might ask questions about which fruit has more seeds. Young learners need to physically see the real seeds lined up in a row to form

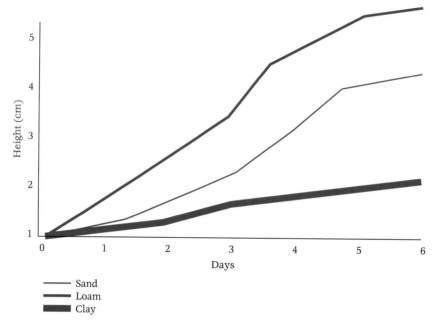

FIGURE 4.9
Growth of grass seedlings in different soil types.

a graph. However, you need to watch for conservation problems. Because the cantaloupe seeds are smaller than pumpkin seeds, for example, young children may say the pumpkin has more seeds. It is critical, therefore, to line seeds up with one another, as if they were the intervals on a graph.

To make the transfer to using numbers in graphs, you first need to work with nonnumerical ideas such as "Which is longer? Which is shorter? Which is bigger? Which is smaller? Which is closer? and Which is farther?" To make the transition to "units," you should use nonstandard units such as blocks, fingers, or shoes. For example, you might ask, "How many blocks high is the bean plant?" "How many fingers wide did they toy car move?" or "How many shoes long did the turtle walk?"

To help young learners make the transfer from concrete graphs to more abstract paper-and-pencil graphs, use pictures of the objects in the paper-and-pencil graphs. For example, to graph the number of seeds in a pumpkin, a watermelon, and a cantaloupe, draw the seeds on graph paper to correspond to the real seeds lined up. Figure 4.10 shows an example of this pictograph technique. Eventually, your students will be ready to make the leap to using numbers

when you match up the seeds on the graph with numbers.

Using Visual Techniques Other nontraditional visualization techniques can be used by students to transform data. Imagine that some students are exploring how different soil types influence the growth of grass. The students decide to measure the height of the grass over time as an indication of growth. One excellent way to represent this data would be to transform it into a graph of the height of the different plants over time. Students could also represent this data by taking photographs of the plants over time. Students studying weather patterns may decide to create a weather map instead of a graph to organize their data.

Combining graphing techniques with other visual techniques should be encouraged strongly at all age levels. When students represent data and ideas in different forms, they are developing deep understanding of the content.

Using Descriptive Statistics Descriptive statistics are another way to transform data. Upper elementary students and middle school students should be encouraged to use descriptive statistics such as differences, averages, and

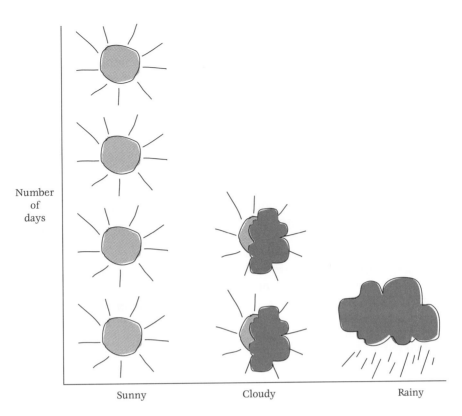

Number
of
days

Sunny   Cloudy   Rainy

FIGURE 4.10
Weather pictograph.

ranges to make sense of their data. Such basic descriptive statistics give a measure of central tendency and variation in their data. For example, a way to transform data about the influence of soil on the height of grass plants is to calculate the average heights of the grasses in each soil type. Students can then create graphs of the average heights of the grass over time. You can introduce young children to descriptive statistics by using such terms as *more, less, big, little, taller,* and *shorter.*

Modeling A model is a simplified representation of a phenomenon that suggests how the phenomenon works. Models, however, have their limitations. Models can be too simplified or too complex to be of value and care must be taken to generate truly useful models. For example, round ball models of atoms have their usefulness in illustrating the particle nature of matter, but they give no insight into the structure of atoms or into how atoms combine to form molecules. There are three types of models: physical, conceptual, and mathematical.

Physical models are actual devices or processes that behave like phenomena. A model airplane and a stream table are examples. Physical models are most obvious to young learners. For instance, a stream table allows students to visualize how the process of the flow of water allows a river and the land around the river to change over time.

Conceptual models link the unfamiliar to the familiar by using metaphors and analogies. Conceptual models depend upon the ability of students to imagine that something they do not understand is similar to something that they understand. Ping-Pong balls bouncing around (an idea that students understand) is a conceptual model for the atomic makeup of gaseous particles (an idea that students don't understand). Because conceptual models are an abstraction, the age and experience of students play a major role in determining the applicability of these models. Direct, hands-on experiences will help students become adept at using conceptual models.

Mathematical models specify a relationship between the variables described and the behavior of phenomena. A mathematical relationship that describes how much work is necessary to move an object is "work = distance × mass." The relationship specifies that the amount of work it takes to move an object is equal to the mass of the object times the distance the object is moved. Notice that this mathematical relationship does not apply in all situations. The relationship assumes that the object is being moved over a frictionless surface. Mathematical models are more abstract than are physical and conceptual models, but although mathematical models are very complex, new computer tools allow students to build dynamic models with a natural language interface. Such modeling programs allow learners to develop an understanding of scientific concepts despite the learners' lack of mathematical sophistication.

The Role of the Teacher   Students will need your support in making sense of data. You have a variety of instructional strategies to use to provide this support. Modeling, sharing, and feedback should be used frequently. You might start by having the class construct either a class table or graph. Next, you might have each student write a summary of what the table or graph means. Finally, have students share and compare their summaries. In addition to these supports that are designed to help students with the cognitive task of making sense of data, students sometimes need support getting along with others in their group.

As students try to make sense of their data, it is likely that they will disagree in their analyses. Such disagreement is healthy because it shows that students are taking responsibility and ownership for their learning. As long as students focus their disagreement on the analysis and do not begin to demean or degrade each other, these disagreements should be encouraged.

You can help students focus their disagreements by having them use evidence to support what they say. (Chapter 5 explores in detail how to manage discussions among students.)

Sharing with Others

Sharing is an essential component of the investigation web. Sharing includes communicating to others your plans and progress throughout the

investigation, your findings and your final products. It also includes receiving feedback on what you have communicated. Sharing helps students gain ownership of their investigation, and students learn new science information when others share with them.

Sharing during the Investigation   Sharing should occur throughout various components of the investigation web. Sharing during the project is critical because it gives learners valuable feedback on their work. This feedback often leads to revisions and new questions. Sharing is also important because students learn new science concepts when they listen and communicate with others. At the early elementary level, sharing aspects of a project or an investigation might be part of show-and-tell. For older students, sharing can be done in science class.

Communicating the Findings   In communicating their findings, students describe in writing the trends they see in their data, they create tables, graphs, or other visualizations, and they make conclusions describing how the data answer the question of the investigation.

Students can communicate their findings in a variety of formats: reports, posters, newspaper articles, hypermedia documents, videos, or e-mail

FIGURE 4.11
Sharing is an essential component of the investigation web.

documents. Figures 4.12 and 4.13 show illustrations from the hypermedia document created by two students.

No matter what form a final report takes it should include most of the following typical components: title, question, background information, experimental design and procedures, data, results, conclusions, and future questions. Figure 4.13 illustrates a conclusion.

Moving into the Next Round of Investigation

The completion of an investigation should lead to the next round of investigation, either as a result of students coming up with new questions or as a result of students thinking of modifications in their experimental design. Students should be provided opportunities to make predictions that are based on the results of their previous investigation, formulate hypotheses based on results of their previous investigation, and apply experimental techniques to new problems. As students conduct their investigation, they should keep a record of new questions that come to mind and of what questions remain unanswered. You need to capitalize on situations in which new questions arise naturally— these are the questions students will be eager to try to answer.

Activity 4.8 gives you the opportunity to connect all that you have read and to perform your own investigation with a partner. Remember to keep track of new questions that arise.

CRITERIA FOR ASSESSING THE VALUE OF AN INVESTIGATION

Too often, teachers and textbooks "do science" for the students. Students don't learn much when most of the investigative work is done

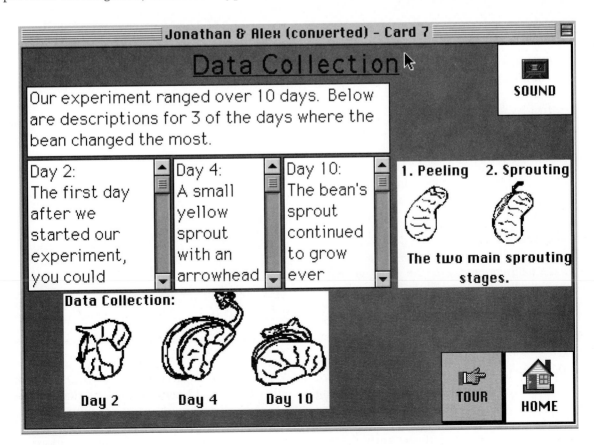

FIGURE 4.12
Hypermedia document communicating findings.

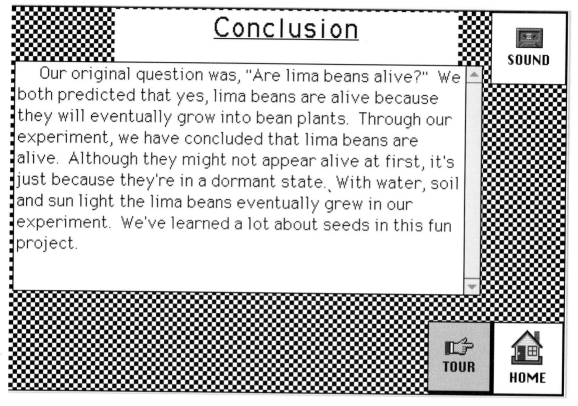

FIGURE 4.13
Hypermedia document communicating a conclusion.

ACTIVITY 4.8

Performing Your Own Investigation

A. Work with at least one partner to observe meal worms (available at most pet stores). Record your observations.

B. What questions come to mine? Are your questions testable? Can you phrase your questions in terms of a hypothesis?

C. What background information do you need? Obtain that information.

D. Design an experiment to answer your question.

E. Carry out the experimental work.

F. How can you analyze your data? Complete the analysis.

G. What conclusion can you draw?

H. Share your experimental work and data with the members of your class.

I. What other questions come to mind? What would you do differently if you did your investigation over again?

J. Document your investigation in your portfolio.

---

for them. It is important that teachers not confuse giving students support with doing the work for students. Table 4.15 lists criteria for determining if the teacher or curriculum materials are performing the cognitive work for students.

Not all of the investigations your students will perform will receive high marks in Table 4.15. Indeed, there are many situations in which you would want lower scores. However, if throughout the year, all your investigations are turning out low scores, you need to ask yourself

TABLE 4.15 Reflecting on the Structure of an Investigation

- To what extent did the students define the investigation?

1	2	3	4	5	6
Closely defined					Not defined

- To what extent did the investigation allow students to ask their own questions?

1	2	3	4	5	6
No opportunities					Numerous

- To what extent was the teacher expecting the right answer?

1	2	3	4	5	6
Pre-defined					Not defined

- To what extent were students allowed to design their own investigation?

1	2	3	4	5	6
No opportunities					Numerous

- To what extent were students allowed to collect data?

1	2	3	4	5	6
No opportunities					Numerous

- To what extent was the investigation meaningful to students?

1	2	3	4	5	6
Not meaningful					Very meaningful

- To what extent was the investigation feasible for students to carry out?

1	2	3	4	5	6
Not feasible					Very feasible

- To what extent was the investigation nontrivial to students?

1	2	3	4	5	6
Trivial					Nontrivial

- To what extent was the investigation real world?

1	2	3	4	5	6
Not real world					Real world

- To what extent did the investigation allow students to analyze data they collected?

1	2	3	4	5	6
No opportunities					Appropriate

- To what extent were students allowed to present their findings?

1	2	3	4	5	6
No opportunities					Numerous

- To what extent were students allowed to revise their work?

1	2	3	4	5	6
No opportunities					Numerous

if you are helping students become responsible for their learning and helping them learn to do difficult cognitive tasks on their own. Your goal should be to move students toward *doing* science. Throughout the school year, there should be increasingly higher scores on the table. Activity 4.9 provides practice in using Table 4.15.

SUMMARY OF CHAPTER

In this chapter, we discussed why investigations should be an integral part of elementary and middle school science instruction. We examined the investigation web and discussed a number of ways to help students implement the web. We considered numerous strategies for getting started, asking and refining questions, changing questions to hypotheses, using predictions, finding information, planning and designing, conducting the experimental work, making sense of data, sharing with others, and moving to the next round of investigation. Finally, we discussed criteria for assessing the value of an investigation.

ACTIVITY 4.9

Comparing Two Investigations

MATERIALS NEEDED:
- a partner
- two thermometers
- two Styrofoam cups
- hot water
- stirring rods

A. Read the following investigations.

Investigation 1: Cooling It by Stirring

Purpose: You will observe how the temperature of a hot liquid changes with stirring.

Materials: Two thermometers, two Styrofoam cups, hot water, and stirring rods.

Procedures for collecting the data:
1. Label one Styrofoam cup "Stirring" and one "Control."
2. Fill the two cups with 150 ml of hot water. **Caution:** Hot water can burn you. Make sure both cups are secure.
3. Place a thermometer in each cup.
4. Gently stir one of the cups of hot water until the end of the experiment.
5. Record the temperature of each cup every three minutes for 24 minutes.

Data analysis: For each cup, make a graph of temperature versus time. Place temperature on the y-axis and time on the x-axis. Place each graph on the same y–x-axis.

Questions:
1. What was the starting temperature of each of the cups?
2. What was the final temperature of each of the cups?

3. Which cup changed temperature first? Why do you think this one changed first?
4. How long did it take before the temperature of the other cup began to change?
5. How does stirring affect the cooling of a hot liquid?

Conclusions: Write a conclusion to support your data.

Investigation 2: Stirring Things Up

Prediction: If one cup of hot liquid is allowed to cool undisturbed while another is constantly stirred for a period of time, will one cool faster than the other? Draw a graph to illustrate your prediction.

Purpose: In this investigation, you will determine if people who constantly stir their coffee are really affecting the cooling process or just exhibiting a case of nerves.

Challenge: Design an experimental procedure to find an answer to the question proposed.

Questions to think about:
1. Did your results agree with your original prediction? Why or why not?
2. Will you continue to stir your coffee? Explain.

Additional investigation: What other factors might have an effect on the cooling process? Set up investigations to explore these other factors.

B. Use Table 4.15 to discuss the two investigations. How are they alike? Different? Which is most like project-based science? Why?

REFERENCES

American Association for the Advancement of Science. 1993. *Benchmarks for science literacy.* New York: Oxford University Press.

Annenberg/CPB. 1997. *Case studies in science education.* Washington, D.C.: Author.

Berg, C. 1994. *Chameleon condos: Critters and critical thinking.* Shorewood, Wis.: Chameleon Publishing.

Berger, C., G. Berkheimer, L. Lewis, H. Neuberger, and E. Wood, 1974. *Pushes and pulls.* Boston: Houghton Mifflin.

Burnett, R. 1992. *The pillbug project: A guide to investigation.* Washington, D.C.: National Science Teachers Association.

Elementary Science Study. 1970. *The ESS reader.* Newton, Mass.: Education Development Center.

Hawkins, D. 1965. Messing about in science. *Science and Children* 2(5):5–9.

Ingram, M. 1993. *Bottle biology.* Dubuque, Iowa: Kendall/Hunt Publishing Co.

Krajcik, J. S., P. Blumenfeld, R. W. Marx, K. M. Bass, J. Fredricks, and E. Soloway. 1998. Middle school students' initial attempts at inquiry in project-based science classrooms. *Journal of the Learning Sciences*. Vol. 7 (3 and 4) pp. 313–350.

Lawrence Hall of Science. 1989. *River cutters*. Berkeley, Calif.: Author.

Metz, K. E. 1995. Reassessment of developmental constraints on children's science instruction. *Review of Educational Research* 65:93–128.

National Research Council. 1996. *National science education standards*. Washington, D.C.: National Academy Press.

Scardamalia, M., and C. Bereiter. 1991. Higher levels of agency or children in knowledge building: A challenge for the design of new knowledge media. *The Journal of the Learning Sciences* 1:37–68.

Schauble, L., L. E. Klopfer, and K. Raghavan. 1991. Students' transition from an engineering model to a science model of experimentation. *Journal of Research in Science Teaching* 28:859–82.

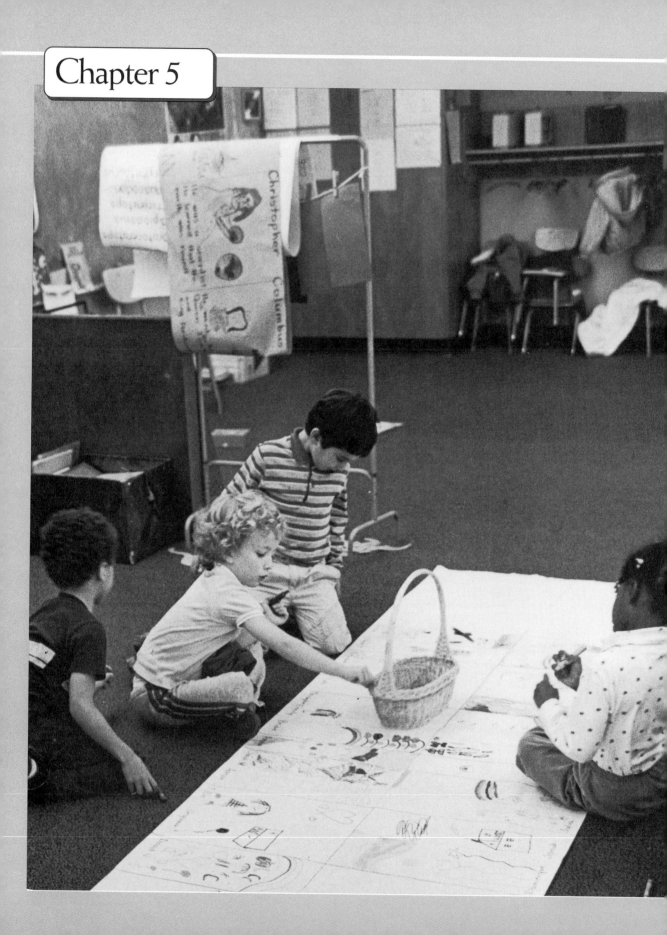

Chapter 5

HOW DO I DEVELOP COLLABORATION IN THE SCIENCE CLASSROOM?

INTRODUCTION

This chapter explores the nature of collaboration and why it almost always works better than individual learning. The topic of collaboration raises a number of questions: How do I get students to work together on intellectually challenging tasks? How do I get members of the community to work with students to find answers to their questions? What are the benefits of such a classroom environment? What is the role of the teacher in a classroom characterized by collaboration? This chapter will address these and other questions. Scenarios will illustrate the various types of collaboration among students, teachers, and members of the community. Because collaborative learning doesn't just happen in a classroom, the chapter focuses on creating a collaborative environment over a long period of time. You will learn about the social skills students need to work in groups with others and how to hold students accountable during collaboration. The chapter concludes with a discussion of ways to overcome challenges that might arise in the implementing of collaborative groups. We'll begin with scenarios of several types of group situations that you may have experienced in elementary or middle school. As you read each scenario, focus on what the teacher is doing or thinking, what the students are doing or thinking, and how students are working together to complete an assignment.

Scenario 1: Group Work with Little Guidance

Your fourth grade teacher covered the topic of dinosaurs for several weeks. When she finished the topic, she explained to your class that you were going to work in teams to complete a project on dinosaurs. The teacher divided your class into teams of four students. She told you that you and your teammates were to write a report on a certain type of dinosaur, draw a picture of the dinosaur, and give a class presentation about the dinosaur. Shelly, who was really bossy, told everyone else in the group what to do, and she dominated the entire project. She decided which dinosaur you would research and how the report would be written. She instructed

Marcus to search through some encyclopedias from the library, but he didn't read them as Shelly had asked. Frustrated, Shelly took the books home, read them, and wrote the report for everyone else. Sarah, who had good handwriting, recopied the report Shelly wrote. You could draw well, so you were left to draw the picture of the dinosaur for the cover. Although you and the others found Shelly's bossy behavior frustrating, you all knew you would receive a good grade because she was smart, so you happily let her do all the work. Shelly made the presentation to the class while you and the others stood behind her. One classmate asked a question; you didn't know the answer because you didn't learn much about dinosaurs anyway, but, luckily, Shelly was able to answer it.

In this first scenario, the topic was selected by the teacher. The teacher placed the students in groups but gave very little guidance or assistance that would ensure that students worked together in a joint intellectual effort. Although the students did cooperate with each other enough to complete the project, they did not have the skills to work together effectively. As a result, students were not motivated. Although all the students received the same grade, not all of you learned about dinosaurs.

Scenario 2: Individual Jobs in Group Work

As a whole class, you read the textbook section on cells. Then the teacher placed you into groups of five to learn about cells. Your group was instructed to learn all you could from reference books. Another group learned how to use a microscope to view cheek (animal) and onion (plant) cells. A third group learned how to use a software program on cells. A fourth group watched a video that compared and contrasted plant and animal cells. The teacher assigned each student in each group a job—one was a runner to get the materials, one was a recorder of the findings, one was a timer to keep the group on time, one was the manager to keep everyone on task, and one was a cheerleader to keep everyone involved. You were assigned to be the runner. You retrieved the encyclopedias from the shelf for your group and then proceeded to watch others in the class. You wished you had been in the computer group because you found reading the encyclopedia boring. When it came time to share your group's work, you wondered where the information came from, because you weren't really paying attention. The other groups shared their information about microscopes, the computer, and the video. Their projects seemed really interesting, and you learned a lot from them.

In this scenario, the teacher assigned each student a "job" so that the work was shared by members of the group. The teacher provided each group some guidance to complete the activity. However, because the teacher had selected the problems and learning approaches for each group, the technique did not motivate all students to learn. Some team projects seemed more fun than others, and some students' attention wandered. They didn't learn the intended material. In addition, not every "job" was equally important, and not every job was critical to completing the task.

Scenario 3: Using Expert Groups

The teacher told you that you were going to investigate the topic of sound. The goal of this lesson was for you to become an expert on one topic or concept and teach it to others. The teacher divided the class into teams of four and assigned each team member a job. One person was a runner who gathered the materials, one was a recorder who wrote down the results, one was a manager who got to do the experiment, and one was the timer who made sure the group completed the project in the time allotted. The teacher also provided you with a sheet of questions to answer to help you determine if you were "expert" enough to teach the concept to other students. Your assignment was to find out what material (air, water, or solids) sound travels through best. Sarah was assigned to be the runner, so she collected the supplies (a bucket of water, a tuning fork, and a paper tube) for the activity. John was the manager, so he got to experiment with the tuning forks to see when they seemed the loudest. You recorded the results after everyone agreed upon the answers. Marcus watched the clock the whole time and an-

nounced the time at ten-minute intervals. Once each of you had become an "expert" and knew that sound travels best in solids, you were put into "learning teams" where you taught this idea to three students who had not been in your group. You engaged the three new students in the same activity with the tuning fork, water, and tube of paper to demonstrate that sound travels best through the solid table, next best through the water, and least well through the air. You were happy that you were able to do the experiment that only John had been permitted to do when you were in your first group. Each of the three other students had become experts in other topics and they taught you what they had learned. You had a great time and really understood which material sound travels best through, but you were still a bit fuzzy on what the other students taught you. On the test the teacher gave, you did well on questions about the type of materials sound travels well through, and you did okay on the items about frequency, pitch, amplitude, and sound insulation that the other expert teams taught you.

In this example, the teacher structured the lesson by choosing the activities and providing all the directions for the students. The teacher provided students with guidance on the criteria for being an expert. In this way, each student was cognitively engaged because she needed to teach the concepts to others. This strategy seemed to work well.

Scenario 4: A Learning Community

Your class had been exploring the driving question "What causes living things to become endangered?" Your teacher lead the class in a discussion of possible threats to plant and animal survival. After you all decided on some causes of endangerment, the teacher let you choose your teammates. One group decided to investigate how pollution affects animals and plants. They conducted experiments on plants with various amounts of acids and other substances, and they researched the decline of frog populations throughout the world. Another group studied the gorilla and the effect of the war in Rwanda on the gorilla population. A third group investigated how the sea turtle in Florida has been affected by humans building along the coastline where they reproduce. Your group decided to learn more about the rainforest and causes of endangerment in the rainforests of the world. In your group, each member discussed his or her interests and ideas for investigating the rainforest. Juanita said, "I read the story called *The Great Kapok Tree* by Lynn Cherry, and I think the animals are dying because they're cutting down all the trees." Monika added, "Yeah, but my dad says it's because we eat a lot of hamburgers. The ranchers cut down trees to raise cows." "I don't know," Brian said. "I think it has more to do with pollution. Pollution is killing the animals." "Yeah, I saw something on TV about frogs dying because of pollution, and there's frogs in the rainforest," said Kameel. "Yeah, but I don't think frogs are the only animals dying in the rainforest," replied Monika. "And what would cutting down trees have to do with frogs dying? They live in water!" said Kameel. Your teacher came over to work with your group to help you figure out how you would finish the task. The teacher also asked you questions to get you thinking about what types of artifacts, products to share, you might create to show what you had learned.

Through collaborative planning and some guidance from your teacher, your group decided to divide this topic into types of endangered animals in the rainforest, causes of endangerment, and solutions to endangerment. As a team, you decided to learn about these three topics by reading books, visiting the zoo, watching a video on rainforests that you noticed in the school library, and e-mailing students in South America to talk with them. You divided into smaller working pairs to answer questions about endangered animals, causes, and solutions. Over the course of a few days, you found out that deforestation is a major cause of endangerment, so you decided to conduct a small experiment to see what would happen to insect populations in a section of the schoolyard when you slowly destroyed their habitat by removing sticks and leaves, cutting the grass, and pulling out the grass. Your teacher helped you understand what types of insects might live in the area by teaching a lesson about insect classification and helping you locate some resources for insect identification.

At each stage, you kept data and developed artifacts to show what you were learning. You decided to take close-up photos of the school yard insect population. Soon after the teacher asked you to give a presentation, you and others in the group analyzed and synthesized what you had learned and decided to present your information to classmates in the form of a poster labeled "Cause" and "Effect." Finally, the big day came. Your group gave its presentation to the class, and everyone applauded. The other students in the class were very interested in your project, but one team commented that you might have left out variables when comparing insect populations to the rainforest. They wondered if you could really compare the two situations because the rainforest is much more complex than a 3 foot by 3 foot area on the playground. You decided that this was a valid point and began to wonder how to address it. The other teams presented the results of their projects, and you learned that there might be other factors that you did not think about such as acid rain, economic factors, and social factors. These ideas gave you some direction for further exploring the rainforest.

In this scenario, the teacher served as an instructional planner and guide. The teacher helped students design questions, provided learning materials, and organized discussions. The driving question "What causes living things to become endangered?" was a meaningful and important question that served to organize the activities. The students in the group formed a learning community. Each negotiated with others in the group to select an investigation. Students shared the work, discussed ideas, and completed portions of the entire project. Differences in opinion were resolved amicably. Members of the community were included in the project. The Internet provided e-mail access to students in South America. The project's direction and outcome were determined by members of the group. The students were involved in "hands-on" investigations of habitats. Students developed "artifacts" that they shared with others. These artifacts and the presentation itself were critiqued by others in the class in a positive manner, thereby providing the group with ideas for future exploration. In this sample scenario, students had a voice in their learning, were motivated, and were cognitively involved. Students worked together to create meaning and understanding. There weren't some "jobs" that were less attractive than others.

ACTIVITY 5.1

How does Collaboration Change the Nature of the Classroom?

MATERIALS NEEDED:
- ◆ two classrooms to observe

A. With the help of your instructor, a school principal, or school curriculum director, identify two teachers for observation. Obtain permission to observe each of these teachers. Make sure you observe at least one group work setting.

B. As you observe both classrooms, analyze how collaboration changes the nature of the classroom. Try to answer the following questions:
- ◆ How are students working together in these classrooms?
- ◆ How does the teacher structure the group work?
- ◆ Are students given jobs or roles to play? Are the roles or jobs meaningful intel-

lectually, or are they only procedural tasks?
- ◆ Are the jobs or roles necessary to complete the task?
- ◆ What is the role of the teacher in the classroom?
- ◆ What are the teacher's objectives in the lesson?
- ◆ What instructional strategies does the teacher use?
- ◆ How does the teacher help students work in groups (by developing interpersonal skills, encouraging students to talk with each other, resolving conflicts)?

C. What do you see as the advantages and challenges of a collaborative classroom? Discuss with peers how these challenges might be overcome.

D. Record your thoughts and observations in your portfolio.

This fourth scenario describes a project-based science classroom in which collaborative learning is one of the major assumptions; it involves students, teachers, and members of society in trying to work through an important problem in which people are interested. Collaborative learning requires students to work with others to solve a problem or conduct an investigation.

These four scenarios illustrated different types of collaborative learning. Activity 5.1 will further clarify the characteristics of different approaches.

THE NATURE OF COLLABORATION

Understanding the nature of collaboration will help you comprehend its importance in project-based science classrooms. In this section, we will explore two questions about collaboration: What is collaboration? and What are the characteristics of collaboration?

What Is Collaboration?

Collaboration is best defined as a joint intellectual effort of students, peers, teachers, and community members to investigate a question or

problem. Students working with others on an intellectual problem to build understanding are a **community of learners.** A community of learners who are collaborating to answer the question "Why does algae grow in the fish tank?" might debate ideas about the cause of algae in an aquarium. This process encourages students to challenge their conceptions and ideas and debate these ideas. They work with others in the class to test their ideas and build understanding. They might set up several aquariums under different conditions such as in the window of the classroom with sunlight, in a dark room without sunlight, in a cool place, and in a warm place. The teacher might present a lesson about algae being an aquatic organism that has some characteristics of plants (it makes its own food through the process of photosynthesis) but that lacks true roots, stems, leaves, and embryos. In the lesson, the teacher has students observe algae under a microscope so that they can see these characteristics. The students might ask the owner of a local pet store how to control algae in an aquarium. In this learning community, the students, teachers, and other community members work together to find resolutions to questions or problems.

Chapter 2 examined Vygotsky's ideas about child development and learning. Teachers can use Vygotsky's (1986) ideas to create learning environments in which students have contact with others with different levels of expertise; that is, with multiple zones of proximal development. Such a learning environment is created by benchmark lessons, lessons that provide students with basic knowledge or skills that will enable them to expand and continue their learning. (See Chapter 6 for more information or benchmark lessons.) Students learning about the cause of algae in an aquarium are exposed to new concepts when the teacher gives a benchmark lesson on how to observe algae under the microscope. The teacher thus provides a scaffold that enables students to learn that algae make their own food through the process of photosynthesis. This concept helps the students understand that an aquarium in the sunlight will grow algae more quickly than will an aquarium placed away from a window. This same type of learning environment is created when a student explains how his family keeps algae from growing in their swimming pool or when the pet store owner explains how she keeps algae from forming on the aquariums in her store.

What Are the Characteristics of Collaboration?

The biggest difference between collaborative learning and other types of group arrangements is that collaborative learning encourages high levels of equality and mutuality (Damon and Phelps, 1989), and students work with others to create meaning. **Equality** is the level of knowledge or ability that members bring to a group. In a collaborative classroom, each member should contribute equally. This does not mean that each member of the group possesses the same knowledge or abilities—in fact, it is desirable that members bring different experiences, varied prior knowledge, and varied abilities. This is different from other group arrangements that encourage only cooperation—getting along or being compliant with others in a group to finish a task. For example, of the students studying algae growth, one has a swimming pool at home

and is familiar with the techniques used to control algae; one has a fish tank in her bedroom, and she has noticed that it has less algae when she keeps it away from the window; and one thinks he has algae growing in his shower at home (where it is warm and moist), so he has theories about cause of algae growth. All three share different, but equal, ideas with the group.

Mutuality refers to the common goals of the students. In collaborative classrooms, mutuality should be high—the students in a group should be working to answer the same question, complete the same task, reach the same goal, or solve the same problem. The students studying algae growth are all investigating why algae grows on the fish aquarium in the classroom. They have a strong driving question that they are investigating together. Other group arrangements sometimes involve each student having a separate "job." The students have different goals—each task corresponds with a different goal. Although the students in Scenario 1 did cooperate to present a dinosaur report to the class, each child's participation in that task had a separate goal. The goal of one student was to make sure the report was illustrated. The goal of another student was to make sure the report was legible. Mutuality was low.

Another characteristic of collaboration is that it creates meaning. In the first two scenarios, students in the groups did not work together to understand the topics. Some students did all of the work; others did not play important roles that would enable them to develop any understanding. Some students' attention wandered, and most did not cognitively engage in the learning process. In contrast, the third and fourth scenarios illustrated students collaborating. In the third scenario, students shared their expertise on various aspects of sound. In the fourth scenario, students worked together and with others (the teacher and members of a broader learning community) to create understanding about the rainforest.

The students studying the question "Why does algae grow in the fish tank?" were also collaborating because they created meaning, and they experienced high levels of equality and mutuality: They all contributed knowledge and skills to the group's effort and they worked to answer the same question. Without creating understanding and establishing high levels of equality and mutuality, students are probably just physically in groups; it is unlikely that they are working collaboratively.

TYPES OF COLLABORATIVE LEARNING

Collaboration can occur among all members of a community. In this section we will explore three types of collaborative learning: among students, between students and teacher, and between students and community.

Among Students

Student-to-student collaboration is a powerful method of instruction that can occur at several different levels, ranging from one-on-one collaboration to various group configurations. In one-on-one situations, one student can tutor another. A pair of students can also work together to investigate science questions. This one-on-one collaboration can occur within a classroom or even across a geographical distance via e-mail or regular mail. Collaboration among groups of students can involve students of a single class working together on a project, students from two or more classes within a school building or district exchanging ideas, or students from one class communicating with other classes via e-mail or regular mail.

Imagine groups of fourth grade students trying to answer the driving question "How do things with wheels help us move?" As students begin experimenting with skateboards, roller blades, bicycles, and other everyday objects with wheels to find out how they help us move, they find that they need to multiply distance by weight to figure out how much work is accomplished. One student in the group does not know how to multiply. Rather than hold the entire group back while the student learns multiplication, the teacher could set up a peer tutoring situation. While the one student worked with another to learn multiplication, the entire group could move ahead with the project.

To encourage student-to-student collaboration, some teachers start by pairing students

FIGURE 5.1
Student-to-student collaboration facilitates science learning.

during group activities. Pairs of students can be given specific prompts to discuss ideas and make meaning from science activities. For example, teachers can ask students to compare and contrast their own ideas with those of their partners. One such open-ended prompt is "My idea is like _____'s because _____, but my idea is different from _____'s idea because _____." Over the course of a school year, teachers can begin to put students in larger groups. As students become comfortable working in groups, some teachers have them share information, debate ideas, and brainstorm solutions with students from other classes within a school building or a district. Teachers of the same grade level can encourage this level of collaboration by having their students all study the same driving question and by providing their students time to meet with members of the other classes. If meeting with other classes is not possible, e-mail or regular correspondence can facilitate collaboration. Finally, once students are skilled collaborators, a teacher can encourage collaboration with other students around the world. National Geographic's programs such as "What's in Our Water?" involve students in one class collaborating with students in another class via the World Wide Web (National Geographic Society, 1991).

There are several reasons for using student-to-student collaboration. First, peers are not authority figures, so students tend not to feel threatened in these situations. Second, students come to school with many different prior experiences that give them different levels of knowledge about subjects. Each student has different interests, personalities, learning styles, and attention spans. As students explore solutions to driving questions, they can use these varied interests, abilities, knowledge levels, personalities, and attention spans to help their fellow students learn new ideas.

Between Students and Teacher

A cornerstone of collaboration is equal participation among members of a learning community. Collaboration between teachers and students is a situation in which students and teachers participate equally. Although students do not have the same level of expertise as the teacher, there are some areas in which students have more experiences or different understandings. Such experiences and understandings can become a valuable resource for the classroom.

Imagine a sixth grade teacher whose class is studying the driving question "Are there poisons in our environment?" The teacher can generate her own questions such as "Is insecticide a poison in our environment?" She also can suggest to students that they are experts when it comes to their own experiences. The student whose parents purchase only organically grown foods might ask, "Are food preservatives a poison?" The student who reads information on the Internet about harmful products around the home might ask, "Are cleaning products poisonous?" The student whose family just purchased a radon detector might ask, "Is radon a poison?" In such a classroom, the teacher can participate equally with the students by asking them to generate questions rather than being the sole director of the lesson.

To enter into a teacher-student collaboration, a teacher must show students that their ideas are important, and that the teacher is a learner in the classroom as well. When a teacher encourages students to contribute questions and ideas to classroom projects, students are empowered: They begin to feel that they have important knowledge, and they no longer perceive the teacher as the sole source of information in the classroom. Students begin to take responsibility for their own learning and help teach the class. Once the imbalance between roles is reduced, students and teachers can begin to collaborate equally.

In establishing a collaborative relationship with students, a teacher must play two roles—that of the collaborator who shares and debates ideas, negotiates meaning, and takes risks as well as that of the instructor who orchestrates instructional events and keeps the class focused on learning goals. Adequately playing both roles can be difficult. The teacher needs to establish trust among students so that students feel comfortable discussing ideas, asking questions, seeking information, and posing probable solutions. This can be accomplished by letting students know that they won't be punished or ridiculed for their ideas. The teacher can also admit to students that she doesn't know everything—that she's a learner in the classroom, too. However, the teacher also needs to maintain control of certain classroom events, maintain appropriate behavior, and keep students on task. This can be accomplished by establishing acceptable classroom behavior, timelines for lessons and projects, limits on use of resources, and overall learning goals. (Classroom management is discussed more fully in chapter 8.)

Collaboration between students and teachers has several benefits. First, it helps students to see classroom projects as real-world problems rather than as "cookbook" lab work with a single right answer. They come to view learning as more meaningful because they begin to see that the solutions to their questions extend beyond the teacher. They come to understand that no one—not even the teacher—has all the answers, and every person must learn how to answer questions posed. They learn that adults continue to learn—learning is an ongoing process. Second, students gain self-esteem because they see that their ideas are valued. Third, they tend to be more motivated to learn because they are excited to find answers to their questions—especially answers that the teacher may not even know!

Between Students and the Community

In collaboration between students and the community, students work with parents, neighbors, friends, relatives, and other community members either by meeting or by communicating over the telephone, via e-mail, or through the mail to share information, investigate ideas, or develop artifacts.

Collaboration with community members can take many forms. A student might call a person at a governmental office to receive information about a given topic. A guest speaker might visit the classroom to demonstrate a concept, discuss an idea, or answer students' questions. Community members might provide resources; schools with limited budgets sometimes cannot afford materials that community members and businesses can provide. Students might correspond with community members, sharing their ideas, questions, and investigations over an extended period. Finally, community members may become mentors for students, working collaboratively with students to answer a driving question and modeling for the students specific strategies or behaviors.

To extend collaboration beyond the four walls of the classroom, a conduit for communication must first be established. There are many ways to establish this communication. A teacher might encourage students to invite to the classroom parents, neighbors, friends, and relatives who have expertise in an area being studied. A teacher might invite community resource people such as doctors, water quality experts, chemists, and veterinarians to the classroom. As students become comfortable working with adults in the community, they can work on their own to contact and interview community members. Another conduit is technology. Telephones, fax machines, e-mail, and Web pages are tools that can connect students to the community. For example, in the acid rain project, students could link via the Internet to experts in the field.

Teachers also need to establish a classroom environment that encourages collaboration with community members. To accomplish this, the teacher needs first to help students understand that she and the science textbook aren't the only sources of information in a classroom—that students can learn from each other and from people in the community. Second, the teacher needs to allot class time for community members to visit and for students to communicate with others outside school. Third, the teacher should help students understand the different roles community members can play in teaching them science.

Individuals in the larger community represent a wealth of information for learners; they can provide resources and ideas otherwise unavailable to students. Through collaboration with the community, students see that science learned in school is relevant to real world problems. They learn about people and their careers. They learn to communicate with adults in a collaborative fashion. Upper elementary and middle school aged students especially seem to appreciate working with adults in the community because the adults treat them as young adults capable of understanding science in the real world.

CREATING A COLLABORATIVE ENVIRONMENT

Collaboration doesn't just happen. Teachers must work to create a collaborative environment in their classrooms. Collaboration is new to many students; it does not resemble the typical interactions that most students have experienced. To understand what real collaboration is, students need experiences and guidance in collaborating. Some students will be frustrated by collaboration at first if they are not used to taking initiative and responsibility for their own education.

For these reasons, it is important to introduce students gradually to collaboration. Over the course of an entire school year, a teacher can create a foundation for collaborative learning. In this section, we will explore some considerations when designing collaborative classrooms: how to form groups, how to develop collaborative skills, and how to get all students equitably involved.

Forming Groups

Before students can collaborate in small groups, the groups must be established. Many factors may be taken into consideration when forming groups: Should groups represent mixed academic ability or similar abilities, mixed personalities or like personalities (all shy students in the same group and domineering students in another group) and single sex or mixed? How many students should there be in a group? Should the teacher create the groups or allow students to select their own group members? Should groups be randomly assigned? Should groups stay together throughout the entire project or should new groups be formed for each activity? As you think about forming groups in your own classroom, on what basis will you determine group composition to facilitate the best collaboration?

One of the most important steps a teacher can take when designing a collaborative classroom is to think carefully about group composition before placing students into groups. Collaboration works most effectively in heterogeneous groups with moderate differences in ability, personality, and prior experience. Each student brings different strengths and weaknesses to the group. Vygotsky's (1986) theory supports the need for situations in which discrepancies among children's views exist to promote cognitive development. Students are exposed to more zones of proximal development when they are grouped with students who may be a little more knowledgeable or have different viewpoints. If differences among students are too drastic, however, problems can arise. For example, a highly competent reader in the fourth grade may become frustrated working with a peer who cannot read beyond a second grade level. This student may even come to reject or mistreat the student who has difficulties reading. Students with extremely incompatible personalities may not work well together either. For example, an extremely extroverted student may totally dominate an extremely introverted student. Drastically different prior experiences may also inhibit students' abilities to complete a task. For example, a student who has never worked with a computer may not be a good choice for working with students who are computer fanatics.

Although heterogeneous groups tend to foster collaboration, there are exceptions to this with regard to gender. Researchers studying equity issues in education have found that girls sometimes feel intimidated in groups dominated by boys. Boys tend to take control of conversations, activities, and decisions. Girls are often relegated to serve as scribes, taking the notes for the group or writing out the results of investigations. These educational researchers have found that girls, particularly upper elementary and middle school girls, tend to participate more in science when they work only with other girls (Baker, 1988; Kahle & Rennie, 1993). To avoid these potential problems, teachers can help make girls feel more comfortable with science by sometimes creating girl-only and boy-only groups. Then, as the girls' confidence increases, the teacher can gradually introduce mixed-gender groups.

The size of collaborative groups is also important. With younger elementary students who are in the self-centered stage of development, smaller groups—such as pairs—work best because such children have not learned to share attention with a large number of other people at once (Edwards & Stout, 1990). There is only one line of communication in pairs (between the two students), and no one is left out. Groups of three can be effective if there are three tasks, roles, or part for students to take. However, there is the risk that two students will pair up, excluding the third. Groups of four seem to work better than groups of three because even with pairing up no one is left out. Groups of four are also physically easy to arrange—four student desks can be put together to form one larger table area for students to work. When more than four students are grouped, behavior management sometimes becomes a problem, and it is more likely that students will be left out of the group dynamics.

It is important to decide whether students will be allowed to choose their own groups or whether you will assign group membership. This decision is not always an easy one. Most teachers find that students who are not used to working in collaborative groups will select team partners who diminish effective collaboration. They tend to select their friends, and this type of group composition can cause off-task behavior and cliques that dominate activities. Some teachers randomly select members of a group because students see this as a "fair" way to select groups. Other teachers make groups based on the physical arrangement of the classroom, such as by dividing the class into quadrants. Another option is to form interest groups. For example, all students who want to explore the same question can be grouped.

Students who have learned to work in collaborative groups have skills that help them overcome the problems inherent in grouping. In fact, older elementary and middle grade students who are comfortable with collaboration will appreciate being given the responsibility of selecting their own groups.

Regardless of who selects groups, it is important to build team identity. Team identity creates team rapport and camaraderie. Young adolescents have a need for peer approval and for feeling that they belong to a group, so it is important to build team identity with upper elementary and middle school students. Some teachers have students select group names, make team banners, write team cheers, or create team slogans. The identity of a team can be related to characteristics of members of the team or to the problem they are solving. For example, a team investigating wetlands might create a team name such as "The Swamp Things."

The decision to keep groups together throughout a project or to form new groups is one that is difficult to make. Some teachers find that, once the momentum has built up in a project, students want to stay together. Further, students in a group build mutual understandings and interpretations that must be built all over again each time new groupings are formed. Other teachers find that students need change to keep them interested in a project. Students may become bored working with the same group members, ideas may become stale in the group, and students eventually may learn all they can from each other. Regardless of what their final decision is, teachers find that it is only through continual monitoring of the dynamics within a group that they can make this decision.

To overcome the problem of switching groups frequently, some teachers form different levels of groups. **Informal groups** are used for short-term activities such as quick brainstorming sessions. Such groups may exist for only a few minutes. **Project groups** may stay together for months while a project is being completed. **Home groups,** groups that are used for check-

ing work and supporting each other, may be used the entire school year. One option is to form base groups and sharing groups. **Base groups** are groups of students who work together on a project. They each become experts in their topic area, on their driving question, or on their problem. After they have finished their project, the students move to new groups—the **sharing groups**—in which they share information about their respective projects.

Developing Collaborative Skills

To foster collaboration, teachers need to help students develop collaborative skills. Most students are not used to collaborating, talking to each other about ideas, and working independently in small groups and may need to learn how to do so. Also, collaboration requires students to take risks. By sharing their ideas, students open themselves to criticism from their peers. Teachers need to provide a safe environment so that students are willing to take such risks, by teaching students how to sensitively give feedback. Collaborative skills are essential in this type of situation as well as many other real world interactions such as completing projects with others in a job situation or getting along as a member of a family. For effective collaboration, students need to learn the skills of decision making, task completion, trust building, communication, and conflict management.

Groups will quickly fail unless the teacher analyzes the collaborative skills needed by students and discusses, models, practices, and evaluates them. In other words, collaborative skills must be taught just as purposefully as academic skills. Before starting a lesson, many teachers discuss the skills that are necessary for collaboration. Activity 5.2 explores ways to purposefully approach collaborative skills.

Another technique that teachers use to develop collaborative skills is to ask students questions such as "What is *negotiating?*" "Why is it important to negotiate?" "Why will your groups work better if you negotiate with each other?" "How do you know if people are negotiating?" A teacher might use a T-chart to teach about this skill (Johnson & Johnson, 1990). The T-chart is simply a chart in the shape of a T. Write the

ACTIVITY 5.2

How Do I Introduce Collaborative Skills to Students?

MATERIALS NEEDED:
- something to write with

A. Elementary and middle grades students need to be introduced to collaborative skills, and these skills need to be developed over time. Children don't naturally collaborate. For each of the following skills, think of questions you might ask children as a means of introduction. For example, imagine you are introducing the skill "agreeing with others." You might ask students, "What does it mean to agree with others?" (to compromise or reach the same opinion on something), "Why should members of a group agree with each other?" (so that arguments and fights are avoided), and "How will the group's ability to complete science projects improve if students are in agreement?" (they can proceed with a project without being sidetracked by disagreements).
Skills
- talking in appropriate voices in small groups
- taking turns using science equipment
- sharing science materials
- acknowledging others' contributions in a group
- staying on task during a project
- completing work on time
- helping others understand science ideas
- using "I" messages (saying what one thinks rather than blaming others, such as "I wish you would redesign that artifact" rather than "You didn't design that artifact correctly")
- criticizing in a positive way
- listening actively
- rephrasing others' science ideas
- being patient
- compromising
- negotiating
- asking for justification for science answers/responses
- probing or redirecting questions in a group

B. Discussing collaborative skills is only a first step in introducing collaborative skills. Develop a collaborative lesson. Decide what you would do to reinforce these skills. How would you develop the skills?

C. Try the lesson. Evaluate how well the introduction worked with students. What else do you need to do?

D. Record your ideas in your portfolio.

name of a skill above the T, descriptions of what the skill looks like to the left of the T, and descriptions of what the skill sounds like to the right of the T. Table 5.1 is a sample T-chart of the skill *negotiating*. The teacher would have students generate examples of what they would see each other doing and hear each other saying if they were negotiating. The teacher could model these behaviors or ask students in the class to model them. Next, students would practice the skill. Finally, after the class period is over, the teacher would have students discuss and evaluate how well they negotiated with each other. In some cases, teachers even videotape the classroom activities and have students watch and analyze themselves to determine how well they worked together. The students would conclude by determining what areas still needed refinement.

In Activity 5.3, you will create your own T-charts to teach students skills that will be helpful in collaborative groups.

Decision-Making Skills   In a project-based science classroom, students take responsibility for making many decisions. Students must make decisions about division of labor (who will do what, what role each person will play, and how the work load can be equitably distributed), timelines and scheduling (when people will complete things and in what sequence), activities (finding possible solutions to problems, deciding which activities to complete, and determining what artifacts to make), and resources (information, supplies, and materials).

As discussed in Chapter 4, a teacher can help students learn decision-making skills by using goal sheets to help students track division of labor,

---

TABLE 5.1 Sample T-Chart

Negotiating

Looks like	Sounds like
◆ heads nodding in agreement or disagreement	◆ "What is your idea?"
◆ students making eye contact with each other	◆ "Can we come up with a compromise?"
◆ students brainstorming more than one alternative	◆ "That's an interesting alternative!"
◆ students not putting down any ideas	◆ "How can we use both ideas?"

ACTIVITY 5.3

Making T-Charts

MATERIALS NEEDED:
  ◆ something to write with

A. Practice developing a T-chart. Make two columns and develop your own ideas for the following:
  ◆ resolving conflicts
  ◆ criticizing ideas, not people
  ◆ respecting others
  ◆ disagreeing politely
  ◆ maintaining self-control
  ◆ showing appreciation
  ◆ taking turns
  ◆ encouraging others
  ◆ praising
  ◆ respecting others
  ◆ accepting differences

B. Try making a T-chart of these skills with others in your group (or with children). How are their ideas different from and similar to yours? How did developing a T-chart help you communicate with the other people in your group? With children?

C. Keep these T-charts in your portfolio so that you can use them at a later time.

---

timelines and schedules to help students plan and sequence their time, and checklists to make decisions about resources. A goal sheet is simply a chart on which students can record their goals for the week and their plans for who will take responsibility for completing certain goals. Table 5.2 is a sample goal sheet.

After students have completed their goal sheets, they can move to developing timelines and schedules. This can be accomplished with the use of a weekly or monthly calendar, or the goal sheet can be expanded to include a plan and timeline. Table 5.3 is an example.

You can use a list to provoke students' thinking and expand their ideas about resources to use to complete their project. A checklist option is shown in Table 5.4. Another option is to work with students to develop their own resource list.

Task-Completion Skills Task-completion skills are necessary to teach students to stay focused

TABLE 5.2 Goal Sheet

What do we need to do?	Who will do it?
Find information about air pollution.	Liz
Contact the EPA.	Jeff
Figure out an experiment we can do to test for particulate matter.	Rosario

on the driving question and complete projects within a reasonable time frame. Once students understand the task at hand, they need to learn how to actually complete the task. To complete a task, students must know how to complete it, remember to complete each step of the task, stay focused, and monitor their time. (Remember that it usually takes more time to cover the same objectives in a collaborative learning environment than in a traditional classroom. Students

TABLE 5.3   Goal Sheet with Plan and Timeline

What do we need to do?	Who will do it?	How will it be done?	When will it be done?
Find information about air pollution.	Liz	Use World Wide Web	by Friday, Sept. 12th
Contact the EPA.	Jeff	Call from home.	at home
Figure out an experiment we can do to test for particulate matter.	Rosario	Look in resource books.	today, by Friday, Sept. 12th

TABLE 5.4   Resources Checklist

What?	Can we use it?	How?
Information		
encyclopedia	yes	Find out more about air pollution.
magazines		
journals		
books		
CD-ROMs	yes	Use in library.
software	no	The school doesn't have any on air pollution.
laserdisk	no	The school doesn't have any on air pollution.
guest speaker	yes	from the EPA
telephone call	yes	to the EPA
e-mail		
interview	yes	of someone at the EPA
World Wide Web	yes	Do a search.
letter		
Supplies and materials		
writing materials		
computers		
drawing materials		
science equipment	yes	Check with the teacher.
calculator		

need time to discuss ideas, work together, build understanding, and complete projects.)

To help students complete tasks, some teachers use a progress report. A progress report is a modification of Tables 5.2, 5.3, and 5.4 in which students review how much they have accomplished at the end of a day or a week. You might have students turn the progress report in to you, share it with classmates, put it in a science journal, or include it in an evaluation portfolio. The main point is to engage students in the reflective practice of examining how much they have completed. This will keep students conscious of starting in a timely manner and avoiding off-task behavior.

Trust-Building Skills Trust-building skills are critical to collaboration so that all students feel comfortable working in small groups. Each student should be at ease giving suggestions or opinions, participating in discussions, and helping answer the driving question. Although students must feel safe when sharing their ideas, an important part of science is the critique of ideas, and students must be willing to have their ideas critiqued. In addition, students need to learn how to critique ideas without offending others. Students can learn to build trust within a group by including everyone in discussions. When all students feel that their ideas are wanted and considered, they will be more likely to trust their peers.

Getting to Know Others If students in the classroom do not know each other or if the school's population is highly transient, an important first step for building trust is helping students get to know each other. Most people are not comfortable sharing ideas with or taking risks among strangers. Students need to introduce themselves to each other and discuss hobbies or interests. They need time to develop some common lines of communication. Teachers who neglect to facilitate students getting to know each other, will find that students are frequently not on task because they are taking the time themselves to build trust by talking about their lives and their interests.

One simple way to accomplish this is to engage students in icebreaker activities. In one icebreaker, children complete a worksheet with the names of their classmates: "Who knows how to play a piano?" "Who has a chemistry kit?" In another icebreaker, students simply interview each other. Activity 5.4 introduces ways to help students get to know each other.

Feeling Needed In building trust, it is not only important for students to know each other, but also for them to feel needed by the group. One way to accomplish this is to identify situations in which not all students are participating and to encourage nonparticipating students. You might draw quieter students into group discussions by inviting them to share their thoughts or ideas. To encourage sharing, you might make it a requirement for each student to share a given number of ideas during a lesson. You might use a "round-robin" approach in which each student must contribute one idea. To encourage equal participation, you might give each student a limited number of tokens. Each time they contribute an idea, they "pay" a token. When they run out of tokens, they cannot contribute more ideas until all the other students have also used up their tokens. Another

approach is to have groups of students break into pairs temporarily to talk or work together before returning to the large group. While students are working in pairs, they will all participate equally. When back in the large group their high level of participation may continue. Activity 5.5 introduces a strategy for teaching students that they must depend on others in their group.

Offering Constructive Criticism After students have learned about one another and have begun to feel needed by the group, they must learn how to critique others' ideas without offending each other. This is probably the most difficult component of trust building to teach. Students often speak before thinking. There are strategies you can use to get students in the practice of thinking about their classmates' feelings and to foster mutual respect. A T-chart, like the one in Table 5.5, can be used to help teach students how to show respect for the ideas of others.

Many children find it difficult to avoid putdowns. You might have students make lists of insulting words they should not use in a group, such as *stupid* or *dumb*. Then, students practice accepting others' ideas and avoiding the list of prohibited words. Another strategy is to have students create lists of acceptable words. For example, students might be tempted to say, "That's a dumb idea." The teacher can have the class brainstorm a list of respectful ways to point out the problems with an idea. Students might list, "You seem to be having trouble with this idea." or "You need to think about this again."

Students also need to be taught to avoid a tone of voice that suggests ridicule. Rules regarding making faces might need to be established. Students will probably need to practice critiquing others' work without being offensive or abusive. Finally, when students disagree with other people's ideas, they need to learn to criticize the ideas—not the people. To learn to criticize ideas rather than people, students can practice using "I" messages rather than "you" messages. For example, saying, "I think this might be a better way to solve this problem" is less threatening than saying, "You cannot solve this problem this way."

ACTIVITY 5.4

How do Children Build Trust Among Members of a Group?

MATERIALS NEEDED:
- ◆ something to write with
- ◆ index cards
- ◆ scissors

A. What follows are techniques for developing trust among members of a group. Try them out with a group of peers or a group of children.

Name Cards

Each participant should write his or her name in the center of a 5 × 8 index card. In each corner, the person should write some type of information about him- or herself. For example, children might list where they were born, personality characteristics, favorite hobbies, favorite science topics, the name of people they admire, accomplishments they are proud of, or favorite school subjects. Participants should gather in groups of four to share their cards. Participants should take on different roles—probers, recorders—to elicit more information about what is written on the cards. Each person in each group should introduce another group member to the whole class.

People Search

Each participant should complete the following chart by circulating among the entire group to find people who meet all the criteria.

Someone who likes comedy shows:	Someone who plays basketball after school:	Someone who likes science:	Someone who has visited a science museum:	Someone who took a vacation last summer:
Someone who collects stamps, coins, stickers, or baseball cards:	Someone who likes pizza:	Someone who has a chemistry kit:	Someone who likes: _____ (fill in the name of a restaurant)	Someone who loves cats:
Someone who loves dogs:	Someone who dances:	Someone who likes: _____ (fill in the name of a TV star)	Someone who has the middle name Marie:	Someone who has lived on a farm: (or in the city)
Someone who walks to school: (or takes a bus)	Someone who owns a computer:	Someone who is shy:	Someone with a science software program:	Someone who likes: _____ (fill in the name of a particular song)
Someone who likes to read science fiction for enjoyment:	Someone who has used a telescope:	Someone who likes to swim:	Some who likes to sleep late:	Someone who likes to get up early:

Partner Interview

All participants should pair up. Each member of a pair should interview the other by asking the following questions:

What is your favorite science fiction movie?	What do you like to do after school?	What is your favorite school subject?	Where have you gone on vacation?	What science museums have you visited?
What is your favorite hobby?	What is your favorite science topic?	What is your least favorite science topic?	What is your favorite restaurant?	Do you have any pets? Which kind?
What is your favorite sport?	What sports do you play?	What is your favorite song?	What is your middle name?	Where do you live?
What science magazine have you read?	What is your favorite computer program?	What would embarrass you?	What do you think you want to be when you grow up?	What makes you laugh?
What's your favorite book? Why?	Who's your favorite actor or actress?	What's your favorite science experiment? Why?	What science topic have you noticed in the newspaper this week?	What science topic would you like to know more about?

Interview Cube

Make paper cubes (or cover some other types of cubes). On each side of each cube write the name of a topic such as favorite science fiction movie, favorite science topic, science-related hobby, or best experiment ever conducted. Participants should form groups of four or five. Each member should "roll" the cube and respond to the topic that rolls face up. For example, if the cube lands on "science fiction movie," the roller must tell the others the title of her favorite science fiction movie. Then members of the group must ask probing questions about the topic. For example, they might ask, "When did this become your favorite movie?" At the end of the activity, each participant should share something interesting about the person next to him or her.

Finding Common Ground

Participants should form groups of four or five and then select a topic such as sports,

science class, TV shows, or school. Each group should discuss its topic until members find a common interest, dislike, or quality that *every* member of the group shares.

Finding Qualities

Participants should circulate around the room to find one positive quality about each other person. Participants should list each person's name with at least one positive quality such as "Is always friendly toward others" or "Helps others understand science ideas."

B. After you have completed some of these activities, analyze how each contributed to building trust among members of a group.

C. Why would it be important for children to build trust before working in collaborative groups?

D. Record your ideas in your portfolio.

ACTIVITY 5.5

What Skills Are Helpful in Cooperative Groups?

MATERIALS NEEDED:

♦ five squares cut up as shown and sealed in envelopes[1]

A. Cut up five squares (all of the same dimensions) as shown in Figure 5.2 for each group of five people. Distribute the five squares among envelopes as shown.

B. Each member of the group should get an envelope. The goal is for each person in the group, *without communicating in any way* (without talking or gesturing or writing notes), to form a square that is the same size as all the other member's squares. Members of the group may hand their own pieces to others in the group, but they may *not* take pieces from another person or point to pieces they want. They can only wait for a person to hand them a piece. They cannot gesture that they do not want a piece; they must accept it and give it to someone else if they do not want it. When a member gives a piece to another member of the group, she must simply hand the piece to the member and not place the piece so as to help complete a square. The activity is not timed, and it may take anywhere from a few minutes to over a half hour to complete.

C. When all the members of the group are finished, discuss what happened. What skills does it take to complete this task? Was it frustrating? Why? Was there collaboration among the members of the group? What skills would facilitate collaboration in elementary and middle grades classrooms?

1. Adapted from Abruscato, J., and J. Hassard. 1976. *Loving and beyond: Science teaching for the humanistic classroom.* Glenview, Ill.: Scott, Foresman.

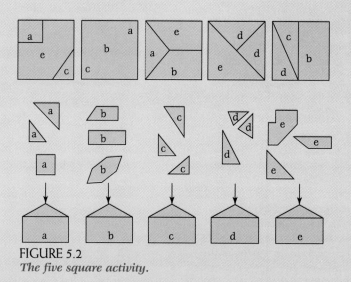

FIGURE 5.2
The five square activity.

TABLE 5.5   Respect-Building T-Chart

Showing appreciation	
Looks like . . .	**Sounds like . . .**
Smiling	"Thanks, I appreciate your help with this."

TABLE 5.6 Elaborating T-Chart	
Elaborating	
Looks like . . .	**Sounds like . . .**
Pointing to an investigation in progress	"Please tell me more about your project."
Holding up an artifact	"I think . . . because. . . ."

Communication Skills Communication skills are critical for success in collaborative situations. There are three components of communication skills. One, students need to learn to talk about learning. Two, they need to learn to speak clearly. Three, they need to listen carefully to what others are saying so that miscommunication doesn't arise. These three components help students communicate clearly with others, and effective communication helps prevent arguments, frustrations, and disagreements among group members.

Talking About Science Learning Children don't automatically know how to talk about science. They need to be taught how to ask questions and generate alternative answers to questions. One way to teach children how to generate questions and answers is to hold a whole group brainstorming session, during which you record questions and plausible answers on the board.

Children also need to learn how to probe for more information and request justification for ideas and evidence for conclusions. If a student says, "I think the aquarium is dirty because the fish go to the bathroom in it," other students might learn to ask probing questions like, "Why do you think that? Fish go to the bathroom in lakes and oceans too." However, often when students are challenged to elaborate, they resort to nonanswers like, "Because." To overcome this problem, teachers can have students practice responding in complete sentences. To help students talk about evidence, you might use T-charts. Evidence might be in the form of observations; data collected; or things read in books, articles, or on the World Wide Web. Students can also create T-charts for skills such as summarizing information, paraphrasing others' ideas, checking for scientific accuracy, elaborating, probing for more information, advocating a position, and justifying a science answer. Table 5.6 shows a sample T-chart on elaborating.

Children also need to learn how to advocate a position. Teachers can foster this skill by engaging students in role-playing situations (such as role-playing whether to report to the authorities a person who litters), mock trials (during which students have to argue for the prosecution or defense), letter writing campaigns (such as to newspaper editors about a local issue), making posters (such as those advocating conservation of energy), or participating in news groups on the World Wide Web (such as those advocating bans on types of tuna fishing that endanger dolphins).

Speaking Clearly Speaking clearly means enunciating words, using appropriate voice levels, and facing others when talking to them. Young children, of course, are still developing a repertoire of words, and they often mispronounce them. They are also losing teeth and sometimes find it difficult to say certain words. In addition, children sometimes get very excited about science and so speak too quickly. Although these are normal characteristics of children's speech, teachers can help their students practice more effective speech by enunciating and talking more slowly so that others can understand, talking at appropriate voice levels so that people want to listen, and talking face-to-face so that others can hear them better.

Listening Carefully Listening is as important as speaking in good communication. Children like to talk but frequently don't listen carefully to what others are saying. They need to be taught active listening, which includes using names and eye contact when speaking to each other, paraphrasing what others say, asking for explanations, and summarizing conversations. Standards can be set about raising hands, taking notes when others talk, and not interrupting others in midspeech.

For example, while working on a display board for an artifact, one student might say, "I think we should do something different." A second student could interpret this to mean that they should make a different type of display. In fact, the first student meant that they should complete their experiment before making the display board. Without understanding what the first student's comment meant, the second student might suggest a different format for the display. This, of course, could lead to confusion and anger. To avoid misunderstanding, the second student could have said, "You said we should do something different. Do you mean that we need to have a different type of display?" The first student can then clarify his intent without causing problems.

Conflict-Management Skills   Even after students have learned decision-making, task-completion, trust-building, and communication skills, conflicts can arise among members of a group. For this reason, students also need to develop conflict-management skills. These skills include the ability to clarify disagreements, negotiate, and compromise.

Clarifying Disagreements   To clarify disagreements within a group, students need to learn to understand the points of view of others. Children frequently have difficulty understanding others' opinions. This is partly developmental (with young elementary children) and partly due to inexperience.

With elementary and middle grade students, teachers foster understanding by using literature, stuffed animals, and pets. A teacher might read a story and ask children to express how the character in the story feels. The *Story of the Three Bears* is a good story to use in this way. A teacher might have students pretend that a favorite stuffed animal or pet can talk and tell stories about how the animal thinks and feels.

With older elementary and middle grade students, teachers can have students pretend (role-play) that they are other people. Students can ask themselves, "What would I think if I were the other person?" Older students respond well to courtroom dramas. Teachers can read a courtroom drama or set up a courtroom simulation in which each student plays a different role. Students can discuss the thinking, feelings, beliefs, values, attitudes, desires, wants, and problems of each person in the drama. Imagine that students disagree about who should contact a guest speaker. One student wants to contact the guest speaker because he thought of the idea; another student wants to contact the guest speaker because his father works with her. By switching roles (pretending each is the other person), the students can try to understand why each believes he is the best person to call the speaker.

Negotiating   Next, students need to learn to negotiate. Negotiation does not mean that one person wins and the other loses. Negotiation results in both parties feeling as if they had won.

To teach negotiation, many teachers use T-charts, or a hybrid of the T-chart, a win-win chart. On each side of the T in a win-win chart, students write the names of the disagreeing parties. The students list under each name how the person or group will win in the situation. Table 5.7 is an example of a win-win T-Chart. The chart illustrates that both Matt and Luther want to feel like they are contributing to the project. Matt wants the students to know that his father knows the speaker. Luther wants the speaker to know that inviting her was his idea. In order for both students to win, Luther will help Matt make arrangements for the speaker's visit. Matt will call the speaker. He will tell the speaker that inviting her was Luther's idea and he will introduce her to Luther when she arrives.

Another way to teach negotiation is to use Venn diagrams for finding common ground. Stu-

---

TABLE 5.7   Win-Win Chart

Who gets to call the guest speaker	
Matt	**Luther**
I can call since my dad knows the speaker.	You can mention that I suggested this.

dents list differences in the outer circle and common ideas in the area of intersection of the two circles. The Venn diagram in Figure 5.3 indicates that students originally wanted to include different types of pictures in their project but agreed upon a photograph.

Students can also send an e-mail about the problem to another school or student requesting new ideas for solving the differences. A group of students having difficulty reaching a consensus on how to build a machine to test for friction, for example, could e-mail their ideas to another school in their district and ask the students at the other school to vote on the best idea.

Compromising If negotiation fails to produce a win-win situation, students need to learn to compromise. In a compromise, students settle differences and reach an agreement in which each "side" or person makes concessions. The resulting decision may combine the best qualities or elements of different ideas.

To teach the skill of compromise, a teacher might have students list all of the major points

in their arguments. Then, the teacher instructs each side in the disagreement to give up one or two of its ideas in an exchange. Slowly, the two sides should come to an agreement that is a fair compromise. For example, students trying to decide how to best measure friction might use ideas from Table 5.8 to compromise. The compromise might turn out to be building a skateboard and measuring the friction of the skateboard across different surfaces using a pulley.

Involving All Students Equitably

One of the essential features of collaboration is equal participation. However, frequently, there are students who are reluctant to collaborate for one reason or another—lack of self-confidence, unfamiliarity with collaboration, and so on. Students need to understand that the products and ideas developed through collaboration must represent every one, including them. Each student should feel that his or her contribution to the collaborative task is essential. A collaborative environment keeps all members of a group equitably involved and needed by others in the group. Some educators call this condition **positive interdependence**—the linking of all group members so that one cannot succeed unless the other group members succeed.

You probably noticed in the first two scenarios at the beginning of the chapter that some students' "jobs" weren't really critical to the success of the group as a whole. Students whose efforts were not critical to the project's success quickly lost interest, got bored, or failed to participate intimately with others in the group. Positive interdependence may be built through establishing common goals or rewards, building common understanding, dividing up labor, and assigning roles.

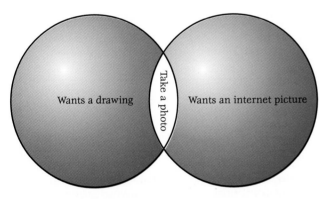

FIGURE 5.3
Venn Diagram

TABLE 5.8 Compromise	
How should we build a machine to test friction?	
Yolanda's ideas	**Anchee's ideas**
Make a skateboard.	Build a pulley system to measure accurately.
Test it on different surfaces.	Drag objects across different surfaces.
See if you fall off the skateboard on rough surfaces.	Chart how hard it is to move the objects.
See if the wheels get hotter going across some surfaces.	

Establishing Common Goals Teachers can establish common goals by teaching students to move from individual ideas to group ideas. During all stages of collaborative learning (designing a driving question, investigating, developing artifacts, and sharing artifacts), students can first write down their own ideas. Open-ended prompts such as "My idea is . . . ," "My plan is . . . ," and "My goal is . . ." are helpful. After students have recorded their own ideas, they can work in small groups to share ideas. Then students can record the ideas and goals of others in the group. Finally, by comparing and contrasting goals, they can develop a common goal. Table 5.9 shows examples of charts that can be used to help students build common goals.

Building Common Understanding To build common understanding, teachers need to have students discuss intellectual ideas. This is no easy task. The first step is to get students to re-ally listen to each other. When one student gives her idea, and another student recites it back to her, two other students can add modifications to the idea, and once all of the ideas are out, students can discuss the similarities and differences among the ideas. Understanding the similarities and differences among ideas helps students listen to each other, and it helps clarify ideas and build understanding among the members of the group.

One technique for facilitating discussion of intellectual ideas is to ask students to think about the validity of their responses. Students can be asked to justify the positions they take, and no one's idea can be included or excluded without a reason. Students can use sentences such as "We think X is better than Y because . . . ," "We think it is . . . because . . . ," "We don't think it is . . . because . . . ," and "I think we should . . . because . . ." At first, charts like the one in Table 5.10 are useful to encourage

---

TABLE 5.9   Charts for Building Common Goals

Driving Question

Ideas	How the idea is like mine	How the idea is different from mine	Our group idea for a driving question
My idea			
Sara's idea			
Richard's idea			
Rahel's idea			

Investigation

Ideas	How the idea is like mine	How the idea is different from mine	Our group idea for an investigation
My idea			
Sara's idea			
Richard's idea			
Rahel's idea			

Artifacts

Ideas	How the idea is like mine	How the idea is different from mine	Our group idea for artifacts
My idea			
Sara's idea			
Richard's idea			
Rahel's idea			

discussions. The charts can be photocopied and distributed to other groups for discussion. Groups can discuss how their ideas are different from those of other groups. For example, the teacher can ask, "Which other group had a prediction similar to your groups?" Over the course of the year, students will gain the skills to discuss ideas without the prompt in the charts. Activity 5.6 illustrates how a group of students can build common understandings.

Dividing up Labor   Division of labor occurs when students collaborate, negotiate, compromise, and interface with others to investigate a driving question. *Division of labor* does not mean *divide and conquer*. Divide and conquer strategies rarely lead to equitable distribution of knowledge, skills, or effort. Someone always seems to carry a larger workload, have a more interesting task, or contribute more information to the group. Students need to learn that true division of labor can only occur when members of

the group participate equally in a task. All students need to take an active role and no one can dominate. In a collaborative environment, it is in the division of labor that the teacher serves the role of guide—making sure students are cued to listen to one another's ideas rather than only to work individually.

One way a teacher can help facilitate a true division of labor is to put students in situations in which they are dependent upon one another's resources. Resources include skills, abilities, knowledge, prior experiences, access to information, and friends and acquaintances. Students who have slightly different prior experiences will all contribute equally in a significant way to answering a driving question—thus dividing the labor. Imagine that students are trying to find out what factors affect plant growth. A student who has grown houseplants in an apartment complex has prior knowledge about window locations, the size of pots, and the amount of water. Another student who lives in a rural area grows food crops. This student brings to the group knowledge about farm machinery, commercial fertilizers, pesticides, herbicides, and crop yields. A third student who lives in a subdivision has a garden in her backyard. This student has experience using a compost pile as a source of fertilizer and organic gardening methods. These students can work together to divide the labor in an equitable fashion based

---

TABLE 5.10   Defending Your Ideas

Idea	Why?
We think _____	because _____
We think it is not _____	because _____
We think _____ is better	because _____

ACTIVITY 5.6

How Can You Help Students Build Understanding?

MATERIALS NEEDED:
- materials to conduct a short science investigation
- a science activity book

A. With the help of your instructor, obtain a science activity book and select an investigation that you can complete with a group of students or a group of your peers. Keep the investigation simple. For example, you might investigate how to light a flashlight bulb using only one wire, one flashlight bulb, and one dry cell.

B. Members of the group should predict the results of the activity. For example,

members can complete the sentence "I predict that the bulb will. . . ." Each member of the group should provide a prediction and recite the previous person's prediction. Have other students add modifications. Once all of the ideas are out, students can discuss the similarities and differences among their predictions.

C. Conduct the investigation.

D. Members of the group should discuss the results and justify the reasons for their beliefs. For example, students can use sentences such as "We think the bulb lit up because . . . ," "We think it did not light because . . . ," "We don't think it is . . . because . . . ," and "I think we should . . . because . . . ."

ACTIVITY 5.7

How Do Roles Facilitate Collaborative Learning?

MATERIALS NEEDED:

- *The Great Solar System Rescue* or *The Great Ocean Rescue,* by Tom Snyder Productions
- a laser disc player with a monitor or a computer with a CD-ROM player (depending upon the version of *The Great Solar System Rescue* or *The Great Ocean Rescue*—both are available in either laser disc or CD format)
- a computer with a cable connection to a laser disc player (optional with the laser disc version)

A. Complete one lesson from either *The Great Solar System Rescue* or *The Great Ocean Rescue.*

B. After you have completed the lesson, analyze how each person's role contributed to the group's success in solving the mystery presented in the activity. Could the mystery have been solved effectively without one of the roles? Explain your views.

C. How did having a particular role contribute to your achievement, social skills, and self-esteem? How do you think the role would affect students engaging in the activity?

D. Record your ideas in your portfolio.

upon their prior experiences. The first student could help the others set up an experiment to grow plants in pots of different sizes under various lighting conditions (in north, south, east, and west windows). The second student could help the others investigate how commercial fertilizers and pesticides help plants grow by setting up conditions in which some plants are treated with fertilizers and pesticides and others are not. The last student could contrast this investigation with one on organic gardening methods.

Assigning Roles   If students are having difficulty working together, assigning roles can alleviate the problem. The assignment of roles ensures that all students participate and that no one dominates. It also teaches responsibility by making each student responsible for a part of the task.

It is critical that each role be important and contribute in a significant way to solving the problem or reaching understanding. **Interpersonal roles** help ensure that members of a group work well together. Interpersonal roles include a facilitator (who makes sure everyone is participating), an encourager (who makes sure all students are participating or provides positive feedback to members of the group), a checker (who keeps notes about how well the group is doing on skills or tasks), and a noise monitor (who makes sure the group isn't too loud). **Managerial roles** include a reader (who reads directions to the group) a timekeeper (who makes sure the group finishes the task in a given amount of

time), a recorder (who writes down the team's answers), and a runner (who gets materials that the group needs). **Cognitive roles,** or roles that require a specific type of thinking or specialized knowledge, include an executive, a skeptic or critic, an educator, and a conciliator. Cognitive roles can also correspond to scientific fields; such roles include a veterinarian, a botanist, a paleontologist, a geologist, an ecologist, a meteorologist, a zoologist, an oceanographer, an astronomer, and a chemist. Activity 5.7 will enable you to experience cognitive roles in collaborative learning.

Interpersonal and managerial roles, more than cognitive ones, tend to focus on separate jobs to get a task finished. Interpersonal and managerial roles are also less likely to be significant for the completion of a task. For example, the job of a student who is a runner is over as soon as supplies are acquired, and the student who is the encourager is likely to lose interest in the role and feel that it is phony or silly. For this reason, interpersonal and managerial roles are best used only with young children or students who lack even extremely basic skills for working together. For older elementary or middle school students (or students with more developed collaborative skills), cognitive roles are more effective. If students are studying acid rain, for example, they might take the roles of chemist, botanist, geologist, and ecologist. The chemist studies how the chemicals determine acidity. The botanist learns about how plants are affected by acid levels. The geologist researches the effect of acid rain on rocks, minerals, and soil. The ecologist looks at the overall picture, determining how acid rain interacts with the environment. With these cognitive roles, each person is needed throughout the project and each contributes equally to the task.

CHALLENGES THAT ARISE WHEN STUDENTS COLLABORATE IN SMALL GROUPS

Students don't automatically collaborate with others, and groups do not always work well together. Students may argue, fail to communicate, or resist compromise. Students' personalities may lead to situations in which some students do all the work and others contribute virtually nothing. Sometimes higher ability students feel they are being taken advantage of by others, or they dominate. Status among members of a group can cause problems—high status members (those with higher academic status, peer status, or social status) may take control of a group. Sometimes, members of a group may make a pact to do the least amount of work possible. Differences in diversity among students (gender, culture, physical ability, or academic ability) can cause problems in small groups. Some students even become socialized to believe they cannot work well in a group. Students can also become socialized to believe that there is a "right answer" for everything and find it difficult to work in project-based science classrooms where students work together to find solutions among many possibilities. Finally, parents, colleagues, or administrators may not understand the nature of collaboration and cause problems by questioning a teacher's techniques.

A Lack of Collaborative Skills

As discussed earlier, students need to learn collaborative skills to be able to work effectively in small groups. Children do not learn these skills overnight; it can take months or years for students to learn to work well in groups. However, without these skills, students may experience unresolved conflicts, aggression, failure to challenge the viewpoints of others, and failure to make meanings explicit.

When problems arise during collaboration, try two approaches: (1) carefully examine the types of collaborative skills students seem to be lacking and work on these specific skills, and (2) get students to try to work out their own problems. Use these two approaches before moving problem students to another group or forming new groups. If you are too quick to move students to a new team, you will only reinforce negative behaviors—students will learn that complaining results in getting to be on a team with the people they want to be with.

If students seem to argue excessively, work with them so that they learn to summarize ideas in a positive fashion, request help, agree with each other, and support other's ideas. Try to get students to understand that they do not need to have arguments, give negative criticism, or overlook the positive contributions of members of the group. Have students work out their own problems, if possible. You might ask some of the following questions:

◆ What have you done to try to resolve the argument?

◆ What could you try next?

◆ What are some other ways to solve this?

When students realize that they are going to be working as a team for a length of time and that they must work together to be successful, they will often work out their problems and get along.

There may still be situations in which students refuse to work together, however. When this happens, you may need to remove a student from the group and let him or her work alone until ready to work with others. Sometimes, isolation and seeing teams enjoying themselves motivate students to want to join the team. A private meeting with an uncooperative student might also reveal reasons for negative behavior. Some teachers ask team members to think of ways to help an uncooperative student participate as a productive member of the team. Similarly, some teachers call class meetings to discuss ways to improve teamwork.

Sound levels can also become a problem in collaborative classrooms—especially if the school building is not built with acoustical tiles, carpeting, and more modern ways to absorb sound. Although talking is expected and desired in a project-based science classroom (students, after all, are debating ideas, constructing understanding, carrying out investigations, and making artifacts), unproductive noise can be distracting. If the teacher must say, "Shhhhh," every few minutes, something is wrong. Either the teacher's expectations for noise level are too strict, or students are too noisy. To determine which is the case, observe the classroom for a moment. Students should not be yelling at each other. Students should be able to talk and hear each other within a group. If you can see that students are struggling to hear one another, reinforce (or establish) ground rules for talking. Turn off the lights, for example, to get the room quiet and then establish appropriate noise levels.

Finally, students may not use collaborative time effectively. If students are talking about subjects other than the project, try to find out why. Is it that the students do not know each other and so are talking about common interests to become acquainted? Are they finished too early and trying to amuse themselves in the remaining time? Are they failing to focus on the driving question? Did they fail to make sure everyone understood the material? It is only through working *with* the groups that you will get to the heart of the problem. You may need to give them time to get to know each other. Perhaps students need more challenging work. You may need to refocus students' attention on the driving question and create new zones of proximal development so that they can sustain collaboration. You may need to show students strategies for making sure all members of the group understand the concepts. For example, students may need to create quizzes for each other or practice giving group presentations to see if each member really understands what has been learned.

Loafing

The "loafer effect" happens when one or more group members allow others to do all the work. Constant monitoring of group member's contributions to the group goal will help you determine if there are any loafers. If you keep groups small (three to four students), you will notice these free riders more easily. As you move about the classroom, you can momentarily conference with each group to discuss what each student is doing. You can try to engage the loafers by directing them to tasks they can complete, ideas they can contribute, or ways they can enhance the group's work. You can also provide support mechanisms that will ensure that all students contribute to completing a project. For example, students can complete daily journals in which they record their contributions to the project. You can collect daily charts in which students document their day's accomplishments and record each group member's contribution. These types of support focus on individual and group accountability and help eliminate the loafer effect.

The Fear of Being Duped and the Dominating of Others

Sometimes a higher ability member of a group fears being "used" by the other members and so doesn't want to collaborate. Sometimes a member of a group uses others to his or her advantage, thereby gaining more than he or she would have alone. By requiring individual accountability and self-assessment, teachers can eliminate either of these effects. For example, a teacher may require each student to complete a daily journal to chronicle individual contributions and learning and to account for the accomplishments of the entire group. In this fashion, students have the opportunity to show the teacher their own work as well as that of the group.

Status Differential

The *status differential effect* occurs when a high status member of a group takes control. Higher status can be caused by many things—cliques, socioeconomic status, older students working with younger ones, or academic achievement (Cohen, 1994). You can approach this type of problem from several directions. First, you can continue to stress collaborative skills so that all members of the group are contributing equally and learning to accept their individual differences. Second, you can form groups carefully in an effort to avoid status differentials. Finally, you can require individual accountability within a group so that all members are recognized for their efforts.

For example, a teacher may purposefully avoid placing a group of students who all play on the basketball team with a student who is not on the team. The collegiality formed among members of the basketball team may cause a clique to form that excludes the one student who is not on the team.

Pacts

When all members of a group make a pact to avoid work and contribute the least amount of effort to complete a task, the result is a poor quality product or inadequate completion of the goal. A teacher who knows the abilities of the students in his classroom will quickly recognize this type of behavior.

When you spot evidence of a pact, stress high standards. You might demonstrate or model what is expected at the end of the lesson by showing a sample finished product. You might establish minimum competencies so that students complete a certain agreeable level of work. For example, you could require each student to have at least two complete artifacts to document science learning or a certain number of entries in a portfolio. Another strategy is to have students complete "learning contracts" in which they establish standards for completion of their work before they begin it. Some teachers promote peer reviews among collaborative groups. Most elementary and middle grade students are motivated to do their best when they know they are going to be required to share their work and be evaluated by other groups. Sometimes, friendly competition between groups helps establish high standards. While the members of a group are collaborating, the groups are competing with each other for recognition of high quality work.

Diversity

Research findings on collaborative learning have shown that, over time, students working in groups learn to appreciate each other's differences including gender, racial, cultural, and physical or mental ability differences (Cohen, 1994; Manning & Lucking, 1992). With collaborative learning, students tend to accept others different from themselves, make friends with diverse members of their class, and raise the self-esteem of isolated students. However, these same differences in gender, culture, physical ability, and academic ability can cause problems in some group learning situations. For example, research in education has shown that male students frequently dominate science activities, and female students are left behind (Baker, 1988).

You may need to directly address differences in gender, culture, race, and physical and academic ability. For example, you can point out situations in which male students are dominating group situations, or you can subtly encourage female students to participate. Sometimes, making gender-specific teams can eliminate this problem.

Problems certainly can arise when students see some group members as *different,* but they also can arise when students see some group members as *better.* The student who is interested and gifted in science and mathematics may be labeled a "nerd" in a traditional classroom environment because she is always the one raising her hand, getting called upon by the teacher, giving the right answers, and being praised by the teacher. Other students may come to resent her because her success makes others look bad. In contrast, members of a sports team do not resent a talented athlete on their team, because the talent of the star athlete is shared with the team—everyone becomes a winner when one person does well. By fostering such a team mentality with your students, diversity can come to be celebrated and students with special abilities can come to be members of the group.

Socially Induced Incompetence

Socially induced incompetence occurs when members of a group ostracize or disparage a student to the point that he or she feels unable to contribute to the group's work. Children and adults are not always aware of how their behavior can affect others, how talking in a certain

ACTIVITY 5.8

Troubleshooting

MATERIALS NEEDED:
- something to write with
- peers to work with
- a teacher experienced with having students work in collaborative groups

A. Think about each of the following situations. As the teacher of an elementary or middle grade classroom, what would you do in each situation? List your ideas.
- Team members are not working well together and one student is begging you to let her out of the group.
- Two students monopolize the activities and discussions.
- The groups are too noisy.
- One shy student doesn't want to work with others.
- You have an ESL student (a student for whom English is a second language).
- Parents complain that their children are being cheated by having to work with others. One father says his child is gifted and is being held behind by working with lesser-ability students.
- A student is habitually absent and so doesn't contribute to her group's work.
- A student in a group complains that he has done all the work.
- A student in a peer tutoring situation complains that the tutor is mean.

B. Now discuss each situation with a group of peers. How do your ideas compare?

C. Discuss these issues with a teacher experienced in using collaborative strategies. How would the teacher handle each situation?

D. Record your findings in your portfolio.

---

tone of voice that is intimidating or making faces or laughing at fellow students can create feelings of inadequacy. You should discuss these problems, model appropriate behavior, and evaluate group work so that students are not socialized to believe they are incompetent. For example, a teacher can purposefully display as a representation of good work an artifact created by a student who has low self-esteem.

A Belief in the "Right Answer"

Even as early as the elementary grades, students are socialized to believe that there are always "right answers" for problems or exercises. In project-based science classrooms, teachers frequently encounter situations where students rely too heavily upon looking for correct answers. You need to work with students so that they come to understand that many problems or situations in real life have many possible solutions and answers. Reliance on correct answers can cause students to continually seek you out for approval, information, or reassurance. You may need to "wean" students from you, slowly teaching them that they themselves are sources of information, that they can help themselves find answers, and that they have the ability to

find resources and information. You need to help them learn that reassurance comes from completing a project as a group rather than from getting minute-to-minute approval from you.

Activity 5.8 will help you think about what to do if collaboration fails to work well in your classroom.

Lack of Support from Parents, Colleagues, or Administrators

Parents, colleagues, or principals may not understand the benefits of collaborative learning. Colleagues or administrators with differing beliefs about learning may view a collaborative classroom as unstructured, noisy, or time consuming. These people think that teaching is not taking place when the teacher is not glued to the front of the room lecturing, writing on the chalkboard, or asking questions of the whole class. Principals, in particular, can become problematic if they are not supportive of the instructional techniques being used in a teacher's classroom. Pressure to conform to traditional classroom methods such as having students sit in rows or keeping students quiet can destroy a teacher's efforts to develop and sustain collaboration.

ACTIVITY 5.9

How Do I Explain Collaborative Learning to Colleagues and Parents?

MATERIALS NEEDED:
- pen and paper or computer

A. Imagine that you are planning to use collaborative learning in your science classroom. Think about how you will explain your teaching strategies so that others will understand your goals, expectations, and management strategies.

B. Write a letter to each of the following groups to explain why you are using collaborative learning and how your classroom will function:
- the principal of the school
- parents or guardians
- a substitute teacher (in case you are absent)

C. File your letters in your portfolio.

One of the major erroneous beliefs that parents or guardians may have is that higher-ability students are harmed in mixed-ability groups. Research does not support this belief. Findings suggest that higher-ability students do just as well or better in mixed-ability, or heterogeneous groups as they do in homogeneous groups (Manning & Lucking, 1992). On the other hand, lower-ability students tend to fall further behind when they are placed in same-ability groups. Parents may also believe that students are not learning when they are talking in small groups.

Changing people's beliefs can be difficult. One way to circumvent problems is to explain to parents, colleagues, and administrators early in the school year what you are doing and why you are doing it. For example, you might write a letter to parents or to the principal explaining your reasons for using collaborative learning. Another strategy is to invite parents, colleagues, or principals into the classroom to engage them in collaborative learning situations. Make them active members of the learning community, not just observers. You can put parents' careers, colleagues' hobbies, and a principal's expertise to work in your learning community. These community members can become sources of information and potential guest speakers. Very often, such a positive experience will convince them of the benefits of collaborative learning. Over time, parents and guardians will see the positive effects of collaborative learning on their son's or daughter's attitudes toward school. Activity 5.9 will help you practice what you might tell a parent, principal, or peer.

WHY COLLABORATION ALMOST ALWAYS WORKS BETTER THAN INDIVIDUAL LEARNING

Collaboration is an essential component of project-based science. It almost always works better than individual learning for seven main reasons:

1. Collaborative learning environments create multiple, overlapping zones of proximal development so that students help one another. The students also interact with the teacher and members of the community, forming additional zones of proximal development.

2. Collaborative learning has been found to be more effective than other teaching techniques for raising achievement, enhancing problem solving abilities, and developing understanding.

3. Collaborative learning helps spread among members of a group the cognitive load that a task or project might demand.

4. Collaborative learning encourages students to become autonomous, self-motivated learners.

5. Collaborative learning tends to lessen anxiety about learning.

6. Girls and minorities—groups traditionally left behind in science classrooms—tend to become essential, active members in a collaborative classroom.

7. In collaborative classrooms, students develop skills necessary for real life situations.

Multiple Zones of Proximal Development

Trying to learn a new concept or skill without the assistance of others is often very difficult. Have you ever taken a correspondence course or tried to learn something new solely from reading a book or watching a videotape? Have you ever tried to learn a foreign language from an audiotape? If you have, you probably know that learning is more likely to occur in a social situation, a situation in which you can see a new skill modeled by a teacher before you try it out on your own or you can receive the assistance of someone more knowledgeable.

In collaborative classrooms, as students interact with others, new strategies for solving problems are introduced by members of the group. Additional, new, or conflicting ideas crop up. Group members create learning scaffolds for one another. These collaborative interactions foster joint formation of ideas, construction of shared meaning, development of new skills, and the creation of different ways of solving problems. Collaboratively, students advance from a state of uncertainty, frustration, or confusion toward understanding.

In a traditional classroom, students compete with each other instead of helping each other learn. Low-achieving or quiet students frequently try to avoid attention and so don't participate or interact with others.

Elizabeth is an elementary teacher whose class is answering a driving question about the effects of acid rain on the environment. Groups of students are working on different sub-questions. One group of students has decided to collect water samples from nearby lakes, rivers, streams, ponds, and puddles. They have measured the pH of each water sample. Now students are contemplating the reasons why the pH in the puddles, which were created by a fresh rainfall, had much higher acid level than did the lake, river, stream, and pond. After all, they think, a puddle is fresh, and standing bodies of water should accumulate higher levels of acid over time. Elizabeth has the group members write down what they believe are the reasons for this surprising finding. Then she has each student share his or her reason by completing the sentence "My idea is . . ." One student says, "My

idea is the air is very polluted and the rain picked up additional acidity when it fell." Another says, "My idea is there was something on the asphalt that was acidic—the rain was simply absorbing acid from the pavement it was sitting on." Another says, "My idea is that cars sitting on the asphalt put acid into the puddle with their exhaust." Still another student says, "My idea is that the puddle is the closest of all the water sources to a factory." Each student, with a different prior level of knowledge about acid, provides a zone of proximal development for others in the class. After students thoroughly discuss the possible causes of this phenomenon, Elizabeth suggests that they test each of the ideas. She provides suggestions for testing the ideas and of people with whom they can talk. Students call the factory and find out that factory officials monitor the air and ground surface around the factory for pollution. Now they know they can obtain information about the acid level of both the air and ground. One student contacts a local automobile dealership owner and receives information about car exhaust and the environment. As the students interact with Elizabeth and with other knowledgeable adults in the community, they continue to be exposed to new zones of proximal development. Each zone provides students with links to higher learning, links that would not have occurred if students had been working alone or in traditional classrooms.

Effects on Achievement, Problem Solving, and Understanding

A number of research studies have shown that when students work in groups, their academic achievement improves (Manning & Lucking, 1992; Slavin, 1992). Recent research has found that collaborative learning is better for improving problem-solving skills and helping students learn concepts—two important goals of the *National Science Education Standards* (National Research Council, 1996). The zones of proximal development discussed in Chapter 2 help explain why this seems to be true. As students interact with others, disagreements usually arise over ideas, methods to test ideas, and answers. The disagreements and their resolutions help students solve problems: In the process of re-

FIGURE 5.4
A community member shares her expertise with the class.

solving disagreements, students construct understanding, improve their reasoning skills, and enhance their problem-solving skills. They are also likely to form richer conceptual understandings. Attempts by students to validate their views help bring about cognitive change. Conflicts brought about by arguments that cause students to defend their views to one another help some students become dissatisfied with their own views and abandon them. Further, students are more likely to retain material learned in collaborative groups because ideas and relationships are formed and modified via communication with others. When students express ideas with others, stronger connections are formed because students must represent ideas in new ways. Students use **cognitive elaboration**—strategies that enable them to form more detailed, thorough mental understanding—when they discuss concepts, debate ideas, and explain concepts to others in their group.

In the acid rain project, as students discuss reasons that fresh rain puddles contain more acid rain than other bodies of water, they begin to disagree and argue. Some students insist that the factory caused the acid rain, and others argue that it had something to do with the asphalt. Because the students disagreed, they decided to test out all their ideas. As a result of this exploration, students learn that the factory exceeds all EPA air quality regulations, enabling them to rule out proximity to the factory as a cause.

Spread of Cognitive Load

Rarely, in today's world, is there a science topic that is simple. Most topics are interdisciplinary—they overlap various science subjects, social issues, mathematics, and technology. The study of acid rain, for example, involves many disciplines. Understanding the formation of acid in the environment is the study of chemistry. Examining the effects of acid rain on the environment includes areas of biology, geology, meteorology, and physical science. Measuring and monitoring acid rain involves mathematics. Evaluating the sources of pollutants in the air that cause acid rain is a social concern.

Many scientific questions and problems have more than one plausible answer. For example, there are numerous ways to limit acid rain in the environment (limit sulfur burning coal factories, add scrubbers to factory smokestacks, find ways to neutralize acid, and so on). New knowledge in science and technology is increasing at such a rapid pace that journals and textbooks, unless they are electronic, cannot keep up with it. It is nearly impossible for people to acquire, synthesize, and assimilate all the information available to answer a question that they find important.

Most children cannot on their own answer many science questions that arise. In collaborative learning situations, however, the cognitive load is spread among members of the group. Not every student in the class has to answer every question, grapple with every idea, obtain information from all community members, or test all possible hypotheses. The cognitive load of acquiring, synthesizing, and assimilating information is spread among members of the class with different learning styles and intelligences. For example, the student with strong interpersonal skills may want to interview business leaders about efforts to control acid rain, whereas the student with visual/spatial skills might build a model to demonstrate the effect of acid rain on the environment. Some students may read journals and books, while others search the World Wide Web for information. A few students can conduct a scientific experiment, while others interview people in various careers.

Promotion of Autonomous, Motivated Learning

Collaborative learning shifts the responsibility for learning from the teacher to the students. Students learn from each other as well as from the teacher and others in the community. A collaborative environment promotes students taking active roles in their own learning as well as in the learning of others, determining what is learned, how it is learned, and when it is learned. When students take an active role in their learning, the subject matter content becomes interesting to them, and they are motivated to learn. This type of responsibility helps students become autonomous learners who know how to ask questions and find solutions to questions.

Collaborative learning reinforces the idea that effort, not solely innate ability, is rewarded. For example, in a traditional classroom, if a student fails a test, she may conclude, "I'm just not smart enough to understand molecules!" In a collaborative environment, students are more likely to conclude that with effort, time, and cooperation, every member of the group can learn to understand molecular theory. This type of success is motivating.

The collaborative classroom environment is particularly powerful with preadolescents and young adolescents because it matches their developmental needs (Barnes, Shaw & Spector, 1989). They desire peer interaction, want to be accepted by others, need to be trusted to make their own decisions, and crave meaningful learning. A collaborative environment also develops students who are intrinsically motivated to learn, thereby reducing or eliminating the need to enforce punishments or give artificial rewards.

In the acid rain project, Elizabeth explores ways to make her relationship with her students more collaborative. She wants to move away from the traditional role of the teacher as holder of knowledge to one in which she is a co-investigator with her students. She accomplishes this by becoming a learner along with her students—asking questions and exploring with students without ever being certain of the solutions that will arise. She empowers her students' status by behaving as if they have important knowledge and experiences that are useful in their exploration of the problem. The students respond by selecting resources to help them investigate the problem. They read local newspapers, consult reference books, and talk with individuals who work in related fields. Some students choose to investigate the topic on the World Wide Web. Others set up experiments to measure acid rain levels and the effect on plant life. The students become responsible for their own learning. The classroom is a democratic one—both the students and the teacher share in the decision making. The traditional roles of the student and teacher change. In Activity 5.10, you will explore how the role of the teacher changes in a collaborative classroom.

Reduction of Anxiety About Learning

In collaborative classrooms, anxiety, or uneasiness and apprehension, about learning science is reduced for several reasons (Sheridan, Byrne, & Quina, 1989). First, students share ideas without fear of being put down or ridiculed. Peers are not typically threatened by one another, so they can engage in quality discussions, share thoughts, and debate ideas without anxiety. Second, collaborative work tends to be supportive rather than competitive. Collaborative learning classrooms are caring environments in which students are committed to kindness, fairness, and responsibility. Third, in collaborative classrooms, the teacher and the students become allies in the learning process. The teacher isn't an authority but rather a guide in the learning process. In addition, the teacher is not the sole disseminator of information; students play an important role in asking questions, finding information, and sharing what they have learned. Fourth, the collaborative classroom stresses that

---

ACTIVITY 5.10

How Do Teacher's Roles Change in a Collaborative Classroom?

A. With the help of your instructor, a school principal, or school curriculum director, identify two teachers—one who does not use much group work and one who uses many collaborative techniques in his or her classroom. Obtain permission to observe and interview each of these teachers.

B. Observe each teacher. Analyze the likenesses and differences between the teachers in terms of

- the academic goals for students;
- the structure of daily lessons;
- the style of classroom management;
- the reactions of students during lessons;
- the level of interaction among students in the class and between the teacher and students; and
- the methods of evaluation in each class.

C. What do you see as the advantages and disadvantages of collaborative learning? How do teachers' roles change in collaborative classrooms? Record your ideas in your portfolio.

---

there aren't short, correct answers but possibly many answers, interpretations, or solutions to questions. In this atmosphere, students know that there are often many ways to answer a question or solve a problem and that their ideas are as valid as those of others.

The students who are learning about acid rain are very comfortable asking questions. Neither the other students in the class nor their teacher, Elizabeth, will make them feel intimidated for asking questions. In fact, students are encouraged to ask as many questions as possible since it is part of the learning process to answer questions. As students take control of their own learning and become more comfortable in the project-based classroom, their self-esteem increases. Their attitudes toward learning about the effects of acid rain are very positive. Elizabeth finds that, over the course of a school year, she is able to get students more involved. All students participate equally, and they don't seem anxious about learning science. Students seem to like school, enjoy science class, and are concerned for others in their group. This caring environment reduces or eliminates the anxiety frequently observed in a traditional, competitive classroom.

Inclusion of Groups Traditionally Left Behind in Science

Research indicates that girls and minorities lag behind others in their pursuit of learning about science, developing science-related interests, se-

lecting science electives in high school, and embarking on careers in science (Kahle, 1985; Pollina, 1995; Rosser, 1990; Seymour, 1995). Collaborative learning has been demonstrated to be a positive teaching strategy for including girls and minorities in science (Baker, 1988; Manning & Lucking, 1992). There are several reasons that collaborative learning helps girls and minorities. First, collaborative learning removes the competitive atmosphere that prevails in some science classrooms in which some girls and minorities feel intimidated. Second, because collaborative learning demands that all students participate equally in investigating a question, students who may not perceive science as a strength do not "fall through the cracks." They must participate in discussions, investigations, and decisions. Third, collaborative learning develops the social and interpersonal skills of all students, making them better able to work with students from backgrounds different from their own and making them more accepting of others and their opinions or ideas.

American Indians, for example, are underrepresented in science, and many drop out of high school and do not attend college. Although there are differences among Native American tribes, there are certain core values that Native Americans hold. For example, Native Americans respect all life and encourage respect for individual people (Soldier, 1989). They teach their children to solve their own problems and look to their elders for wisdom. Many Native American children are part of extended families in which they learn to cooperate, share, and live in harmony with others. Traditional classroom environments that stress competition for grades, individual work rather than group work, and the authority of the teacher conflict with basic Native American values. Collaborative classrooms, on the contrary, promote cooperation, group work, sharing, and respect for all individuals in a group. Further, collaboration in a project-based science classroom encourages student-directed learning; the teacher is not the authority but rather the guide who might be sought out for his or her wisdom—a concept of teacher that is consistent with American Indian culture.

In the acid rain project, a quiet girl named Maria is confident enough to share her ideas with three other classmates, but she tends to fail to participate in whole-class situations. Maria's family, originally from West Virginia where coal mining is a major industry, believed very strongly in the benefits of burning coal to produce energy. As a result of sharing her experiences with classmates about the economy in West Virginia, others in the group learned to accept her and had greater tolerance for her ideas. They began to explore ways that factories could still use sulfur-burning coal and not damage the environment.

Development of Real Life Skills

Collaborative learning helps develop the abilities and skills students need in real life. The Labor Secretary's Commission on Achieving Necessary Skills (Brock, 1991) identified five minimum competencies (called the *new basics*) necessary for all adult citizens. These are the abilities to work with others; acquire and use information; identify, organize, and allocate resources; understand complex interrelationships; and work with a variety of technologies. To work with others, for example, a person must be able to participate as a member of a team, contribute to a team's efforts, negotiate with others, resolve differences, and work with people of diverse backgrounds. These types of skills are developed in collaborative learning situations.

As students in the acid rain project investigate the driving question, they develop skills they will use throughout their lives. They need to work effectively with other students in their group. This project requires them to communicate with others, compromise, develop new ideas together, and resolve differences. Although they come from diverse backgrounds and have different opinions, they must learn to work together. To acquire and use information, the groups of students need to read the local newspapers, identify appropriate journals and books to read, and synthesize information from these readings. They figure out how to obtain related information from the World Wide Web. To conduct their plant experiments, they need to identify, organize, and allocate such resources as pH meters, plants, sources of acid rain, and locations to take samples. To understand the effect of acid rain on the environment, they have to make sense of complicated interrelationships such as the effects of biological factors on plants, the physical effects of acid rain on buildings and other surfaces, the chemical relationship between sulfur-burning coal and the formation of acid rain, and the geological processes that take place in the atmosphere and hydrosphere. They use scientific equipment and tools that include pH meters, microscopes, computers, fax machines, and telephones.

Activities 5.11 and 5.12 ask you to revisit the activity you completed at the beginning of this chapter and reassess the nature of collaborative classrooms now that you know more about it and to learn about available curriculum resources that use collaborative strategies.

ACTIVITY 5.11

***How Does Collaboration Change the Nature
of the Classroom?***

MATERIALS NEEDED:
- two classrooms to observe

A. Reexamine your answers to these questions
   from Activity 5.1:
   - How are students working together in
     these classrooms?
   - How does the teacher structure the group
     work?
   - Are students given jobs or roles to play?
     Are the roles or jobs meaningful intellec-
     tually, or are they only procedural tasks?
   - Are the jobs or roles necessary to com-
     plete the task?
   - What is the role of the teacher in the
     classroom?

- What are the teacher's objectives in the
  lesson?
- What instructional strategies does the
  teacher use?
- How does the teacher help students work
  in groups (by developing interpersonal
  skills, encouraging students to talk with
  each other, resolving conflicts)?

B. What do you see as the advantages and
   challenges of a collaborative classroom?
   Discuss with peers how these challenges
   might be overcome.

C. How have your thoughts changed (if at all)
   about collaborative strategies?

D. Record your thoughts and observations in
   your portfolio?

SUMMARY OF CHAPTER

In this chapter we discussed the nature of collaboration among students, teachers, and members
of the community. Because collaborative learning
doesn't just happen in a classroom, the chapter
focused on ways to create a collaborative environment, including forming groups, developing
collaborative skills (such as decision-making,
task-completion, trust-building, communication,
and conflict-management), and getting all students equitably involved (through establishing
common goals, building common understanding, labor, and roles). We discussed ways teachers can overcome challenges that arise during
the implementing of collaborative groups.
Specifically, we discussed what to do when students lack collaborative skills and how to deal
with particular situations such as students failing to work in groups or not being accepted by
peers. We discussed how to work with parents,
colleagues, and administrators who may not be
familiar with collaborative group work. Finally,
we discussed reasons why collaboration is almost always better than individual learning,
such as the development of zones of proximal
development; improvements in achievement,
problem solving, and understanding; the spread
of cognitive load; the promotion of motivated
learning; the reduction of anxiety about learning; the inclusion of groups traditionally left behind in science; and the development of real life
skills.

ACTIVITY 5.12

What Curriculum Resources Use Collaborative Strategies?

MATERIALS NEEDED:

- a variety of curriculum resources listed in the following activities

A. In recent years, a variety of curriculum materials that use various collaborative strategies have emerged on the market. Obtain several of the following curriculum materials and investigate them. If possible, use the materials with a class of students:

- *Science for Life and Living: Integrating Science, Technology, and Health.* 1992. BSCS, 830 N. Tejon, Suite 405, Colorado Springs, CO 80903, or Kendall/Hunt Publishing Company, 4050 Westmark Drive, P.O. Box 1840, Dubuque, IA 52004-1840. An elementary science textbook series.
- *Decisions, Decisions Series.* 1990, 1991, 1993. Tom Snyder Productions, 80 Coolidge Hill Rd., Watertown, MA 02172-2817, 1-800-342-0236. Different simulation programs about colonization, immigration, revolutionary wars, environmental issues, and more.
- *The Great Solar System Rescue.* 1992. Tom Snyder Productions. Simulation in which students work to find space probes lost in the solar system.
- *The Great Ocean Rescue.* 1993. Tom Snyder Productions. Simulation in which students work to solve environmental problems about the oceans.
- *Fizz and Martina.* 1991. Tom Snyder Productions. Cooperative learning activities for mathematics.
- *The Geometric Supposer.* 1987. Education Development Center, Inc. Sunburst Communications Inc., 39 Washington Ave, Pleasantville, NY 10570, 1-800-431-1934. Cooperative learning activities to teach about geometry.
- *What's in Our Water?* 1991. Washington, D.C.: National Geographic Society. A curriculum supported with software that allows schools to share data across the country.

B. How are these materials different from other curriculum materials you've seen for teaching science to children?

C. How well do the materials utilize the following philosophical framework for project-based science?:

- **Focus on a driving question.** Students investigate meaningful and important questions that orchestrate activities and organize concepts and principles.
- **Investigations.** Students investigate the driving question by asking and refining questions, making plans, designing experiments, debating ideas, collecting and analyzing information and data, drawing conclusions, and communicating ideas and findings to others.
- **Generation of products or artifacts.** As a result of performing inquiries, students develop a series of artifacts or products that represent their knowledge in a variety of ways.
- **Learning communities and collaboration.** Students, teachers, and individuals outside the classroom collaborate to investigate the driving question.
- **Use of cognitive tools.** Learners represent and share ideas and support their research efforts with cognitive tools such as computers.

REFERENCES

Baker, D. April 1988. Teaching for gender differences. *Research Matters to the Science Teacher* (30):3. National Association for Research in Science Teaching (NARST).

Barnes, M. B., T. J. Shaw, and B. S. Spector. 1989. *How science is learned by adolescents and young adults.* Dubuque, Iowa: Kendall/Hunt.

Brock, W. E. 1991. Continuous training for the high-skilled work force. *Community, Technical, and Junior College Journal* (61):4, 21–25.

Cohen, E. G. 1994. *Designing groupwork: Strategies for the heterogeneous classroom.* New York: Teachers College Press.

Damon, W., and E. Phelps. 1989. Critical distinctions among three approaches to peer education. *International Journal of Educational Research* 13:9–19.

Edwards, C., and J. Stout. 1990. Cooperative learning: The first year. *Educational Leadership* 47 (4):38–41.

Johnson, D. W., and R. T. Johnson. 1990. Social skills for successful group work. *Educational Leadership* 47 (4):29–33.

Kahle, J. B. 1985. *Research matters to the science teacher: Encouraging girls in science courses and careers.* Cincinnati, Ohio: National Association for Research in Science Teaching.

Kahle, J. B., and L. J. Rennie. 1993. Ameliorating gender differences in attitudes about science: A cross-national study. *Journal of Science Education and Technology* (2):1, 321–34.

Kohn, A. 1996. *Beyond discipline: From compliance to community.* Alexandria, Va.: Association for Supervision and Curriculum Development.

Manning, M. L., and R. Lucking. 1992. The what, why, and how of cooperative learning. In *Relevant research,* ed. Marcia K. Pearsall. Washington, D.C.: The National Science Teachers Association.

National Geographic Society. 1991. *What's in our water?* Washington, D.C.: National Geographic Society.

National Research Council. 1996. *National science education standards.* Washington, D.C.: National Academy of Science.

Pollina, A. 1995. Gender balance: Lessons from girls in science and mathematics. *Educational Leadership* 53 (1):30–33.

Rosser, S. V. 1990. *Female-friendly science.* New York: Pergamon Press.

Seymour, E. 1995. The loss of women from science, mathematics, and engineering undergraduate majors: An explanatory account. *Science Education* 79 (4):437–73.

Sheridan, J., A. C. Bryne, and K. Quina. 1989. Collaborative learning: Notes from the field. *College Teaching* 37 (2):49–53.

Slavin, R. E. 1992. Achievement effects of ability grouping in secondary schools: A best evidence synthesis. In *Relevant research,* ed. Marcia K. Pearsall. Washington, D.C.: National Science Teachers Association.

Soldier, L. L. 1989. Cooperative learning and the Native American student. *Phi Delta Kappan* 71 (2):161–63.

Vygotsky, L. 1986. *Thought and language.* Cambridge, Mass.: MIT Press.

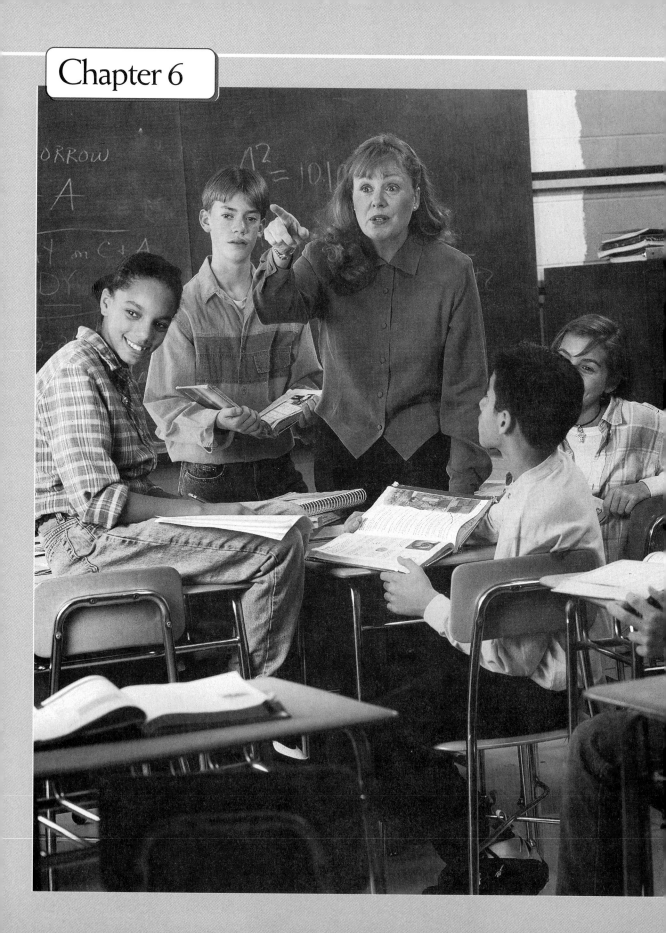

Chapter 6

HOW DO I DEVELOP AND USE BENCHMARK LESSONS?

INTRODUCTION

This chapter focuses on the various ways teachers can represent science content and concepts in benchmark lessons to help students develop meaningful understandings in a project-based science environment. The topic of benchmark lessons raises a number of questions: What is a benchmark lesson? How do I use benchmark lessons? How do I plan benchmark lessons? This chapter will address these and other questions. The chapter will also discuss the use of student-developed concept maps as a way to express ideas. Because good questioning techniques are an essential component of conducting benchmark lessons, we will also focus on questioning techniques to promote student thinking. Finally, we will discuss how teachers can prepare benchmark lessons.

Benchmark lessons are teacher-directed classroom activities that present concepts, principles, or skills that students need in order to understand the work of a project. Benchmark lessons may involve giving demonstrations, facilitating discussions, role-playing, presenting information, making concept maps, going on field trips, and using literature. Before beginning our discussion of benchmark lessons, consider the following three scenarios on the presentation of scientific ideas. These scenarios will illustrate the importance of a project approach and how to use benchmark lessons in your teaching.

Scenario 1: Reading About Insects

Mrs. Patterson, your fifth grade teacher, started class like this: "Okay, let's open our science textbook and turn to page twenty-eight. Today, we are going to read about the variety of insects that live in our world. Karen, would you please read the first paragraph?" At the end of each paragraph, Mrs. Patterson asked a different student to read the next section and made sure to write new vocabulary words on the board. After about twenty minutes of reading and summarizing, Mrs. Patterson said, "Now turn to page forty-one and answer the first four questions about insects. Make sure to use complete sentences and check your spelling." You turned to

page forty-one, took out a piece of paper, and started to answer the questions.

You followed most of the reading, but occasionally you drifted and thought about playing soccer after school. You were happy that you answered the questions in the amount of time Mrs. Patterson gave you. You weren't sure why you were reading about the insects. Some of the pictures of the insects were pretty cool and you wondered if you had insects like that in the school yard or in your backyard.

Sound familiar? Chapter 1 referred to this method of science instruction as *read about science.* Although important new terms are introduced to students with this method, students experience science as a reading activity. The concepts of science are not shown to be linked to everyday life. Reading is an important component of science learning, but when reading about science is not tied to a larger picture that has meaning for students, it can become a routine and uninteresting way of learning.

Scenario 2: Using a Microscope

Mr. Michaels, you fifth grade science teacher, started class by saying, "Today we're going to find out about how to use a microscope." Mr. Michaels gave a number of cautions about handling a microscope and then gave a demonstration. For the remainder of the class period and the next day, you and your partner practiced using a microscope and looked at some "neat" stuff under the microscope. Mr. Michaels wanted you to draw what the objects looked liked when viewed through a microscope. You examined and drew pictures of onion skin, human hair, and a fly wing. You heard "oohs" and "aahs" during class as students looked at the various objects under the microscope. You and your partner did not fully understand why you learned to use the microscope, but you remember Mr. Michaels mentioning that scientists used it to make discoveries.

In Chapter 1, you learned that this kind of science teaching is called *process science teaching.* Although it was awesome to see things under the microscope and the activity generated excitement in the classroom, learning to use the microscope wasn't tied to a larger purpose.

Mr. Michaels used the activity to meet one of the district's curriculum objectives: use scientific tools to make more precise observations. Although you learned how to make observations using a microscope, the observations were not connected to new ideas or to answering your questions. Although at the elementary and middle school level it is important to develop students' skills, skills learned in isolation are often not transferred to new situations. As we discussed in Chapter 4, you don't learn to play tennis by learning one skill; the skills must be practiced in context.

Scenario 3: Observing Insects

Your class was exploring the question, "When do various insects appear on our playground?" As part of your project activities, you were observing when various insects appeared on the playground and in the small wooded area behind the school. As part of your work, you decided to draw the various insects and to write down the date when you first saw them. A number of the children in the class asked your teacher, Ms. Fisher, how they could better observe the insects. Ms. Fisher, noticing your activities, decided that it would be beneficial for the class to learn how to make more careful observations with either a microscope or a magnifying glass. She also realized that a benchmark lesson on microscopes and magnifying glasses would help meet one of the district's objectives: using scientific tools to make more precise observations. She decided to plan a lesson on how to use a magnifying glass and a microscope to observe and identify insects. Ms. Fisher started the next science class by explaining what she had observed about the students and what questions students had asked. She then said, "How can we better observe the insects we see on the playground?" After several students' responses, Ms. Fisher summarized and elaborated on what the students said: "Scientists often use various tools to help them in their work. Tools that can help people better see the insects are magnifying glasses and microscopes." She demonstrated how to use a microscope, showed the class how to make slides to observe various parts of the insects, and gave a number of cautions about how to handle a microscope. She also demonstrated how to use a

magnifying glass. For the remainder of the class period and the next day, you and your partner practiced using a microscope and looked at some "neat" stuff under the microscope. You looked at onion skin, human hair, and a fly wing. "Oohs" and "aahs" could be heard throughout the class as students looked at the various objects under the microscope. Once you knew how to use the microscope and understood the cautions about using it, Ms. Fisher allowed you and your partner to use your new tool to continue your observations of insects. Science was fun, you did some new activities, and you learned how to use a tool to help you answer questions you had about insects.

This third scenario illustrates an example of a project-based science environment and how a teacher uses a benchmark lesson to help students further their work in the project as well as meet some curriculum objectives. The students learned how to make observations with a microscope, but their learning was connected to learning new information that would help them answer their questions. The project and the benchmark lessons exposed the students to new ideas, allowed them to interact with materials, held their interests, and were meaningful.

THE ROLE OF BENCHMARK LESSONS IN PROJECT-BASED SCIENCE

One question that practicing and preservice teachers frequently ask is if activities traditionally performed in school science, such as demonstrations or hands-on activities, have a place in a project-based science environment. As Scenario 3 illustrates, teacher-lead activities do have an important place in project-based science. During a project, the teacher frequently must trigger students' thinking about a phenomenon, present particular concepts so that students will develop deeper understandings of the concepts in the project, or illustrate procedures that are necessary to carry out the experimental work in the project. Often, these benchmark lessons are related to the curriculum objectives of the district or state. Or they may match up with curriculum objectives advocated by national organizations such as the Association for the Advancement of Science or the National Research Council. When activities or lessons are tied to projects, they are known as *benchmark lessons* (Hunt & Minstrell, 1994). Teachers help students learn the principles and concepts of projects by interspersing the project work with benchmark lessons related to content and skills that students need to further their project work. Students can also use these concepts and skills in subsequent discussions and project work.

Benchmark lessons can take many forms: demonstrations, teacher-lead discussions, teacher-lead activities, or presentations of new information involving a variety of visual aids and powerful analogies. They can be as short as fifteen minutes or as long as several class periods, depending on their purpose.

Benchmark Lessons: A Critical Component of Project-Based Science

Benchmark lessons are critical to the structure of project-based science. Benchmark lessons can help students learn difficult concepts during project activities, illustrate important laboratory techniques, develop investigation strategies that they will need to complete a project, model thinking, or stimulate curiosity.

Help Students Learn Difficult Concepts   One of the most appropriate uses of benchmark lessons is to help students learn key scientific concepts and principles associated with a project. Imagine that a fourth grade class is exploring the question "What chemicals are found in the home?" The teacher might use a benchmark lesson to help students develop ideas about chemical properties, chemical change, or chemical reactions. Such lessons might focus on the chemical properties of simple cooking items like flour, salt, sugar, and baking soda. The teacher might explore chemical reactions by showing the students how a gas is formed when vinegar is mixed with baking soda. Finally, the teacher might decide to show a video that explains what chemical changes occur in the mixing of vinegar and baking soda.

Imagine that a class is exploring the question "Is my water safe to drink?" The teacher might use benchmark lessons to introduce students to

concepts such as groundwater, aquifer, runoff, point pollution, or nonbiodegradable. These are all concepts that students must understand to be able to effectively explore the question.

Young children learning about plant growth need to learn some basic concepts as well. The teacher might give benchmark lessons on parts of the plant (stems, roots, and leaves) and functions of plants (plants make their own food, take in water, and give off oxygen).

What makes a benchmark lesson differ from a traditional lesson is that in benchmark lessons students are not just learning the concepts for the sake of learning them. Rather, they are learning the concepts and principles to help them understand and find solutions to the driving question of the project. During a benchmark lesson, it is important to refer often to the driving question of the project so that students see how the lesson connects to their project. If a class is exploring the question "When do various insects appear on our playground?" the teacher might give a benchmark lesson about the life cycle of insects. Students need to understand that insects go through several stages during metamorphosis. Otherwise, they may think they are observing different insects instead of different stages of the same insects. Although the life cycle might be a sophisticated concept for some students to learn, it will be easier for them to understand if connected to the driving question.

Illustrate a Laboratory Technique   Benchmark lessons are also critical for illustrating how to perform a laboratory technique. Again depending on what a teacher needs to illustrate, lesson time will vary. Imagine that a third grade class is exploring the driving question "How can I get large pumpkins to grow in my garden?" As part of the project activities, students are comparing the growth of different kinds of pumpkin seeds. The teacher knows that the students will need to understand how to use a ruler to measure the height of the plants, so once students have planted their seeds, the teacher gives a benchmark lesson on how to read a ruler. First, he explains that to measure the height of a plant, everyone will need to know how to read a ruler. Next, he demonstrates how to read a ruler and has students practice the skill. Finally, he has the class measure a number of objects and compare their readings. The teacher ties the skill of reading the ruler to the students' work in the project.

Imagine a first grade class is exploring the question "What is alive?" As part of this project, students might explore if various seeds are alive and what it means "to grow." As part of the project activities, the teacher wants students to observe a seed germinating, so she will need to illustrate how students might do this. In a benchmark lesson, she shows them a technique in which they can use resealable plastic bags, seeds, and moist paper towels to sprout seeds and watch them grow.

The science activities routinely performed in elementary and middle school are seldom tied to large projects or students' questions, and, as a result, often fail to be meaningful. Tied to projects, benchmark lessons that illustrate laboratory skills have meaning for students.

Build New Inquiry Abilities Teachers can also use benchmark lessons to help students learn important inquiry strategies like asking and refining questions, evaluating information, justifying and building arguments, analyzing data, and drawing conclusions. Again, the time for such lessons will vary. For instance, in the project on the growth of various pumpkin seeds, a teacher might observe that not all students are recording their results in a systematic manner. She decides to review with the class the importance of systematically recording observations. Because the class had explored this idea earlier, the teacher feels that only a short discussion with the class is necessary. However, during the project, the teacher realizes that students will need a way to compare their results. Because the students have not been introduced previously to bar graphing, she decides that a lesson on bar graphing would be appropriate, and she knows it will take several days to teach since it is an unfamiliar concept. See Chapter 4 to learn about more ideas for developing lessons to help teach investigation strategies.

Model Thinking Benchmark lessons are also valuable techniques for modeling thinking. This type of benchmark lesson overlaps with the other types described so far; however, because it is so critical for teachers to model thinking, it

deserves special consideration. During various parts of projects, there will be many opportunities to model thinking. Model thinking includes asking yourself questions, reflecting aloud, and wondering what might be done differently.

Imagine that you want to illustrate to students the importance of questioning information found on the World Wide Web. During a project exploring the driving question "Does my environment influence my health?" students might find information about the effects of smog on the health of young children. One way to help students evaluate this material is to model the thinking process that you would use to evaluate it. For instance, you could model questioning the source of the materials: "Does it matter if the source is the manufacturer of cars, an environmental advocacy group, or a university group?" or "How can I determine if this is a reputable source of information?"

In the project on growing pumpkin seeds and using bar graphs to compare results, a teacher could think aloud about how she came to the decision to use bar graphing. One technique would be to introduce the bar graph lesson by saying, "Today we are going to learn bar graphing so we can compare the heights of the pumpkin plants." Although this tells the children why the teacher is introducing bar graphing, it isn't the most powerful technique because it doesn't capture student curiosity and it doesn't model thinking. Another technique is to model coming to the decision to use bar graphs. The teacher might, for instance, start by asking, "How are we going to compare the data we have on the heights of different kinds of pumpkin seeds?" Next, the teacher could ask the students for their ideas or she could continue to think aloud. She might say, "Let's see. Putting the data in a table might help, but it won't allow me to see trends easily. What kind of visual representation might I use? Aha! A bar graph would let people see the trends."

Stimulate Curiosity Although projects should be propelled by driving questions that students find important and interesting (and also contain worthwhile information), children are children. Their curiosity may need to be stimulated throughout a project, and benchmark lessons can help accomplish this task. It might be important at the beginning of a project to illustrate to students the importance of the topic. For instance, a teacher could give a benchmark lesson presenting information about the largest pumpkin recorded in the *Guinness Book of Records*. The lesson could point out to students that it is important to investigate how to grow large pumpkins, because they might want to grow a garden themselves, and they might want to eat the largest produce or sell it to customers at a roadside produce stand.

Sometimes in the middle of the project a teacher will sense that students are losing interest in the topic. When this happens, it is beneficial to use a benchmark lesson to refocus the students' attention on the goal and value of the project. For example, imagine that students are losing interest in exploring when insects appear. To refocus their attention and get them motivated, the teacher might introduce a benchmark lesson on some fascinating feature of insects (such as the behavior of the praying mantis or the camouflage features of the walking stick). The teacher might also have students share interesting aspects of their project with others in the class. This sharing sometimes stimulates students to become more interested in the topic.

Chapter 3 and Chapter 4 offered additional suggestions for stimulating curiosity in a project. For example, a benchmark lesson in which students go on a walk to observe their surroundings can stimulate curiosity. To raise curiosity in a project with the driving question "How many different birds live in my neighborhood," a teacher might take students on a walk around the school grounds to look for different birds. Discrepant events, discussed later in this chapter, also help stimulate curiosity.

When to Plan a Benchmark Lesson

How do teachers know when a benchmark lesson is in order? There are three ways to identify the need for a benchmark lesson: the use of concept maps, observing and listening to students during a project, and the KWL technique (Ogle, 1986).

Concept maps are visual representations of the relationships among concepts. As such, concepts maps are an external representation of

ideas an individual holds. Concept maps (Novak & Gowin, 1984) allow learners (students and teachers) to link ideas and concepts, helping them construct integrated understanding. By developing concept maps of a project, a teacher can identify the major concepts students will need to understand to complete the project and can plan benchmark lessons. Later in this chapter, we will explore how students can use concepts maps as external representations of their understanding and how teachers can use them to guide the flow of a project and ensure that students are exploring worthwhile science content.

Another way to identify the need and content of benchmark lessons is to observe and listen to children during a project. As teachers observe students during project work, they notice what concepts and skills students need to complete the project. For example, the teacher described in Scenario 3 noticed that students needed to know how to use a microscope and a magnifying glass to better observe insects. That's when she planned a related benchmark lesson.

A third technique is a strategy frequently used in reading instruction, the **KWL technique** (Ogle, 1986). In this technique, the K stands for "what you already know," the W stands for "what you want to know," and the L stands for "what you learned." K and W are typically determined prior to beginning a topic, investigation, or lesson. L is determined after instruction or the investigation. Frequently, determination of L is used as an assessment technique.

Using Concept Maps   Before we can discuss how to use concept maps to identify benchmark lessons, we need to further examine what a concept map is. A concept map is an educational tool used to tap into a learner's cognitive understanding and to externalize that understanding. On a typical concept map, each word representing a *concept* is enclosed by an oval, circle, or rectangle, and the concepts are connected by *lines* and *linking words*. Together, the linking words and concepts form a *network*. A very simple concept map would consist of just two concepts connected by a linking verb to form a *proposition*. For instance, the concept *chemical reaction* could be linked with the concept *products* by the verb *form* to make the proposition *chemical reactions form products*. However, most

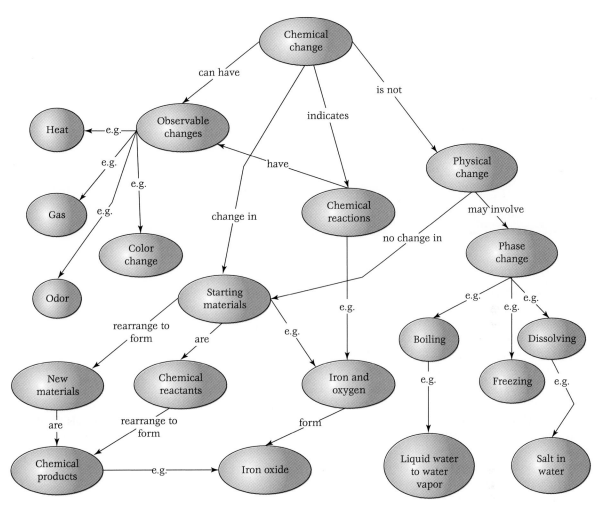

FIGURE 6.1
Concept map of chemical change.

concept maps are much more complex. Figure 6.1 shows an example of a concept map drawn with a computer program. Although there are some advantages to using software programs to draw concept maps, students can make concept maps with paper and pencil, index cards and tape, or even poster board and yarn.

The relationships between concepts are *hierarchical*. The more general concepts (*superordinate*), chemical change, chemical reaction, and physical change, are located toward the top of the hierarchy, and the more specific concepts (*subordinate*), iron oxide and salt in water, are located below, to reflect the degree of their generality. Linking words are used to connect the various concepts. *Cross-links* are formed to show

the *interrelationships* among the concepts included on the map. Activity 6.1 will help you develop an understanding of what a *concept* is.

The mental images you saw when you thought about *dog* are your concepts of *dog*. You might have pictured a golden retriever or a French poodle or a mutt. You probably pictured other associated concepts as well, such as a dog snuggling up to you on a chair or a dog barking and chasing you down the road. All affiliated images form your conceptual map (framework) of *dog*. When you heard the terms *oxidation* and *stomata*, you probably did not see as rich images. In science teaching, we want to create understandings that are as rich and detailed as those that occurred when you thought of *dog*. One goal of

---

ACTIVITY 6.1

What Is a Concept?

MATERIAL NEEDED:
- something to write with

A. Think of the word *dog*. What comes to your mind? What images do you see? Close your eyes and think about the word *dog*. Open your eyes. Write down all the words that describe what you see.

B. Share the list with members of your group. How do your ideas differ?

C. Now do the same thing with the words *oxidation, photon, stomata* or *xerophytes*. Close your eyes and write down all the words that describe what you see.

D. Share the list with members of your group. How do your ideas differ? Note: Just about any word can be used, but the idea of *dog* seems to work well.

E. Record this in your portfolio.

---

science teaching is to develop concepts that have numerous associated concepts and that can grow and change as students learn more information.

A good way to start developing a concept map is to brainstorm all the concepts related to the topic of the project. You can also leaf through books to help you identify various concepts. Once you have developed your list of concepts, identify which concepts are superordinate (the most general) and which are subordinate (the most specific). Identify the most superordinate concept and link it to subordinate concepts. Remember that on a typical concept map, each concept word is enclosed by an oval, circle, or rectangle and that the concepts are connected by lines and linking words. If you are like most learners, you will find it difficult to determine the exact hierarchy on your first attempt. When first developing a concept map, you might use sticky notes, small index cards, or scraps of cardboard because these methods allow you to easily make changes. Place one concept on each index card, sticky note, or piece of cardboard. The sticky notes, index cards, or pieces of cardboard can easily be moved around. Computer programs such as *Inspiration* (Helfgott & Westhaver, 1997) also allow you to make easy changes.

Linking words are used with concept words to construct sentences with meaning. Table 6.1 shows a number of different types of linking words. The first row in Table 6.1 shows general linking words. The second row shows linking words that signal an illustration. The third row contains linking words that show a relationship between concepts. The fourth row shows

TABLE 6.1   Linking Words

Types of linking words	Examples
Common linking words	are, where, the, is then, with, such as, as in the, by the, has
Illustration linking words	is for example, is needed by, is made of, can be, is in a, comes from, is in, determines, depends on, is the same as
Relational linking words	is bigger than, is faster than, contains, live in, is part of, leads to, helps, divides into, is based on, is done to, occurs when, is essential for, involves, depends on, describes, is a kind of
Process linking words	causes an increase, produces, consumes, changes, uses, results in, aids in, employs, is formed from, comes from, goes into, washes away

process linking words, which are used to show how one concept affects another concept.

Activity 6.2 will give you the opportunity to practice building a concept map for a project of your choice. We illustrate the procedure using a project with the driving question "What happens to all our garbage?"

The various concepts drawn on a concept map can help you identify potential benchmark lessons. For instance, in Figure 6.2 because *food chain* is the uppermost concept, a teacher might

ACTIVITY 6.2

Building a Concept Map

MATERIALS NEEDED:
- paper and pencil (with a good eraser!)
- sticky notes, index cards, or scraps of cardboard (or a computer program like *Inspiration*)

A. Brainstorm or use resources to make a list of concepts related to a project you might want to do. For example,

producers, cow, consumers, sunflower, decomposers, fungus, plants, food chain, animals, herbivore, carnivore, omnivore, lion, algae, and bacteria

B. Order the concepts from the most inclusive (superordinate) to the most specific (subordinate). For example,

food chain, producer, consumers, decomposers, herbivores, carnivores, omnivores, plants, animals, sunflower, cow, lion, algae, fungus, and bacteria

Don't worry if you don't get the order right the first time. It usually takes a number of trials to develop a concept map; use sticky notes or index cards to help you determine the hierarchy.

C. Show the relationships between the superordinate and subordinate concepts. Link the superordinate concept with subordinate concepts using arrows and linking words. If there is a directionality to the relationship, use an arrow to show the direction of the directionality. Make sure to include cross-links. Figure 6.2 is an example.

D. Review the concept map you have developed. Share it with a classmate and discuss the connections. After this discussion, make revisions if necessary. Put this in your portfolio.

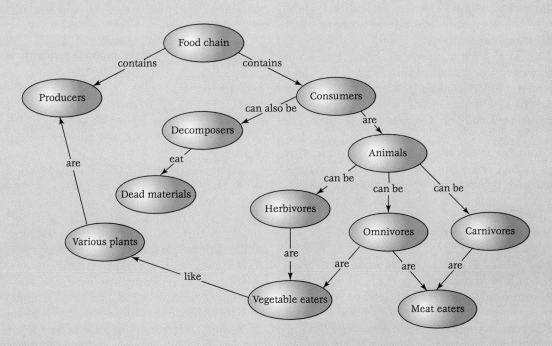

FIGURE 6.2
Concept map of food chain.

ACTIVITY 6.3

Developing a Concept Map to Identify Benchmark Lessons

MATERIALS NEEDED:

- pencil and paper (or a computer program like *Inspiration*)

A. Imagine that you are teaching second grade, and your class is pursuing the driving question "How do we take care of our class pets?" Follow the procedure for developing a concept map to develop a map for this project.

B. Brainstorm a list of concepts or use various resources to identify concepts.

C. Order the concepts from the most inclusive (superordinate) to the most specific (subordinate).

D. Show the relationships among the superordinate and subordinate concepts. Make sure to include cross-links.

E. Show the concept map to a classmate. Discuss it. How would you revamp your map based on your discussion?

F. Identify benchmark lessons that might be used to help students learn important concepts or skills. How did the concept map help you identify benchmark lessons?

---

want to have an ongoing benchmark lesson in which the children in the class create a drawing of a food chain, showing what animals eat what animals and plants. Other benchmark lessons might teach students about producers, consumers, and decomposers.

You may need to redo or expand a concept map during a project. Like the children in a class, a teacher will develop understanding as a project progresses. When you revise a concept map, you may identify additional benchmark lessons. For example, students might become interested in the nutritional value of being a vegetarian. This might lead to new benchmark lessons on various aspects of health such as cholesterol, vitamins, and fiber. Activity 6.3 will give you additional opportunities to practice making concept maps and identifying benchmark lessons.

Using Observations and Listening   A second way to identify necessary benchmark lessons is by observing and listening to your students. During a project, you might notice that students are having particular trouble understanding or applying a concept, employing a laboratory technique (like using a microscope), or perhaps using a procedure (like calculating the mean of a list of numbers). Based on your observations, you could plan a benchmark lesson for the next day. Or you might change the plans for the day and carry out an impromptu lesson. You might

hold a discussion to help clarify a concept that students were having difficulty with at the moment. Chapter 7 contains a more in-depth discussion of listening and observing students during project work.

Using KWL   The KWL technique (Ogle, 1986) is another good strategy for determining what benchmark lessons to use during project activities. As already mentioned, the *K* stands for "what you already know," the *W* for "what you want to know," and the *L* for "what you learned."

Asking students what they already know and what they want to learn helps teachers determine what benchmark lessons to use. The *K* assesses students' prior knowledge and so helps teachers better understand what concepts and skills will be needed in the project. This can identify students' current understandings. The *W* helps teachers develop lessons based upon students' interests. The *L* can be used to develop new investigations—once you have an understanding of what students have learned, you also have an idea of what they still need to learn.

Imagine that students are exploring the project question "When do various insects appear on our playground?" A teacher might start this project by creating three columns on the board, one labeled *Know, Want to know,* and *Learned.* The teacher asks the students, "What do you

TABLE 6.2 KWL Chart

Know	Want to know	Learned
Insects are dangerous.	_____	_____
Insects come from eggs.	_____	_____
Insects come out in the spring.	_____	_____

TABLE 6.3 KWL Chart

Know	Want to know	Learned
Insects are dangerous.	I want to know how insects are born.	_____
Insects come from eggs.	I want to know what insects are dangerous.	_____
Insects come out in the spring.	I want to know where insects live in the winter.	_____

know about insects?" The teacher is not critical of students' answers; she allows students to generate as many ideas as possible. Some of the students' responses are not accurate, but the teacher doesn't try to correct them at this point. Students might say, "Insects are dangerous," "Insects come from eggs," and "Insects come out in the spring." These responses inform the teacher that students need benchmark lessons on insect characteristics, metamorphosis, insect defense mechanisms, and seasons. The KWL chart the teacher is creating so far looks like the one in Table 6.2.

Next, the teacher asks, "What do you *want* to know about the insects?" and records responses. The teacher lets students brainstorm questions for the list. Students might generate questions like, "I want to know how insects are born," "What insects are dangerous?" and "Where do insects live in the winter?" These questions help the teacher plan benchmark lessons on metamorphosis and insect behavior. The chart now looks like the one in Table 6.3.

To begin a study of insects, the teacher has students observe insects on different 3-foot by 3-foot plots on the playground. Once this activity is completed, the teacher has the students list their observations. Throughout the project, the teacher has students update this list and the two columns of the chart, correcting what they thought they knew or adding to what they want to learn.

At the end of the project, the teacher refers again to the chart and asks the students, "What did you learn?" Students might say, "We learned that insects go through several stages called *metamorphosis*," "Insects lay eggs that stay dormant during the winter and hatch in the spring," and "Insects can camouflage themselves to hide from predators." Answers like these help the teacher develop new benchmark lessons such as one on defense mechanisms other than camouflage. The final KWL chart looks like the one in Table 6.4.

PLANNING A BENCHMARK LESSON

Although the best planned lessons don't always succeed, unplanned lessons rarely succeed. Planning is critical for a successful lesson. As a beginning teacher (or even an experienced teacher trying project-based science for the first time), you will spend much time planning your

TABLE 6.4   KWL Chart

Know	Want to know	Learned
Insects are dangerous.	I want to know how insects are born.	We learned that insects go through several stages called *metamorphosis*.
Insects come from eggs.	I want to know what insects are dangerous.	Insects lay eggs that stay dormant during the winter and hatch in the spring.
Insects come out in the spring.	I want to know where insects live in the winter.	Insects can camouflage themselves to hide from predators.

benchmark lessons, thinking through each step. You will need to ask and answer a series of questions: What am I teaching? What are the learning outcomes? How is what I am teaching related to the driving question? What materials are needed for the lesson? How will I proceed with the lesson? How will I evaluate students? With practice, you will find that you are asking yourself many of these questions automatically. However, it will still be essential for you to make plans to structure your benchmark lessons so that you can help students learn what you are trying to teach them.

FIGURE 6.3
Benchmark lessons require careful planning.

Creating a Lesson Plan for a Benchmark Lesson

Think of a lesson plan for a benchmark lesson as a road map. You wouldn't plan a trip to an unknown region without consulting a map. Similarly, you shouldn't perform a benchmark lesson without constructing a lesson plan. When planning a benchmark lesson, it is a good idea to use a lesson plan format. Lesson plan formats vary—the following format is useful for science teachers in a project-based classroom. (Later we will discuss two additional strategies that can be used in the instructional sequence stage: the learning cycle model and the 5-E model.)

Lesson Plan Format

- **Learning objectives:** What do I hope to accomplish in the benchmark lesson? What concepts or inquiry skills will students develop? Will students develop background experiences for the project?
- **Relationship to the driving question:** How is the lesson related to the driving question of the project?

- **Materials:** What materials will I or the students need?
- **Instructional strategies:** What strategies or learning activities will I use to help students reach the learning objectives? Will I use demonstration or discussion, for example?
- **Time required:** How much time will it take to complete the benchmark lesson?
- **Instructional sequence:** How will I proceed through this lesson?

   1. Introducing the lesson: How will I introduce the lesson to the students? How will I motivate and capture students' attention? How will I find out about students' prior knowledge?

   2. Representing the content: How am I representing the content students will learn? What explanations or learning

activities am I using? How will I connect the ideas to students' prior knowledge?

3. Establish links to the driving question: How is the activity related to the driving question? How will I point out to students how what they are learning is related to the driving question of the project?

4. Evaluating learning: How will I determine if students met the learning objectives? What is the relationship between this benchmark lesson and student products or artifacts?

◆ **Cautions:** Are there any dangerous or hazardous components of the activities associated with the lesson? What precautions need to be taken?

Sample Benchmark Lesson Plan Let's look at a specific plan for a benchmark lesson that helps middle grades students develop the idea that when chemicals react, they often give observable evidence. The benchmark lesson is situated in a project with the driving question "What chemicals are in my home?" When developing a benchmark lesson, you need to ask yourself a series of questions based on the lesson plan format. The answers given here pertain to the chemical reaction lesson:

◆ **What are the learning objectives for this benchmark lesson?**
Based on the concept map you developed for the project (see Figure 6.1), you decide that students need to gain an understanding of what is meant by a chemical reaction.

◆ **How is the lesson related to the driving question of the project?**
The driving question was selected so that the study of basic chemical ideas could be introduced to students. This is necessary to help them be able to identify chemical changes that occur in their home.

◆ **What materials are needed?**
You will need about ten tablespoons of sulfur (this can be purchased through any science catalog); steel wool; a magnet; a Pyrex test tube; and a propane torch, Bunsen burner, or Sterno can.

◆ **What instructional strategies or learning activities will you use to help students reach the learning objectives?**
You will use a teacher demonstration.

◆ **How much time is needed to complete the benchmark lesson?**
At least forty minutes will be required.

◆ **How will you sequence the various instructional strategies?**
Students should sit in groups of four. At each table there should be a sample of steel wool and sulfur. Ask students to describe what the steel wool and sulfur look and feel like. Let the students test the magnetic properties of steel wool with the magnet (the magnet will attract to the steel wool). Have groups share their observations. Ask students to come to a class consensus about the descriptions.

Ask students to predict what will happen if you heat the sulfur and steel wool together. Also ask them to give justifications for their predictions. Next have students share their predictions and explanations with the class. Write predictions and explanations on the board or newsprint paper.

Now place about two tablespoons of sulfur and a small amount of steel wool in a beaker. Heat the two materials using a propane torch, a Bunsen burner, or Sterno can. Caution: Wear safety glasses and don't point the mouth of the test tube toward the children.

Once all of the sulfur has burned off or reacted with the steel wool, walk around the classroom, showing the students the material in the test tube. Ask them to describe what they see.

Once the test tube has cooled, pass out a small sample to each group. (Note: You may have to break the test tube to get the sample out of it.) Again ask students to describe what the material looks and feels like. Have them test the magnetic properties of this material (it is no longer magnetic). Ask them to compare what they observed with their predictions. Have them try to explain why their predictions are different from their observations. Have the students share their observations with the class.

Ask students to discuss in their groups what occurred. Ask them if the material that was in the tube is the same as the sulfur and steel wool (iron). Ask them to explain their reasons. Have the groups share their ideas with the class.

Share with the class a verbal explanation of *chemical reaction.* The material sulfur and the material iron reacted (came together) to form a new substance called *iron sulfide.* This new substance has different properties than the original substances. It looks different. It is not magnetic. Tell them that this is an example of a chemical reaction: Starting materials come together to form a new material. Ask them how they know a new material was formed.

This demonstration could be followed up by another showing that chemical reactions usually give evidence. For instance, you could break water up into hydrogen and oxygen through electrolysis (running electricity through it with a 9 or 12 volt battery). With a little practice, this demonstration is not difficult to do. Another idea is to follow up this demonstration with a student activity. For instance, you could have students mix baking soda and vinegar and then starch and iodine together.

◆ **What Cautions Are Involved in Doing the Benchmark Lesson?**
Good safety precautions should be followed throughout the demonstration. You should wear safety goggles. This will both protect your eyes and model good laboratory practice. Also, do not point the mouth of the test tube toward the children. Finally, the test tube will get hot. Do not let the children touch it. Wear heat-resistant gloves or use hot pads. Practice the demonstration before doing it in class.

This sample benchmark lesson was a demonstration, and the instructional sequence provided in the lesson plan format worked well for this activity. However, there will be times when you will want to provide students with the opportunity to explore concepts on their own. These situations call for the use of two different models during the "instructional sequence" stage: the learning cycle model and the 5-E Model. Both models are supported by constructivist theory, because they take into consideration children's prior experiences, and they let students construct understanding from activities in which they have been actively engaged.

Learning Cycle Model   The **learning cycle model** is a three-phase model for teaching developed by Robert Karplus who was a professor of physics from the University of California at Berkeley (Renner & Marek, 1988). It is based upon the belief that students need to first *explore* a concept using concrete materials. After children explore a concept, the teacher can introduce or *invent* the concept by relating what the children explored with the concept that is to be learned. Finally, the teacher can provide opportunities for children to *apply* the concept to a new situation or further explore the concept. Let's look at each stage more closely.

Exploration   In the exploration stage, students are given time to construct knowledge and understanding of a concept. Most students have at one time or another memorized things that had little meaning, perhaps the words to a song in a school play or vocabulary words for a test. There was a little boy who knew his baby-sitter was studying to become a teacher. He asked her on several occasions who Richard Stands was. Each time she said that she did not know. One day the child grew frustrated with her and yelled, "You're going to be a teacher, so you better find out who Richard Stands is!" When she asked him where he had learned about "this Richard Stands guy," the boy said that they pledged to him every day—"I pledge allegiance to the flag of the United States of America, and to the Republic for Richard Stands, one Nation, under God, invisible [as opposed to indivisible] with liberty and justice for all." This type of confusion also happens in science. Students sometimes encounter concepts that are totally foreign to them. Unless they have the opportunity to explore the concepts, develop understanding of them, put words to them, and expand upon them, the concepts have little real meaning. This is the purpose of the exploration stage in the learning cycle model—to provide children with the opportunity to create meaning from phenomena or engage in knowledge construction.

Now, imagine a child about the age of seven who is learning about magnets. She places the magnet near a paper clip, and it is picked up. She places it near a pile of paper clips, and they are all picked up. She slowly moves the magnet across the top of a table, and, to her surprise, a paper clip jumps over to the magnet before the magnet actually touches it. She tries this again. She holds the magnet about an inch above the paper clips, and several jump into the air to the magnet. She places the magnet below the table and moves it around under the pile of paper clips. They follow the magnet across the table. She thinks about the refrigerator magnets used to hold up her schoolwork, so she places a sheet of paper over the paper clips and places the magnet over the paper. Sure enough, the magnet lifts both the paper and the paper clips.

What has this child discovered? She knows that the magnet is attracted to the paper clips, and she knows that the magnet can "go through" air, paper, and desk "to attract" the paper clips. Does she know that this phenomenon is called the *magnetic field*? Does she know that the magnetic field can pass through nonmagnetic materials? Does she know that magnets attract to materials such as iron and nickel? Conceptually, she understands the answers to many of these questions, but she simply hasn't put the words to them.

Contrast her situation with that of the child whose teacher gives him the definitions of *magnetic field* and *magnetic attraction*. Does the child have any real understanding of the concepts this way? Maybe, but it is unlikely that a seven year old really understands these concepts very well after having only been given definitions. Most children will not really understand such concepts unless they have had prior experiences with them. The central purpose of the exploration phase of the learning cycle is to let a child construct knowledge and assimilate new concepts into those learned during previous experiences. The child who thought about the refrigerator magnet holding up her work was assimilating new experiences (of the magnet being able to attract paper clips through air) with those she already has (about magnets going through paper).

Concept Invention   In the concept invention stage, the teacher discusses and provides formal instruction about a concept by putting words to the understandings the students have just created. In the magnet lesson, the teacher might gather the children to discuss what they discovered. Students would share their findings about the magnet being able to "pass through" air, paper, and desk to pick up a paper clip. The teacher would introduce the related concepts to the students, explaining that these findings showed that the magnet's *magnetic field* can pass through *nonmagnetic* materials. Since the students have constructed their own understanding of these concepts, they will be able to use the scientific terminology with much less confusion. The scientific words most likely substitute for the words they have been seeking. A child who has been searching for a word to explain the magnet's ability to "go through" things can accommodate the term *magnetic field* easily into his or her mental structure or schema.

Concept Application   Once a child has assimilated and accommodated new ideas about magnetic fields and magnetic materials into her understanding, she is ready to integrate these new ideas with related concepts. In the concept application phase of the learning cycle, the teacher expands upon the ideas learned, and students use their newly learned concepts and vocabulary. The teacher might engage students in another investigation in which they explore whether the magnet will attract through plastic, glass, aluminum, metal cookie sheets, and other objects. Students expand their current understanding to encompass the idea that magnetic fields will pass through nonmagnetic materials but not other magnetic fields. The teacher might also show a video, have students watch an educational television program, or read related text passages.

The learning cycle stages support a constructivist approach. Students explore phenomena, tie experiences to concepts and reinforce their ideas. Students construct their own understanding and meaning with real materials, and they are provided more than one experience with the concept. The learning cycle, however, must not be viewed as a hierarchical model for teaching. Although we have examined a three-step learning cycle in this section of the chapter, it does not need to proceed in this order. The teacher

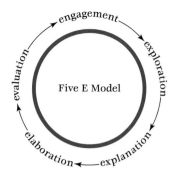

FIGURE 6.4
The 5-E model.

might take three separate lessons to accomplish the cycle. The teacher might also lead students in and out of the various phases several times in one lesson.

5-E Model   The learning cycle has been expanded in recent years by the Biological Science Curriculum Study (BSCS) program into a five-stage model. The **5-E model** shown in Figure 6.4 includes the stages of *engagement, exploration, explanation, elaboration,* and *evaluation.*

Engagement   In the engagement stage, the teacher tries to make some type of connection between students' past experiences and the present lesson. The purpose is to focus students' thinking on the current concept or skill to be learned. There are many ways to accomplish this. The teacher might provide the students with an advance mental organizer (such as telling them they are about to read about electricity), tell a story, create an analogy, recall a previous experience, ask about students' experiences, or remind students of a lesson or investigation done earlier in the year.

In a benchmark lesson used to teach about electrical circuits, conductors, and insulators, a teacher would read a passage from the story *Dear Mr. Henshaw* by Beverly Cleary. The passage is about a boy named Leigh Botts who keeps having his dessert stolen out of his lunch. He decides he wants to build a burglar alarm so that he can catch the dessert thief. The teacher asks students how they think Leigh might build this burglar alarm. This sets the stage for learn-

ing about circuits, conductors, and insulators, and it enables the teacher to find out about students' prior knowledge about electricity.

Exploration   As in the learning cycle, in the exploration stage students develop understanding about a concept by engaging in concrete experiences with materials. They develop an understanding by exploring on their own; the teacher does not tell them what concepts they need to learn.

In the electricity benchmark lesson, the students use dry cells, wires, and bulbs to try to construct their own circuits to light the bulbs. They test various materials in the circuit pathway, such as rubber bands, pop can tabs, coins, erasers, wires, and paper clips, to see if they will light the bulb.

Explanation   In this stage, the teacher introduces formal vocabulary or students verbalize understanding about the explorations in which they have been engaged. The intention is to focus the students mentally on the concepts they are exploring. This stage is similar to the concept invention stage in the learning cycle.

In the electricity lesson, the teacher directs students at this stage to notice that there are two types of circuits: series and parallel. She formally introduces the word *conductor* for the items that let the bulb light when they are in the circuit pathway and the word *nonconductor* to those items that do not let the bulb light when they are in the circuit pathway.

Elaboration   This stage is similar to the concept application stage in the learning cycle model. During elaboration, students can gain a deeper understanding of the concept by engaging in additional activities related to the concept.

In the electricity benchmark lesson, students make a simple switch that, when connected, will set off a buzzer. This extends students' learning about circuits (the circuit is closed when the switch is on and it is open when the switch is off) and conductors (the metal in the switch conducts electricity when the switch is on).

Evaluation   The last stage in the 5-E instructional model is evaluation. In the electricity benchmark lesson, students are evaluated on

---

ACTIVITY 6.4

Planning and Teaching a Benchmark Lesson

MATERIALS NEEDED:
- paper and pencil or computer
- a video camera
- teaching supplies and equipment as planned

A. Using the lesson plan format presented earlier, prepare a short benchmark lesson, no more than ten or fifteen minutes long, on a topic of your choice. You may use the instructional sequence provided in the first example, or you may use the learning cycle or 5-E model during the instructional sequence.

B. Situate the benchmark lesson into a project. What is the driving question of the project?

C. Teach the benchmark lesson to a small group of your peers. Arrange to have your lesson videotaped.

D. Watch yourself on videotape and analyze your lesson:
   1. How did you help students understand the concepts or skills?
   2. What kinds of questions did you ask?
   3. What did your classmates think of the benchmark lesson?

---

their knowledge of circuits, conductors, and insulators when they complete the following task: Figure out a way to "alarm" a lunch box so that when it opens, the buzzer goes off. Students must have working knowledge of circuits, conductors, and insulators to be able to figure out how to make the buzzer come on when the lunch box opens. Some students have constructed the lunch boxes so that the electrical circuit is connected when a piece of metal (a conductor) touches a loose metal end of the buzzer when the lid of the lunch box is pulled up (thus closing the circuit).

The BSCS instructional model, while essentially the same as the learning cycle, clarifies the constructivist theories by stressing two additional items: engagement and evaluation. The engagement stage is consistent with the constructivist model because it provides the teacher a chance to activate or explore students' prior understandings and experiences before starting the exploration stage. The evaluation stage is in accord with the constructivist theory that advocates embedded assessment.

Activity 6.4 will help you synthesize what you have learned about the lesson plan format, learning cycle model, and 5-E model.

At this point in this chapter, you have learned why benchmark lessons are a critical component of a project-based classroom, you have learned some techniques for knowing when to plan a benchmark lesson, and you have learned some strategies for planning a bench-

mark lesson. The remainder of this chapter will explore in more detail techniques and strategies that can be used in benchmark lessons.

USING DEMONSTRATIONS

Think of a **demonstration** as showing something to someone. In a project-based science classroom, the purpose for showing something to students is to prepare them to find solutions to the driving question or to conduct their own investigations. Imagine that a fifth grade class is exploring a stream that runs next to the school. One of the questions that the students want to explore is how the temperature of the stream changes throughout the school year. Before sending students to the stream, the teacher needs to demonstrate how to use a thermometer to measure the temperature and how to use a secchi disk to measure water turbidity.

The Purpose for Demonstrations

Demonstrations can be a particularly effective strategy for benchmark lessons. They can be used to teach a difficult concept, model a new skill, show something that would be too difficult or too dangerous for students to do on their own, or encourage children to question and wonder.

A teacher can use a demonstration to illustrate a difficult concept associated with a project. For instance, during a weather project exploring

"When are skies blue?" a teacher might demonstrate a number of properties of air pressure. Also, a demonstration can illustrate or model a laboratory technique/skill or show how to use an apparatus. For instance, if students wanted to measure pH, a teacher would need to demonstrate how to use a pH probe.

Although it is important for students to experience science for themselves, there are some activities that children, depending on their age and maturity, should not do on their own. Sometimes, the teacher needs to perform a demonstration for safety purposes. For instance, in a project on "What chemicals are found in my home?" the teacher might demonstrate how some household substances like vinegar (acetic acid) and "Drano" (sodium hydroxide) can generate very high temperatures if mixed together. Such a demonstration would illustrate to students how dangerous some chemical reactions can be, illustrate safety techniques (such as the use of a safety shield) for some investigations, and teach students about the properties of certain chemicals.

A final purpose for demonstrations is to have students begin to question and wonder. In a project about "How safe is our water to drink?" a teacher might demonstrate what happens when various substances, such as cooking oil, car oil, and lemon juice, are added to water and how some substances mix and others don't. Such a demonstration could provoke some students to ask, "How do we know what is dissolved in water?" or, "How do we remove materials that sink to the bottom but don't dissolve?"

Presenting Demonstrations to Learners

What techniques should a teacher use to present a demonstration and how can teachers engage students during demonstrations? Demonstrations can be conducted in an interactive manner that stresses inquiry and engages students. In any demonstration, teachers can ask students to make predictions about what will happen and list the predictions on the board. For instance, the teacher can start by asking students what they think will happen when cooking oil is added to water. Next, he can ask students to describe what they see and to compare their observations with their predictions. Again, the

teacher can list their observations on the board. Do all students agree? Finally, the teacher can engage students in a discussion to explain their observations. Predicting, observing, and explaining should be central features of all demonstrations because they help students practice important inquiry skills and they keep students cognitively engaged.

Besides engaging students in demonstrations, teachers need to make sure that all students in the class can see what is happening. Nothing is worse than sitting in the back of the room and not seeing what is going on. Make sure demonstrations are visible to all by standing in an appropriate place in the room, moving students' desks to help them see, or removing obstructions. You may want to refer to Chapter 8 for more information about classroom arrangements.

Make certain that demonstrations do not become dry, boring, information sessions. Students typically find demonstrations more interesting and motivating when the teacher is exciting. This can be your chance to ham it up. Some teachers tell jokes, act silly, or dress up when presenting demonstrations.

Cautions in Giving Demonstrations

Demonstrations can be exciting as well as informative. They can also be dangerous. Fire comes out of a test tube, we hear a loud bang, a top blows off a can, a can is crushed when placed in water. Because of potential hazards, a demonstration is sometimes preferred to student activity. However, there are safety precautions that you, too, must follow when leading a demonstration:

- ◆ Practice good laboratory technique by always wearing safety goggles. At times, you might need a safety shield. Protect your eyes and eyes of the students.
- ◆ Students frequently want to crowd around the teacher during a demonstration. Although this is never good practice, it is especially poor practice during a demonstration that involves safety hazards. Teachers should make sure students are at all times at a safe distance from the demonstration area. Make sure students are not standing in the way of objects that might project toward them.

ACTIVITY 6.5

Heating Water in a Paper Cup

MATERIALS NEEDED:
- a paper cup
- water
- a Sterno can
- a thermometer
- matches

A. Fill a paper cup with water. Measure the temperature of the water. Light a Sterno can and heat the cup of water over the Sterno. If

you have a ring and ring stand, you might want to suspend the paper cup filled with water on the ring.

B. Predict what will happen. How hot can the water become? Will the cup start on fire? Why or why not?

C. What do you observe happening? Record your observations. Explain the observations.

D. How do your predictions compare to your observations? Record your ideas in your portfolio.

- As with any instructional technique, teachers should practice demonstrations before giving them in front of the class. Practice will help you understand what precautions to take and make you aware of what can go wrong. Practice will also help ensure that the demonstration will work when it is performed in front of the class.

Discrepant Events

Discrepant events comprise a special class of demonstrations. A **discrepant event** consists of a grabber—an event that goes against what students expect and thus provides an open-ended question to stimulate student thought. The unexpected event captures the attention of the class, and the open-ended question involves students intellectually. Demonstrations featuring discrepant events can be used to contextualize a project, stimulate curiosity and interest, and provide focus to a benchmark lesson on central concepts.

Discrepant events can be used to grab student attention at the start of an investigation or a new project. For instance, in a project with the driving question "How can I stay on a skateboard?" a teacher can start off the project by demonstrating the center of mass of an odd-shaped object (that appears to defy gravity by balancing in an awkward position). A discrepant event can also be used as the central focus of a benchmark lesson to help students learn important concepts linked to the project. For instance, in a project on weather forecasting with the

driving question "Will we have blue skies?" the teacher might demonstrate the force that air pressure can exert by crushing a pop can with air pressure.

An excellent source of discrepant event ideas is *Invitations to Science Inquiry* by Tik Leim (1981). To familiarize you with some discrepant events, complete Activity 6.5.

In Activity 6.5, you probably did not expect the result you observed; you probably thought that the paper cup would catch fire, and you were probably very surprised that you could boil water in a paper cup. This discrepant event probably caused some dissonance between what you observed and what you thought should occur. As a result, you are probably curious about the reasons for what you have observed. Your interest is raised and you are more likely to want to learn more. Just like you, after students have seen a discrepant event, they invariably ask, "Why?" and they are motivated to find an answer. Students are very likely to remember discrepant events for a long time because they engage them intellectually. Activity 6.6 presents another discrepant event.

Student Demonstrations

Demonstrations don't always have to be performed by teachers. Students can also perform demonstrations. Several positive results occur when children lead demonstrations. First, when children make a presentation, most other children find it extremely motivating. Presenting a demonstration is a good time for students to

---

ACTIVITY 6.6

The Inverted Jar

MATERIALS NEEDED:
- ◆ a glass jar
- ◆ water
- ◆ a note card
- ◆ a group of elementary or middle school students to work with

A. Slowly pour water into a jar. Fill the jar to the edge. Place a note card over the mouth of the jar. Now hold the card in place and turn the jar and card over. Ask students to predict what will happen if you let the card go. Let the card go. What happens?

   Variation 1: Stretch two layers of cheesecloth over the mouth of a jar and hold them in place with a rubber band. Pour water into the jar slowly. What do students think will happen if you quickly turn the jar over? Try it. What happens?

   Variation 2: To add some humor and excitement, have a student sit in a chair and turn the jar and card over the student's head (do this only after you have practiced a few times).

B. What concepts are covered in this discrepant event that serve as a central focus in a benchmark lesson? For what driving question might this discrepant event provide a benchmark lesson?

C. Interview the students. What are their questions? What do they want to learn more about after having seen the discrepant event?

D. Record your observations and thoughts in your portfolio.

"show off" in a productive manner. Second, when students have to present and explain the material to others, they themselves develop a better understanding of the concepts involved. Many experienced teachers realize the value of explaining a concept for the first time. Numerous accomplished teachers have experienced the "ah ha!" phenomena when explaining a concept for the first time. In the process of teaching, they think, "I finally get this." Third, by making a presentation, students experience presenting in front of a large group and practice presentation skills. Such an experience is also motivating to many students because the demonstration is being given to a real audience.

An example of a student demonstration that serves as a benchmark lesson to help answer the driving question "When do various insects appear on our playground?" is a demonstration of how to use a magnifying glass. Early elementary students can demonstrate how to hold the magnifying glass, focus it on an insect, and clean it without scratching the lens.

LARGE GROUP DISCUSSION

Large group discussions are often necessary in a project-based science classroom. Large group discussions help students pull together ideas and arrive at shared understanding of the project. Imagine that a third grade class is completing a project on the behavior of pillbugs. Students have just finished making observations of pillbugs, estimating their size and looking for behavior patterns. The teacher now wants to synthesize these various observations and determine how many of the children agree to them. A classroom discussion is an appropriate strategy for accomplishing this synthesis.

Value of Discussions

Throughout a project, a teacher may want to hold numerous large group discussions. These benchmark lessons do not have to be long; they can last for as few as ten minutes and still provide valuable information to both the teacher and the students. First, discussions can provide teachers with *feedback* regarding how the project is going and let them know if they need to provide any additional benchmark lessons. Second, a discussion can help students synthesize ideas. For instance, during a project with the driving question "Is our water safe to drink?" a discussion about the various water quality indices (such as biological and chemical indices) will serve not only as a *review* of the indices, but also as a way to *synthesize* the ideas. Students will find discussions *engaging* because they enable them to share their ideas and findings. Discussion is also an excellent instruction technique for building *student-to-student interaction*. Students can also hear *different view points* during discussions, which can help scaffold the learning of new ideas.

Leading a Discussion

Good discussions don't just happen. Getting students engaged and able to express themselves is a difficult task. Knowing how to lead a discussion that fosters thinking and student interaction will take much thought on your part. Discussions must be carefully planned out beforehand. A common mistake often made by beginning teachers is to blaze into class and lead a discussion without preparation. Many class periods are frustrating and unsuccessful because the lessons the teacher planned were "discussion." Learning to lead a discussion will be a life-long process. Learning how to lead an excellent discussion will come about only with much practice, preparation, and thought.

How do you start the discussion? How do you help students discuss ideas among themselves and not just with you? How can you help students to more clearly express their ideas? One way to plan a discussion is to prepare beforehand a set of questions to guide the discussion. Asking open-ended questions is critical: such questions promote in-depth responses and foster student-student interaction. "What" and "how" questions tend to be effective: "What observations did you make?" "What other observations were made?" "Who doesn't agree with this and why?"

Techniques for Improving Classroom Discussions

Several techniques can help teachers improve discussion techniques. Wait-time, probing, and redirecting are specific techniques that encourage better dialogue among students, engage more students in discussions, facilitate the flow of discussions, and increase student interaction.

Wait-Time **Wait-time** refers to the amount of time teachers wait to call on specific students after asking a question and to the amount of

time that elapses between a student answer and the teacher responding. Mary Budd Rowe, a former professor at Stanford University, and Pat Blosser, a former professor at Ohio State University, researched questioning in classrooms and found that with increased wait-time, students' responses improved in duration, quantity, and quality; students' confidence increased; the number of questions among students increased; responses from students who typically don't respond increased; and more students became involved in answering questions. These results were evident when teachers waited from only three to five seconds (Blosser, 1990; Rowe, 1996; Swift, 1983; Wilen, 1987). This amount of time allows the students time to think about, reflect on, improve, and elaborate on answers.

Teachers must use wait-time if they want more students to engage in discussions and give thoughtful answers. When you first try to wait three to five seconds, it may seem as though an eternity is passing and as if you are wasting time. At first, you may feel a bit nervous about the "empty time." Science education researchers have found that teachers fear wait-time for three reasons: (1) they feel as if they have too much material to cover to slow down, (2) they think fast-paced questions keep students motivated, and (3) they fear that discipline problems will occur if they wait too long between questions (Swift, Gooding, & Swift, 1996). Research does not, however, support these teacher fears. When too much material is covered, students aren't really learning it; fewer students participate in fast-paced drills; and because fewer students are engaged, it is more likely that classroom discipline problems will erupt with fast-paced questioning. Don't worry that wait-time will cause problems or waste time. Try it. To make sure you really wait a few seconds after asking a question, try silently counting to ten before calling on someone. Most teachers find that with longer wait-times, more students get involved in class discussions and give more thoughtful responses.

Probing Another useful technique for improving classroom discussions is **probing**. Probing is asking students to elaborate on their answers. This technique is especially useful for identifying students' prior conceptions and possible misunderstandings. It is also useful to help students clarify understandings and form new conceptions. Imagine a teacher has just dropped a toothpick into a gallon of water and asked, "Why did the toothpick float on top of the water?" If an elementary child answered, "Because it is lighter," a teacher might assume that the child understood that the toothpick was less dense than the water and move on to the next question. However, the child could mean that the toothpick is lighter than air, not water. The teacher probes the response by asking the child, "What do you mean, it is lighter?" The child answers, "Well, it's lighter. It floats because it is small compared with the gallon of water." This response tells the teacher that the child is comparing the tiny toothpick to a gallon of water and concluding that, because of their relative sizes, the toothpick must be lighter. The child is not comparing the density of the material—the amount of mass in the same amount of space. The teacher probes the child's answer further and, through questioning and further explorations, directs the child's thinking to the idea that the toothpick would float on a much smaller amount of water. Teachers also can probe students' responses by asking for more information: "Tell me a little more about what you mean by that?" "How did you come to that answer?"

Redirecting   Many teachers do all the talking in a classroom. They ask all the questions and provide feedback to all student answers. Sometimes, in the rush for an answer, teachers even answer their own questions. In fact, many students have been conditioned to wait to answer the teacher's questions and *not* to respond to their neighbors' questions or comments. In a project-based science classroom, teachers want students to evaluate themselves and their peers. They want students to have discussions with other students, not just with them. How do teachers accomplish this? If students are not talking to each other, asking each other questions, or critiquing each other's responses and ideas in classes, teachers might start by **redirecting** students' answers to other students in the class. For example, if a child cannot elaborate on her answer or express why she thinks the toothpick is lighter, the teacher might redirect the question to another student in the class: "Anissa, could you provide more information to Jessica's

answer?" "Is there anyone else who could help provide information?" This redirecting is not meant to ridicule Jessica for her inability to elaborate on her answer. Care should be given to make sure that there is a sense of trust in the classroom and that students feel free to give answers without worrying about being wrong or being perceived as failures (see Chapter 8 for more information about class climate). The teacher could ask Jessica to respond to Anissa's answer. This type of redirecting encourages students to talk with each other. It stimulates student-to-student discussions.

Keeping Track of Your Comments

During a discussion, keep track of your comments so that you can evaluate how well you are using discussions. The scheme in Table 6.5 was developed by Vincent Lunetta, a professor from the Pennsylvania State University, to track teachers' verbal commentary.[1] This table will help you complete Activity 6.7.

In Activity 6.7, you will lead a discussion. Try to make responding (student-centered) and initiatory (questioning) comments. Try to ask extended-answer questions that foster an environment suitable for project-based science.

PRESENTING INFORMATION

At times, you will find it necessary to present information to students to further the work of a project. We all learn by listening to what others say. However, there is strong evidence that merely presenting facts will not help children develop understandings that they can apply and build upon. Several techniques, however, can be used to present information in powerful ways. Using analogies and metaphors, graphs, movies or videos and educational television programs, and diagrams or pictures are ways to powerfully represent information. Guest speakers often can present information in interesting ways that tie to a project, and community resources are great sources of information.

Teachers can also present information in more active ways. For instance, teachers can present information to students by setting up

1. Modified from Vince Lunetta (1977).

TABLE 6.5 Tracking Teacher's Verbal Comments During Discussions

Initiatory (talking)

◆ lectures (presents information) or gives directions (for example, tells the students to get out a pencil, paper, and magnifying glass.)
◆ makes statements or asks rhetorical questions (for example, says "The magnifying glass is a good way to observe the insect in your jar.")

Initiatory (questioning)

◆ asks short-answer questions (for example, says, "What kind of insect do you think you have in your jar?")
◆ asks extended-answer questions (for example, says, "How are the insects in your jar alike or different from those found by other students in the class?")

Responding (teacher-centered)

◆ rejects students' comments, answers, or questions (for example, says, "No, that isn't quite correct.")
◆ accepts students' comments or answers (for example, says, "Yes. That's correct!")
◆ confirms students' comments or answers (for example, says, "John's ideas regarding how insects are alike and different is right on target!")
◆ repeats students' answers or comments (for example, says, "Did you hear Lesley's ideas about insect behavior? She said she thinks insects behave this way to protect themselves.")
◆ clarifies or interprets what students said (for example, says, "Do you mean to say that insects are protecting themselves against predators who might eat them?")
◆ answers students' questions (for example, student asks, "Do all insects have six legs?" and teacher responds, "Yes, that is true.")

Responding (student-centered)

◆ asks students to clarify or elaborate (for example, says, "Could you please explain what you mean by 'protect themselves'?")
◆ models questions he or she wants students to ask each other (for example, says, "You will want to ask your partner a question that makes him or her use observations of the insects, such as, 'What color is your insect?' "
◆ uses students' questions or ideas (for example, says, "That idea of protection is a good one. How could we test this idea further?")
◆ asks for other ideas (for example, says, "Does anyone else in the class have an idea as to why this insect is holding up its tail in the air?")

ACTIVITY 6.7

Leading a Discussion

MATERIALS NEEDED:
◆ paper and pencil or a computer
◆ a video camera

A. Prepare a short discussion, no more than ten or fifteen minutes long, on a topic of your choice. Situate the discussion in a project. What is the driving question of the project?

B. Lead the discussion with a small group of your peers. Make sure to videotape the session.

C. Watch yourself on videotape and analyze the discussion. Use the categories in Table 6.2 to track your verbal behavior:
   1. What was the average number of questions you asked per minute?
   2. What kind of questions did you ask?
   3. What is your pattern of asking questions?
   4. Did you use wait-time, probing, and redirecting?

D. How would you like to change your questioning? Record your ideas in your portfolio.

short activities for them. Role-playing, investigation centers, and field trips are also active ways to present information.

Metaphors, Similes, and Analogies

Metaphors, similes, and analogies actively involve students in constructing meaningful knowledge by linking new ideas or concepts to prior knowledge or previous experiences. Educational researchers (Vosniadou & Brewer, 1987) suggest that metaphors, similes, and analogies can help students develop understandings.

Metaphors are a figure of speech in which a word or phrase that ordinarily designates one thing is used to designate another, making an implicit comparison between the two. For example, a teacher might say, "The heart is a pump," or, "Don't eat garbage food." The first metaphor lets students picture the heart (an unfamiliar object) as a pump (a familiar object). In the second metaphor, the use of the word *garbage* helps students picture something that is not good and compares it with unhealthy snack foods.

A **simile** is a type of metaphor that makes a comparison between two things using the words *like* or *as*. For example, a teacher might say, "An exoskeleton of an insect is like a shield of armor," "The iris in the eye is like a shutter in a camera," "Dots and dashes in Morse code are like DNA in genes," or "The arteries of the body are like the plumbing of a house." Each of these similes has students picture a familiar object and then has them compare it to an unfamiliar object. The similes also help students understand relationships between ideas. For example, understanding that a camera shutter opens and closes helps students understand that the iris in the eye opens and closes.

An **analogy** is a comparison between seemingly unlike things that points out a similarity between them and thus infers that they might be alike in other ways as well. For example, "the circulatory system is to the body what a transportation system is to a country" helps people envision that the circulatory system transports things for the body. Once a person has begun to think of the body as a country, it is a small leap to think about the nervous system as analogous to a country's information system. The skeletal system might then be compared with the economy of a country, and the immune system in the body can be compared to a country's military. Such analogies help students make connections among all the things they are learning, improves their retention of new information, and encourages them to anticipate new information, which increases motivation.

Diagrams, Graphs, and Pictures

A picture says more than a thousand words. This old adage still applies and perhaps does so even more in today's media driven society. Often, key ideas can be expressed by showing students diagrams, graphs, and pictures that represent the ideas. The use of these media helps learners form links between ideas, helping them build deeper understandings.

Imagine a class is exploring why the land around the school has the form that it does. Water that cut through the school's neighborhood made a meandering stream. A teacher could describe to students what a meandering stream looks like; however, showing them aerial views of meandering streams or perhaps even an aerial view of the stream in question would do much more for understanding than a description. After showing the students the meandering stream, a teacher could have them describe what they saw.

New technologies such as video disks, CD-ROMs, and the World Wide Web are excellent sources of a variety of diagrams, graphs, and pictures. The images available on the Web can bring real meaning into the classroom. Using a video disk or a CD-ROM might be the better choice for finding illustrations of a meandering stream; however, the World Wide Web might have pictures and diagrams not yet available on video disks or CD-ROMs. Imagine that a class is completing an activity on "Can life exist on Mars?" As of this writing, some excellent, current pictures of Mars are available on the World Wide Web at the NASA site but not available elsewhere.

In Activity 6.8, you will search for images on the Web.

Movies, Videos, and Educational Television

If a picture says more than a thousand words, then a video says more than a book. Although it certainly can be overused, when video is used

---

ACTIVITY 6.8

Finding Images on the World Wide Web

MATERIALS NEEDED:
- a computer connected to the WWW

A. Complete a search of the World Wide Web to find some educationally important images that would not be available through other media. Topics that often meet this criterion include

- current news events,
- recent scientific discoveries, and
- live information (such as minute-to-minute weather maps or global atmospheric maps).

B. How can these images help students answer a driving question?

C. Keep the addresses of interesting and important Web sites in your portfolio.

---

judiciously, there are many beneficial educational outcomes.

Videos can be used to help set the context of a project, and they can be used to enhance the context. A teacher completing a project on air pollution could use a video to show children the influence of acid rain on the environment. Time-lapsed photography would give students the chance to watch the changes that occur on a rock as a result of acid rain. Showing and discussing a video would help contextualize the project for students. The *Jasper Woodbury* series developed by Vanderbilt University (Cognition and Technology Group at Vanderbilt, 1992), the *Scientist in Action* series developed by Vanderbilt University, and *The Great Ocean Rescue* (1992, 1994) and the *Rainforest Researchers* (1996) developed by Tom Synder productions are excellent examples of video-related material available on compact disc or laser disc that contextualize an instructional unit.

Videos also let children experience phenomena that would be too dangerous or costly to experience firsthand. Imagine that students are doing a project on weather and exploring the driving question "What will it be like outside tomorrow?" Although most children never experience a real tornado, videos about tornadoes can represent for children the power of this natural phenomenon without their actual involvement. Similarly, videos of earth quakes and volcanoes also show children the power of natural phenomena in a safe but dramatic manner.

Videos can also be used to raise issues or help pull together a number of ideas raised throughout a project. Imagine that students are exploring the driving question "Why do we need to recycle?" A number of excellent videos could be used in this project. One of the best is the Dr. Seuss video *The Lorax* (Geisel & Geisel, 1971), which raises a number of central issues regarding conservation and recycling in a style that both young and old children (including adults) find entertaining. The *Twentieth Earth Day Special* produced by Time-Warner is another video that raises a number of conservation issues.

Guest Lectures

Teachers certainly want their students to see them as people who like to learn, who are knowledgeable, and who care about their learning, but it would be unreasonable to expect teachers to be experts on all subjects. Guest lecturers can easily fill in gaps in expertise. Guest lectures can offer informed perspectives, share in-depth information, create excitement, and present ideas in new ways. Guest lectures also share careers, serve as role models, bring in resources not normally found in schools, and build community ties. Don't be shy when it comes to asking community members to come into the classroom; many of them will embrace the request with open arms.

Imagine that students are completing a project exploring the question "How do we care for our classroom pets?" This is a perfect opportunity to invite in a local veterinarian to explain to the class how to care for pets. The veterinarian will further explain some of the concepts discussed already in class and introduce many new ideas that will help the children develop better understandings of some central concepts such as nutrition, health needs, and anatomy.

Community Resources

Teachers also have opportunities during a project to make use of community resources. Community resources provide valuable sites for field trips and sources of educational materials and experiences. During a project exploring the weather with the driving question "Will we have blue skies?" a class could take a trip to a local weather station. The local meteorologist could explain how to predict the weather using a variety of different scientific instruments. Although the meteorologist might explain some concepts the class has already explored, he will also bring in new ideas, such as the influence of weather on crop growth and local economies that will help the students understand the material in greater detail, and the review will also help the students develop further understandings of how weather impacts daily life. Students will also be able to see how new technologies and new visualization tools are used in predicting the weather.

Science museums provide students with hands-on displays, interactive experiences, and special programs. Many science museums have wonderful hands-on displays of principles of motion such as large, swinging pendulums. During a project related to motion that addresses the question, "Why do I need to wear seat belts?" a trip to a science museum could enhance children's experiences by allowing students to interact with various exhibits dealing with force and motion. Other community resources are local zoos, parks, hospitals, police stations, courts, radio stations, universities, and businesses. In Activity 6.9, you will explore the educational benefits of various educational resources.

Active Strategies

To enhance the learning that takes place during a project, teachers need to create opportunities for students to develop understanding of the key ideas of the project. Information can be presented to students with active strategies, including role-playing, teacher-planned activities, investigation centers, field trips, and literature.

Role-Playing   Role-playing can cause excitement as well as help students develop deep understanding of the issues, concepts, and principles of a project. Through role-playing, students may explore subject matter and their attitudes and values, which are more clearly seen in these simulated situations. Role-playing can also help students develop greater comfort in expressing their feelings. Role-playing allows learners to put themselves in the roles of experts—scientists, doctors, local politicians, or teachers. Role-playing can also allow children to imagine themselves in situations that they can't actually experience. For example, students cannot see digestion as it occurs, but they can role-play the human body digesting a hamburger.

Placing children in these role playing situations, allows them to "act out" or represent their understanding. This acting out also allows children to develop stronger understandings of what they know because it allows them to represent understandings in another way. Howard Gardner has written a number of books about multiple intelligences (1983, 1993). In these books, he asserts that people have many types of intelligences (verbal/linguistic, logical/mathematical, visual/spatial, bodily/kinesthetic, musical/rhythmic, interpersonal, and intrapersonal). Role-playing is a powerful method of reaching students with strong visual/spatial and bodily/kinesthetic skills, enabling these students to learn in a way that is consistent with their forms of intelligence. Because children act out their understandings during role-playing, it can be considered another form of embedded assessment. Chapter 7 addresses this issue in greater detail.

Imagine a class is exploring the driving question "Why do I need to wear a seat belt?" Students could engage in a role-playing activity about revoking the law that mandates the wearing of seat belts. During a mock court debate, one or several students could take on the role of physicists explaining why seat belts can prevent injuries. Others might role-play scientists explaining how seat belts can cause injuries. Students can also take the parts of lawyers, judges, community members, and insurance agents.

Teacher-Planned Activities   Another way to present information in an active manner is through short, teacher-directed activities. Teacher-directed activities can help students learn important concepts or skills associated with a project. For instance, during a project focused on exploring whether the community has acid rain, a class could explore the concept of

ACTIVITY 6.9

What Educational Value Do Community Resources Have?

MATERIALS NEEDED:
- pencil and paper or a computer

A. On a sheet of paper or on a computer, make two columns—one marked *Community Resource* and the other marked *Scientific Educational Value.* For each of the following community resources, identify a scientific educational value. For example, a radio station can teach students about sound production and broadcast and expose them to a science-related career.

Community resource	Scientific educational value
radio station	◆ teach students about careers ◆ teach students about sound production and broadcast
zoo	
park	
hospital	
police station	
fire station	
library	
water treatment plant	
sewage treatment plant	
court	
universities	
retail businesses:	
photocopy store	
grocery store	
pet store	
bookstore	
welding business	
furnace and air-conditioning business	
restaurant	
gas station	
auto dealership	
mechanics shop	

B. Select one community resource and an elementary or middle school in your own geographic area. Pretend you are teaching at the school. How would you answer the following questions?
1. What is educational about a field trip to this location? Is there a clear purpose for going there?
2. What travel arrangements could you make?
3. Who would handle the arrangements?
4. Is there any legal liability? Do you need parents' permission? Does the community resource have any particular rules concerning student age, safety, or behavior?
5. What is the cost?
6. How long would the trip take?
7. What is the area of expertise of the people at the community resource?
8. Do these people know how to handle and talk to children?
9. What arrangements will you make to visit the location yourself in advance so that you know what the students will encounter?
10. What is the phone number of the resource person to contact?
11. How much lead time is required to arrange a trip to this resource?
12. How will you keep track of the students when you are there? Will you need parent assistance?

C. If possible, contact this community resource and find out the answers to the questions you were unable to answer on your own. What have you learned about community resources? Record this in your portfolio.

acidity by first investigating the acidity of various household materials. Next, students might explore how acids affect different materials. Such activities would need to be teacher-directed since they would involve potentially dangerous chemicals and since students would not necessarily be able to envision how to arrange them on their own.

Teacher-directed activities also help children learn how to use various scientific instruments, like microscopes, graduated cylinders, or rulers. The teacher might lead a classroom activity in which students learn how to use a pH meter by measuring the pH of various household chemicals like bleach, ammonia, shampoo, and detergent.

A teacher-lead activity on how to use an instrument is an efficient strategy; however, for such an activity to have meaning for the learner, it must also be related back to the project. Students must understand that learning how to use a pH meter is related to their driving question about acid rain.

Investigation Centers   Another way to actively engage students in learning concepts, principles, or skills is to have students work at **investigation centers.** Investigation centers are self-instructional science learning activities that help small groups of students learn particular science concepts, principles, or laboratory skills associated with a project. Investigation centers typically provide a set of detailed instructions for students to follow on their own without further direction and science materials needed to complete the activity. An investigation center need not be elaborate—it can be as simple as a shoe box containing the materials, instructions, and maybe a list of instructional objectives, a glossary of scientific terms, and a posttest for assessing learning. Usually, the center requires the learner to submit a product (such as observations, a posttest, or a self-evaluation checklist) to the teacher.

Imagine that a class is investigating how many birds visit the classroom bird feeder. One possible instructional objective is for students to notice subtle differences among birds so that they can identify them. The teacher might set up an investigation center where students examine subtle differences among several objects such as sea shells, buttons, or nuts, bolts, and screws. By investigating differences (such as size, shape, color, and luster), students improve their observation skills. After this activity, the teacher might set up an investigation center near the window with the bird feeder where students use a bird guide to identify the types of birds coming to the feeder. After completing the independent activities, students might turn in an observation sheet describing the different types of buttons they found and a checklist of birds they saw at the feeder.

Field Trips   During a project, many opportunities to make connections with the community will arise. Let's continue to explore the investigation of "What birds live near school?" One project-related opportunity is a visit to a zoo to learn about birds that live in different environments. Students might take a field trip to a local natural preserve or wildlife refuge to see what other types of birds live there. Field trips, like other strategies for presenting information, should be related to project activities. Such related activities help students build a deeper understanding of the concepts and principles being explored in the project.

Field trips in the community do not need to be elaborate. Often the best trips are those around the school such as visits to streams, ponds, fields, woods, or playgrounds. Have students mark off a 1-meter by 1-meter area of the playground and record everything they see and hear in the area during a five- or ten-minute period. They will learn a great deal from this simple field trip about the animals and plants that live in the area, and they will learn about people from the litter they find.

Make sure children know the purpose of the field trip. To prepare students for a trip to a community resource, use the KWL model (Ogle, 1986). Ask students what they know (K) about the location you are visiting. List their ideas on the board or have students record them. Next, have students tell what they want to learn (W). Again, record these questions or ideas. After the trip, summarize what was learned (L). Record these ideas, too. Another technique is to give students a list of questions they need to answer during the trip or on the bus back from the trip. Providing students the questions ahead of time gives them an advanced organizer for focusing their attention during the trip.

Activity 6.10 asks you to prepare another benchmark lesson. The purpose is for you to continue to synthesize what you have learned about benchmark lessons.

USING LITERATURE

Reading is a critical aspect of project-based science. Through reading, students can learn valuable background information, they can find information related to their projects, and they can

---

ACTIVITY 6.10

Planning and Teaching Another Benchmark Lesson

MATERIALS NEEDED:
- paper and pencil or a computer
- a video camera
- teaching supplies and equipment

A. Prepare a short benchmark lesson, no more than twenty to thirty minutes long, on a topic of your choice. Situate the benchmark lesson in a project. What is the driving question of the project? Make sure you use some of the strategies already discussed, such as demonstrations, discussion, activity centers, and role-playing.

B. Teach the lesson to a small group of your peers. Videotape the lesson.

C. Watch yourself on videotape and analyze your lesson:
  1. What strategies did you use?
  2. How did you help students understand the concepts?
  3. What kind of questions did you ask?
  4. What would you do different next time? What would you change? What would you keep the same?

---

learn new ideas associated with the project work. Reading, abstracting information, and evaluating what is read is a central focus of project work.

Many teachers new to project-based science think that students don't read in a project environment. While this is not the case, it is true that in project-based science students don't read from a single textbook. As they explore their question, they read from a variety of sources, including various textbooks, magazines, trade books, newspapers, and World Wide Web postings. For example, during a project related to air quality, sixth grade students might search the Web for related articles, read the local paper, and read trade books about pollution. In a project about insects in the neighborhood, first graders might look through insect picture books to identify insects they found.

Children's Literature

Children's literature and trade books can serve as powerful resources in a project-based science environment. With its illustrations and high accessibility, children's literature tends to capture the attention of students in a way that textbooks don't. Children's literature prompts children to *imagine* science concepts, and the writing often relates concepts to the lives of children.

Imagine that a class is exploring the driving question "Will humans always be on earth?" As part of the project, the teacher needs to teach a benchmark lesson on dinosaurs. Dinosaurs are

FIGURE 6.5
Children use various printed resources to find information related to their project.

one of those topics that are difficult to teach since dinosaurs are not around for students to observe. However, children's literature provides an excellent resource for teaching about these magnificent creatures. *Dinosaur Dreams* (1990) by Dennis Nolan (New York: Macmillan Publishing) helps children imagine what life would be like if dinosaurs still lived today. *My Visit to the Dinosaurs* (1969) by Aliki Brandenburg (New York: Harper & Row) tells children about characteristics of dinosaurs. *Dinosaur Babies* (1991) by Lucille Recht Penner (New York: Random House) explains how dinosaurs hatched from eggs and how they survived. *Digging up Dinosaurs* (1981) by Aliki Brandenburg (New York: Harper & Row) teaches children how archaeologists find dinosaur fossils and learn about dinosaurs from the fossil remains. *The Day of the Dinosaur* (1987) by Stan and Jan Berenstain (New York: Random House) tells children all about dinosaurs. *How Big Is a Brachiosaurus?* (1986) by Frederic Marvin (New York: Platt & Munk Publishers, a division of Grosset & Dunlap, Inc.) helps children conceptualize the size of a Brachiosaurus by relating it to the size of more familiar objects. Give children's literature a try; many teachers find that it is a great resource for the science classroom.

If you are not familiar with children's literature, your first stop should be the children's section of a local library or bookstore. Children's librarians are usually very eager to assist you in locating books on a given topic. The National Science Teachers Association's journals, *Science and Children* and *Science Scope,* publish annual lists of recommended children's literature stories that can be used to teach science. These journals also often feature reviews of new books. The number of children's stories and trade books available today is enormous, so these reviews are excellent ways to keep up on what is being published. Other good sources of ideas for using children's literature in science include the following:

Brainard, A., and D. H. Wrubel. 1993. *Literature-based science activities: An integrated approach.* New York: Scholastic.

Butzow, C. M., and J. W. Butzow. 1989. *Science through children's literature: An integrated approach.* Englewood, Colo.: Teacher Ideas Press.

Cerbus, D. P. 1991. *Connecting science and literature.* Huntington Beach, Calif.: Teacher Created Materials, Inc.

Gertz, S. E., D. J. Portman, and M. Sarquis. 1996. *Teaching physical science through children's literature.* Learning Triangle Press. New York.

Mayberry, S. C. 1994. *Linking science with literature.* Greensboro, N.C.: Carson-Dellosa Publishing Company, Inc.

Staton, H. N., and T. McCarthy. 1994. *Science and stories: Integrating science and literature—Grades K–3.* Glenview, Ill.: Goodyear Books.

Staton, H. N., and T. McCarthy. 1994. *Science and stories: Integrating science and literature—Grades 4–6.* Glenview, Ill.: Goodyear Books.

Magazines and Periodicals for Children

There are many magazines and periodicals written for children that make great resources in a project-based science environment. These resources can be used to broaden the context of a project, present new information, or review ideas explored previously in project work. Just like literature books, children's magazines and periodicals are written to capture children's attention, and they are filled with wonderful illustrations and photographs. In addition, because magazines and periodicals are printed monthly or quarterly, they contain more up-to-date information than do books. Activity 6.11 will familiarize you with some of these resources and help you identify ways to use them in the classroom.

The World Wide Web

Resources found on the World Wide Web have several advantages over text-based materials. First, the content is more current. Using resources on the Web, students can obtain information that may be just minutes old. For example, weather data are continuously updated on the Web. Second, the Web offers a great deal of primary-source material, firsthand information. For example, weather data comes from the U.S. National Oceanic and Atmospheric Administration (NOAA); there is no more primary source of these data. Scientists, too, use NOAA's databases for this reason. Third, Web content is comprehensive. In typical libraries used by children, only subsets of popular and scholarly material on a given subject are available. The Web widely expands the range of content enormously thereby giving students access to an unprecedented range of information sources. For example, although students will find plenty of information about weather in books found in the library, the WWW contains an enormous

---

ACTIVITY 6.11

How Can I Use a Children's Science Magazine?

MATERIALS NEEDED:
- pencil and paper or a computer
- one or more of the following children's magazines (visit your local library, if necessary):
  - *Ranger Rick*
  - *My Big Back Yard*
  - *Science World*
  - *The Curious Naturalist*
  - *World*
  - *Zoo Books*

A. Read through as many magazines as you can. Identify ways you could use these resources in a project-based science environment. What would be the driving question of the project? How could you use the magazine in a benchmark lesson?

B. If possible, have an elementary or middle school student look through each of the magazines. Interview the student about his or her opinion of the magazines. What do students like and dislike about them?

C. Record the ideas in your journal.

---

amount of information about weather phenomena including real-time weather maps, satellite images of hurricanes, and historical data on weather patterns. Fourth, Web resources are represented in various formats, including digital form, which can then be manipulated easily by students. Information can also be conveyed through video and sound—imagine dynamic views of the ozone holes and the sounds of a tornado. These new ways of conveying information are particularly helpful for students who are visual/spatial learners. Fifth, students can publish their own work on-line, sharing it with a wide audience. Many students find this sharing valuable and motivating, because immediate contact with others makes their work more meaningful. Sixth, Web content is readily accessible. Information on the Web is in a single source, obtainable from a single point of access (the computer).

Clearly, the World Wide Web offers a wide range of learning opportunities. However, some of the Web's advantages have the potential to become disadvantages. Although advanced learners might find it valuable to read from the same sources that scientists do, such material presents the possibility of confusing young learners. Also, the materials available on the Web are sometimes too comprehensive and difficult to sift through for a young student. Projects like the University of Michigan's Middle Years Digital Library project (http://www.umich.edu/~aaps/) provide a structured environment in which sixth, seventh, and eighth grade students can have positive and productive Web experiences.

Making Sense of Written Material

The most difficult aspect of reading is making sense of what is read. Students can use a number of strategies to help them construct meaning from text. One strategy is to ask a variety of questions before, during, and after reading. Before a student starts to read, he might ask himself, "What do I want to learn from reading this text?" During reading he might ask, "What are the author's goals and purposes?" After reading, he might ask, "How can I summarize what I just read?" Table 6.6 lists a variety of questions that students can ask to make meaning of text.

Another key aspect of reading is monitoring what is read. A learner might ask, "Do I understand what I just learned?" Evaluation is another critical habit that good readers employ consistently. A learner might ask, "Do I agree with arguments made in the text?" Table 6.7 lists questions that learners can ask themselves to help monitor and evaluate the materials they are reading.

CONCEPT MAPS

Concept maps are visual representations of the relationship concepts have with one another and, as such, make external representations of understanding. Concept mapping empowers learners by making them aware of their own thinking. Concept maps help learners develop meaningful understanding by structuring the information into long-term memory (Eggen & Kauchak, 1992), thereby connecting or linking new ideas or experiences with existing ones.

TABLE 6.6   Constructing Meaning from Text

Before reading

- What are my goals for reading this text? What do I want to learn?
- How can I use the text structure to help me learn? (headers, side bar questions, key words)
- Which parts of this text will most likely contain relevant information (for my goal)?
- What are my initial ideas about what the text is about?
- How might this text or reading relate to what I already know?

During reading

- What is the important information?
- Where are the key words?
- Where are the topic sentences?
- What are the writer's goals and purposes?
- What was the last sentence or section about?
- What do I think will happen next?
- What were my initial ideas about the materials? Were they correct? If not, what are some new ideas?

After reading

- Am I rereading sections that were unclear?
- What important information is in the text?
- How did my ideas work out? Why?
- How can I summarize the material?
- Do I understand what I read?

TABLE 6.7   Monitoring and Evaluating Text Materials

Monitoring

- Am I finding appropriate information for my goal?
- Do I reread sections when I need to?
- Do I agree with what the author said?
- Am I finding definitions to unfamiliar terms?

Evaluating

- Do I agree with arguments made in the text?
- Are the examples clear?
- Is the writing clear?
- Is the content trustworthy? Can I believe the material?
- What are my reactions to the text?

Each link in the network increases the meaningfulness of the concept, because it represents a connection with another related topic. Through this networking, the learner develops a working schema. Once information is stored, mapping aids in the retrieval of the information from long-term memory and facilitates through a greater number of associations the transfer of a new idea to another setting. Through mapping, learners can take charge of their learning—in essence, they can learn how to learn.

Joseph Novak, a professor at Cornell, created the concept map as a tool to assess the changes in conceptual learning that were occurring in the science students he was studying over a twelve-year span of schooling (Novak & Gowin, 1984). However, assessment is only one way to use concept mapping in project-based science. Concept maps can be used before a project starts. This technique helps students elicit their understandings prior to the project, giving an indication of students' initial understandings. Using concepts maps is an excellent way for students to track the concepts they are developing during a project and integrate them with the understandings they are developing. As the project continues, students make new concept maps, helping them form links between concepts. By comparing earlier versions of their concept maps with later versions, students see how their conceptual understandings are developing. Another useful approach is to have students compare their concept maps with those of other students. This technique allows them to see the connections formed by other students, sparking new connections for themselves. Concept maps developed at the end of a project help students tie together the concepts explored and serve as a form of assessment (see Chapter 7 for more assessment information). For additional ideas on how to use concept mapping with young children see Novak and Gowin, 1984.

Issues to Consider When Using Concept Maps

There are a number of issues you need to consider when introducing students to concept maps:

Concept mapping is a very difficult cognitive activity for most children (as for most adults). Don't be surprised to find students dislike making concept maps. One way to help students learn about concept maps and see their value is to have them start by creating concept maps of familiar things—the grocery store, movies, songs, or sports. The maps they create about what is familiar will flow easily and show students how rich their ideas are. This activity also isolates learning about concept maps from learning about a particular concept, focusing students' attention and energy on one learning task at a time. For example, if students don't know how to create a concept map and they are trying to map new ideas related to decomposition, they will struggle with both making the map and understanding the links among the new concepts.

Students don't always recognize all of the concepts that can go in a concept map. You need to help students identify additional concepts. One way to do this is to have students brainstorm concepts and ideas. For example, you might have students brainstorm ideas about rooms in a home, such as a bedroom, a bathroom, a garage, a kitchen, a den, and a basement. Then, they might brainstorm as many things as they can that might go in a garage. By brainstorming as a class, students usually exhaust most possibilities of concepts that should be included on a map. Some teachers keep a running list of concepts and ideas that they have taught. Students can be encouraged to add to the list when they find new concepts. This makes them aware on a daily basis of the new concepts they are learning, and it provides them with a prompt of ideas for mapping. Finally, some teachers help students identify concepts that should be included in a map by having them refer to field trips, guest speakers, textbooks, books, activities, the Web, and other project materials and experiences. The act of remembering all that has been experienced during the course of the project often will help students remember concepts that should be included on the map.

Students will show reluctance to creating a hierarchy. You need to encourage students to search for inclusive concepts and order less-inclusive concepts under more-inclusive ones. Again, a useful strategy to

help students learn how to develop hierarchy is to pick a familiar concept, like a home, and elaborate on all the subconcepts associated with it. First, have students identify rooms in a home. Second, have students list what is found in these various rooms. Third, develop the hierarchy of the concepts listed. For example, the rooms in a home (such as a bathroom) can be superordinate concepts, and the things found in the room (such as tissue paper, soap, shampoo, and toothpaste) are subordinate concepts. Record each concept on sticky notes, index cards, or scraps of cardboard so that students can easily move them around. Fourth, have students share their ideas with a partner and together generate a hierarchy. By working with others, students usually see new and more detailed ways to link ideas.

Students sometimes fail to use linking words to connect concepts in a concept map. Linking words are critical in clearly communicating hierarchical relationships. Stress to students the importance of selecting linking words. At first, you will need to help students choose good linking words. Posting a chart similar to the one in Table 6.1 will give students a resource of potential linking words to use. You might pair students and have them discuss the relationships among the concepts. As one student tells the other about the relationships among the concepts, the other double-checks the meaning and then writes down the linking words on the line connecting the ideas. A conversation between students might sound like this:

"I connected the rooms like *bathroom, garage, mom and dad's bedroom, my sister's bedroom, kitchen,* and *family room* all to the word *house* because they are all in the house."

"So these rooms are all in a house?"

"Yeah."

"So, we could say the link is *contains a*—the house *contains a* bedroom, bathroom, etc."

"Yeah, that's right. Write down 'contains a' on each of those lines."

Students frequently don't use arrows on their links. You need to encourage students to do so, however, because arrows show the direction of relationships, and it is crucial for students to indicate direction. Pairing students, as described, can help students use arrows. Another way to stress the value of arrows is by asking questions of students as they work on their maps. For example, you could ask, "So, are you saying that a bathroom is made of toothpaste?" Children will laugh and say, "No. Toothpaste is found in a bathroom!" You might then say, "Oh, so what direction should the arrow go so that I don't get confused about that?"

Students are unlikely to produce good maps on the first attempt. To encourage better maps, have students revisit and redraw their maps whenever possible throughout a project. Students very often will be surprised to compare their initial maps to their final project maps. Filing maps in portfolios is an excellent way to track how students' understandings change throughout a project. Show that you value the process of revision by giving students time to work on their maps. Show that you value the revisions themselves by having students compare, in class discussions, how their maps have changed or by acknowledging improvement on maps (either with verbal praise, points, or grades).

USING QUESTIONS

Questioning is a central aspect of project-based science teaching. Why is this so? It is important to have children manipulate real materials, but manipulating materials is not an end in itself. Hands-on science is a means to the end, an end that requires students to be mentally engaged in the process. Questioning is one of the key ways to engage students mentally.

Project-based science teachers seek out and use students' questions and ideas to guide lessons and projects. They encourage students to discuss, elaborate upon their response, and challenge others' ideas. Questioning techniques help the teacher identify prior conceptions, understandings, and possible misconceptions. These techniques also help students create, refine, and elaborate upon their understandings.

Types of Questions

Over the last few decades, many researchers have examined questioning strategies used in classrooms. Researchers have found that teachers ask many questions. Unfortunately, most questions are too low level and factually oriented (Gall, 1984; Wilen, 1987). This means that teachers ask questions that only require students to *tell* about, *define*, *recite*, *list*, or *identify*. Few questions ask students to *analyze*, *differentiate*, *contrast*, *imagine*, *create*, *prove*, or *evaluate* things. In other words, most teachers are simply stressing rote memorization of factual material. In a project-based science classroom, higher level questions need to be stressed.

The types of questions teachers ask will greatly affect the quality of the answers they receive from students and the character of classroom discourse. Educators classify questions as divergent and convergent or higher order and lower order. Here we will put questions into two general classifications: higher level and lower level. **Higher level questions** require complicated thinking, such as evaluation, synthesis, or application. **Lower level questions** can often be answered without understanding of ideas or much thinking.

Consider this question: "What is the best way to clean up an oil spill?" The question has more than one answer, requiring students to think about multiple possibilities and evaluate the best one. The question takes more intellectual thought than just, for example, recalling an explanation given in a textbook. Now consider this question: "What is a vertebrate?" This question is a lower level question, that narrows the thinking of the learner to one scientifically acceptable answer. A student could also simply memorize a definition for the word *vertebrate* without having a true understanding of the concept.

Teachers want to plan what major questions they will ask in a benchmark lesson. Although a lesson should always be flexible—lessons would probably resemble drills if teachers did not allow for deviation from planned questions—few effective teachers let all questions surface serendipitously during a lesson. They usually plan in advance a list of higher level questions to cover during the lesson.

Table 6.8 presents a classification scheme for both lower level and higher level questions. These clue words in Table 6.8 will help you plan

TABLE 6.8 Question Classification Scheme*

	Level of question	Clue words
Lower level questions	Knowledge	Give me the *definition* of . . .
		Locate the word for . . .
		List examples of . . .
		Name as many . . .
	Comprehension	*Describe* what happens when . . .
		Retell what happened when . . .
		Explain what . . .
		What are some . . .
Higher level questions	Application	*Make use of* the information . . .
		Produce an example of . . .
		Illustrate how you could . . .
		Apply what you learned to . . .
	Cause and Effect	*Explain* the effect that A had on B.
		Tell what caused this.
		What are some reasons for this effect?
	Analysis	*Differentiate* between . . .
		Analyze this situation to . . .
		Compare and contrast the . . .
		Give an *alternative way* to . . .
	Synthesis	*Create* a new way to . . .
		Invent an alternative to . . .
		Improve this situation by . . .
		Produce a way to . . .
	Evaluation	*Decide* if you would . . .
		Prove that . . .
		Judge the circumstances in . . .
		Evaluate the situation and . . .

* From Bloom (1956).

lessons, form questions, and facilitate higher level thinking. Although at times you will want to ask lower level questions, the most effective questioning you do will be questioning that sparks higher order thinking.

In Activity 6.12, you will determine the levels of questions and practice writing your own higher level questions.

As you can see, teachers should be very concerned with developing their questioning skills. Many of us went through school experiencing the bombardment of low level questions, focusing on giving "correct responses" to questions in a designated textbook or a teacher's lecture. This recitation method of questioning was short and fast paced. It went something like this:

Teacher: "What is a molecule?"

Student: "A building block."

Teacher: "A building block of what?"

Student: "Of everything."

Teacher: "Good. What are all molecules made of?"

Student: "Atoms."

Teacher: "Right. What are atoms made of?"

Student: "Protons, neutrons, and electrons."

Teacher: "Right."

This type of recitation leads students to believe that science questions always have one "correct answer." Such questioning does not demand much thinking, and it does not lead to discussion.

ACTIVITY 6.12

Identifying Higher Level and Lower Level Questions

MATERIALS NEEDED:
- ◆ pencil and paper
- ◆ an interesting newspaper article

A. Using the information you have learned about questioning as well as Table 6.9, identify each of the following questions as either lower level or higher level.
  1. What are the causes of animal extinction?
  2. Explain what happened in your investigation.
  3. What is a *molecule*?
  4. Why would you or wouldn't you want a low level toxic waste site in your town?
  5. What causes oil to float on top of the water?
  6. What might life be like on Mars?
  7. How are frogs different from toads?
  8. How effective is your state at handling solid waste problems?
  9. Do you think that the spotted owl should be protected? Why or why not?
  10. What is *evaporation*?
  11. What causes evaporation?
  12. How might you stop water from evaporating from a swimming pool?
  13. How might you increase water evaporation from a wet towel?
  14. What are the characteristics of a reptile?
  15. Who invented the light bulb?
  16. How is sedimentary rock formed?
  17. What is a fossil?

B. After you have identified each of these questions as higher level or lower level, meet with a small number of classmates to discuss your answers. Come to a consensus on the level of each of the questions.

C. Form teams. In your team, locate an interesting article in the local newspaper that covers an important current event that might be discussed in an elementary or middle school classroom. Try to find a different article from the other teams. Write three lower level questions and three higher level questions for your article. After you have accomplished this task, pair up teams and trade articles. Then ask your paired team the three higher level questions from your team and take notes about their responses. Do not ask them the lower level questions.

D. Analyze the answers to the higher level questions. What did you notice? What types of thinking occurred? Did team members demonstrate knowledge of the lower level questions when they answered the higher level questions? If so, what does this tell you about the lower level questions? Record your ideas in your portfolio.

Because of teachers' prior experiences and beliefs about teaching, multiple answers, uncertain responses, tentative answers, opinions and judgments, and divergent answers may seem frightening to them. Because many teachers have limited science preparation, they fear open-ended and divergent questions, questions to which there are no answers written in the textbook. Consider this type of questioning:

Teacher: "What did you find out about landfills from your research?"

Student 1: "I found out that landfills are filling up, and the state has laws prohibiting the opening of new ones unless you go through a lot of regulations and red tape."

Student 2: "We also found out that our city doesn't allow grass clippings or tree branches in the garbage."

Student 3: "Yeah, and my subdivision doesn't allow composting, so what are we supposed to do?"

Student 1: "What do you think we should do?"

Student 3: "I don't know. Maybe write to the city."

Teacher: "What do others in the class think?"

Student 4: "I think we should make posters and hang them up in town to tell about this problem."

Teacher: "Do you think this would be beneficial?"

Student 4: "Yeah, it would make people aware of the problem, and maybe they'd do something about it."

Teacher: "Is there anything else we could do and is there any 'red tape' that we'd encounter?"

ACTIVITY 6.13

Analyzing Your Questioning Style

MATERIALS NEEDED:
- ◆ a video camera
- ◆ a videotape
- ◆ a prepared lesson

A. Prepare a short benchmark lesson, no more than ten or fifteen minutes long, on a topic of your choice. Teach it to a small group of your peers while you are being videotaped.

B. Watch yourself on videotape and analyze your lesson:
1. What was the average number of questions you asked per minute?
2. What percentage of your questions were lower level? Higher level? Procedural (just part of organizing the lesson)?
C. After analyzing your lesson, list in your portfolio ways that you could improve your questioning strategies. What are you doing well?

As you can see, the teacher is asking very open-ended questions. There are many possible responses. The teacher may not know the answers to the questions asked. Remember: Science is a process and a way of thinking. Use community resources, guest speakers, the Web, and other resources to find the answers you don't know. You don't need to be afraid: In a project-based classroom, everyone participates in finding solutions.

Does asking higher order questions increase student achievement? Research findings have found mixed results on this important question, but some research supports the assertion that higher order questions followed by longer wait-times, probing, and redirecting have resulted in greater student achievement (Wilen, 1987). Activity 6.13 will help you analyze your own questioning style.

SUMMARY OF CHAPTER

In this chapter, we explored the role of benchmark lessons in a project-based environment and discussed their importance. Benchmark lessons serve several purposes. They help students learn difficult concepts, they illustrate laboratory techniques, they build new inquiry abilities, they model thinking, and they stimulate curiosity. The chapter introduced ideas to help teachers know when to plan benchmark lessons, including using concept maps, observations, and the KWL method. Several lesson plan formats and models for structuring lessons were presented, including the learning cycle model and the 5-E model. We explored many strategies and techniques that teachers can use in benchmark lessons, including demonstrations, large group discussions, presentations (metaphors, diagrams, graphs, videos, guest lectures), and community resources. We considered strategies to make benchmark lessons more active, such as role-playing, teacher-planned activities, investigation centers, and field trips. We discussed ways that teachers can use literature, including children's books, magazines, and the World Wide Web. We also discussed ways that teachers can help students make sense of textual material. Finally, we discussed the use of concept maps and questioning. In project-based teaching, information should never be presented in an isolated manner, not even in benchmark lessons. Ideas and principles must be related to a driving question that is meaningful to the students.

REFERENCES

Berenstain, S., and J. Berenstain. 1987. *The day of the dinosaur*. New York: Random House.

Bloom, B. 1956. *Taxonomy of educational objectives: The classification of educational goals*. New York: D. McKay.

Blosser, P. March 1, 1990. *Using questions in science classrooms. Research matters to the science teacher*, NARST, no. 9001.

Brandenburg, A. 1981. *Digging up dinosaurs*. New York: Harper & Row.

Brandenburg, A. 1969. *My visit to the dinosaurs.* New York: Harper & Row.

Cleary, B. 1983. *Dear Mr. Henshaw.* New York: William Morrow.

Cognition and Technology Group at Vanderbilt. 1992. The Jasper series as an example of anchored instruction: Theory, program description, and assessment data. *Educational Psychologist* 27:291–315.

Eggen, P., and D. Kauchak. 1992. *Educational psychology: Classroom connections.* New York: Macmillan.

Gall, M. 1984. Synthesis of research on teachers' questioning. *Educational Leadership* 42:40–47.

Gardner, H. 1993. *Multiple intelligence: The theory into practice.* New York: Basic Books.

Gardner, H. 1983. *Frames of mind: The theory of multiple intelligence.* New York: Basic Books.

Helfgott, D., and M. Westhaver. 1997. *Inspiration 5.0.* Portland, Ore.: Inspiration Software, Inc.

Hunt, E., and J. Minstrell. 1994. A cognitive approach to the teaching of physics. In *Classroom lessons: Integrating cognitive theory and classroom practice,* pp. 51–74, ed. K. McGilly. Cambridge, Mass.: The MIT Press.

Leim, T. 1981. *Invitations to science inquiry.* Lexington, Mass.: Ginn Custom Publishing.

Lunetta, V. N. 1997. The role of the laboratory in school science. In *International handbook of science education,* ed. D. Tobin and B. J. Fraser. The Netherlands: Kluwer.

Marvin, F. 1986. *How big is a brachiosaurus?* New York: Platt & Munk Publishers.

National Research Council. 1996. *National science education standards.* Washington, D.C.: National Academy Press.

Nolan, D. 1990. *Dinosaur dreams.* New York: Macmillan Publishing.

Novak, J. D., and D. B. Gowin. 1984. *Learning how to learn.* Cambridge, England: Cambridge University Press.

Ogle, D. 1986. A teaching model that develops active reading of expository text. *The Reading Teacher* 39 (2):564–70.

Penner, L. R. 1991. *Dinosaur babies.* New York: Random House.

Renner, J. W., and E. A. Marek. 1988. *The learning cycle and elementary school science teaching.* Portsmouth, N.H.: Heinemann.

Rowe, M. B. September 1996. Science, silence, and sanctions. *Science and Children* 34:35–37. Reprinted from March 1969 issue.

Seuss, Dr. (Geisel, T. S., and A. S. Geise). 1971. *The lorax.* New York: Random House.

Swift, J. N. November 1983. Interaction of wait time and questioning instruction on middle school science teaching. *Journal of Research in Science Teaching* 20:721–30.

Swift, J. N., C. T. Gooding, and P. R. Swift. October 23, 1996. *Using research to improve the quality of classroom discussions. Research Matters to the Science Teacher,* NARST no. 9601.

Tom Snyder Productions. 1996. *Rainforest researchers.* Watertown, Mass.: Author.

Tom Snyder Productions. 1992, 1994. *The great ocean rescue.* Watertown, Mass.: Author.

Vosniadou, S., and W. F. Brewer. 1987. Theories and knowledge restructuring in development. *Review of Educational Research* 57 (1):51–67.

Wilen, W. W. 1987. *Questioning skills, for teachers.* Washington, D.C.: National Education Association.

Chapter 7

HOW IS STUDENT UNDERSTANDING ASSESSED?

INTRODUCTION

This chapter focuses on ways that we can assess student understanding in a project-based science class. You may have many questions about assessment. How do I assess science understanding? Are some ways to assess better than others? What are portfolios and how do I use them in science classes? How do I know that all students are learning? This chapter answers these and other questions about assessment. The chapter also explores the benefits of authentic assessment. We start by discussing the purpose of assessment in science classes, the term *authentic assessment,* and the ways authentic assessment differs from traditional forms of assessment. Next, we consider numerous strategies for gathering assessment information such as conducting observations, using concept maps, and doing performance-based assessments. We discuss artifacts as ways to form lasting memories in students' minds, strategies for assembling information into artifacts, and ways that students can present information. After that, we will consider information about using scoring rubrics to evaluate assessment information. Before we begin deliberating the purpose of assessment, let's examine two classroom scenarios that focus on assessment.

Scenario 1: Paper and Pencil Tests

"Now that we've finished grading the pop quiz in science, I have a few reminders for you. Remember, boys and girls, next Friday is the last day of the quarter, so you will be taking tests each day next week that will be included in this grading period. On Monday, you will have a test on Chapter 3 of the social studies book, which covers the Revolutionary War. Tuesday's test in math will cover division of decimals. Wednesday, we will have a test on Chapter 4 of the science book on simple machines. On Thursday, you will take a test on possessive nouns, and Friday's test will be the regular week's spelling list. Oh, I almost forgot, make sure you take home the letter I gave you this morning about the Iowa Test of Basic Skills that you'll be taking in two weeks. Study hard and have a nice weekend!"

Do these words bring back memories of school testing? In the past, teachers commonly administered paper and pencil tests as the sole form of assessment. Students were expected to pass these tests, which for the most part, determined their letter grades in each school subject. These tests were usually multiple choice, true/false, matching, or essay, and they were administered to the whole class after the class covered a chapter or some other unit of study. After completing the designated chapter or unit, the teacher rarely brought up the topic again for the rest of the year. *Assessment* was synonymous with *test,* and *test* meant *grades.* The whole idea of testing caused nervousness, anxiety, and perhaps sweaty palms.

Scenario 2: Embedded Assessment

Students in a third grade class asked, "Why do pumpkins decay after Halloween?" To answer this question, they planned several investigations. Some students thought that pumpkins rotted when they froze outside, because they had noticed that fresh fruit is mushy after being frozen. That group investigated how fast a pumpkin decays when it is frozen and when it is left inside the building. Another group of students investigated whether "germs" have anything to do with the decay. They washed one pumpkin with an antibacterial soap and left another one alone to investigate which decayed first. Another group buried pumpkins in some leaves and soil to see what effect this had. Some students compared carved and uncarved pumpkins, while another group left their pumpkins in the sun and in the shade. Between team investigations, the teacher taught several lessons on bacteria, decay, and mold growth. The class also visited a compost site where the city dumped leaves to generate fertilizer for sale. Some students wrote to grocery store managers to see how they stopped fruit and vegetables from decaying.

Next, the teacher had students design a poster (an artifact) depicting what they learned as they completed their investigation. The poster was divided into two sections labeled "Things that cause a pumpkin to rot" and "Things that stop a pumpkin from rotting." Students drew pictures and took photographs of the things that were listed on each side of the poster to illustrate. Students included with the poster a short essay on the benefits of decomposition in their daily lives.

This second scenario is characteristic of project-based science. What did the students learn in

---

ACTIVITY 7.1

What Is the Purpose of Assessment?

MATERIALS NEEDED:
- pencil and paper or a computer

A. Think about why we assess students. What do you think is the purpose of assessment? On a sheet of paper or on a computer, make three columns. Label the first column "Know," label the second column "Want to know," and label the third column "Learned" (Ogle, 1986). Take a few moments to list in the first column as many things as you know about why we assess students.

B. Interview a classmate to see why he or she thinks we assess students. How does his or her viewpoint compare with yours? Find another classmate (or a teacher) with a different viewpoint. Compare and contrast these two colleagues' ideas about assessment.

C. Interview an elementary or middle grade student (preferably a student in grades four, five, six or higher in which testing becomes more frequent) and ask the student why he or she is assessed or tested in school. How does the student's view of assessment compare with the teachers'? With yours?

D. After conducting these interviews, list as many things in the second column that you can think of that you want to know about assessment. At the end of this chapter, you will assess your own learning in this chapter by filling in the third column, "Learned," indicating what you have learned about assessment.

E. Place your ideas in your portfolio.

---

this investigation? They learned to ask questions and devise investigations. In the process, they learned about the effect of freezing on plant cells, about bacteria and using soap to kill bacteria, and about composting and the relationship of sunlight and oxygen to decomposition. They used communication skills to write letters, and they learned about community efforts to compost leaves. Their learning did not occur in a single, discreet step but unfolded gradually through a variety of activities in a learning community. Not all students were required to do the same activities at the same time.

As you can imagine, assessment for this project environment would need to be different from traditional assessment in order to accurately measure what students had learned. Students could take a multiple choice test with questions like, "What is decomposition?" and answers like, "a. dead plants and animals, b. rotting, c. separation of matter into its basic components, d. breaking up of elements, e. none of the above." However, such questions would fail to assess the multitude of ideas students learned. They wouldn't measure students' ability to work as a team. They would fail to identify the most important ideas students learned. They would not show how students could apply their knowledge and skills to everyday life. They would not show that they could plan investigations or interpret data. Paper and pencil tests are not consistent with the philosophy of project-based science because they do not measure the kinds of understandings students gain while in the process of pursuing answers to driving questions.

Assessment techniques in a project-based science environment differ considerably from the technique depicted in the opening scenario. First, various forms of assessment (not just tests) are used so that a wide variety of understandings, skills, and attitudes are measured. Second, assessment takes place during instruction as well as after. Third, higher level cognitive skills such as asking questions, designing investigations, gathering information, and drawing conclusions are assessed as are affective outcomes such as curiosity, skepticism, and open-mindedness. Fourth, students are involved in assessment decisions along with their teachers. Fifth, assessment is a continuous process, embedded in learning, not an end in itself.

Although some teachers stubbornly refuse to move beyond paper and pencil assessment practices, most teachers have learned to use a variety of techniques to assess their students. After reading this chapter, you should understand why the opening scenario does not exemplify assessment practices recommended today. Before we move to the next section, Activity 7.1 will help you think about the purpose of assessment.

THE PURPOSE OF ASSESSMENT

Assessment can be thought of as any method used to judge or evaluate an outcome or help make a decision. Assessment is a fervent topic in education today, and it is scrutinized at the public level and within our educational system. At the public level, it seems that we face almost daily issues pertaining to assessment. For example, there are news articles about how our nation's students compare on standardized tests with previous generations or with students in other countries. Policy makers, community leaders, parents, and school administrators are demanding that students be held accountable for certain levels of performance and understanding. As a result, many states have debated and implemented new educational standards that include proficiency testing or high school graduation qualification testing. Many people believe that these externally mandated paper and pencil tests inform the public about how our schools are doing. They are intended to be a measure of the nation's educational achievement. Increased achievement in science is, in fact, a national goal in *America 2000* (USDOE, 1991).

Within our educational system, however, many people are debating the relevance of traditional paper and pencil tests and are looking for alternative means of assessment. Most educators believe that assessment should measure the many types of learning that occur in our classrooms. The *National Science Education Standards* (NRC, 1996), for example, argues for a greater emphasis on "assessing what is most highly valued" (as opposed to what is easily measured); "assessing rich, well-structured knowledge" (as opposed to discrete knowledge); "assessing scientific understanding and reasoning" (as opposed to only knowledge); "assessing to learn what students do understand" (as opposed to what they do not know); "assessing achievement and opportunity to learn" (instead of only achievement); and "engaging students in ongoing assessment of their work and that of others" (as opposed to end-of-term assessments given by teachers) (p. 100).

Traditional paper and pencil assessments usually measure only knowledge about something and therefore are viewed by many today as an insufficient means of meeting the assessment standards found in the *National Science Education Standards* (NRC, 1996). In contrast, good assessment strategies measure when a student can use knowledge in a meaningful way. For example, a student who can repeat a memorized definition of *density* may possess little to no understanding of density, whereas a student who can use scientific equipment to figure out the density of an object has in-depth knowledge of the concept. It is this in-depth knowledge that educators are encouraging and trying to measure.

Assessment should improve curriculum and instruction by determining what knowledge and skills children bring to science lessons and by identifying what students know and can do following instruction. It should convey expectations to students and their parents in a way that motivates and helps students to learn. Assessment should also assist teachers in making decisions about what instruction has not been effective, helping, therefore, to modify instruction. We view assessment as an ongoing process that occurs during as well as after project-based science instruction and helps students, teachers, and parents monitor individual student's learning. Activity 7.2 examines teachers' views of and beliefs about instruction and assessment.

THE NATURE OF AUTHENTIC ASSESSMENT

Just as instruction in project-based science has certain characteristics that distinguish it from traditional science teaching, assessment best suited for a project environment has special characteristics that distinguish it from traditional assessment as described in the opening scenario. Assessment that is appropriate for project-based science has many different labels: active assessment, direct assessment, performance assessment, alternative assessment, and many others. This book uses the term **authentic assessment** because *authentic* means "genuine or justifiable," and assessments that most closely measure what happens during instruction are more genuine and justifiable.

Assessment in a project-based science environment serves a much broader purpose than simply determining students' grades and mea-

---

ACTIVITY 7.2

How Do Teachers' Beliefs About Instruction Affect Their Methods of Assessment?

MATERIALS NEEDED:
- ◆ materials to conduct an interview

A. Interview several teachers about their beliefs on teaching and assessment. Try to determine whether each teacher believes teaching is "telling students information" or "helping students construct their own

understandings." Ask each teacher how he or she typically assesses students. What types of assessment do they use? What do the assessments measure? How do the teachers determine grades?

B. Analyze the difference between the "teller" teachers and the "constructivist" teachers. How does the curriculum vary? What about instruction? Assessment?

C. Record these ideas in your portfolio.

---

suring achievement. Authentic assessment has the following features:

1. It measures students' understanding, skills, and motivation in situations that closely match real life.

2. It helps teachers plan instruction, determine students' conceptions of science, and revise curriculum and teaching accordingly.

3. It is designed to continuously monitor student progress. It looks like instruction, differing only in purpose. In fact, it is embedded throughout the instructional process.

4. It measures academic progress fairly and accurately by using a variety of assessment techniques and various sources of information.

5. It helps students become self-reflective, self-regulated learners who monitor their own learning. It is something teachers and students do together, not something the teacher does to the student.

6. It assesses the progress of individual students rather than group norms or comparing students to one another.

In addition to measuring understanding of science knowledge, authentic assessment monitors students' mastery of skills and attitudes. When you were in school, the teacher probably focused almost solely on measuring your attainment of scientific facts. You may remember asking the teacher, "Is this going to be on the test?" You and your classmates were probably keenly aware that tests measured certain content, and you

wanted to make sure you memorized the particular knowledge that you would be asked to give. It is unlikely that your teacher paid much attention to whether you had misunderstandings about scientific ideas and whether you were able to ask and refine questions, plan and design investigations, collect data, make sense of data, or report your findings. It is even less likely that your teacher was concerned with measuring your attitudes and dispositions toward learning science or your motivation to learn.

Teachers using project-based science are concerned that students attain scientific knowledge, but the type of knowledge now considered most important differs from knowledge valued in the past. Traditional science teaching focuses almost entirely on content knowledge, while project-based science focuses on content, inquiry, and epistemic knowledge (see our description in chapter 2). Traditionally, students were expected to know vocabulary words such as *vertebrate, invertebrate, crustacean, mollusk,* and *reptile.* For almost all students, this type of knowledge didn't have much relevance outside of school. It was thought that knowing such vocabulary words would build a foundation for understanding science. Today, science educators see the teaching of such concepts as a much more complex process than simply requiring students to memorize definitions and recognize examples. Today, teachers are concerned with examining students' prior beliefs about the scientific world and their understanding of its major concepts. Science educators also see knowledge as something that helps students analyze a question, solve a problem, or conduct an investigation in a way that is meaningful to them. This type of knowledge is

ACTIVITY 7.3

How Can I Choose a Good Assessment Technique to Measure Understanding?

MATERIALS NEEDED:
- paper and pencil or a computer

A. What follows are several objectives that might be contained in a typical elementary or middle school curriculum. Form a team of three students. Read each objective and decide what would be the most beneficial ways to measure whether students have gained understanding of the topic. Keep in mind that good assessment should
  1. be valid and reliable;
  2. match instruction and reflect goals;
  3. reflect the needs and unique cultural aspects of our society;
  4. be consistent with learning theory; and
  5. measure deep understanding.

  Objectives
  - After investigating simple machines, each student will understand how machines help us do work.
  - After investigating what animals need to eat, each student will be able to distinguish between a consumer and a producer.
  - After investigating what types of trees are in our environment, each student will be able to identify two types of trees.
  - After investigating where garbage goes, each student will be able to tell why it is important to recycle.

B. As a team, develop a lesson to teach one of the objectives. Develop two different ways of assessing the objective after you have taught it. Teach the lesson to another team in your class and try the two different methods of assessment.

C. Ask the team you taught which method of assessment best measured what they learned. How do that team's beliefs about good assessment techniques compare to yours?

D. Record your ideas in your portfolio.

---

not superficial. For example, rather than focusing on the definition of *invertebrate, crustacean,* and *reptile,* a teacher might have students analyze how a crustacean (with a hard outer covering) and a reptile (with a hard shell) are alike and different. This knowledge of similarities and differences would help students set up a functioning aquarium to investigate a driving question about how some crustaceans and reptiles can co-exist in a saltwater tank with poisonous invertebrates. In Activity 7.3, you will develop your own assessment procedure for measuring understanding.

If a group of students actually assembled a functioning aquarium, they would be applying their knowledge and skills. As a result, the assessment of such an activity would extend beyond measuring declarative knowledge. Students cannot investigate driving questions without using such problem-solving skills as observing, comparing, classifying, measuring, hypothesizing, analyzing, and concluding. Interpersonal skills used in daily life such as communicating, resolving differences, and solving problems are also essential to collaborative investigation. Authentic assessment serves the purpose of measuring the attainment of these investigative and social skills.

Authentic assessment also monitors the affective side of learning which is so prominent in a project-based science classroom. Students are encouraged to ask questions, become excited about an investigation, remain open-minded about new ideas, be thorough in their investigation, stay fair in their conclusions, and be honest in their presentation of evidence. Imagine that a group of students is investigating the driving question "Where does all the garbage go?" The students could become aware of landfill problems, discuss their attitudes about the situation, and create artifacts that depict the problem without exhibiting positive dispositions or taking action, two other objectives of the project. It would be better if students responded to the landfill problem by recycling aluminum cans and encouraging others to recycle. It would be even better if students organized a schoolwide recycling program for all possible school products—glass, aluminum, steel cans, paper, cardboard, and plastic. By focusing assessment on the knowledge, skills, and attitudes of students, authentic assessment broadens the purpose of assessment and treats it as a process that matches instructional goals and life outside of school.

Characteristics of Authentic Assessment

Authentic Assessment Is Responsive to Context As depicted in the opening scenario, assessment traditionally was thought of mainly as a measure of students' understanding of declarative knowledge. It was not used to determine what should be taught. It did not influence teachers' day-to-day lessons or provide a means for revising lessons and teaching techniques. On the other hand, assessment in a project-based science environment is context-responsive. It is used to help plan instruction, guide day-to-day interactions with students, and, if necessary, revise instruction on a moment-to-moment basis.

Teachers in a project-based environment use assessment techniques to diagnose students' prior knowledge of science and any problems they may have with science learning. Teachers also examine students' interests. These diagnoses assist teachers in planning and carrying out lessons. For example, if students are having difficulty making meaning of the effects of seasonal change on the behavior of animals and the growth of plants, a teacher would revisit the concepts in a different way and plan new experiences to help students better understand the concepts. If students are extremely interested in Venus's flytrap, the teacher might use this interest as an avenue for teaching about types of plants, including carnivorous ones.

Authentic assessment techniques also provide teachers with information that may alter their moment-to-moment and day-to-day decisions. Since authentic assessment is used to monitor understanding, skills, and attitudes, teachers using these techniques are less likely to blindly continue lessons without regard to how students are progressing. In other words, teachers using this type of assessment become reflective practitioners. They think about, ana-lyze, and mentally debate what should be done to most effectively teach particular students at any given moment. Such teachers continually ask themselves questions like, "Are the students interested in the lesson?" "Was the student misbehavior a result of my management and questioning?" "Did I choose the best instructional strategy to get across the concept?" "Was my pacing okay?" "Did I call on the same students or many different students?" "Did I wait long enough after I asked questions?" "Did I give good examples?" "Were my transitions good?" "Did I end the lesson in a way that summarized what was learned today?" Such ongoing reflection frequently results in teachers changing the direction of their questioning, instructional strategies, choice of curriculum, and classroom environment.

Authentic Assessment Is a Continuous Process Embedded in Instruction In the opening scenario, traditional assessment was portrayed as something that always happens at the *end* of instruction. Such assessment is a discreet event separate from instruction. Authentic assessment in a project-based science classroom looks like instruction. It is a *continuous process* that is *embedded* in instruction. It is contextualized and realistic rather than contrived or staged. It does not occur under artificial testing conditions; rather, it matches classroom instruction and real life. Teaching, learning, and assessment are thought of as reciprocal. Authentic assessment continuously monitors student learning; it is not solely an end product of learning. Assessment with these characteristics looks more like the assessment discussed in scenario two.

Imagine that you took a month-long vacation to Australia, you have only brought black and white film, you only have enough to take one photograph per week, and your camera has only one setting. How well would these photographs portray your vacation experiences? How could you improve the documentation of your vacation? First, you might bring more film so that you would not be limited to one picture per week. You might also bring color film, and you might use a 35 mm camera so that you could change the focus. If you brought a wide angle lens and a zoom lens, you could take panoramic pictures and close-up photographs. You might even bring a video camera so that you could document continuous sights as well as sounds, and you might keep a diary so that you could write down your impressions of Australia. Finally, you might gather souvenirs to take back home with you.

This analogy is very similar to a teacher's efforts to document students' progress in school using authentic assessment techniques. Traditional forms of assessment supply the teacher with only blurred monochrome snapshots of what students know, can do, and are like. Authentic forms of assessment are more analogous to use of the video camera, 35 mm camera, and journal and the gathering of souvenirs—strategies that gather a wide range and depth of information. In a project-based classroom, teachers and students will continually collect information during the instructional process. The "souvenirs" of science, which are the artifacts of a project, are especially important because they are often the most remembered and therefore the most meaningful for students and teachers. Therefore, students will create many different types of "science souvenirs" or artifacts that can be used to assess their knowledge, skills, and attitudes.

Authentic Assessment Is Multidimensional Assessment in a project-based science classroom aims to make fair and accurate judgments about student progress, and the most legitimate judgments come from diverse sources of information. Traditional paper and pencil assessment techniques often ignore differences in students' learning styles, interests, attention spans, or types of intelligences. For example, on traditional tests, a student might not correctly identify the definition of *metamorphosis* from five choices provided. However, the student might be able to demonstrate understanding of *metamorphosis* by drawing a diagram illustrating stages of growth or choreographing a performance depicting changes occurring in an animal's life cycle. A student who demonstrates understanding of *metamorphosis* in one of these ways has exhibited deeper understanding of the concept than has a student who can only choose a response.

For teachers who work in schools that require letter grades, the alternative assessment techniques used in project-based science can be of great assistance. Using diverse forms of assessment information helps teachers make more

valid decisions about students' grades. Students also tend to learn concepts in a more in-depth manner, so they are more likely to score well in other types of assessments.

Authentic Assessment Engages Students in the Assessment Process In a project environment, teachers and students engage collaboratively in assessment. At each stage of the assessment process, teachers and students work together to collect data, make decisions about individual progress (as opposed to comparing students to statistical norms or to other students), document progress, and set goals. This collaborative process helps students become self-reflective, self-monitoring learners who regulate and take responsibility for their own learning.

Imagine that students are engaging in an investigation. During the investigation, they make numerous observations and record this information in their science notebooks. While students engage in this process, the teacher makes notations in his journal about the students who are having trouble making observations and recording information. Later, while students work in collaborative groups to make decisions about the artifacts they will present to the class, the teacher assembles information from the students' notebooks to file in their portfolios. The teacher judges each student's depth of understanding from the items contained in his or her portfolio. After the artifacts are presented to the class, the entire class engages in a critical dialogue. Later, the teacher discusses with each student the items contained in his or her portfolio. The teacher reviews individual progress with each student and together they devise strategies to improve the student's academic growth. Students are involved in every step of the assessment process, which has been designed to help them become motivated, self-regulated learners.

THE BENEFITS OF AUTHENTIC ASSESSMENT

So far, we have considered numerous reasons for using authentic assessment instead of traditional paper and pencil measures of achievement in project-based classrooms. All of these reasons, however, fall into five general categories of benefits of authentic assessment. First, authentic assessment is a more valid and reliable way than traditional assessment to appraise students' knowledge, skills, and attitudes. Second, authentic assessment more closely matches today's educational goals. Third, it better accommodates cultural diversity. Fourth, it is consistent with cognitive learning theory. And fifth, authentic assessment techniques measure deep understanding.

Authentic Assessment Is Valid and Reliable

Good assessment is both valid and reliable. *Valid* assessment is fair and allows the teacher to make accurate generalizations about a student's knowledge. Invalid assessment does not permit a teacher to make accurate decisions about what students know and what they are ready to learn. Each one of us can provide examples of tests or assessments from our own educational experience where we remarked, "The test wasn't fair!" We agonized over the results of the test because we knew in our minds that it didn't represent what we really knew or what we were capable of doing. Therefore, any generalizations made from the test about us were incorrect or at best only partially correct. Validity, therefore, pertains to collecting the kind of information needed to make accurate generalizations about students' learning. Since authentic assessment focuses on more than simply the attainment of declarative knowledge, uses diverse sources of information, and involves the student in the assessment process, it is less likely that it will result in biased conclusions or errors.

Reliable assessment provides consistent results across different trials. In other words, a reliable assessment tool will yield similar results on different occasions or will result in different assessors coming to similar conclusions about the student being assessed. Think about your car. If it starts one day but not another under similar weather conditions, you would say that the car isn't reliable. The results are not consistent, so the car isn't trustworthy. Of course, if this happened only once, you could not blame your car for being unreliable. If, however, your car repeatedly starts one day and not the other, you could assuredly conclude that it isn't reliable.

With traditional assessment techniques, a single "snapshot" of students' abilities is taken at the "conclusion of learning." Many factors such as testing conditions, the assessment items themselves, and a student's frame of mind can influence the reliability of these snapshots, and so the results are not always trustworthy. Authentic assessment techniques are more reliable because they give students many opportunities and ways to demonstrate their abilities, thus eliminating variables that may alter results.

Authentic Assessment Matches Today's Educational Goals

It is widely recognized today that learning should be active and integrated; the knowledge explosion has made it futile to ask students to memorize large quantities of facts as they will quickly become outdated. In our information age, labor force experts are calling for students who can learn to solve problems, make decisions, learn how to learn, collaborate with others, and manage themselves (*SCANS Report,* 1991). Educators think it is important for students to be able to understand how they have arrived at an answer, transfer knowledge to real life situations, think critically, document and communicate information, and analyze and synthesize information.

These new educational goals have required changes in the way we teach. Active and integrated strategies such as collaborative learning, which is used in project-based science, are stressed. Assessment practices need to be holistic and complex. If a teacher were trying to measure declarative knowledge, or knowledge that is concerned only with what facts students have acquired, selected response assessments such as true/false and multiple choice tests would be adequate. However, teachers today are trying to measure much more: knowledge, skills, and attitudes in situations relevant to out-of-school experiences. Students are assessed on their abilities to solve problems, make decisions, and collaborate. Not only do authentic assessment techniques *match* today's goals, but they also help to meet them: by engaging students in the assessment process, authentic assessment pushes students to become independent learners, responsible for their own learning.

ACTIVITY 7.4

How Does Science Reform Affect Assessment Practices?

MATERIALS NEEDED:
 ◆ reference materials including *Benchmarks for Science Literacy* (AAAS, 1993), *Project 2061: Science for All Americans* (Rutherford & Ahlgren, 1989), and *National Science Education Standards* (National Research Council, 1996)

A. On a sheet of paper, list as many answers as you can to the question, "What is a science-literate person?" You completed a similar list in Activity 1.5 in Chapter 1. You might refer to your notes in your portfolio.
B. How you could asses whether a person had met this criteria?

C. How many of the items did you choose to assess with traditional multiple choice, true/false, and essay questions? How many required different approaches to assessment? Why is this so?
D. Compare your list of characteristics of scientific literacy to those in major national reform reports such as *Benchmarks for Science Literacy, Project 2061: Science for All Americans,* and *National Science Education Standards.* How do your criteria for scientific literacy compare with the criteria in these policy reports? What effect do you think these reports will have on curriculum, instruction, and assessment?
E. Record your ideas in your portfolio.

Activity 7.4 asks you to compare assessment practices with several reform documents that have established today's educational goals.

Authentic Assessment Accommodates Cultural Diversity

Recent policy reports in science education have called for changes that will attract all students to science learning (National Research Council, 1996; Rutherford & Ahlgren, 1989). When considering the diverse needs, interests, and abilities of students in our country—particularly girls, minorities, students with disabilities, and those with limited English proficiency—it becomes obvious that traditional assessment techniques are appalling. They overlook the prior experiences, learning styles, multiple intelligences, and interests of our diverse population. Authentic assessment techniques, on the contrary, allow for students' unique differences.

For example, a student with limited English proficiency might have difficulty answering essay questions about the process of metamorphosis. This test, however, would more likely be assessing her ability to write English sentences than her understanding of metamorphosis. An assessment that asked her to draw pictures of the stages of life that an insect goes through from egg stage to adult stage would more likely measure her understanding of the concept.

Authentic Assessment Is Consistent with Cognitive Learning Theory

In Chapter 2, we examined how students construct understanding, the social nature of learning, and the need for science to be anchored in students' daily lives. Social constructivist theory has several implications for assessment in a project-based science environment. What follows are a number of constructivist learning principles and the authentic assessment practices that derive from them (adapted from Herman, Ashbacher, & Winters, 1992).

People generate knowledge through an active process of creating personal meaning from mixing new information with prior knowledge. This principle implies that assessment should *encourage* more than one answer to questions. For example, in project-based science, some students might make posters to demonstrate what they have learned, while others might create a video documentary. This principle also implies that assessment should measure how students relate new learning to personal experiences and prior knowledge. Finally, assessment should measure how well students apply what they have learned. For example, students investigating why the water in the classroom faucet doesn't flow well might present their data to the city water department, a perfect opportunity for assessment.

Students of all ages and abilities can think and solve problems. This principle implies that assessment techniques should engage students in problem-solving activities and investigation. Because learning does not happen in discreet, small steps, assessment should measure holistic knowledge and abilities. When students present artifacts, they are demonstrating a wide variety of knowledge, skills, and attitudes they learned—not isolated facts.

Children differ in learning styles, attention spans, memory, and developmental rates. This principle implies that assessment techniques should be varied and multidimensional. Students should be given more than one chance to demonstrate their competence, and they should have time to complete tasks. Students should be allowed to revise work and show improvement over time. Finally, students should be able to demonstrate their various abilities, whether they be academic, artistic, verbal, or social. Student production of artifacts presents an opportunity for appropriate assessment because students can construct the products over time and present information in whatever format best matches their learning styles. After presenting their artifacts to a public audience, students receive feedback, which can then be used for revision or further development of the artifacts.

People need to know when to use knowledge and how to adapt it. They also need to learn how to manage their own learning. This principle suggests that students should be able to participate in their assessment, consulting with the teacher, reflecting upon their own work and progress, and helping set their own learning goals.

Motivation and effort affect learning and performance. This principle implies that students should play a part in identifying what they will do, how they will do it, and how it will be evaluated, because motivation and effort are enhanced when learners are able to set their own goals and when the criteria for assessment are demystified.

Learners also need clear guidelines about expectations, and they need to see the connection between their efforts and their results. When students determine what artifacts to include in their portfolios for assessment, their motivation increases. They play active roles in selecting, developing, and giving presentations that will be assessed. They participate in assessing the presentations and artifacts of their classmates.

Learning occurs within a social context. This principle implies that assessment of group work should be included in evaluation. As students work together, they construct understanding and find solutions to questions and problems. As a result, it is critical to assess the products that emerge from students working together.

Authentic Assessment Measures Deep Understanding

Do you remember memorizing answers for a test and not understanding what you were memorizing? What is Avogadro's Number? What is the equation that represents the process of photosynthesis? What type of lens focuses light to a single focal point and then inverts it to enlarge the image? What are the names of the three bones in the ear? What is a vacuole? What are the six simple machines? If you cannot answer these questions, it's probably because you learned them by rote memorization in order to regurgitate them

FIGURE 7.1
Today's educational goals require a variety of techniques.

on a paper and pencil test at the end of a chapter or quarter. It is likely that you have never used or applied these concepts since and that you lack a deep understanding of them.

Paper and pencil tests are typically true/false, multiple choice, matching, short essay, fill-in-the-blank, and circle the correct picture. Although these types of tests can be structured to measure deep understanding of concepts, they frequently are not. Students can easily memorize terms and guess at correct answers based on shallow and disconnected understanding of material. Sometimes ambiguous words, unclear questions, or vague sentences make it difficult for students to even respond during these types of tests. Imagine a question that instructs children to look at pictures of plants to identify which plant needs the least amount of water. Two of the plants pictured are a cactus and a head of cabbage. The "correct" answer is supposed to be the cactus. However, students could reason that since the head of cabbage is dead (since it has been cut from its roots), it no longer needs *any* water to live. Choosing the head of cabbage actually demonstrates a deeper understanding of the concept in question. Whether or not paper and pencil test questions are poorly written, however, they fail to measure what students know; instead, they measure what students do not know.

Paper and pencil tests don't often measure higher level thinking, requesting instead low level, factual answers that fail to assess depth of understanding. True/false, sequencing, and multiple choice tests limit student answers. Students often, however, take paper and pencil tests on state-wide assessments. For this reason, some teachers like to use paper and pencil tests in their classrooms. For more information regarding the construction of good paper and pencil tests, you may want to refer to Miller & Erikson's (1990) *How to Write Tests for Students* or Peter Airasian's (1996) *Assessment in the Classroom.*

Authentic assessment, on the contrary, measures deep understanding by stressing open-ended answers rather than a single "correct" one. Students engage in higher level reasoning through discourse with others (teachers, peers, members of the community). Creating artifacts is more complex and engaging than is selecting answers from a multiple choice list. Artifacts demonstrate higher level thinking skills such as

planning, inventing, and making conclusions. Students construct knowledge rather than simply repeat memorized information. Finally, students engage in self-reflection which develops self-regulation and personal responsibility.

Imagine that your students have spent considerable time investigating the driving question "Why does flooding cause so much damage?" You could try to measure students' understanding of water pressure on levees by asking a multiple choice question such as, "What is water pressure? a. the amount of pressure a given amount of water exerts on an object, b. the amount of water that presses down upon the earth, c. the amount of pressure on water from the air above it." Or you could assess understanding of water pressure on levees using an authentic assessment technique—a performance assessment. You could provide students with 2-liter soda bottles, each with three holes about 2 inches apart—one near the top, one in the middle, and one near the bottom. Instruct students to tape the holes and then pour water into their bottles. Ask students to explore what happens as they remove the tape from each hole. Ask them to explain the results of the activity. Ask them to compare the results of this activity to the breaking of levees during the Mississippi River flood of many towns in the Midwest in 1993 or during the wet El Niño weather of the winter of 1997–1998. Question them about their opinions on building levees along a river.

Which of these examples of assessment measures deep understanding? A student could memorize a definition of *water pressure* from a textbook and really not understand the concept. However, to explain the results of an investigation on water pressure, a student must have a deep cognitive understanding of it. The student must construct meaning to explain why the water in the bottom hole flows out faster and at a different angle. The student must also have a deep conceptual framework to discuss how the results of the investigation resemble the Mississippi River flooding and whether levees are ultimately helpful or harmful.

In Activity 7.5, you will compare traditional assessment techniques with authentic assessment techniques and examine the pitfalls of traditional testing in order to better understand the merits of authentic assessment.

ACTIVITY 7.5

What Are the Pitfalls of Traditional Testing?

MATERIALS NEEDED:
- ◆ traditional textbooks and accompanying commercial tests

A. Reread Scenario 1 at the beginning of this chapter. Make a list with two columns labeled *Traditional assessment* and *Authentic assessment.* Under each of these headings, make two additional columns labeled *Advantages* and *Disadvantages.* Identify as many advantages and disadvantages as you can for each type of assessment.

B. With a few classmates, compare and discuss the advantages and disadvantages. Make a list of what you all agree are the most important advantages and disadvantages. How do the advantages of each category help students learn, help teachers administer assessment, help parents understand student progress, and help students understand their own progress?

C. Discuss whether the advantages of authentic assessment techniques outweigh the disadvantages? How can the disadvantages be overcome?

D. Examine the commercial tests that accompany a traditional elementary or middle grade textbook. How many of the following can you find in the tests or assessments?

1. a variety of testing formats including whole class, small group, and individual
2. a variety of formats including artifacts, performance-based tests, teacher observations, essays, student-produced products, student self-evaluation, inventories, and concept maps
3. assessment throughout the learning process
4. measurement of higher level cognitive outcomes
5. measurement of skills
6. monitoring of affective outcomes
7. student monitoring of own progress and time to continue to learn content until it is mastered
8. measurement of relationships, the nature of science, critical thinking, problem solving, and interrelationships between school science and life outside of school
9. measurement of student understanding of the subconcepts within the test
10. feedback beyond a letter grade or percentage score

E. As a classroom teacher, what steps would you need to take to make a traditional test accompanying a textbook series more "authentic" in its assessment method?

F. Record your thoughts in your portfolio.

ASSESSMENT OF STUDENT UNDERSTANDING

Thus far, we have defined *assessment* and *authentic assessment,* and we have discussed the nature and benefits of authentic assessment. In this section, we will discuss how teachers assess student understanding in a project-based science environment.

The process of assessing student understanding might be thought of as a three-step procedure. First, you and your students gather information that will help in forming generalizations about students' learning. Second, after securing information, you and your students assemble and present the information in some fashion. Third, you and your students evaluate the assessment information. The purpose of evaluation is to make judgments about student growth, to set goals, and to report information to students and their parents.

Imagine a group of third grade students investigating how insects grow and change. Students could record in their notebooks information about the length, mass, and appearance of the insects at different stages of growth. During inquiry, the teacher could observe the students and keep information about their progress on a checklist. To assemble and present information, students might draw pictures or take photographs of the insects at each stage and share them with classmates. The teacher could place copies of these items into each student's portfolio. Finally, to evaluate progress, the students might keep a journal in which to enter their personal reflections. The teacher could use a scoring rubric (described later in this chapter) to determine levels of understanding or skill attainment on a performance-based assessment. The following sections will discuss specific methods of collecting, assembling, and evaluating authentic assessment information.

Gathering Assessment Information

Classroom teachers have many assessment options. No matter which options they choose, teachers need to be able to collect sufficient information so that they can make generalizations about students' learning and make good planning decisions. The information needs to be relevant to teaching and the goals desired in the classroom. Therefore, the information-gathering techniques presented in this section are only options, not recommendations. It is up to you, the expert on your classroom, to continually reflect upon your curriculum, your teaching methods, your students' performance, and your goals in order to select and develop methods for gathering information that meet the particular needs of your classroom.

Observation-Based Assessment   Observation is a great technique for gathering data. Observations can help teachers make valid decisions about curriculum and instruction and determine how much progress students are making. Observations play a firm role in a teacher's minute-to-minute decision making during a project. A puzzled look on a student's face might provide you with the evidence that a student is having difficulty with a concept or task. Off-task behavior by students might indicate problems with methods of instruction. These types of observations can help you make "in-flight" curricular or instructional decisions that refocus a lesson.

Observations are often informal. For example, you might notice that a particular student raises her hand often during social studies but very rarely during science, indicating that she understands social studies topics but is having difficulty with science concepts. However, observations can be planned and formal. For example, you may intentionally ask groups of students questions about the driving question and their investigative plans. You can also purposefully listen to and watch a particular student while he solves a problem, reads aloud, or creates a project to identify problem areas as well as areas of mastery.

Observations are inevitably subjective to some degree. When you observe a particular behavior, you interpret what you see. For example, there once was a college student who wore a portable radio with headphones during his science methods class. During the first week of class, the professor interpreted his behavior as rude and inattentive, and she decided that he was a mediocre student. However, after talking with him about the headset, she discovered that he was taking sixteen quarter hours and working two jobs to pay for his tuition. The science methods class was his last class of the day, and he was listening to music to stay awake during class. Incidents like this demonstrate why it is preferable to use a variety of observation techniques that provide varied information than to rely on a single technique. There are several observation techniques that you can use to ensure that you gather varied information. These include discussion-based observations, anecdotal records, checklists, and clinical interviews.

Discussions   During the instructional process, discussions can provide a rich array of information about students' understanding of important science concepts. Discussions can also be used to identify students' process skills and thinking patterns during investigations. Finally, discussions can be used to check students' attitudes. Using discussions to extract information about students' knowledge, skills, and attitudes is also less threatening to most students than are traditional forms of testing and, consequently, invites broader student participation.

Unfortunately, teachers' lack of discussion skills often limits the information they glean from students during a discussion. They sometimes ask too many superficial questions, give students too little time to formulate answers to their questions, or call on the same students all the time. To obtain better answers from more students during a discussion, teachers should learn the techniques of wait-time, probing, and redirecting. These techniques were discussed more thoroughly in Chapter 6. With good questioning technique, teachers can find out from students how well they really understand science concepts.

Teachers can also engage students in discussions about their thought processes and their investigative procedures. For students to discuss their thought processes, teachers sometime have them "think aloud"—that is, talk about what they are thinking during an investigation. Ensuing discussions can then focus on their reasoning, beliefs, and misconceptions.

Discussions in project-based classrooms can also be used to detect students' attitudes. For example, students investigating why frogs are disappearing in their state might discover that sulfur-burning factories in the area have increased the acid in the air to a level that is toxic to frogs. Students can then discuss whether they would vote for stricter air pollution laws. This type of value-oriented discussion is good for making students confront their own beliefs and forcing them to apply those beliefs in the area of social policy.

Anecdotal Records In elementary and middle grade classrooms with twenty to thirty students, teacher observations can easily be forgotten or associated with the wrong students. For these reasons, many teachers choose to keep anecdotal records of their observations. **Anecdotal records** are written records of student behaviors made at or near the time that the behaviors occurred. These records can be kept in a teacher's notebook, in folders, on index cards, on sticky notes or labels, or on the computer. After a class period, you might make notations about students' understandings, types of questions, and possible misunderstandings. Some teachers have all students jot down their responses on paper before calling on anyone to give an answer. This technique gives each child the time to think about and compose his or her response before the question is discussed, and it gives the teacher a written record of students' thinking. Hand-held or palmtop computers permit teachers to effortlessly make observations *during* instruction instead of after.

One technique is to keep a file with an index card on each student. At the end of each day, take a moment to write down any significant observations about students on their cards. These cards

will be very beneficial when it is time to write up individual student progress reports or have discussions with parents at parent-teacher conferences.

Checklists To keep track of students' observations, teachers often keep checklists. These checklists can be used to evaluate knowledge, skills, or attitudes. For example, on a class roster you can easily tally the frequency of students' participations in classroom discussions. Or you might maintain a checklist of important concepts and check off students who demonstrate understanding of the concepts. For example, on a list with items such as "understands why machines make work easier," "sees why we lubricate machines to reduce friction," and "knows how energy is transferred in a system," you could jot down students' names under the appropriate list heads.

You can assess skills by observing students and recording on a checklist which skills they use. During a lesson, walk around the room with your checklist while students are working. Choose a few students to observe, and mark on the checklist the skills in which they seem to be proficient. Imagine that your students are working on a project that explores the kinds of trees in the neighborhood. As part of the project, they are observing leaves, classifying them into groups, and graphing the numbers of trees in each classification. You might use the checklist in Table 7.1.

Checklists are time savers: Teachers can rapidly mark off on a checklist evidence of a

---

TABLE 7.1 Project-Specific Checklist

1. Observation

_____ 1.1 Can identify major characteristics of the leaves

_____ 1.2 Notices similarities among the leaves

_____ 1.3 Notices differences among the leaves

2. Classification

_____ 2.1 Can determine a method of grouping leaves into two groups

_____ 2.2 Can determine a way to group leaves within groups

_____ 2.3 Can explain why leaves are classified

_____ 2.4 Can classify a new leaf into the existing classification scheme

TABLE 7.2   Generic Checklist

Questioning	**Gathering data to explore questions**
The student can	The student can
_____ explore ideas	_____ observe characteristics
_____ form a question	_____ identify ways to measure data
_____ remain curious	_____ seek additional information
_____ design an investigation	_____ use science equipment
_____ formulate a hypothesis	_____ measure accurately
_____ note discrepant events	_____ estimate answers
_____ notice problems	_____ examine more than one variable
_____ challenge ideas	_____ select variables
_____ remain skeptical	_____ name an object

Examining data to answer questions	**Answering questions**
The student can	The student can
_____ classify objects into groups	_____ communicate results
_____ make predictions	_____ summarize information
_____ analyze results	_____ make revisions
_____ describe observations	_____ make decisions
_____ make comparisons	_____ demonstrate knowledge
_____ graph information	_____ identify limitations
_____ order or sequence data	_____ make inferences
_____ search for patterns	_____ describe discrepancies
_____ tabulate information	_____ establish criteria
_____ identify errors	_____ offer evidence
_____ interpret data	_____ verify results
_____ control variables	_____ solve problems
_____ calculate	_____ generate new questions
_____ make drawings or diagrams	_____ establish relationships

skill or the meeting of an objective. You might keep an observation sheet for each student in a three-ring binder, making a functional grade book for tracking student progress. This method of observation has the added benefit of keeping you focused on your lesson objectives. It also helps you make sure that no one falls between the cracks and goes unnoticed. Finally, it provides documented evidence of progress for grade cards or progress reports or for discussions with students and their parents.

Checklists can be either project specific, as with the leaf-classification checklist, or generic. Table 7.2 shows a generic checklist designed to gather information about general skill development.

In Activity 7.6, you will try your hand at developing a skills checklist.

Checklists can also provide you with a list of affective attributes to look for in a project-based science classroom. Table 7.3 is an inventory of dispositions to be used as a guide when observing students.

In Activity 7.7, you will develop an assessment for monitoring affective attributes.

Clinical Interviews   Interviews with people seeking jobs can tell an employer a great deal that résumés, grade transcripts, or applications cannot. For example, an interview can provide insight into a candidate's motivation and rapport with people. Also, during an interview, a candidate has time to elaborate on specific items in his or her résumé, transcript, or application. Interviews are also common for candidates seek-

---

ACTIVITY 7.6

Developing a Skills Checklist

MATERIALS NEEDED:
- materials to teach a lesson developed in this investigation

A. Design a lesson that requires a great number of skills such as observing, measuring, classifying, inferring, and concluding. Teach this lesson to a team of classmates after you design a checklist of all the skills you might observe while your classmates are engaging in the investigation. Try to keep track of your classmates' performance while they participate in your lesson.

B. Share the checklist with your classmates. Discuss whether it was an accurate measure of the skills they used. How might it be improved?

C. Put the checklist in your portfolio.

TABLE 7.3   Affective Attributes of Students in Project-Based Science

ambition to investigate	honesty in artifacts	satisfaction with artifacts
compromise with others	independence	self-confidence
cooperation with others	objectivity	self-discipline
curiosity about the world	open-mindedness	self-reliance
dependability	patience with others	sensitivity to others
disciplined thinking	persistence with a task	skepticism about results
enthusiasm to continue	precision	thoroughness
excitement about science	questioning attitude	tolerance for change
fascination with findings	respect for evidence	willingness to change
flexibility with ideas	responsibility to project	

ACTIVITY 7.7

Assessing Affective Attributes

MATERIALS NEEDED:
- pencil and paper

A. Evaluate a science lesson (one you participated in during this course or one you taught to children). What affective attributes (attitudes or dispositions) do you think would be important to the lesson? List them.

B. Create a method to monitor the dispositions. Would it be a formal attitude inventory, an interview, a journal?

C. Some educators do not believe that monitoring attitudes or dispositions is an important teacher activity. Write an essay presenting your opinion on the matter or debate the idea with others in your class.

D. Put your essay or notes about your discussion in your portfolio.

---

ing master's or doctoral degrees. During these one- or two-hour interviews, university committee members can ask candidates unanticipated questions, and candidates can demonstrate in greater depth what they know.

Classroom interviews with your students can serve similar purposes. In an interview, students can explain in greater detail what they understand, how they're progressing, what problems they're having, and what steps they or you might take to improve learning. In an interview, you can get to know students, work on individual student goals, and clarify misunderstandings and concerns. Interviews provide a depth of information that other forms of assessment cannot. They also provide opportunity for clarification of classroom observations. For example, you might observe that a student never raises her hand during class and conclude that she's having difficulty with the topic. However, an interview with the student may reveal that she is simply bored, tired, or shy.

Interviews with students can be either informal or formal. Informal interviews, which resemble teacher-student discussions (written notes can be made after the discussion), are less stressful to students than are many other forms of assessment. Imagine that in an informal interview about a water quality project you ask, "Why did you use the balance scale to measure the amount of water?" and the student answers, "I wanted to see which weighed more." To probe for more in-depth understanding and to ascertain why the student is only interested in a general level of measurement ("more water" versus "less water"), rather than an exact measurement in milliliters, the teachers might ask "Tell me what you mean by 'more'?"

Formal interviews may seem more stressful, but they don't have to be. What differentiates formal and informal interviews is the greater structure of formal interviews. You might set up formal interviews, for example, to elicit the same information from each student. A list of guiding questions will keep you focused on your objectives. Some guiding questions you might ask are "What is your driving question?" "What is the design of your investigation?" "What materials or equipment are you using?" "What have you accomplished so far?" "Are you having any problems?" "What kinds of results have you obtained?" "What are your conclusions so far?" and "What do you intend to do next?" However, guiding questions only provide the foundation to a formal interview: You will need to ask additional questions to clarify student answers and elicit in-depth answers.

Open-ended questions are a great way to start either formal or informal interviews. An open-ended question gives a child a cue to explain what she thinks. Compare these two types of opening questions: "Lisa, how many stages did the butterfly go through?" "Lisa, what can you tell me about butterfly stages?" and "Lisa, what have you learned about butterflies this week?" The first question squelches conversation and limits the child's response. She will have answered the question if she only says, "Five." The teacher could just have easily obtained this amount of information with a written test. The second question, while still focusing on butterfly stages, permits a richer explanation. However, the third question gives Lisa the greatest opportunity to elaborate on what she knows and doesn't know about butterflies, and it may lead to some unexpected responses. The teacher can then ask probing questions to see if Lisa has any misunderstandings and to find out how much she knows about butterflies and their stages of growth.

Another effective technique for either informal or formal interviews is the "what if" question. For example, a teacher might ask: "What if the balance scale were used to measure the helium balloon? What would you see?" This type of question probes students' understanding even further by forcing them to think about new variables and different situations.

Keeping records of both informal and formal interviews provides a rich source of information for portfolios, parent-teacher conferences, and future discussions with students. After an interview, jot down your thoughts about students' understandings and misunderstandings. If you take notes during interviews, some children will become intimidated and stop talking. Also, jotting down a note about each question makes the interview process too time-consuming.

Assessment Based on Concept Maps   In Chapter 6, we learned that concept mapping can be used to link new ideas or experiences with earlier ones. Concept mapping can also be a powerful method of assessing individual students' conceptual understandings or the understandings being formulated among groups of students.

Examine the concept maps shown in Figures 7.2 and 7.3. If a fourth grade student had completed the first map to show prior understanding about magnets, what would you be able to say about the student's misunderstanding? What major concepts are missing? First, magnets are not attracted to all types of metal, so this demonstrates an incomplete understanding. Second, opposite poles attract and like poles repel, but the student depicts both the north and south poles attracting to the north pole. Third, the map fails to include some major concepts such as temporary and permanent magnets, natural and human-made magnets, and magnetic fields.

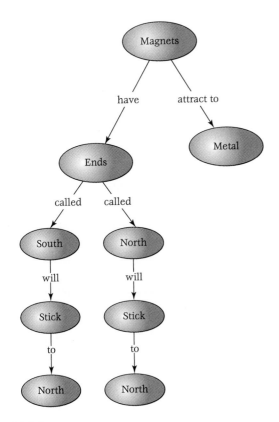

FIGURE 7.2
Limited concept map.

In short, you could use this concept map to diagnose the student's knowledge of magnets and adapt instruction accordingly. If the same fourth grade student completed the second concept map following a project that investigated magnets, you could conclude that the student's conceptual understanding of magnets had improved dramatically.

Some teachers use concept maps with groups of students during discussions, interviews, and group projects. A concept map drawn on the board or projected on an overhead transparency or LCD pad can form the basis for a class discussion about the relationship among ideas that surface while investigating a driving question. Concept maps can be used to probe students about their interpretations of investigation findings. Finally, students can collaborate on their own concept maps to illustrate the relationships among their findings.

Concept maps can also be evaluated. Students' concept maps are commonly scored according to the complexity of the conceptual relationships they illustrate (Novak & Gowin, 1984). For example, students might be awarded one point for every hierarchical level in a concept map, quantifying the complexity of their

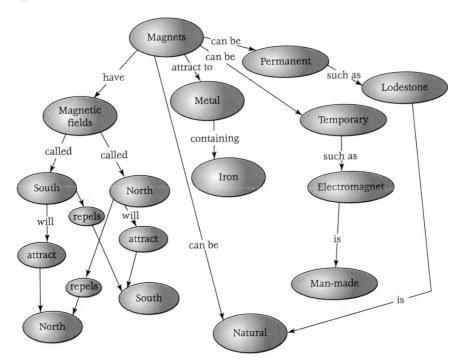

FIGURE 7.3
Complex concept map.

thinking. A point could also be given each time a concept was branched into new categories. For example, in the second concept map, the student has branched the idea of magnetic fields into two subcategories, north and south. Likewise, students may be awarded points for cross-links such as those between human-made magnets and electromagnets and between natural magnets and lodestone. You might award more points for branches and cross-links that occur at higher hierarchical levels.

Performance-Based Assessment **Performance-based assessment** refers to methods of directly examining students' knowledge, skills, and dispositions. With these methods, teachers collect assessment information while observing students as they perform some targeted activity. The activity can be a natural part of a lesson (observing something under a microscope), or it can be a prompt given to provoke an observable action (setting up equipment and providing a set of directions asking students to assemble a slide and focus a microscope).

In project-based science environments, students must integrate a complex combination of knowledge and skills in order to carry out their investigations, create artifacts, and present their projects to others. Performance-based assessments involve similar integration and consequently are a good fit with project-based science. For example, students who have been investigating how to set up and maintain an aquarium may have learned about acids and bases (pH), nitrogen cycles, life cycles of fish, salt- and freshwater, and classifications of animals. They may also have used a variety of science skills such as *observing* the behavior of fish, *measuring* the pH or temperature of the water, *classifying* the types of fish that can get along together, *making inferences* about fish that die, and *forming conclusions* about appropriate conditions for their fish. A performance-based assessment might consist of giving students a pH test kit and five water samples. A prompt tells the students that certain tropical fish can only survive in pH levels ranging between 7 and 8. Students are then asked to determine which of the water samples would be safe for the fish. This question could be extended to measure problem solving skills by asking students what they could

do to make the inappropriate water samples livable for the fish. This performance-based assessment item integrates students' abilities to measure water accurately, interpret a chart, understand pH, and draw a conclusion.

To summarize, good performance-based assessment seeks to put students in realistic situations in which they must integrate relevant knowledge and skills in order to perform a target activity. A good performance-based test item usually includes the following characteristics:

It reflects important curriculum targets. Good performance-based assessment reflects those curriculum goals that have been the objects of classroom instruction. For example, if students have been investigating the weather, they needed to learn how to use a thermometer. It is, thus, more *realistic* in an assessment to have students use a real thermometer to measure and record the temperature of air than it is to have them identify the temperature on a picture of a thermometer.

It asks students to create a product (artifact). Good performance-based assessment encourages students to create a product. For example, students might make their own barometer to measure air pressure. Being able to do so would indicate understanding of the purpose of a barometer, of how it works, and of the effect of barometric changes on the weather.

It asks students to collaborate and use resources. Collaboration and use of resources is another key feature of good performance-based assessment. Students learn to work with others and with equipment, materials, or resources to solve a problem and create a product. For example, students might work in a collaborative team to solve a problem about what types of ground cover collect the most heat in the summer. The team might decide to use a thermometer to measure and a computer spreadsheet to record temperature of four different materials— stone, grass, asphalt, and sand.

It encourages active investigation. Good performance-based assessment encourages the type of active investigation mentioned in the ground cover example. Students engage in exploration of ideas and questions rather than in passive activities such as listening to the teacher, watching a movie, reading about a concept, or watching a demonstration.

It permits multiple approaches. Performance-based assessment permits multiple approaches to solving a problem. For example, students might be asked to construct an "ear" that would be a good sound collecting device.[1] There is no one answer to this task. Students could design a cone-shaped ear that looks like a megaphone. They could make a long, narrow ear like a rabbit's. They could draw pictures of their ears and explain the design of the human ear in accompanying text.

It integrates ideas. Performance-based assessment also requires the integration of ideas. If students create an "ear" that is cone-shaped and has "hairs" in it, they have combined the ideas that funnel shapes gather sound waves and that hairs (which are solids) carry sound waves better than does air. They will also have used their artistic skills to design the ear and their literacy skills to explain the design.

It requires higher order thinking. Performance-based assessment demands higher order thinking, and it emphasizes concepts over individual facts. For example, it requires students to understand the bigger ideas of how air pressure affects the weather or how well sound travels through various objects as opposed to memorizing the definition of *air pressure* or *frequency* and selecting the "correct answer" from among a list of possible answers.

It is interesting. Good performance-based assessment is inherently more interesting than traditional paper and pencil tests. Making a barometer or an "ear" is more challenging and motivating than selecting from a list of definitions. Because students enjoy the learning process involved in the assessment item, they feel less anxiety. As a result, assessment results are more reliable.

It is developmentally appropriate. Performance-based assessment emphasizes the characteristics promoted as developmentally appropriate for both early childhood and young adolescent students (NAEYC, 1986; NMSA, 1995). These characteristics include the use of concrete materials rather than passive paper and pencil tasks. Performance-based assessment stresses problem solving processes over memorization of abstract ideas. It doesn't punish students who are nonreaders or poor readers. It engages students in direct, purposeful experiences rather than in contrived assessment tasks. It integrates subject areas. By allowing multiple approaches, it builds self-esteem and allows for differences in learning types, ability, and development. Finally, it is interesting and motivating.

How do you go about designing a performance-based assessment? First, you must decide what science content to include in the performance. For example, your instructional objective might be "Students will understand how energy is transferred in an electrical system." Second, you must determine what skills or complex processes to observe while students engage in the activity. For example, students assembling an electrical system will classify objects according to whether they conduct electricity or not. They will make inferences about the type of energy that is used in a dry cell. They will make conclusions about how the energy is transferred from the dry cell to the wires and the light bulb to give off light. Third, you must generate the activity for the performance assessment. For example, you might decide to set up an activity in which students are given light bulbs, dry cells, wire, and a small motor and asked to make the motor work using only the items provided. Fourth, you must test the assessment item by letting students try out the activity. Fifth, you must revise the performance-based task based upon trial runs.

In recent years, performance-based tasks have become such a popular technique for collecting assessment information that large assessment companies, such as the Educational Testing Service (ETS), are now developing and

1. Credit for this idea goes to colleagues in science education, Dr. Jodi Haney at Bowling Green State University and Dr. Andrew Lumpe at Southern Illinois University.

ACTIVITY 7.8

Developing a Performance-Based Assessment

MATERIALS NEEDED:
- materials to teach a lesson developed in this investigation

A. Following are two ideas an elementary or middle grade teacher might want a student to develop in a project-based environment. These require a complex combination of knowledge and skills. Form a team of three. Read each idea and decide what would be the most authentic ways to measure whether students have gained the pertinent knowledge and skills.
- Each student will be able to observe the differences between two types of soils and determine which one is the best to plant a cactus.
- Each student will be able to read a weather map and determine what the weather will be like tomorrow.

During your decision making, consider the following criteria of good performance-based assessment:

1. It reflects important curriculum targets.
2. It is consistent with instruction.
3. It asks students to collaborate and use resources.
4. It encourages active investigation.
5. It permits multiple approaches.
6. It integrates ideas.
7. It requires higher order thinking.
8. It is interesting.
9. It is developmentally appropriate.

B. As a team, develop a lesson to teach one of the two objectives. Develop two different ways of assessing the objective after you have taught it. Teach the lesson to another team in your class and try the two different methods of assessment.

C. Ask the team you taught which method of assessment best measured what they learned. How did their beliefs match yours about good techniques for assessing complex combinations of knowledge and skills?

D. How do these findings fit with your state science proficiency model? Record your lesson, assessment methods, and conclusions in your portfolio.

---

adopting these types of tests. This should not be surprising. In all other aspects of our lives we make evaluations on the basis of actual performance. We want our automobiles to run, our doctors to rid us of our ailments, our dentists to fix our cavities, and our plumbers to fix our sinks. We expect artists to generate emotions, entertain, and challenge and athletes to amaze us with their physical abilities. Why, then, do we expect our students only to regurgitate answers and not also to do what it is that they should be able to do? Activity 7.8 asks you to develop a performance-based assessment.

Assembling and Presenting Assessment Information

After teachers and students have collected assessment information, they must assemble it into a presentable form for others to see. In project-based science, there are two main ways to assemble and present information: artifacts and portfolios.

Artifacts are the products that result from an investigation: writing samples, journals, physical models, drawings, videotapes, or multimedia documents. Artifacts, which represent students' work and emerging understandings, provide a concrete product that can be assessed. They have long been a natural part of assessment in the arts, but they are now being recognized for their contribution to science education.

What do you think of when you look at the shells you collected at the ocean, the turquoise jewelry purchased in the Southwest, the miniature lighthouse you bought in Maine, the Alligator-shaped mug you collected in Florida? What do your parents think of when they look at your baby pictures, that Mother's Day card you drew in first grade, that graduation tassel? Like souvenirs and keepsakes, artifacts that have been assembled for the purpose of assessment form lasting memories in our minds. Students are more likely to remember their science products if they culminate in some type of public presentation: a presentation about landfills given to younger students, a poster about recycling displayed at the mall, a videotape about weather that becomes a tool for future instruction.

Why are students more likely to remember artifacts than abstract knowledge? First, through the creation of artifacts, knowledge is constructed in students' minds. As students reflect upon what they have learned and develop artifacts, they actively manipulate science knowledge and thereby generate understanding. Second, the fact that learning does not occur in linear, discrete steps argues against traditional tests that are constructed around small, discrete bits of information, whereas artifacts let students display their learning in a fashion consistent with real-life learning, which unfolds as a continuous process. Third, all students learn differently, and in developing artifacts, students can use varied ways of displaying their learning that are compatible with their learning styles. Students who are interested in drama might role-play their understanding. Those interested in music might write songs to describe what they learned. Artistically inclined students can create models, posters, and murals. Talented writers can compose reports and papers. Fourth, students are more likely to remember what is meaningful to them. Do you remember an obscure lesson from fifth grade that involved calculating the area of a 4-inch by 3-inch square? Probably not. However, if you ever had to measure a floor or wall to purchase carpeting or wallpaper, you might remember making those calculations because there was a real purpose to them. Likewise, when students develop artifacts to share with an audience, they are more likely to remember the experience since it has social meaning. Fifth, artifacts developed as part of a collaborative process provide social experiences students are likely to remember.

When you think back to your own education, you probably have vivid memories of friends you played with or collaborating on a school play. Do you have similar memories of routine classroom lessons? Social experiences form lasting memories that we tend to cherish. Because project-based science stresses development of student artifacts in collaborative settings, students are far more likely to have lasting memories of these group experiences than they are of typical school lessons that involve little social interaction.

Portfolios, which are collections of student artifacts, can be thought of as both objects and

FIGURE 7.4
Teachers provide thoughtful feedback to students.

methods of assessment. As objects, they are a place for holding materials such as papers, photographs, or drawings that are representative of students' work and progress. As methods of assessment, portfolios are ways to continuously collect and assess student work.

Assembling Artifacts There are many ways of assembling information into artifacts. We will focus on writing samples, daily journals, physical products, drawings, music, videotapes, and multidimensional documents.

Writing Samples Students can demonstrate understanding in a number of ways using writing samples, and there are several good reasons for using this technique to assemble information. First, writing samples provide a creative and accurate measure of student understanding. Second, writing is a curriculum-based task; it matches goals of instruction and integrates the language arts. Third, writing is active rather than passive like traditional test taking. Fourth, writing is complex and allows students to provide rich interpretations of their investigations. Fifth, writing is directed at learning styles and targets students with verbal/linguistic abilities. Finally, writing is a task that students consider worthwhile.

There is nothing wrong with report writing, and it is necessary to teach students how to write a report. Having children write reports assesses their ability to obtain and synthesize information and to communicate through reading and writing. Also, students can learn a great deal from writing independent reports on given topics. However, there are many other types of writing samples that can be used to evaluate understanding. Students can write stories, create poetry, make television commercials, produce plays or puppet shows, create newspaper articles, write documentaries, draft letters, compose essays, keep diaries, write computer presentations, or create comic strips. Students also can write reactions to guest speakers, films, videos, or software programs; they can develop biographies or autobiographies; and they can create annotated bibliographies. Each of these samples can be a powerful way to assess science understanding.

Imagine that fifth grade students write stories to tell about parasitic and symbiotic relationships. One boy writes a clever story about a flea named Billy. Billy wanted a new world away from the familiar scene he had on the back of an old, outdoor dog. The story tells of the flea's adventures in the big city—almost getting run over by a car, fumigated by a pest control sprayer, and stepped upon by a pedestrian. The flea was hungry, scared, and tired. He decided that there was no place like home and returned to the back of the dog where he was safe and well fed. Of course, the dog wasn't too happy about Billy the Flea's return![2] Using a story format, this student is able to explain most of what he knows about this particular parasitic relationship. This same student might have failed a test item that asked him to identify the correct definition of *parasite*. Would the teacher accurately have measured the boy's understanding with a test item? Would he have been able to elaborate on the parasitic relationship with the depth and richness that he displayed in this story?

Here are some other writing ideas that can be used in science classes. Have students take the viewpoints of other people to illustrate their understandings of particular concepts. For example, a student might present a lesson on evolution from the point of view of Charles Darwin—

how would Darwin argue about evolution? Or imagine that students have launched an investigation into the changes in Lake Erie over the last century. After learning about the history of the lake, they might create a travel brochure telling about the lake's geological and environmental features and the impact of humans. Students could draw maps, diagrams, or illustrations of the area for the travel brochure.

Daily Journals Daily journals are personal records of events and experiences and reflections that offer several advantages over other forms of assessment. First, they let students assemble some of their own assessment information. Second, they permit the teacher to conduct assessment at the most convenient time. Third, journal writing encourages students to connect science to their daily lives. Fourth, journals encourage candid teacher-to-student or student-to-student communication.

The typical elementary or middle grade teacher's day is very busy and hectic. Teachers are usually responsible for teaching all subjects to twenty-five to thirty students of varying ability levels and cultural backgrounds. Journal assessment helps teachers out in several ways. First, when students make their own observations about what they have learned from a particular activity and about what continues to present difficulty, the teacher is relieved of some of the assessment burden. Second, teachers can read journals after school hours when things aren't so hectic.

Journal writing also encourages students to associate science with their everyday lives. For example, a teacher might encourage students to keep track of the science-related literature stories they read, of science-related news items, and of science-related shows they see on television. Students could keep annotated reading lists in their journals. They could also comment on what they learn in science class and how it is related to their lives.

Communication between students and teachers is typically enhanced with journal writing because students often open up in journals and write things in their journals that they would not say publicly. Students are often more willing to write than talk about what they learn, and they commonly describe their feelings, attitudes

2. Credit for this story goes to one of Charlene's former fifth grade students, Robert Coggin.

and fears in a journal. When teachers respond to what students have written, what results is an ongoing dialogue that helps guide instruction. For example, if a student were to share in her journal that she is nervous about presenting in front of her classmates, the teacher could take steps to alleviate this fear—perhaps by having the student present with a partner.

Some teachers encourage students to communicate with each other by trading journals. By writing back and forth with a friend, students can discuss their science class, construct understandings in a social context, and compare what they are learning to what others are learning.

Physical Products If you wanted to buy a new automobile, would you rather read about and see the car in a catalog or see the real product? What's the difference? The real product provides you with a *realistic* assessment of the car's riding comfort, sound quality, road handling, acceleration rate, turning ratio, workmanship, and design. Reading about it might only give you the opinions of others. Similarly, to see what students really know and can do, teachers need to make evaluative judgments from actual student products. The finished work of students is the best evidence of the knowledge and skills used and applied in a given situation.

A product can be a book, a physical model of some kind, or a working apparatus that a student makes to demonstrate what she has learned. For example, imagine that students were interested in the human lung. They could develop a project in which they researched how human lungs worked; write a report about lungs; develop a physical 3-D model of the lung using ordinary household objects such as straws, balloons, sponges, and cups; and give a presentation on how smoking is harmful to lungs. When finished, students would have demonstrated their ability to collect and synthesize information, to communicate and to solve problems, and to create a product.

Teachers should always inform students about their expectations for a project and about how they will be evaluated on it. Expectations and evaluation criteria can be communicated verbally or in the form of checklists. Checklists are particularly effective because they can be shared with parents and because teachers easily can convert them into scoring rubrics to evaluate products. Figure 7.5 shows an example of a parent letter and checklist for the human lung project.

Drawings Drawings give students a chance to represent scientific understanding in diverse forms such as murals, bulletin boards, posters, and bumper stickers. For example, students investigating the types of animals and plants in their neighborhood might create a mural of the neighborhood. Students might create posters of what they found in their school trash that will end up in a landfill. Finally, they might create bumper stickers using permanent markers on strips of contact paper to communicate their opinion of local recycling policies.

Drawing, as a form of assessment, offers the following advantages to students. First, it lets visual/spatial learners demonstrate their knowledge in a way that is comfortable for them. Second, drawings are sometimes a more accurate way to measure understanding because children can depict ideas such as the water cycle more completely than they could say through exposition (words). Third, drawings can be used to express attitudes or feelings about science through pictures, color, and texture. Fourth, drawings are particularly effective for assessing science understanding in early elementary grades when student aren't able to read and write well. The following examples illustrate some of the benefits of assessments based on drawings.

Imagine that you are teaching seventh grade students how to use a microscope to observe cheek cells (a common activity in which students swab the insides of their mouths and rub the cells on a slide) and onion cells (an activity in which students place a single layer of onion skin on a slide) because they are investigating how plants and animals differ. Your objectives for the students might include learning to use a microscope correctly (a skill) and learning the differences between animal and plant cells (knowledge). While an elementary grade student could probably describe to you the differences between cells, if you want students to notice that animals cells are rounded with a cell membrane and plant cells are stiff and rectangular with a cell wall, then having the students draw what they observe will give you a good way to measure your objectives.

Dear Parents,

Your son/daughter has been learning about the human body in science. So far, we have learned about the skeletal system and the circulatory system. The students have become interested in how the lungs work and are now investigating this topic. The project they are working on will show what they learned from their investigations and will be shared with classmates on November 15th.

The project is designed so that your son/daughter will work as part of a collaborative team investigating this topic. However, you can help by taking him/her to the library or helping obtain materials that could be used to develop a project. The project may require some common household materials such as straws, balloons, sponges, paper, cups, and glue, but you should not spend any significant amount of money on these materials.

When your son/daughter shares the project on November 15th, it will be evaluated on the following criteria:

1. The report answers the question "How do our lungs work?"

2. The report is thorough enough to answer the question completely.

3. Teams are expected to use at least two references in the report with only one of the references being an encyclopedia.

4. Pictures or diagrams should be used to help communicate this information.

5. Teams will construct a physical model that demonstrates how the lungs work.

6. Each team member should be able to explain how the model represents a real lung.

7. Each team member should be able to explain why smoking harms the lungs.

If you have any questions about this project, please contact me at school.

Sincerely,

Mrs. Czerniak

FIGURE 7.5
Parent letter.

Imagine a third grade classroom in which students are learning about how animals see. The teacher has taught students how the eye works, and students participated in a teacher-lead activity in which they used flashlights to observe how classmates' pupils expanded or contracted in the presence or absence of light. To assess students' understanding, the teacher asks them to draw pictures that explain how their eyes work. One child draws a picture of rays shooting out of the eyes toward an object and then returning to the eye. This drawing tells the teacher that the child has an inaccurate conception of sight and thinks that we see because of rays that come from our eyes. Drawings help teachers identify when children are having difficulty understanding science concepts.

Imagine a classroom in which students are drawing pictures of scientists. This technique, called *draw a scientist,* examines students' beliefs and attitudes about science (Barman, 1996; Boylan, Hill, Wallace, & Wheeler, 1992; Huber & Burton, 1995; Rampal, 1992; Sumrall, 1995). Researchers have found that students commonly depict scientists very stereotypically, as white, balding men wearing glasses and white lab coats. Of course, the scientist is usually surrounded by glassware out of which vapors are rising. Frequently, he has a disheveled or evil appearance. This activity can be used to monitor students' beliefs about who can become scientists and about what scientists can do in their careers.

Music Students who possess strong musical/rhythmic intelligence can demonstrate their understanding of science by creating songs, raps, jingles, or cheers. They can engage in choral readings or set plays to music. A number of commercial science songs provide students with stimuli for their own writing. Song writers such as Raffi and the Banana Slug String Band have created science-related songs, such as "Baby Beluga" and the "Water Cycle Boogie," that are popular among elementary students.

Videotapes Students can record the images and sounds of their investigations on videotape. Videotapes are useful forms of assessment for several reasons. First, creating a videotape is easy. Second, the videotapes can be edited, which is akin to revision in writing. Third, they permit subsequent playback or broadcasting to public audiences. Fourth, they conveniently document long-term projects. Fifth, videotapes form vivid memories in students' minds. Sixth, the act of creating a videotape can force students to focus on the main ideas learned.

Almost all schools now have access to a video camera and a VCR. In addition, it is relatively simple to create a videotape. The technology has advanced to the point at which even young elementary students are able to use it. Since videotapes can be played back for broadcast, they are records that can be used for assessment and for instruction.

Because video can be filmed in sections, edited, and stored until additional footage is captured, videotapes are a convenient way to document long-term projects. An investigation about why leaves drop from trees in the fall might span an entire school year. Video footage could be collected over a long period of time to document this year-long process.

Remember the exotic vacation analogy? Videotaping a vacation provides continuous sight and sound documentation. For this reason, videotapes form vivid memories in students' minds. In one fifth grade classroom, students made an 8 mm movie of William Tell. To this day, many years later, one of the authors of this book remembers more about Swiss history than about the history of any other European country.

Videotapes can be used to generate unique and complex presentations, vividly capturing what students know. For example, older elementary students can connect video cameras to microscopes and computers to add new dimensions and edit video and audio footage.

The process of creating a video can force students to focus on main ideas. If students, for example, are required to present their science project to classmates in a fifteen-minute video, they must focus on only the most important concepts and best examples. This editing process can help students sift out the most important information from a mass of facts or unrelated data.

Multidimensional Documents Making the artifacts that we have discussed so far can be meaningful for students and result in thorough and useful assessment. Multidimensional documents that combine writing, illustrations, photographs, videotapes, audiotapes, computer applications, and other media can enrich conceptual understanding and assessment even further. Multidimensional documents give students an opportunity to present their understandings more fully than words alone ever could. In addition, they give students the opportunity to depict learning in ways that are most consistent with their learning styles.

For example, student photographers in your classroom might enjoy documenting their learning with photographs. Computers enable students to combine images and scan them into their written documents. Students can take photographs with digital cameras, and these digital pictures easily can be added to documents. Students can readily collect data and create graphs using computer programs. Quicktime movies enable students to add short clips of footage to their writing. Hypercard programs let students combine writing, audio, and visual images into a single document.

Presenting Artifacts   Any of the artifacts (writing, journals, products, drawings, music, videotapes, and multidimensional documents) already discussed can be used in presentations to groups of younger students, peers, parents, or community members. Presentations don't necessarily have to involve artifacts, however. For example, students who possess a strong bodily/kinesthetic ability may enjoy engaging in debates, simulations, plays, and role-plays. Whatever the format, presentations can motivate students and enhance their self-esteem.

Students are more motivated to complete investigations and put forth their best effort to develop artifacts when they see a purpose to the activity. Too often in elementary and middle grade classrooms, students complete work that is only seen by the teacher. Presenting an artifact to a real audience provides an investigation with a real, meaningful purpose and gives students the experience of dialoguing with others about their work.

Developing Portfolios   Portfolio assessment is a process of collecting representative samples of students' work over time for purposes of documenting and assessing their learning. Typically, four types of documentation are contained in portfolios: artifacts, reproductions, attestations, and productions (Collins, 1992). As

already discussed, artifacts include writing samples, journals, physical products, drawings, music, videotapes, and multidimensional documents produced in the normal course of a science investigation.

Reproductions are documents attesting to the learning process—not the actual items produced. They include photographs of projects, videotapes of projects, or audiotapes of presentations. The difference between artifacts and reproductions is that artifacts are created during the investigative process, whereas reproductions are created after to document a project. A student's photographs of trees taken during the year to track seasonal changes are artifacts. A teacher's photographs of students' leaf collections is a reproduction.

Attestations are testimonials about a student's work prepared by someone other than the student, such as the teacher, a parent, or a peer. Some examples are a critique by a peer, a letter from a parent, and a report card from the teacher.

Productions are documents that help explain the contents of a portfolio. They include such items as goal statements, personal reflections, captions, and descriptions of what the items in the portfolio represent.

While studying neighborhood trees, students might take photographs of trees throughout the seasons, write reports about trees, collect samples of leaves or needles, map the locations of the trees and draw pictures of the seeds of trees. Some or all of these artifacts could be placed in a portfolio. Since the actual leaf collection would not hold up well in a portfolio, a photograph of the set (a reproduction) could be added to document the learning. The portfolio might also include a testimonial (an attestation) from a parent telling about a child's trip to a local park to identify different types of trees. Students could reflect on their experiences and add to the portfolio a letter to the teacher (a production) telling the most important idea they learned about trees in the neighborhood.

A portfolio can be contained in a file folder, a box, or any other suitable container for student work. However, a portfolio is not just a random collection of student work. It is a carefully planned collection that includes representative samples of student artifacts, reproductions, attes-

---

ACTIVITY 7.9

Creating Your Own Portfolio

A. Think about the major items you've learned in your science teaching methods course. List them on a sheet of paper. You might refer to your instructor's syllabus for help on this or talk to your instructor about it.

B. Now think about things you've done in class that could provide evidence that you've met the objectives. What artifacts could you include in the portfolio? Are there reproductions or attestations from the instructor, cooperating teachers, peers and children that you can include? What productions will you add? List as many things as you can that will provide evidence

of your learning. You might include photos of your teaching; videotapes; assignments from class; your philosophy of teaching science; lesson plans; unit plans; samples of student work; letters from students, parents, cooperating teachers, and instructors; samples of your own writing; reflections on your teaching; evaluations from instructors and cooperating teachers; letters of recommendation; and lists of your educational activities.

C. Begin a teaching portfolio. Think about items that a prospective employer might want to see. What items would add value to your portfolio and help you obtain a job or get a good evaluation from a principal?

---

tations, and productions collected over the entire school year organized so as to clearly represent learning for the viewer. Like documentation of vacation that includes photographs, diaries, videotapes, and personal mementos, a good portfolio contains a carefully assembled sample of student work that encourages reflection.

There are many questions and issues to think about when implementing portfolios in a project-based science classroom. First, the purpose of the assessment should be established before starting the portfolio. Working together, the teacher and student should decide what kind of documents will best demonstrate the student's knowledge and abilities. Will the portfolio contain only the "best" samples of work or samples of varied quality? Must the evidence be individual student products or should the work be completed and documented through a collaborative effort of several students? How much evidence should be in the portfolio? What criteria will be used to judge each piece of work? Teachers frequently construct their criteria, scoring rubrics, checklists, or other methods of judgment prior to selecting the student work to be included in the portfolio. Teachers must also decide if all students will be evaluated by the same criteria; determine how often and by whom the portfolio will be evaluated; decide where the portfolio will be kept and what access students will have to it; help students select samples of their

work that accurately represent their abilities; and periodically critique the portfolio for its effectiveness in helping make decisions and in determining what students know, can do, and are like.

A portfolio can be useful for teachers as well. Activity 7.9 will help you develop a teaching portfolio.

Evaluating Assessment Information

The purpose of evaluation is to make judgments about student growth, set goals, and report information to students and their parents. In the past, teachers used assessment mostly for reporting grades, and only the teacher had a voice in determining how well students were doing. Today, authentic assessment techniques give students a voice in the assessment process. In this section, we will discuss how scoring rubrics can be used to assess artifacts, performances, and portfolios. We will also address the processes of self-assessment and peer assessment.

Scoring Rubrics One helpful technique for evaluating an artifact, performance, or portfolio is to use a scoring rubric. A scoring rubric is a brief, written description of different levels of student performance. It often uses the same set of observable criteria that goes into a checklist.

TABLE 7.4 Analytic Scoring Rubric	Excellent	Good	Satisfactory	Poor
Uses logical inferences	4	3	2	1
Is scientifically accurate	4	3	2	1
Has supporting data	4	3	2	1
Has supporting rationale	4	3	2	1
Has supporting diagrams and drawings	4	3	2	1

Typically, rubrics are classified as either *holistic* or *analytic.*

Holistic rubrics measure the overall quality of an artifact, performance, or portfolio. They evaluate criteria like creativity, relevance to real life, impact, clarity, completeness, and organization. For example, the following holistic rubric contains four general criteria. Although the rubric provides a general framework for scoring students, it does not provide *specific* criteria such as the focus of the scientific content or what characteristics would make the project creative, complete, and clearly presented:

◆ **3 points:** The student makes logical inferences supported by data collected in the investigations, gives rationales for the inferences, and supports the inferences with diagrams and drawings.
◆ **2 points:** The student makes inferences supported by data collected in the investigations but does not support them with rationales.
◆ **1 point:** The student makes a logical inference, but it is not supported by the data collected in the investigations.
◆ **0 points:** The student fails to make a logical inference.

Analytic rubrics measure artifacts, performances, or portfolios in a quantitative manner by assigning (or taking away) points for criteria that are present (or missing). For example, a teacher who is evaluating the investigative process and students' abilities to make inferences might use the analytic scoring rubric shown in Table 7.4. It contains five observable criteria: logical inferences, supporting data, supporting rationale, and supporting diagrams and drawings.

Imagine that students have been investigating how sound travels and how animals use their ears to collect sounds. They have learned that sound travels best through solids, next best through liquids, and least well through air. They have discovered that sound can be collected or projected in a cone-shaped object. As an artifact, students create a model of an animal ear to demonstrate what they have learned. How will the teacher assess this model ear? The following rubric might be used to accomplish this task:

◆ **5 points:** The students designed an ear that clearly demonstrates all four sound concepts learned from the investigations—sound travels best through solids; sound travels better through liquids than air; sound travels least well through air; a funnel/tunnel shape can be used to collect and amplify sound waves so that they sound louder. The students can explain why the ear would help an animal obtain food and avoid predators and they provide evidence from their investigations to support their design.
◆ **4 points:** The students designed an ear that demonstrates at least three of the four sound concepts learned from the investigations—sound travels best through solids; sound travels better through liquids than air; sound travels least well through air; a funnel/tunnel shape can be used to collect and amplify sound waves so that they sound louder. The students can explain why the ear would help the animal obtain food and avoid predators, but they fail to support their design with data from their investigations.
◆ **3 points:** The students designed an ear that demonstrates at least two of the

concepts learned from the investigations—sound travels best through solids; sound travels better through liquids than air; sound travels least well through air; a funnel/tunnel shape can be used to collect and amplify sound waves so that they sound louder. The students can explain why the ear would help an animal obtain food and avoid predators, but the explanation is not linked directly to their investigations.

- **2 points:** The students designed an ear that demonstrates at least one of the concepts learned from the investigations—sound travels best through solids; sound travels better through liquids than air; sound travels least well through air; a funnel/tunnel shape can be used to collect and amplify sound waves so that they sound louder. The students can explain why the ear would help an animal obtain food and avoid predators.

- **1 point:** The students designed an ear and can give a logical explanation about how it would help an animal obtain food and avoid predators. However, the students do not demonstrate any of the four sound concepts covered in the investigations.

- **0 points:** The students designed an ear but are unable to explain how it would help an animal obtain food and avoid predators, and the design is not logical or consistent with concepts learned about sound.

By including evaluative criteria in the scoring rubric, the teacher establishes an objective basis for judging the artifact, performance, or portfolio. Scoring rubrics also provide students with feedback or data supporting grades and evaluations. When students know the criteria on which they were judged, they can take steps to expand their knowledge and improve their skills.

The criteria used in scoring rubrics depend upon the teacher's goals and objectives for the lesson. Some criteria will be mandated by state and local school districts' curricula guidelines, while others are likely to follow national trends or curriculum frameworks such as the *National Science Education Standards* (National Research Council, 1996) or *Benchmarks for Science Literacy* (AAAS, 1993). In project-based science class-

rooms, the following criteria may be used to design scoring rubrics:

- **Understanding of concepts.** Determine whether students have developed shallow or deep understanding by examining the level of detail in the artifact, performance, or portfolio. Note missing links and levels of differentiation or completeness in the explanations.

- **Use of higher order thinking.** Determine whether students are using higher order thinking by examining such factors as their ability to formulate and answer questions, interpret or explain decisions, and discuss assumptions that underlie the artifact, performance, or portfolio. Also assess their ability to explain relationships and formulate new problems or questions and apply information to new situations or problems.

- **Ability to answer driving questions.** Judge how well students are able to answer the driving question. Was there a weak or strong relationship to the driving question? Did students specify the relationship in clear, specific terms?

- **Relatedness to the world.** Determine how strong the connections are between the artifact, performance, or portfolio and the real world. Did students apply information to a real life example in a strong convincing manner?

- **Level of collaboration.** Does the artifact, performance, or portfolio show interaction with others? Is the sharing of ideas and the use of other resources, especially community resources, evident?

- **Level of creativity.** Does the artifact, performance, or portfolio reveal a high level of creativity? Does it construct new ideas or connect existing ideas with new ones? Does it use ideas in novel ways or translate ideas from other subject areas?

- **Presentation.** Did students thoroughly explain the key ideas that answered the driving question? Were their classmates engaged? Did they answer classmates' questions? Did they use enough detail to support their conclusions?

ACTIVITY 7.10

Developing a Scoring Rubric

MATERIALS NEEDED:
- paper and pencil
- the results of Activity 7.8

A. After completing Activity 7.8 (or another performance-based activity), develop a scoring rubric to evaluate the performance. Use the following steps:
  1. Determine how an "expert" would perform in the situation. List the knowledge, skills, or dispositions an "expert" might have.
  2. If possible, examine work that students have completed to see the range of possible answers and responses.
  3. Identify the observable differences between "excellent" and "poor" performance.
  4. Turn the "good" and "poor" performance into a range of possible performances.
  5. Try to assess students with the range of performances you identified.
  6. Revise the criteria as needed.

B. Work in teams to try scoring the performance using the rubrics created. Did the rubrics seem accurate and fair? How might they be revised?

- **Use of cognitive tools.** Did students use cognitive tools such as print media, computers, software applications, and telecommunication. Determine the level of use of these types of tools.

After you have determined the criteria for your scoring rubric, you need to create the rubric. First, determine how an "expert" would perform in the situation. List the knowledge, skills, or dispositions an "expert" might display. Second, examine samples of related student work to get a feeling for the range of possible answers and responses. Third, identify the observable differences between "excellent" and "poor" performance. For example, a student who has mastered an understanding of sound waves is able to explain the science concepts, why the ear is designed to collect and amplify sound, and how the ear helps an animal obtain food and avoid predators. In contrast, the student who has a poor understanding of sound may be able to create an "animal ear" and explain how it helps an animal avoid predators but is unable to explain the science concepts related to the design of the ear. Fourth, turn the "good" and "poor" performance into a range of possible performances. For example, students are able to identify all four concepts, three of the concepts, two of the concepts, one concept, or none of the concepts. Fifth, try to assess students with the range of performances you identified. Sixth, revise the criteria as needed. In Activity 7.10, you will develop your own scoring rubric.

Assessment of Portfolios After students have collected a wide range of items for their portfolios, they need to reflect upon each item and sort out those that best represent what they have learned. Some teachers have students think about "added value." What additional evidence will an item add to the portfolio? If nothing is gained by including an item, it should be left out. For example, while investigating why pumpkins rot, students might produce a short report on decomposition, photographs of their investigation, notes, audiotapes of interviews with a grocery store manager, transcripts of the audiotaped interview, drawings of the various stages of pumpkin rot, graphs of decomposition over time, and journal entries. After reflecting upon their accumulated evidence, they would probably decide that the journal entries and the audiotape of interviews did not help to depict what they learned and omit these items from the portfolio.

After they have selected items to include in the portfolio, it is important to have students reflect upon their progress and overall growth. This reflection can occur in different ways. Teachers frequently have students write captions for each artifact to explain what learning it depicts. Some teachers have students write letters describing all the items in their portfolios and explaining why each artifact is evidence of learning. Others have students create tables of contents to organize their portfolios in a meaningful way. A table of contents might be arranged in a linear fashion to show progression, or it might be arranged around themes to show the relationships among concepts learned.

Finally, it is meaningful for students to evaluate their portfolios by engaging in "portfolio reviews" with the teacher, parents, or peers. The portfolio review is a time for the students and teacher to discuss progress, achievement, and goals. Students can share their portfolios with parents or peers, either in small groups or before the whole class. This final step encourages positive critiques from significant others, and it helps students celebrate with others their progress and success.

Self-Assessment Self-assessment can encourage thinking about such things as learning styles, what was learned, the quality of that learning, and personal goal setting. When students think about their own learning styles and preferences, they are thinking about how they best learn: through reading, hands-on manipulation of physical objects, or working collaboratively with others, for example. The list of ways to learn is practically endless. When students reflect on what they learned, they also think about how they feel about their learning. When they think about the quality of their learning, they examine how well they are doing and how much they have improved and their strengths and weaknesses. Using such self-assessment information, students can then decide what steps to take to improve. As students progress further down the path of self-regulated learning, their intrinsic motivation to learn also grows, and this, of course, is what teaching and learning are all about—the production of highly motivated, self-regulated learners.

Several useful techniques can be used to encourage self-evaluation. You might have students keep journals detailing what they learn in their investigations. However, some students fail to open up in journals and make useless entries such as "I did my math homework after school. Then I worked on my science investigation." This type of information doesn't reveal much about the student's thinking, learning, or problems. To encourage true self-assessment, you might provide students with guiding questions. Students can answer these questions directly, or they can answer them as part of a journal, portfolio, or interview. Guiding ques-

tions might include "Look back over your science report—what did you find easy about writing the report?" "What was difficult for you?" "What was the most important idea you learned?" "Why?" "How does this relate to the driving question?" "What do you like about your artifact?" "What do you feel are its strengths and weaknesses?" "What would you like to improve or change?" "What skills would you like to work on?" "Are you satisfied with your progress in answering the driving question?" "What else do you need to investigate?" "What areas of science do you think you have improved in the most?"

You might choose to base self-assessment on open-ended statements. For example, you could have students complete the following statements:

- The things I am still wondering about are . . .
- I discovered . . .
- I'm beginning to wonder why . . .
- I learned . . .
- I could improve by . . .
- I never realized that . . .
- I was surprised that . . .

You might assess curiosity by determining how many things a student is wondering about. You might use "attitude inventories" that ask students open-ended questions about their interests and beliefs:

- The thing I like best about science is . . .
- My favorite topic to study is . . .
- My favorite subject is . . .

These open-ended self-assessment techniques also encourage students to continue wondering or questioning—affective attitudes valued in a project-based science classroom.

Finally, students can assess their own attitudes about science with a formal assessment instrument. For example, if you are interested in measuring how excited the students are about studying natural disasters, you could ask them the following questions:

a. How excited are you about learning about hurricanes, floods, tornadoes, and earthquakes? (1) Very, (2) somewhat, (3) not at all.

Stage	Technique	Advantages
Gathering information	◆ Observations of students during instruction—e.g., watching students while they conduct an investigation	◆ Helps in minute-to-minute and day-to-day decisions ◆ Can be formal or informal
	◆ Focused questioning of students—e.g., asking students why they completed an investigation in the manner they did	◆ Provides teachers with in-depth information about students' understanding ◆ Can be formal or informal
	◆ Anecdotal records—e.g., notes about student performance jotted on index cards	◆ Is helpful for determining progress at end of a term ◆ Is useful for parent conferences ◆ Helps teachers remember information about students
	◆ Checklists—e.g., list of concepts (understand causes of weather), skills (can record data accurately), and dispositions (appreciate usefulness of weather predictions)	◆ Can be used while students are working ◆ Cuts down time charting assessment information ◆ Keeps teacher focused on obtaining data from all students
	◆ Clinical interviews with students—e.g., sitting down with each student and asking, "What is the design of your investigation?" "What have you accomplished so far?" "What kinds of results have you obtained?" and "What do you intend to do next?"	◆ Provides teachers more detailed information about students' learning ◆ Enables teachers and students to better know each other ◆ Can clarify any misinterpretations made of students while observing them
	◆ Concept maps—e.g.: 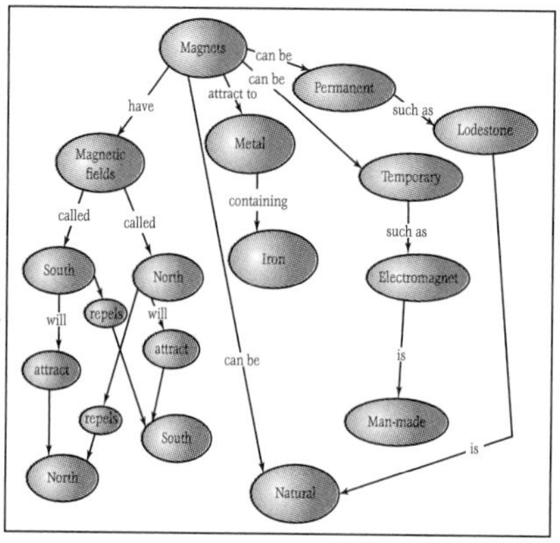 	◆ Lets students demonstrate complex understanding of concepts ◆ Can diagnose misunderstandings
	◆ Performance-based assessment—e.g., providing students a prompt to complete a skill-based activity	◆ Is based on actual classroom activities ◆ Measures complex skills and depth of knowledge ◆ Is linked to instruction ◆ Is concrete and active

FIGURE 7.6
The assessment process.

b. How important was your investigation in terms of answering the driving question? (1) Very, (2) somewhat, (3) not at all.

Whatever self-assessment method you choose, it will foster intrapersonal skills that make students more aware of what they are learning, how they are investigating, and how they are feeling about science.

Peer Assessment In peer assessment, students give feedback to other students in the class. Most students respect the opinions of their peers and value their input. Peer assessment, therefore, can be an effective motivator for many students. In addition, when students know that they will be presenting artifacts to a real audience, they are more likely to see a purpose for their work.

In collaborative learning groups, students can assess the contribution each member made to successfully completing a task. Teachers frequently have students evaluate such things as how well their group members were able to work quietly, carry out assigned tasks, stay on task, share materials, monitor their own time,

Stage	Technique	Advantages
Assembling and presenting assessment information	◆ Student writing samples—e.g., stories, poetry, a television commercial, a play, a puppet show, a newspaper article, a documentary, letters, an essay, a diary, a computer presentation, a comic strip, student reactions to guest speakers, videos, or software programs, biographies or autobiographies, and annotated bibliographies	◆ Is curriculum-based (matches goals of instruction and integrates language arts) ◆ Is active ◆ Is complex (allows students to provide rich interpretations) ◆ Is directed at learning styles (targets verbal/linguistic abilities) ◆ Is a task that students will consider worthwhile (writing has a purpose)
	◆ Daily journals—e.g., journals between student and teacher or student and student	◆ Is kept on a regular basis ◆ Involves students in the assessment ◆ Helps students connect science to their daily lives ◆ Encourages student-teacher and student-student interactions
	◆ Products—e.g., a book, a 3-D model, or a working apparatus	◆ Is embedded in instruction ◆ Demonstrates complex learning
	◆ Drawings—e.g., sketches, murals, bulletin boards, posters, or bumper stickers	◆ Helps artistic/spatial students ◆ Is more authentic in some situations (e.g., explaining things seen with microscope)
	◆ Music—e.g., songs, raps, jingles, cheers, or choral readings	◆ Is good for students who have musical/rhythmic intelligence
	◆ Videotapes—e.g.,tapes of a long-term investigation or project	◆ Is interesting and motivating for students ◆ Can be edited and shown at a later time ◆ Forms lasting memories
	◆ Multimedia productions—e.g., documents that combine writing, illustrations, photos, video- and audiotapes, computers, and other media	◆ Encourages creativity ◆ Measures complex understanding ◆ Is motivating and interesting to students
	◆ Portfolios—e.g., long-term collection of assessment information	◆ Shows progress over time ◆ Allows for multiple sources of information ◆ Encourages student reflection, self-monitoring, and goal setting
Evaluating assessment information	◆ Scoring rubrics—e.g., a holistic or analytical device for making judgments about artifacts, portfolios, or performance-based activities	◆ Helps teacher make accurate and equitable judgments about each student ◆ Provides feedback or data to students, supporting grades ◆ Provides students information they can use to improve
	◆ Self-assessment—e.g., student letters about their progress filed in their portfolios	◆ Encourages responsibility for one's own learning ◆ Encourages goal setting ◆ Increases self-esteem
	◆ Peer-assessment—e.g., other students' critiques on presentations and feedback for improvement	◆ Is valued ◆ Provides students a purpose for their work (to share it with others) ◆ Is consistent with collaborative/cooperative learning

FIGURE 7.6—*Continued*

listen to each other, ask questions, generate alternative answers, contribute ideas, take different perspectives, summarize information, encourage each other, show respect for one another's ideas, and challenge ideas.

Be careful, however, when you first start to use peer assessment in a project-based science environment. Students need to trust each other before they can function well in such an environment. Before trying this method of assessment, build a trusting classroom environment. As discussed in Chapters 5 and 8, this is accomplished by developing interpersonal skills and encouraging collaborative group work.

Figure 7.6 summarizes what you have learned about the assessment process. Now that you know more about student assessment in a project-based science classroom, what type of report card would you develop? Activity 7.11 helps you answer this question.

ACTIVITY 7.11

Creating a Report Card

MATERIALS NEEDED:
- ◆ pencil and paper or a computer

A. Think about the report card you remember receiving as an elementary or middle grade student. What kinds of things did it tell about your performance in science? What do you wish it had included?

B. Imagine you are on a committee to design a new report card. It is your task to design the section for reporting science learning in a project-based classroom. Design a report card that you think best reflects what students and parents should know. Share the report card with others in your class.

C. Would your report card have letter grades? Debate with others whether letter grades should be obsolete.

D. What are the major implications of constructivist theory that would influence your report card?

E. How would you explain to parents that your assessment procedures and report card are authentic?

F. File a copy of your newly developed report card in your portfolio.

ANOTHER LOOK AT ADVANTAGES OF AUTHENTIC ASSESSMENT

Assessment in a project-based science classroom, regardless of the method used, should be designed to help the teaching and learning process—not humiliate, demean, or trick students. Good assessment matches instruction and helps diagnose, monitor, and evaluate students' acquisition of concepts, skills, and attitudes. It is an ongoing process that guides curriculum selection and instruction. Teachers in project-based science think of assessment as a responsibility shared between teacher and student for the purpose of informing students, parents and teachers.

We are reminded of a story told about a college student who took an ornithology class. He learned about different types of birds. He learned how to identify them by color, plumage, shape, size, and song. He learned where they live, what they eat, and whether they are endangered. The final exam consisted of fifty pictures of bird's legs. It asked students to identify the birds only by their feet. The student, frustrated and exasperated, told the professor that the test was unfair as it did not measure what had been taught in the course and that he wasn't going to take it. The professor replied, "That is fine. I will just record a zero in my grade book for this test. Now, what is your name, young man?" The student pulled up his pant leg and said, "I'm not going to tell you. See if you can identify me by my legs!"

This story makes a point very well. In project-based science classrooms, teachers purposefully, carefully, and thoughtfully design and implement assessment procedures. When assessment is carefully crafted and executed, there are numerous advantages for teachers, students, and parents.

Advantages for Teachers

The alternative assessment techniques used in project-based science classrooms encourage teachers to become more reflective in their practice. They force them to think about the design of their curriculum and instruction and about ways to revise and adapt their lessons so that all students learn. They also encourage teachers to take students' comments into account when planning their instruction. Teachers and students thus become allies in the learning process. Assessment is not an end in itself, but a means to a mutually sought end—student learning.

Teachers come to know their students better when using assessment consistent with project-based science. All students become important, and it is less likely for students to fall between the cracks. Because each student works with the teacher, the teacher can discern each child's capacity, style of learning, and rate of learning. Teachers become more constructivist in their practices because they arrive at a deeper understanding of what students know and how they have come to know it. If a school requires letter grades, alternative assessment provides teachers with a more honest and valid appraisal of students' learning on which they can base letter grades.

Advantages for Students

Most educators feel that assessment in a project-based environment encourages student involvement in their own learning and helps them become reflective, self-regulated learners. Teachers and students work together to determine which pieces of work are most representative of a student's ability and how the work will be evaluated. Students can analyze the strengths and weaknesses of their own work and establish their own goals for improvement. This self-monitoring behavior, or metacognitive thinking, helps students develop intrinsic motivation to learn and strengthens their relationship with their teachers.

Assessment also allows for individual differences in student abilities, since the focus is on student improvement rather than on comparison with others. Students are encouraged to chart their own improvement over time. Unlike *criterion-referenced tests,* which grade all students according to a single set of preestablished standards, assessment that focuses on individual student improvement tends to promote self-esteem.

Alternative assessment techniques also promote collaboration with peers. Students work with classmates to develop and share artifacts and portfolios, and they learn to seek suggestions for improvement. During this process, students develop important social skills. They learn to support and coach others and to work collaboratively and cooperatively. Finally, alternative assessment techniques provide a less-threatening environment for evaluation since evaluation is an ongoing part of instruction rather than an occasional, anxiety-producing situation.

Advantages for Parents

Parents and guardians play a crucial role in the education of their children. Many people believe that the alternative assessment techniques used in project-based classrooms accomplish for parents what other forms of assessment cannot.

Standardized (normed) test scores are simply comparisons with the scores of all the other children who have taken the test. A 50th percentile score on mathematics, for example, means only that half of the students who took the test did better and half of the students who took the test did worse. This kind of information tells parents little about children's capability, progress, strengths, and weaknesses. It tells nothing about children's motivation to improve.

Letter grades usually offer little more information since most are based on memory-oriented, criterion-referenced tests. These tests are usually administered at the end of a chapter or other unit of study, and a child's single score determines his or her letter grade. For example, a C grade tells the parent only that the child answered approximately 75 percent of the questions correctly. Was the test valid and reliable? Did the child learn more things about science than the test measured? Is the child interested in science? Has the child developed scientific thinking and problem-solving skills? Formal criterion-referenced tests do little to answer such questions in parent-teacher conferences.

Alternative assessments offer to parents a strong, multidimensional approach to understanding their children's learning. By viewing samples of work over time, they gain a better understanding of the entire learning process and of a child's improvement. However, since many schools require criterion-referenced letter grades, alternative assessments are often used in conjunction with other methods.

It is the job of teachers in project-based classrooms to communicate with parents about their children's progress and explain why project-based science requires different forms of assessment. Parents may need to be won over to these new ideas through involvement in the assessment process.

To involve parents in the assessment process, teachers can, for example, have parents help select some of their children's work to be included in a portfolio. Parents might also play the role of teacher by holding a conference with their children about their work, progress, strengths, weaknesses, and future goals. Parents can also supply valuable observations of their children's learning at home. For example, a parent might supply information about a child's trip to a science museum and resulting interest in building paper

ACTIVITY 7.12

Efficiency of Authentic Assessment

MATERIALS NEEDED:
- pencil and paper or a computer

A. Some educators have argued that authentic assessment, while more valid and reliable, costs a considerable amount of money to implement and uses an exorbitant amount of teacher time. Interview several classroom teachers about this issue.

B. Write a short essay explaining you own beliefs on this issue.

C. If time allows, have a debate in your classroom about the "costs" and "benefits" of authentic assessment techniques.

D. Investigate how computers, hand-held computers, laser discs, and CD-ROMs are making assessment easier and saving time. Examine specific products such as *Learner Profile* by Sunburst/WINGS company, *Grady Profile* by Aurbach and Associates, and *Performance Plus* by National Computer Systems (NCS).

E. Record your findings in your portfolio.

---

airplanes and rockets or Lego structures. Parents might even help fill out checklists of science skills, attitudes, or abilities that they have observed at home. Most teachers who have used alternative assessment techniques and kept in close communication with parents find that the parents appreciate the depth of understanding the teacher has about their children. In short, assessment in project-based classrooms brings together all the stakeholders (students, teachers, and parents) in the learning process.

Although authentic assessment techniques offer many advantages, some educators are concerned about the cost and time it takes to use these techniques. You will explore the efficiency of authentic assessment in Activity 7.12.

SUMMARY OF CHAPTER

In this chapter, you learned about authentic assessment. You discovered the reasons for using authentic assessment methods, and you learned about specific techniques that teachers can use to assess learning. The topic of assessment is overwhelming, and so this book cannot cover all of its aspects. You may want to consult other resources for more information:

Airasian, P. W. 1996. *Assessment in the classroom*. New York: McGraw-Hill.

Hein, G. (Ed.). 1990. *The assessment of hands-on elementary science programs*. Grand Forks, N.D.: University of North Dakota.

Herman, J. L., P. R. Ashbacher, and L. Winters. 1992. *A practical guide to alternative assessment*. Alexandria, Va.: Association for Supervision and Curriculum Development.

Kulm, G., and S. M. Malcom. 1991. *Science assessment in the service of reform*. Washington, D.C.: American Association for the Advancement of Science.

Marzano, R. J., D. Pickering, and J. McTighe. 1993. *Assessing student outcomes: Performance assessment using the dimensions of learning model*. Alexandria, Va.: Association for Supervision and Curriculum Development.

Perrone, V. 1991. *Expanding student assessment*. Alexandria, Va.: Association for Supervision and Curriculum Development.

Raizen, S. A., J. B. Baron, A. B. Champagne, E. Haertzel, I. V. S. Mullis, and J. Oakes. 1989. *Assessment in elementary school science*. Washington, D.C.: The National Center for Improving Science Education.

Also, the National Science Teachers Association published special issues on science assessment of *Science and Children* (October 1994) and *Science Scope* (March 1992).

Now that you have finished the chapter, you should better understand why the opening scenario does not exemplify assessment practices recommended for project-based science. To assess your own learning in this chapter, complete Activity 7.13.

Although we have covered a lot of ground, there are other assessment factors that remained unexamined. For example, the chapter

ACTIVITY 7.13

What Have You Learned About Assessment?

MATERIALS NEEDED:

♦ the KWL list from Activity 7.1

A. In Activity 7.1, you made three columns on a piece of paper or with a computer word processing program. You listed in the first column as many things as you knew about assessment, and in the second column you listed what you wanted to know. Reread your second column. Think about what you learned about assessment in this chapter. In the last column, now list everything you learned in this chapter that answered the questions you had before you read the chapter.

B. How did your beliefs about teaching elementary and middle grades change after reading this chapter?

C. Record your ideas in your portfolio.

ACTIVITY 7.14

High Stakes Testing

MATERIALS NEEDED:

♦ reference materials

A. High stakes testing is testing that has a significant consequence for students— testing that is required for high school graduation, placement in "remedial" or "advanced" classes, or for national and international comparisons. Find out more about this type of testing by researching your state's testing policies; national tests such as NAEP, SAT, and ACT; and international tests such as the International Science Study. Report your findings.

B. Why do some people feel these tests are important? Why do others dislike them?

What are the advantages and disadvantages of this type of assessment? Why do you think it has become more popular in recent years? Will high stakes testing improve our educational system? Include in your report your opinion of high stakes testing.

C. Find out what other countries do in terms of assessment. Are there high stakes testing programs? How do teachers assess within classrooms? Countries you might want to investigate include Japan, Germany, England, Singapore, and Australia. Good sources of information on this topic are the TIMSS Web pages at http://nces.ed.gov/ and http://wwwcsteep.bc.edu/timss.

D. File your report in your portfolio.

ignored the topic of high stakes testing. You may find it interesting to explore this topic in Activity 7.14.

In this chapter we discussed the purpose and nature of assessment. The phrase *authentic assessment* was used to describe the type of assessment strategies most compatible with project-based science. We examined the characteristics of authentic assessment. It is embedded in instruction, is a continuous process, uses multidimensional techniques, and engages students in the assessment process. We examined the benefits of authentic assessment: that authentic assessment is more valid and reliable, matches today's educational goals, accommodates cultural diversity, is consistent with cognitive learning theory, and measures deep understanding. The chapter presented methods of assessing student understanding as a three-phase procedure: gathering information, assembling and presenting assessment information, and evaluating assessment information. We explored numerous techniques for gathering information including making observations, keeping anecdotal records, using checklists, using interviews, using concept maps, and performance-based assessment. We also considered a number of methods for assembling and presenting information including student writing samples, daily journals, physical products, drawings, music, videotapes, and multidimensional documents. Emphasis was given to the use of portfolios and artifacts to present information. The chapter introduced four techniques that can be used to evaluate assessment information: scoring rubrics, portfolios, self-assessment, and peer assessment. Finally, we looked again at the advantages of authentic assessment for teachers, students, and parents.

REFERENCES

Airasian, P. W. 1996. *Assessment in the classroom.* New York: McGraw-Hill.

American Association for the Advancement of Science. 1993. *Benchmarks for science literacy.* New York: Oxford University Press.

Barman, C. 1996. How do students really view science and scientists? *Science and Children* 34 (1):30–33.

Boylan, C. R., D. M. Hill, A. R. Wallace, and A. E. Wheeler. 1992. Beyond stereotypes. *Science Education* 76 (5):465–76.

Collins, A. 1992. Portfolios for science education: Issues in purpose, structure, and authenticity. *Science Education* 76 (4):451–63.

Herman, J. L., P. R. Ashbacher, and L. Winters. 1992. *A practical guide to alternative assessment.* Alexandria, Va.: Association for Supervision and Curriculum Development.

Huber, R. A., and G. M. Burton. 1995. What do students think scientists look like? *School Science and Mathematics* 95 (7):371–76.

Miller, P. W., and H. E. Erikson. 1990. *How to write tests for students.* Washington, D.C.: National Education Association.

National Association for the Education of Young Children. 1986. *Developmentally appropriate practice in early childhood programs serving children from birth through age 8.* Washington, D.C.: Author.

National Middle School Association. 1995. *This we believe: Developmentally responsive middle level schools.* Columbus, Ohio: Author.

National Research Council. 1996. *National science education standards.* Washington, D.C.: National Academy Press.

Novak, J. D., and D. B. Gowin. 1984. *Learning how to learn.* Cambridge, England: Cambridge University Press.

Ogle, D. 1986. A teaching model that develops active reading of expository text. *The Reading Teacher* 39 (2):564–70.

Packer, A. H. 1992. Taking action on the SCANS report. *Educational Leadership* 49:27–31.

Rampal, A. 1992. Images of science and scientists: A study of school teachers' views. I. Characteristics of scientists. *Science Education* 76 (4):415–36.

Rutherford, F. J., and A. Ahlgren. 1990. *Science for all Americans.* New York: Oxford University Press.

Sumrall, W. J. 1995. Reasons for the perceived images of scientists by race and gender of students in grades 1–7. *School Science and Mathematics* 95 (2):83–90.

U.S. Department of Education. 1991. *America 2000: An education strategy. Washington, D.C.*

Chapter 8

HOW DO I MANAGE THE PROJECT-BASED SCIENCE CLASSROOM?

INTRODUCTION

Project-based science creates many unique challenges for managing the elementary or middle grade classroom. To be successful, teachers need to create a learning environment of trust and self-responsibility, a task that may raise numerous questions for you: What does a teacher need to do to establish a positive classroom climate? How do I organize a classroom? How do I structure the school day? What can be done to make sure students are safe? How do I manage student behavior? In this chapter, we will explore how teachers can create learning environments that support project-based science. We will focus on classroom climate, classroom organization, and management strategies.

In the classroom climate section, we will consider ways to establish a positive learning environment and examine a framework for thinking about classroom climate in the context of constructivism. We will discuss the roles of teacher and students, the relationship between teacher and student, and classroom interactions.

In the classroom organization section, we will review how to arrange a science classroom, structure the school day, and maintain a safe classroom. We will explore how to prepare for a lesson and what to do when off schedule.

In the section on management strategies, we will examine ways to foster positive student behavior, anticipate problems, distribute materials, make transitions between classes, deal with disturbances, and reinforce good behavior. We also will consider ways that teachers can handle multiple groups of students working on the same activities as well as groups of students working on different activities at the same time. Techniques are outlined to help teachers deal with diverse abilities of students and students who finish activities at different rates.

Although this chapter offers realistic management strategies, it is not a panacea for problems in the classroom. Building a classroom learning environment that supports project-based science takes a great deal of hard work. The trade-offs for the hard work are the positive results seen in student learning and motivation.

What follows are several scenarios of lessons that could be used in a project-based classroom to teach about pesticides in a food chain. As you read each scenario, focus on various features of the instructional setting. What are the students doing? What does the classroom climate seem to be like? What is the role of the teacher? What is the relationship between the teacher and the students? What instructional supports does the teacher provide? How has the teacher managed the instruction? How is the room arranged?

Scenario 1: Reading About Science

Sixth grade students are sitting at individual desks. They are about to read a section of their science textbook that is about pollution in a food chain. Ms. Jung decides to use the KWL method to focus the students' reading (see Chapters 6 and 7 for more information on KWL). Before students begin reading, Ms. Jung asks the students what they already know about food chains. She lists this information under the *K* column, representing what students know. Next, she asks students what they want to know more about. She lists these responses under the *W* column, representing what students want to learn. Ms. Jung then selects one student at a time to read a paragraph in the book. When the section is completed, she asks the students to answer in writing the two questions at the end of the chapter. The two questions will be used to focus a discussion about what students learned—the *L* on the KWL chart. A few students seem eager to begin reading the assignment, because they want to complete an investigation tomorrow that focuses on pesticides in a food chain. Most of the students begin to answer the two questions: "What is pollution?" and "How does pollution affect the animals at the top of a food chain?" Ms. Jung walks around as students are answering the questions to check that each student is on task and quiet. Rita, who is sitting at the front of the class, is playing with something in her desk and laughing with another student. Ms. Jung reminds Rita that the classroom rules require students to be quiet when they are reading. After five minutes, Ms. Jung notices that Robbie has not started his assignment. She asks him if he has any questions, and she helps him focus on the topic of the paragraph—pesticides. Dr. Sylvia

Brown, the principal, walks in to ask Ms. Jung a question and smiles as she sees the students working diligently. Ten minutes later, Ms. Jung collects the students' answers so that she can give them feedback. She also holds a discussion with the class about what they learned from the reading. She lists these items under the *L* column on the chart at the front of the room. Next, she informs the students that they will begin to design an investigation the next day that is about pollution found in a food chain. The students seem excited about this and begin to talk about some ideas that they have. After a few ideas have been shared, Ms. Jung instructs the students to take out their mathematics books.

Scenario 2: Direct Science Instruction

In a sixth grade classroom down the hall, Mrs. Hamilton is teaching the same topic. She has ten students wear signs made of envelopes indicating that they are playing the role of mice, ten students wear signs made of envelopes showing that they are snakes, and five students wear signs made of envelopes showing that they are playing the role of hawks. The twenty-five students are told that mice eat grains, snakes eat mice, and hawks eat snakes or mice. Next, Mrs. Hamilton engages the class in a discussion. She says, "We will be going outside to play a game. We will be running around on the playground during this game. How can we make sure that everyone learns and that no one gets hurt during this activity?" The students decide that they need to stay away from playground equipment, and they should have a discussion after the game is over to see what people learned from it. Mrs. Hamilton and the students go outside. The game begins by the mice eating "grain" represented by an assortment of white and colored bits of paper. The mice put the bits of paper into their sign envelopes as they "eat" it. Then the snakes are allowed to tag or "eat" the mice, and the hawks are allowed to tag mice or snakes. As the students tag each another, they collect the sign envelopes of the "prey" that they tag. Students are laughing and enjoying the game of tag. Mrs. Hamilton cautions a few students that they are near the playground equipment.

After a proportion of mice and snakes are "eaten," Mrs. Hamilton asks the students to come back into the classroom. The students are excited by this outdoor activity, and they arrive at their classroom in a noisy fashion. Mrs. Hamilton models for the students how they should get quiet as they enter back into the school, and the students seem to do this quickly. Dr. Sylvia Brown, the principal, is waiting for Mrs. Hamilton as she returns to the room with her students. The principal is happy to see that the students are enjoying science, and she joins the class so she can see what all of the excitement is about. The students begin to count how much "food" they "ate" and how many white and colored bits of paper are contained in the envelopes they collected. Mrs. Hamilton informs the students that the colored bits of paper represent food that is contaminated with a pollutant called DDT. If an animal ate any food that included any colored bits of paper, the animal will become sick and its offspring might be deformed. If an animal's food supply consisted of at least as many colored bits of paper as white, the animal will die from the pollution. Students complete the task of counting their bits of paper, and Mrs. Hamilton engages the students in a discussion about the effects of this pollution. She asks them to think about the effect that DDT may have on other animals, particularly humans if they eat animals that have been exposed to it. Finally, she instructs the students to compare how the mice, snakes, and hawks were affected by DDT. The students notice that the animals at the top of the food chain, the hawks, collected a lot more DDT than did the other animals. Mrs. Hamilton finishes the lesson by having students draw a picture of how the pollution was passed through the food chain. A few students finish early, so Mrs. Hamilton asks them to go to the computers to see if they can learn more about the substance DDT. As remaining students finish their pictures, they file them in their portfolios. The students who finished early share the information they found on the World Wide Web about DDT. Students in the class are so interested in this topic that they keep talking about the fact that DDT is still found in our environment even though it was banned in the United States years ago. Mrs. Hamilton is surprised that this lesson has run over a half hour longer than she planned. At the end of the lesson, Mrs. Hamilton helps the students determine how they will structure their investigation tomorrow.

Scenario 3: Process Science

A few students in Mr. Smith's class bring to class an article about the level of PCBs found in fish from a local lake. In the article, students find that PCBs are reported to be in the fish caught in the lake. The article refers to *ppm,* and students wonder what *ppm* means. Mr. Smith approaches the topic of PCBs in food chains by using a laboratory activity as a benchmark lesson. Following directions, the students fill small plastic cups with red food coloring. The red food coloring is a 1 part per 10 solution. Next, the students take one drop of this red food coloring and transfer it to a clean plastic cup, and they add 9 drops of clear water. This becomes a 1 part per 100 solution of red food coloring. After they have done this, they take one drop from this cup and transfer it to a clean plastic cup and add 9 drops of clear water. This becomes a 1 part per 1000 solution of red food coloring. The students continue this procedure until they have mixed up a 1 part per million (1 ppm) solution. Mr. Smith notices that Martin is not following directions, and he reminds him about the contract they made for him to complete assignments in class. Next, Mr. Smith tells the students that pollution is frequently measured in parts per million (ppm) or parts per billion (ppb), and he tells the students that these tiny amounts of pollution can enter the food chain through many different sources (through plants we eat, animals that we eat, or plants that animals we eat have eaten). The students in the class seem excited to learn this information; they now understand what the term *ppm* means. Tomorrow they will conduct an investigation in which they will measure pollutants from a local stream and report them in ppm.

Scenario 4: Multiple Investigations

Mrs. Kimble is teaching her sixth grade classroom about food chains. Students in her class are investigating the question "How do chemicals affect an animal's food supply?" Several groups of students decided to investigate different topics, so Mrs. Kimble sits down at her desk to grade some papers.

One group of students is studying the effect of pollution on the bald eagles in the Great Lakes region of the United States. Today these students are working on the computer, and they are communicating with a group of students in California who are studying a similar question: the effects of pollution on the condor. The students from both schools are comparing the pollutants found in their regions.

A second group of students is reading an article from the local paper about consumption of fish caught in the Great Lakes. They learn that there are recommended limits for consumption of fish from some of the lakes because of pollutants called *PCBs* and *mercury,* which are found in the fish. These students are discussing whether they could set up an experiment to test the effects of pollution on fish in an aquarium in their classroom. The discussion is getting very loud and is disturbing other groups. Mrs. Kimble gets up from grading papers and walks over to this group to question the students about their plan and helps the students understand procedures and regulations governing research conducted on vertebrate animals. She also points out that they need to keep their voices down.

A third group of students is studying the topic of biotechnology, investigating whether there are any known effects on humans who drink milk from cows given chemicals to increase their milk production. These students have decided to invite a guest speaker to come to their classroom to talk about research findings on their dairy production product, and they are excited at the prospect of calling the speaker.

Another group of students is studying the effects of pesticides and herbicides on fruits and vegetables. These students are trying to find out whether these chemicals are harmful to humans who eat the foods. They want to locate two farmers with different opinions about the use of pesticides and herbicides: one who uses organic farming practices and one who uses the chemicals. They are asking other students in the class if they know any local farmers who use these methods.

Like the scenarios you read in Chapter 1, the first three scenarios you just read represent what is called *read about science, direct instruc-*

tion, and *process science teaching.* Each type of science instruction can be used in a project-based environment as long as it supports student investigations. In these scenarios, the *read about science, direct instruction,* and *process science teaching* lessons are used as benchmark lessons to give students basic information about food chains and pesticides that will enable them to conduct investigations later. The last scenario illustrates students working on separate activities. Each scenario demonstrates different classroom management characteristics. The *climate* (prevailing feeling or state of mind of members of the class), *organization* (how the teacher structures classroom activities and space), and *management style* (how the teacher sets, models, and reinforces classroom behavioral expectations) of these four classrooms vary, but the management objective is the same in all of them. In this chapter you will be learning about managing a project-based science classroom. You'll start by analyzing in Activity 8.1 (next page) the opening scenarios to glean from them some basic aspects of managing a project-based science classroom.

As you completed Activity 8.1, you probably discovered that the objective of each lesson in the scenarios was the same—students will be able to define pollution, and they will understand the effect that pollution has on a food chain. During your comparison, you probably grappled with many issues. What should a classroom look like? How noisy or quiet should it be? Should students be moving around or sitting down? Should they be laughing and talking, or should they be quiet and attentive? Should they read from the textbook? Can they learn if they are playing a game? What kind of classroom environment best facilitates learning? Will they learn more if they are having fun? It is not always easy to answer these questions. Numerous factors influence how teachers organize their classrooms and they also affect classroom climate.

In the next sections, we will discuss three basic aspects of managing a project-based science learning environment: classroom climate, classroom organization, and management strategies. Although some of the topics and techniques introduced here are applicable to any subject area, each of these sections is designed to help teachers deal with some of the unique concerns and challenges associated with a project-based science environment.

CLASSROOM CLIMATE

The opening scenarios in this chapter depicted very different classrooms. One way they differed was in terms of climate. What factors determine classroom climate? Why is it important to facilitate a good classroom climate? In this section, we will examine a constructivist rationale and framework for thinking about classroom climate. We consider ideas for establishing a climate in which students solve classroom problems. We also discuss some basic concerns and challenges associated with classroom climate and the responsibilities of the teacher in creating an effective classroom climate. We will consider how the teacher must be a role model, select good curriculum, promote a positive attitude toward science, enhance positive affective factors, balance the relationship between student and teacher, and ensure equality. Before we begin to discuss these topics, use Activity 8.2 to explore classroom climate.

Your descriptions of positive classroom experiences probably featured classrooms in which teachers boosted your self-esteem and made you feel important and capable. Your ideas were valued, and you were pushed to try harder, take risks, and think for yourself. The teachers probably had senses of humor and cared about students. They did not favor some students and did not discriminate against students for gender, socioeconomic status, or race. The classroom was a safe haven, and students enjoyed being there. There was a sense of belonging. Lessons were interesting and motivating. The teachers seemed to enjoy teaching the subjects. There were few classroom management and student behavior problems. You probably still think of those teachers as role models.

A Constructivist Rationale and Framework for Thinking About Classroom Climate

The work of Alfie Kohn (1996), *Beyond Discipline: From Compliance to Community,* provides a rationale and framework for thinking about

ACTIVITY 8.1

Managing a Science Classroom

MATERIALS NEEDED:
- pencil and paper or a computer

A. Compare and contrast the four classrooms described in the opening scenarios. How are they alike and different with respect to climate, organization, and management? What are the advantages and disadvantages associated with the management of each classroom? Use the following list of questions in your comparison.
Climate
- What are the classroom goals and expectations? Do students have a role in making the rules? What happens when someone doesn't follow the rules?
- Does the teacher smile a lot? or frown? Do students seem to be enjoying themselves—or do they seem unhappy?
- Are students encouraged to take initiative and be autonomous, or are they expected to follow the directions of the teacher?
- Do students talk with each other and with the teacher, or is the classroom discourse only between students and teacher?
- Do students' ideas and responses help drive instruction and behavior in the classroom, or does the teacher determine the topics, activities, and behavioral expectations?
- Do students share responsibility for classroom decisions with the teacher, or does the teacher make all decisions?
- Does the teacher focus on "correct answers" to science questions, or are students encouraged to come up with many different answers?
- Are students encouraged to critique the teacher and give suggestions about improving instruction that will help them learn?
- How does the teacher assure that each student's self-esteem is improved?
- Does the teacher believe that all students can learn science? How does the teacher show this? What does the teacher do to assure that all students are successful?
- How are girls and minorities treated in science classes? What does the teacher do to encourage all students in science?
Organization
- How are students' desks arranged? How is the furniture in the classroom organized?
- Are students free to move about the classroom? Do they sit at their desks?
- Where are materials stored? How are they set up for student use?
- How does the teacher structure the day?
- How many minutes are given to each subject?
- How does the teacher structure a lesson? How are materials introduced and used? What comes first and last?
- What does the teacher do to make a transition between subject areas?
- How is the classroom set up so that students' safety is considered?
Management Strategies
- What is acceptable student behavior? Who establishes this, the teacher or the students and teacher working together?
- Does the teacher use contracts to establish and reinforce good behavior?
- How does the teacher create a climate for good behavior?
- Does the teacher anticipate problems that might occur and plan for them?
- How are materials distributed?
- How does the teacher deal with disturbances?

B. What do you think an elementary or middle grade classroom should look like? What should be going on in the room? What should the teacher and the students be doing? Imagine looking through a window or a door into a project-based science classroom. Compose a description of your view of a classroom with respect to organization and climate.

C. Compare your views with those of others. How are each of your views similar and different? How might you work with colleagues with differing viewpoints on classroom management? How would you work with a principal or administrator who has different ideas of management?

D. If possible, visit an elementary or middle grade science classroom. Videotape the classroom and take detailed notes about the climate, organization, and management of the room. How would you characterize the teacher's management style? What is your opinion of the classroom environment?

E. Record your observations in your portfolio.

ACTIVITY 8.2

What Makes a Positive Project-Based Science Classroom Climate?

MATERIALS NEEDED:
◆ pencil and paper or a computer

A. Although it may not be comfortable or fun, reflecting on negative classroom experiences in your educational career is an important activity. If you have not had any, good for you. However, it is likely that sometime in your thirteen or more years of formal education that you have had some negative experiences—miserable or boring classroom situations that made you uncomfortable; circumstances in which teachers seemed to favor others; and practices that seemed unfair. Think for a while about these negative experiences. What specifically, made the classroom climate so unpleasant?

B. Now think about your most favorite classes. What specifically made the educational experience pleasant?

C. What would you conclude about developing a positive classroom climate?

D. Record your ideas in your portfolio.

---

classroom climate in a constructivist classroom. Kohn asserts that most unwelcome classroom behaviors can often be traced to the larger classroom context and the curriculum. Kohn argues that many discipline plans try to do things *to* children rather than *with* them and are, therefore, not constructivist in nature. He argues that making students act "appropriately" is not consistent with constructivist classrooms: "My argument is that the quest to get students to act 'appropriately' is curiously reminiscent of the quest to get them to produce the right answers in academic lessons. Thus, the constructivist critique, which says that a right-answer focus doesn't help children become good thinkers, also suggests that a right-behavior focus doesn't help children become good people" (p. xv). He writes, "This approach is strikingly similar to the traditional model of academic instruction, where information or skills are transmitted to students so they will be able to produce correct answers on demand. For anyone who understands the limits of the 'right answer' approach to learning, it can be illuminating to see that classroom management is basically about eliciting the 'right behavior.' This analogy also may help us to think about what we could be accomplishing instead" (p. 66). A classroom with a positive climate in a constructivist framework is not one characterized by forcing or coercing children to comply with the teacher's demands. Rather, it is one in which students are asked to reflect on what they should do and to solve problems together.

If you asked a group of teachers to think about the long-term goals they have for their students (what they would want students to know, be like, or act like long after they had been their teachers), what would they say? Probably, they would hope that the students would be responsible, caring problem solvers. Most classroom management programs, however, are totally inconsistent with this long-term goal. Kohn (1996) writes, "It is unsettling because it exposes a yawning chasm between what we want and what we are doing, between how we would like students to turn out and how our classrooms and schools actually work" (p. 61). He adds, "No one says, I want my kids to obey authority without question, to be compliant and docile" (p. 61). He argues that there is conflict among our ultimate goals, short-term goals (class management), and methods (coercion, threats, punishment, bribes, and so on). In order for there to be cohesion between the goals of a project-based curriculum, which urges inquiry and collaboration and classroom management, the management system too must urge inquiry and collaboration.

Creating an Effective Classroom Climate

It takes hard work to establish a positive classroom climate. One of the first steps is to give students real choices. Why should students have choices? Kohn (1996) gives several reasons:

◆ People of any age ought to have a say in what happens to them.

◆ If they have a say, it is more likely that they will do essentially what we want.

- Misbehavior will diminish when children feel less controlled.
- Children are more respectful when their need to make decisions is respected.
- Children become more self-disciplined when given choices.
- Choices help children grow into ethical and compassionate people.

What are *real choices*? Real choices are ones that are not contrived by the teacher. A good way to have students make real decisions in a classroom is to ask them, "What do you think we could do to solve this problem?" The teacher depicted in Scenario 2 asked the students to work out how to play a game on the playground. With this question, students were given a chance to reason through a real problem related to their behavior, analyze possibilities, and negotiate solutions. Asking, "How do you want to line up to come in from recess?" however, does not present a real choice. A real choice would be "Should we line up?" or "How can we best come into the room from the playground?" In science the question "Do you want to raise your hands during the discussion or do you want to take turns?" does not offer a real choice. Asking, "What do you think would be the best way for us to share our results with minimal problems?" does offer a real choice.

Children may not be used to making real choices, however, and a teacher may have to work with them throughout the year to get them ready. For example, in the beginning of the year, students might be asked to select one method from a list of ways to control noise during investigations. Later, the teacher should move students toward making their own list of possibilities. Or a teacher might have students vote on the best way to take turns at the computer. Later, the teacher should move students toward coming to a consensus. Or a teacher might hold a class meeting to discuss ways for students to critique classmates' artifacts without insulting them. Later, the teacher should move students toward making their own decisions about behavior continually throughout the day.

Being a Role Model Teachers who are role models in a project-based science class exemplify the behavior appropriate for inquiry sci-

ence. Such teachers seek answers to questions and model how to find these answers. For example, a teacher might say, "Class, I read in the newspaper last night about some people over on Waterford Street who were getting sick from their drinking water. I was wondering if I could find out what was causing the problem. I think I could probably investigate this." The teacher models curiosity and questioning and shows the students how to find answers through reading, conducting investigations, or contacting members of the community. The teacher might say, "You know, I think I could find out what is causing the water problem by reading about water pollution on the Web." The teacher models using technology by logging on to the Internet. Teachers show students that they themselves are members of a learning community. The teacher might say, "I found a lot on the Web, but I don't know where to start to solve this problem. Maybe I need to call someone from the Environmental Protection Agency." Finally, teachers model the sharing of artifacts. The teacher might share with the students a synthesis of articles she found on the Web, notes from her inquiry, and the conclusions she formulated.

Selecting Good Curriculum to Promote Positive Classroom Climate An essential contributing factor to classroom climate (and the way students behave) is the curriculum. Kohn (1996) writes, *"When students are 'off task,' our first response should be to ask, 'What's the task?'"* (p. 19; italics Kohn's). He adds, "If discipline programs studiously refrain from exploring whether an adult's request was reasonable and, more generally, how the environment created by the adult might have contributed to a student's response, their most salient omission must surely be the curriculum. A huge proportion of unwelcome behaviors can be traced to a problem with what students are being asked to learn" (p. 18). The curriculum is often too simple, boring, or too difficult. Students need rich curriculum that extends thinking, elicits curiosity, and helps students answer questions that are important to them (p. x). Kohn suggests that we should ask if the curriculum is worth doing, meaningful, and relevant (p. 19). In project-based science, meaningful and important questions serve to organize and drive activities.

Promoting a Positive Attitude Toward Science

Attitudes are one of the strongest predictors of behavior (Ajzen & Fishbein, 1980; Bandura, 1986; Pajares, 1992), and a teacher's attitude can influence the learning environment. It is critical that elementary and middle grade teachers exude a positive attitude toward science. They should enjoy teaching science, give it a substantial amount of time in the curriculum, and encourage students to explore science topics.

A teacher needs to display genuine interest and enjoyment in science by talking about science topics and being excited about teaching the subject. A teacher's enthusiasm about science will rub off on the students. In fact, the *National Science Education Standards* (NRC, 1996) states, "Teachers who are enthusiastic, interested, and who speak of the power and beauty of scientific understanding instill in their students some of those same attitudes" (p. 37). Imagine that a third grader is excited about his new pet guinea pig and wants to bring it to school the next day. A teacher who wants to promote a positive attitude toward science will build upon this interest and show excitement about the topic. This could result in a visit from the guinea pig to the classroom or some other type of investigation about pets.

A teacher who wants to promote a positive attitude toward science will also spend time teaching science. Research findings (Nelson, Weiss, & Capper, 1990; Nelson, Weiss, & Conaway, 1992; Weiss, 1978; Weiss, 1987) indicate that science is often the subject that gets the least attention in the elementary curriculum. Elementary teachers must make science an equal priority with other subjects. Science cannot be considered a subject that "we'll get to if we have time after everything else has been taught." In the next chapter, we discussed ways that science can be integrated throughout the curriculum and be given sufficient time in the school day.

Finally, a teacher who promotes a positive attitude toward science will encourage students to explore science topics. The third grader who comes to school excited about his new guinea pig might, for example, be encouraged to investigate the types of foods his guinea pig needs and likes. Teachers in a project-based science classroom listen to students, ask questions, and seek information about students' interests so they can encourage science inquiry. Students' ideas and responses help drive instruction in the classroom; the teacher is not the only person who determines the topics and activities.

Promoting Positive Affective Factors

Affective factors include curiosity, excitement, persistence, enthusiasm, flexibility, skepticism, and open-mindedness. Teachers promote positive affective factors when they themselves display them and when they encourage them in students. Rather than discouraging multiple answers in science and emphasizing a single right answer, a teacher who is fostering open-mindedness will seek more than one solution to a question and encourage students to do the same. Table 8.1 provides a few illustrations of ways to promote positive affective factors. In Activity 8.3, you will add to the chart.

Maintaining a Balanced Teacher-Student Relationship

Teachers in a project environment need to maintain a delicate balance between being the ones in charge and being members of the collaborative group. The teacher cannot be too authoritative or the collaboration will be squelched because students will tend to look to the teacher for answers rather than collaborating with peers. However, if the teacher is too relaxed, she may fail to achieve basic curricular outcomes required by the school district or state. Teachers in project-based science classrooms need to continually reflect on desired goals and outcomes, daily lessons, students' academic progress, students' skills, and classroom climate. Through this reflection, teachers can analyze where collaboration is succeeding or failing and take steps to sustain collaboration.

A second factor to consider in maintaining a balanced teacher-student relationship is whether students are encouraged to critique the teacher and give suggestions for improving instruction to enhance their learning. Many educators using constructivist theories (Brooks & Brooks, 1993; Taylor, Fraser, & White, 1994) believe that students should have a "voice" in establishing classroom practices. This means sharing some decisions that are made in the class. Sharing decision making with students (such as about

TABLE 8.1   Ways to Promote Positive Affective Factors

Affective factor	Teacher strategy
Curiosity about the world	◆ The teacher shows her own curiosity about what she reads in the paper by talking about it with the students.
Excitement about science	◆ The teacher brings in science books to read.
Enthusiasm to continue	◆ The teacher encourages students to keep trying to find an answer by pushing them to find other sources of information.
Ambition to investigate	◆ The teacher encourages students to ask, "Why?' "What if?" and "Could we?" questions.
Sensitivity to others	◆ The teacher asks, "How could I help you with this problem?"
Disciplined thinking	◆ The teacher encourages students to analyze potential flaws in their thinking.
Respect for evidence	◆ The teacher says, "Do you think your conclusion is supported by your data?"
Willingness to change	◆ The teacher shows that the schedule can change if students are really interested in a topic.
Questioning attitude	◆ The teacher says, "I wonder if we could find an answer to this question."
Fascination with findings	◆ The teacher says, "Wow! I didn't realize that. Isn't that interesting!"
Responsibility to project	◆ The teacher asks students how they should play a role in completing the project.
Skepticism about results	◆ The teacher says, "You know, I am wondering if this is correct. Do you think we should try it again to see if we get the same results?"
Tolerance for change	◆ The teacher shows a willingness to change a classroom rule if it isn't working.
Confidence in self	◆ The teacher encourages a student by saying, "I know you can do this. You are really good at asking questions."
Open-mindedness	◆ The teacher shows a willingness to accept students' ideas.
Dependability	◆ The teacher demonstrates that he or she can be depended upon—for example, she brings something to school that she promised the students.
Independence	◆ The teacher encourages students to think for themselves.
Self-reliance	◆ The teacher says, "I think you can do this by yourself."
Willingness to compromise	◆ The teacher models compromise by saying, "I see your point. Let's compromise."
Willingness to cooperate	◆ The teacher encourages students to get along with others in their group.
Honesty in artifact	◆ The teacher stresses that students should be honest—it is not acceptable to lie about data just to create a good artifact.
Objectivity	◆ The teacher says, "Well, let's wait till we get some more evidence."
Flexibility with ideas	◆ The teacher encourages students to try different ideas.
Patience with others	◆ The teacher doesn't get frustrated when a student is having difficulty understanding something.
Precision	◆ The teacher encourages students to measure things accurately.
Thoroughness	◆ The teacher models thoroughness by asking students to take meticulous notes.
Satisfaction with artifacts	◆ The teacher tells students they should be proud of their product.
Self-discipline	◆ The teacher says, "I'm going to put mind over matter and finish this."
Methodicalness	◆ The teacher models being organized.
Persistence with a task	◆ The teacher says, "I think you could answer this if you just stuck with it a little longer."

ACTIVITY 8.3

Promoting Positive Affective Factors

MATERIALS NEEDED:
- pencil and paper or a computer
- Table 8.1

A. Fill in additional ideas in the second column of Table 8.1

B. Meet with members of your class to discuss the ideas that you all came up with. What new ones did classmates think of? Keep these ideas in your portfolio.

C. How do these affective factors contribute to a positive classroom climate? How do they compare with your memories of positive and negative classroom experiences?

---

class rules, norms, topics to be studied, group arrangements, and methods of assessment) requires a delicate balance between teacher as adult with authority and student autonomy. When this balance is achieved, students are encouraged to take initiative and be autonomous, and the classroom learning environment fosters inquiry.

Teachers also balance teacher-student relationships by using various questioning strategies that encourage students to talk to one another (see Chapter 6 for more information). Not all classroom discourse should be between the students and teacher. When students interact with each other, the classroom becomes a community of learners. Teachers can also create a positive classroom climate by asking questions that promote creativity, critical thinking, and many different answers. For example, a teacher can ask, "How might we look at this differently?" or "Do you think there might be another way to solve this problem?" This type of climate invites students to take risks without fear of failure.

Ensuring Equality   One essential component of the current national reform efforts in the United States is the premise that *all* students need to be scientifically literate (Rutherford & Ahlgren, 1990; NRC, 1996). Teachers need to believe that all students can learn, and they must treat all students equitably. Research on equity issues finds, however, that girls and minorities still lag behind their white male counterparts in achievement and interest in science (Campbell, 1996).

One way to measure your students' self-images when it comes to science is to have them draw pictures of scientists. The "draw a scientist" activity has been done with many populations of people, and the typical drawing is very stereo-typed (Barman, 1996; Boylan, Hill, Wallace, & Wheeler, 1992; Huber & Burton, 1995; Rampal, 1992; Sumrall, 1995). The scientist is usually drawn as a white man who is either bald or has wild, unkempt hair. He is usually wearing a lab coat while working in a laboratory with chemicals and glassware. Often, he is pictured with a sinister look on his face. He wears eyeglasses, and he usually has a pocket protector filled with pens and pencils. Activity 8.4 gives you the opportunity to test for yourself science-related self-image.

Although girls start in elementary school with similar interests and abilities as boys and overall gender differences in science achievement are decreasing, the gap between high achieving girls and boys is increasing. Girls do less well. Between 1978 and 1990, boys were the top-scoring students in school (Campbell, 1994; Wilson, 1992), and the TIMSS study shows that boys continue to have significantly higher achievement in science literacy than girls (TIMSS, 1998).

Middle-class girls now take about the same number of high school math and science courses as do middle-class boys. However, in college, these girls are much less apt to major in math, science, or engineering fields than are similarly talented boys. They also drop out at faster rates. Low-income girls have had access to far fewer programs than have middle-class girls (Campbell, 1996). The end result is that women are still greatly underrepresented in fields like physical science, engineering, and technology (Pollina, 1995). White women and minorities continue to be underrepresented in science and engineering employment (Campbell, 1996). Current workforce projections indicate that unless more

ACTIVITY 8.4

Draw a Scientist

MATERIALS NEEDED:
- paper and drawing materials
- the following chart
- a group of students

A. Give children drawing paper and drawing materials and ask them to draw pictures of scientists. Do not give them any other directions.

B. Analyze the students' pictures according to the following list. How many students draw their pictures with these characteristics?

Gender

Male _____

Female _____

Race or ethnic background

White _____

Hispanic _____

Asian _____

African-American _____

Other _____

Work environment

Laboratory _____

Office _____

Outdoors _____

Other _____

Personal characteristics

Frizzy/wild hair _____

Eyeglasses _____

Pocket protector with pens/pencils _____

Bald head _____

Mean or sinister look _____

Other _____

C. Ponder this: In 1957, Margaret Mead and Rhoda Metraux published a report entitled "Image of the Scientist among High-School Students" in *Science* (vol. 126 p. 387). They found that

The scientist is a man who wears a white coat and works in a laboratory. He is elderly or middle aged and wears glasses. He is small. He may be bald or may be unshaven or unkempt. He may be stooped or tired. He is surrounded by equipment: test tubes, Bunsen burners, flasks and bottles, a jungle gym of blown glass tubes and weird machines with dials. The sparkling white laboratory is full of sounds: the bubbling of liquids in test tubes and flasks, the squeaks and squeals of laboratory animals, the muttering voice of the scientists. He spends his days doing experiments. He pours chemicals from one test tube into another. He peers aptly through microscopes. He scans the heavens through a telescope (or a microscope!). He experiments with plants and animals, cutting them apart, injecting serum into animals. He writes neatly in black notebooks.

D. Has the image of a scientist changed since 1957? Why do you suppose it has or has not?

E. What effect do you think these images have on girls' and minorities' career aspirations? What might a classroom teacher do to counter these images?

F. Record your ideas in your portfolio.

---

women and minorities are attracted to science, the United States will not have the trained personnel necessary to meet its needs (Campbell, 1996).

A number of different factors have been associated with the gender and racial differences in science. Some studies indicate that girls and women and minorities are socialized to believe that science is for white boys and men (Hardin & Dede, 1992). Television shows and movies that depict scientists as weird "geeks" continue to reinforce this stereotype. Patricia Campbell (1996) suggests that even the news reinforces the stereotype that boys are better than girls in science and mathe-

matics. She writes, "Research that supports math and science stereotypes gets much more attention in the media than does work that challenges them. For example, "When one researcher says boys' higher SAT scores mean that boys are biologically superior to girls in math, she gets invited to the "Today Show" and is written up in *The New York Times.* But when another researcher says that society and test bias cause boys' higher SAT scores, she gets to go home and make dinner. Her results aren't considered news" (Campbell, 1996).

Parents may contribute to biases against science. It is not uncommon for parents to expect

---

TABLE 8.2 Equitable Classroom Practices

- The teacher helps girls and minorities by making sure that they are provided with challenging activities and that they succeed in the activities.
- Girls and minorities are active participants in the lesson rather than passive observers or recorders of information.
- The teacher has high expectations of all students (for example, he or she doesn't give the girls the answers and expects that they can complete the work in science).
- Girls use manipulative materials in science classes.
- The teacher fosters collaboration so in science girls have equal roles to boys.
- The teacher chooses language carefully (doesn't use male pronouns only to refer to doctors, engineers, or scientists).
- If students are in mixed-gender groups, rules are established to make sure girls have a chance to participate equally with boys.
- The teacher exposes students to women and minority role models in science so that students of all backgrounds can think of science as a possible career area.
- Girls and minorities are encouraged to do well in science and mathematics (and to take these subjects in school).
- Girls use computers in the classroom as much as their male counterparts.
- Girls and minorities are involved in science and mathematics competitions (such as MathCounts and Science Olympiad) and extracurricular science and math activities (attendance at science museums, science clubs, and reading science journals).
- Girls are called on in class as much as their male counterparts are.
- Girls' answers are elaborated upon (teachers don't simply say, "Okay," and move on).
- The teacher uses interdisciplinary curriculum materials.

---

different behaviors from boys than from girls. Boys often are expected to be tough, play basketball, and be active in outdoor activities, while girls are expected to be soft, play with dolls, and stay neat and clean while playing indoors. Gender-biased toys still permeate television ads—boys are more likely to be shown playing with erector sets, microscopes, and chemistry sets, while girls are more commonly shown playing with dolls, makeup, and stuffed animals (Hardin & Dede, 1992).

School practices also tend to contribute to gender and racial differences in science. Kahle and Lakes (1983) found that teachers give boys more opportunity to engage in science and math tasks. Teachers speak to boys more often, ask boys more high-level questions, and favor boys' responses (Baker, 1988). They have boys elaborate more on their answers than they do girls and they let boys dominate classroom conversations (Baker, 1988; Sadker & Sadker, 1992). Finally, Guzzetti and Williams (1996) found that boys dominate laboratory experiences by manipulating lab equipment, and girls are given the job of recording information in journals.

Textbook publishers have made concerted efforts to depict girls and women and minorities doing science, but Bazler and Simonis (1992) found that illustrations, photos, and text of boys and men far outnumber those of girls and women. Further, textbooks portray life science as a female interest and physical science as a male domain (Kahle & Lakes, 1983).

To help develop a project-based science classroom in which girls and minorities feel comfortable with science and are encouraged in science as much as their white male counterparts, teachers need to be cognizant of their curriculum and instructional practices. Table 8.2 illustrates some of these practices (Rosser, 1990; Sanders, 1994; Tobais, 1992; Wilson, 1992).

Activity 8.5 will help you think about equitable classroom practices.

CLASSROOM ORGANIZATION

Classroom organization is the second major topic of classroom management that we will examine. In this section, we discuss three aspects

ACTIVITY 8.5

Equitable Classroom Practices

MATERIALS NEEDED:
- a classroom to visit or teach in
- videotaping equipment if you teach the lesson

A. Obtain permission and watch a teacher teaching a science lesson or film yourself teaching a science lesson. Interview the teacher about his or her views about equitable practices in schools or watch the videotape of your lesson.

B. Analyze the classroom interactions and interview for the following:
- How did the teacher help girls and minorities be successful?
- Were girls and minorities active participants in the lesson rather than passive observers or recorders of information?
- Did the teacher have high expectations of girls and minorities (didn't give them the answers and did expect that they could complete the work in science)?
- Did girls and minorities use manipulative materials?
- Did the teacher foster collaboration so that girls and minorities had equal roles to the boys?
- Did the teacher choose language carefully (didn't use male pronouns to refer to doctors, engineers, or scientists)?
- If students were in mixed-gender groups, were rules established to make sure girls had a chance to participate equally with boys?
- Did the teacher expose students to women and minority role models in science so that students of all backgrounds could think of science as a possible career area?
- Were the girls and minorities encouraged to do well in science and mathematics (and to take these subjects in school)?
- Did girls and minorities use computers in the classroom as much as their male counterparts did?
- Were girls and minorities involved in science and mathematics competitions (such as MathCounts and Science Olympiad) and extracurricular science and math activities (attendance at science museums, science clubs, reading science journals)?
- Were girls called on in class as much as their male counterparts?
- Were girls' answers elaborated upon (teachers didn't simply say, "Okay," and move on)?
- Did the teacher integrate science throughout the curriculum?

C. Record your ideas in your portfolio.

---

of classroom organization: planning the physical arrangement of a project-based science classroom, structuring the school schedule, and maintaining a safe classroom. In each area, we will consider some practical strategies for dealing with student behavior and maintaining a productive and safe classroom environment. Finally, we will review in each section management tools that can help teachers organize and maintain a project-based science environment.

Arranging the Classroom

In a project-based science environment, the physical arrangements of the classroom need to be carefully planned to facilitate student investigation and collaboration and to minimize behavioral problems. To stimulate and encourage students to investigate their world around them, the classroom should offer science attractions for students to observe and manipulate, stimulating materials to read, and computers with telecommunication access. To facilitate investigation, science equipment should be readily available, and there should be areas where students can work on particular aspects of projects.

Depending on the project, the physical environment will change. For instance, the classroom might be overflowing for several months with plants while students are investigating the effect of fertilizers on plants, but later when they are studying pollution, the room might be filled with air and water quality testing equipment. Even though the physical organization of the room continually changes in a project-based science classroom, there are fundamental features that must be maintained.

Most teachers don't have the luxury of determining the size and shape of their classrooms, but teachers usually have a great deal of flexibility to move desks and tables, decorate, and arrange materials. A smooth running classroom doesn't just happen. Teachers who have effective, productive, stimulating classrooms are very aware of how they have organized students' desks, equipment, and supplies. Evertson and colleagues (1984) have identified four keys to good physical arrangement of a classroom: (1) keep high traffic areas free of congestion, (2) be sure students can easily be seen by the teacher, (3) keep frequently used teaching materials and student supplies readily accessible, and (4) be certain students can easily see instructional presentations and displays (pp. 4–5).

Keep High Traffic Areas Free of Congestion
What are high traffic areas? These can include, but are not limited to, doorways, the area around the trash can, the teacher's desk, the area around the pencil sharpener, sinks, bookshelves with literature or encyclopedias, investigation centers, and the drinking fountain. It is best to keep high traffic areas away from each other. Keep aisles wide and clear around these areas so that they are easy to get to. Be aware of maintaining accessibility for wheelchair users or students with mobility problems. All students should be able to reach necessary items during the course of the school day. It is also a good idea to keep quiet areas like reading centers away from the high traffic areas. Classroom pets and aquariums should also be kept away from high traffic areas, because animals can easily become stressed from too much noise or movement around their cages.

When people first start teaching, they often give little attention to the logistics of their rooms and instead arrange things so that they look good, designing and putting up fancy bulletin boards. Although an attractive classroom is certainly part of classroom organization and climate, attractiveness is not the primary consideration; a well-conceived classroom can facilitate learning and help minimize behavior problems. One beginning teacher mistakenly placed a set of encyclopedias near a science learning center where students were supposed to work with magnets. While individual students were working in the science center, other students had to walk past to get encyclopedias from the shelf.

Students at the center were continually distracted, often by passersby looking at what they were doing with magnets.

In a project-based classroom, different areas will become high traffic areas at different times, depending on the project. For example, when students are investigating plants, the window area might become a high traffic area, but when students are investigating wheels, they might never go near the windows. Areas that are typically high traffic, regardless of the project, are areas with resources (reference materials, children's literature, and children's magazines), computer areas, areas where laboratory equipment is housed, and office supply areas (where students might obtain construction paper, tape, and glue, to construct artifacts). Since students often work at their desks or at tables in collaborative groups in a project-based environment, it is wise to try to arrange sets of desks away from other sets of desks. In this way, one collaborative group will not interfere with another.

Be Sure Students Can Be Seen Easily by the Teacher Good instruction and good behavior management depend a great deal on teachers' abilities to *see* all of their students. This is especially true in a project-based science classroom where students will be moving about and collaborating with each other. There is nothing more annoying to a teacher than hearing students talking or misbehaving but not being able to see who they are. To help solve this problem, teachers arrange their classrooms so that they have a clear line of sight to all student desks, bookshelves, learning centers, table areas, and science storage facilities.

One beginning teacher arranged a free-standing literature bookshelf so that the shelf created a private study area where there was a bean bag chair. The book shelf obstructed the teacher's view of any student sitting in the bean bag chair, making it a prime site for misbehavior.

Project-based science teachers need to be able to see students in order to facilitate discussions, diagnose learning problems, and help students as needed. If teachers cannot see students, they cannot engage them in conversation or notice if they are struggling with reading material, a question, or an activity. In Scenario 4 at the beginning of this chapter, the teacher sat down to grade papers while the students worked on multiple activities. This is when students became loud and disruptive. Moving about the room to help students, facilitating discussions, or keeping them engaged with prompts and questions will minimize misbehavior. Just being able to see students and the related outcome that they know they can be seen will go a long way to keeping the classroom running smoothly.

Another important reason for making sure that all areas of the room are visible is that even simple science materials, such as a glass jar, can become dangerous if dropped and broken. Teachers need to be able to keep an eye on students while they are using equipment to make sure they are not in danger of hurting themselves and to respond quickly when accidents happen.

Keep Frequently Used Teaching Materials and Student Supplies Readily Accessible   Keeping often used materials and supplies readily accessible saves time for the teacher and students, and when off-task time between activities and lessons is curtailed, invitations for students to misbehave are minimized. Frequently used teaching materials include student textbooks, science equipment, and office supplies (rulers, tape, glue, and paper).

Clear shoe boxes and zipper-closure bags make good storage containers for science equipment and supplies. They can be handled easily by students distributing materials, and they make collecting materials easy and fast. Because such storage containers are clear, the teacher and the students can easily see what is inside. They can be stored on shelves or in larger boxes. Rolling carts (the type that libraries use for returned books) make great locations for storing frequently used textbooks, reference materials, and magazines. The movable carts let teachers rearrange their classrooms as needed, and the carts can be moved out of the way when not in use.

In a project-based science classroom, it is useful to have materials for investigations and for making artifacts readily accessible. Keep magnifying lenses and simple microscopes accessible at all times. This accessibility promotes curiosity and inquiry since it lets students examine objects any time of the day. Other objects to keep readily available are measuring cups, measuring spoons, bowls or containers, bug cages, eye droppers or dropper bottles, balance scales, rulers, flashlights, mirrors, and tweezers. Materials that are com-

FIGURE 8.1
Careful attention to classroom arrangement will facilitate project-based science.

monly used to create artifacts include rulers, tape, glue, cardboard, tagboard, paper, stencils, crayons, markers, and construction paper.

Be Certain Students Can See Displays and See and Hear Instructional Presentations   The obvious reason for making presentations and displays accessible and visible is that students need to be able to see them in order to learn. The less obvious reason is that students become bored or frustrated when they can't see what you and the other students are talking about, and boredom and frustration often lead to misbehavior.

Teachers sometimes erroneously blame students for misbehaving during presentations. In one classroom, a teacher was demonstrating a science technique (how to accurately focus a microscope) to approximately twenty-five students. The sole microscope was sitting on a desk in the front of the room where the teacher was demonstrating the techniques for adjusting the stage, adjusting the mirror, moving the knobs, and fine-tuning the view. Since the microscope was placed at the eye-level of the students in the first row, the rest of the class could not see what was being demonstrated. Some students in the back began to misbehave, and the teacher became frustrated and angry with them. When students were given the microscopes to use, most did not know how to use them, and the teacher again became angry and frustrated. It did not occur to her that the primary cause of the problem was the position of the microscope.

In Chapter 6, we discussed benchmark lessons. These lessons are designed to teach students basic information or skills they need to be able to investigate and answer driving questions. We discussed how benchmark lessons might include demonstrations, discrepant events, presentations (diagrams, pictures, graphs, movies, videos, and television shows), and guest lecturers. Make sure that students can easily see and hear all such presentations and guest speakers. Keep displays such as diagrams, pictures, or graphs in locations where students can see them. Position televisions, screens, and monitors so that all students in the class have a clear view of them. Make sure that students have a clear view and that other students' heads or classroom objects aren't in the way. Make sure that objects to be viewed are positioned at proper distances and heights. Check that glare from overhead lights or the sun doesn't interfere with viewing. In addition, make sure all students can hear the presentation.

Table 8.3 presents a summary of key considerations to think about with regard to the physical arrangement of elementary and middle grade science classrooms.

In Activity 8.6, you will imagine that you are setting up a classroom. Try to think about the aspects of classroom organization just discussed as you design a classroom setting.

Structuring the School Day

Although a teacher may not be able to structure the entire school day, given that there are often fixed schedules for art, music, physical education, meetings, and assemblies, a teacher generally has a great deal of flexibility to structure the day within the classroom. The structure of the school day includes the number of minutes a teacher allocates to various subject areas, the delivery of science as a subject (discontinuous and presented as a separate subject or integrated and continuous), and the day's schedule of activities ("set in stone" or flexible). In this

---

TABLE 8.3   Arranging a Classroom

Keep high traffic areas free of congestion

- Arrange high traffic areas away from each other.
- Keep aisles wide and clear.
- Pay attention to accessibility or wheelchair users.
- Make sure students can easily get to and reach necessary items.
- Keep quiet areas away from the high traffic areas.
- Keep classroom pets and aquariums away from high traffic areas.
- Try to arrange sets of desks away from other sets of desks.

Be sure you can easily see students

- Arrange the classroom so that you have a clear line of sight to all student desks, bookshelves, learning centers, table areas, and science storage facilities.
- Watch for potential safety problems.

Keep frequently used teaching materials and student supplies readily accessible

- Keep student textbooks, science equipment, and office supplies in readily accessible areas.
- Use clear shoe boxes and zipper-closure bags as storage containers.
- Use rolling carts.
- Keep materials used in investigations readily accessible.
- Keep materials used for making artifacts readily accessible.

Be certain students can see displays and see and hear instructional presentations

- Make sure that students can easily see and hear presentations and guest speakers, discrepant events, or demonstrations.
- Keep displays where students can see them.
- Position televisions, screens, and monitors so that all students have a clear view.
- Consider height, angle, distance, and glare.

---

section, we will discuss each of these aspects of structuring the school day.

The Number of Minutes Allocated to Subjects

The number of minutes allocated to a subject area is determined by many different factors: the students' knowledge, skills, and abilities;

ACTIVITY 8.6

Arranging a Project-Based Science Classroom

MATERIALS NEEDED:
- drawing materials such as pencils, rulers, and compass
- paper or a computer with a drawing program
- a classroom to observe

A. Using the four principles of good classroom organization you just read about, design a 20-foot by 40-foot classroom so that it contains all of the following items:
- twenty-five flat-topped (not slanted) student desks
- twenty-five student chairs
- a 12-foot by 3-foot table
- ten extra chairs
- a free-standing bookshelf
- a teacher's desk and chair
- a five-foot–diameter round table
- a file cabinet
- an overhead projector
- two computers on carts
- an aquarium with fish
- a cage with gerbils
- four plants in pots
- a pencil sharpener
- textbooks
- student belongings
- the teacher's supplies

Permanent features of the classroom are as shown in Figure 8.2.

B. Describe how your classroom organization will facilitate project-based science learning. You may want to review chapters that discussed benchmark lessons, collaborative learning, and other techniques that facilitate learning science.

C. What specific types of learning centers, bulletin boards, and visual displays would you design to interest students in science and promote the development of driving questions and investigations?

D. Visit an elementary or middle grade classroom to determine whether the classroom follows the four guidelines for good organization. If not, what would you do to change it?

E. Record your ideas and file your design in your portfolio.

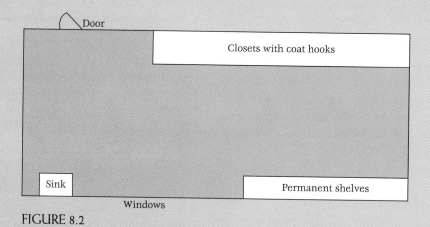

FIGURE 8.2
Permanent Features of Classroom

state and local curriculum guidelines; and the driving question being investigated. These factors can sometimes dramatically alter a teacher's preplanned lesson. You might prepare a forty-minute lesson and take only five minutes to teach it. You might prepare a forty-minute lesson and take 3 days to teach it. The teacher in Scenario 2, for example, was surprised that her lesson took longer than planned. However, while plans always change, it is important to plan, including determining the number of minutes a lesson should last. Without a plan, the day will likely become disorganized and chaotic.

The number of minutes that a teacher allocates to different subject areas depends greatly on the knowledge, skills, and abilities of students, which often have to do with the age and experience of students. Imagine that a group of first grade students is investigating the driving question "What animals live in my neighborhood?" Because first graders are only beginning to learn to read, a teacher may spend more minutes teaching reading than teaching science. However, children can practice their reading skills by reading science tradebooks. Because first graders are unlikely to know how to use a magnifying glass or a simple microscope, the teacher will need to spend a great deal of time developing these skills before students can investigate what animals are in a pond, for example.

With experience, allocating amounts of time for particular benchmark lessons becomes easier for teachers. However, because sometimes even the most experienced teacher is fooled about the amount of time needed to cover a topic, develop a skill, or conduct an investigation, good teachers always think ahead to have contingency plans ready. Otherwise, classroom management problems can arise. In anticipation of lessons that go more quickly than expected, it is a good idea to have extra specimens for students to observe, science tradebooks available for students to look at, and computer-based activities or other activity centers set up to which students can move when they are finished with work. The teacher in Scenario 2 had students learn more about the topic of DDT through computer research when they were finished with their work. Table 8.4 lists activities for students to engage in when there is extra time.

Some state and local curriculum guidelines predetermine the number of minutes a teacher must allocate to a given subject area. For example, some schools may tell teachers that they need to spend forty-five minutes a day on reading and writing and thirty minutes a day on science at the first grade level. Good teachers understand their curriculum thoroughly enough that they can often blend science throughout the curriculum. They do not worry, as a result, about the exact number of minutes they spend on a subject. They realize that a smooth-flowing school day facilitates good classroom management, and a smooth-flowing school day is not always characterized by a specific number of min-

TABLE 8.4　What to Do When There's Time Left Over

Students might

- look up related topics in tradebooks;
- consult the encyclopedia for more information;
- engage in silent reading for personal enjoyment;
- use the World Wide Web to find more information on the topic;
- explore additional examples of the same topic;
- brainstorm related topics to investigate;
- design an activity that classmates could participate in;
- make an entry into a journal or portfolio;
- make a drawing or model to explain what they learned today;
- create a quiz for classmates;
- explore the same topic through a different subject (art, music, mathematics, social studies, language arts, reading, or physical education);
- "peer tutor" other students in the room;
- play an educational game; or
- go to activity centers to explore new topics or ideas.

utes and a schedule set in concrete. They plan their days so that, ultimately, all subjects are covered and outcomes are reached. For example, on one day a teacher had students read about animals for an hour and plan an investigation for fifteen minutes. The next day, students spent forty-five minutes completing the investigation. Then students spent fifteen minutes working with the teacher to write stories about their investigation. Next, the students *read* their investigation "stories" to others in the class for fifteen minutes. On this second day, then, the class spent forty-five minutes on science and thirty minutes on reading and writing. Over the course of two days, the students spent a total of ninety minutes on reading and writing and sixty minutes on science. This is equivalent to the recommended number of minutes of reading/writing (forty-five minutes per day) and science (thirty minutes per day).

The driving question that is being investigated can dramatically influence the number of minutes allocated to science. The type of project, where the students are in the project, and the level of student motivation are all factors influenced by the driving question. For example, a project that investigates "What animals live in my neighborhood?" may take more time to prepare and finish than a project investigating "What do our classroom pets need to be healthy?" simply because it takes more time to get children ready to go outside, walk outside, investigate, and return to the school to resume other work than it takes to observe a pet eating in a cage in the classroom.

Where the students are in the project will also influence the time spent on different subjects. When students are beginning an investigation, the teacher may need to teach many benchmark science lessons to provide students with the knowledge and skills needed for their investigations. The science investigations themselves take time. As students finish their investigations and begin to make artifacts, the teacher may spend more time teaching writing skills.

Finally, student motivation will influence the amount of time spent on a topic. One driving question may really motivate students, and it is difficult to get them to stop their investigations. For other driving questions, it may be difficult to get students to finish their investigations.

Activity 8.7 will work you through planning times for subjects during the school day.

ACTIVITY 8.7

Preplanning the Number of Minutes Allocated to Subjects

MATERIALS NEEDED:
- pencil and paper or a computer

A. Imagine that students in your third grade class have decided (with your guidance) to investigate the driving question "How can magnets be used around school and home?" Think about the knowledge and skills that third graders would need to begin investigating this driving question and make a list of them. Then, think about lessons that might meet these needs and make a list of these as well.

B. Using these parameters, plan a week's worth of lessons focusing on the amount of time that you think it will take to cover various topics (make sure you include all subject areas: science, mathematics, social studies, and language arts/reading). Use Table 8.5 as your planning grid.

C. If possible, meet with a practicing classroom teacher to discuss your plans. Are they feasible? Where does the experienced teacher think you need more time and less time?

D. Find out what guidelines the teacher must follow with regard to the number of minutes per subject area. Does the state or local school district stipulate the number of minutes to allocate to various subjects? What is the teacher's experience with this in his or her classroom?

E. Record your findings and file your plan in your portfolio.

TABLE 8.5   Planning Grid

Monday	Tuesday	Wednesday	Thursday	Friday
9:00 School starts	9:00 School Starts	9:00 School starts	9:00 School starts	9:00 School starts
11:00–12:00 Art class with art teacher				
12:00–12:45 Lunch	12:00–12:45 Lunch	12:00–12:45 Lunch	12:00–12:45 Lunch	12:00–12:45 Lunch
		1:00–2:00 Physical education class with PE teacher		
			2:00–3:00 Music class with music teacher	
3:00 End of Day	3:00 End of day	3:00 End of day	3:00 End of day	3:00 End of Day

The Delivery of Science as a Subject You probably discovered in Activity 8.7 that the structure of the school day is influenced by how the teacher presents science and other subject areas. If the teacher presents each subject area separately, the school week might look like what is shown in Table 8.6.

TABLE 8.6 Sample Schedule

Monday	Tuesday	Wednesday	Thursday	Friday
9:00 School Starts	9:00 School starts	9:00 School starts	9:00 School starts	9:00 School starts
9:00–10:00 Reading/writing: Read first chapter of *How to Eat Fried Worms* and discuss.	9:00–10:00 Reading/writing: Read second chapter of *How to Eat Fried Worms* and discuss.	9:00–10:00 Reading/writing: Write an opinion piece about whether you would be willing to eat fried worms.	9:00–10:00 Reading/writing: Read third chapter of *How to Eat Fried Worms* and discuss.	9:00–10:00 Reading/writing: Read fourth chapter of *How to Eat Fried Worms* and discuss.
10:00–11:00 Science: Test whether opposite ends of a magnet attract or repel.	10:00–11:00 Science: Use iron filings to see evidence of magnetic fields at the end of a magnet.	10:00–11:00 Science: Test what magnets stick to and don't stick to.	10:00–11:00 Science: Plan an investigation to see how we use magnets in our daily lives.	10:00–11:00 Science: Carry out science investigation.
11:00–12:00 Art class with art teacher	11:00–12:00 Mathematics: Introduce graphing.	11:00–12:00 Mathematics: Make a graph showing how many students in the class have blue, brown, and green eyes.	11:00–12:00 Mathematics: Teach about types of graphs (bar, circle, and line).	11:00–12:00 Mathematics: Practice making one of each type of map using student eye color.
12:00–12:45 Lunch	12:00–12:45 Lunch	12:00–12:45 Lunch	12:00–12:45 Lunch	12:00–12:45 Lunch
12:45–1:00 Silent reading	12:45–1:00 Silent reading	12:45–1:00 Silent reading	12:45–1:00 Silent reading	12:45–1:00 Silent reading
1:00–2:00 Mathematics: Finish lesson on adding two digit numbers and give end-of-chapter test.	1:00–2:00 Social studies: Introduce symbols on a map (keys, north, south, east, west).	1:00–2:00 Physical education class with PE teacher	1:00–2:00 Social studies: Learn about geographical features on maps and identify key features in state.	1:00–2:00 Social studies: Make a map of the neighborhood, including directional key and geographical features.
1:00–2:00 Social studies: Discuss how maps are used in everyday life. Examine a map.	2:00–3:00 Health: Introduce lesson on nutrition and food pyramid.	1:00–2:00 Social studies: Look at a map of the United States and locate regions based on directional keys.	2:00–3:00 Music class with music teacher	2:00–3:00 Reading: Write a summary of chapters read in *How to Eat Fried Worms*
3:00 End of day	3:00 End of day	3:00 End of day	3:00 End of day	3:00 End of day

In Table 8.6, each subject area was treated separately, and seldom was there a connection among the subject areas. If a teacher presents science as a continuous subject integrated with other subjects, the week will look very different. Imagine a teacher starts out the week by reading a fifteen-minute story about how magnets are used in everyday life. Next, the teacher explains to students that they will need to know something about magnets to explore the driving question "How can magnets be used around school and home?" In a benchmark lesson, the students spend about an hour learning that magnets have a north and a south pole, and they test poles of the magnet to learn that opposite poles attract and like poles repel. The teacher explains that maps are used in everyday life and that maps have directional arrows on them to indicate north, south, east and west. The teacher introduces the idea that the earth has a magnetic north that can be identified with a compass. The teacher spends about an hour showing the students how to use a compass. After lunch, the class discusses situations in which maps are used, and they identify objects on a map (such as cities, states, roads, streams, and lakes) using the compass. Finally, the students are given a home assignment requiring them to investigate how magnets are used in their homes.

The next day, students discuss the findings of their home assignment. They begin a portfolio where they gather pictures that illustrate how magnets are used in everyday life. They create descriptions of how the magnets are used to accompany the pictures. The teacher notices that many of the descriptions in the students' portfolios contain incomplete sentences and lack end punctuation, so he includes a lesson that will teach students about complete sentences and end punctuation. Next, the teacher explains to students that they will be graphing information about magnets and that they may develop artifacts that display information in graph form. The teacher introduces graphing by having students sort objects that stick to a magnet and objects that don't stick to a magnet. Students make a bar graph to display data about the number of objects that attracted or did not attract the magnet. Students make two pie graphs to show what types of items (such as metal, paper, and plastic) attracted or did not attract the magnet.

On the third day, the teacher reviews how to use a compass for finding directions and contrasts this method with using the grids and coordinates on a map. Students practice finding various geographical features and sites on a map of their state. Next, the teacher holds a discussion about how students could use a compass if they were lost and did not have a map. The class goes outside and practices finding various things on the playground using a compass. After lunch, the teacher returns to the driving question "How can magnets be used around school and home?" The students discuss investigations that they might develop to answer this question. One group decides to investigate how a magnet could be used to keep things open or closed. Another group decides to investigate how magnets are used to keep things together. A third group decides to investigate how magnets are used in machines and other technology. A fourth group decides to investigate how magnets are used in hobbies and crafts.

The next day, each group works to come up with subquestions and a preliminary investigation plan. They write down the plans. Table 8.7 shows the groups' plans.

After lunch, the teacher helps students locate resources, supplies, and materials needed to conduct the investigations, and students begin their investigations.

On Friday, the morning begins with students continuing their investigations. The teacher notices that one group is having difficulty adding up a list of numbers of machines found that use magnets. This prompts him to take some time to teach a lesson about adding two-digit numbers. After the lesson, students are ready to continue with their investigation.

After lunch, the teacher shows the students how to summarize information using a chart. At the tops of the charts, students write down statements that reflect the topics of their investigations. In the charts, they list all the things they found. Students use the topics at the tops of the charts to form the topic sentences of their summaries, and they use the items in the charts to make supporting sentences. The teacher has students summarize in writing what they have done so far in their investigations. Students

TABLE 8.7   Preliminary Investigation Plans

Group 1: How can magnets open or close things?

Plan: Using magnets of various sizes and shapes, investigate how magnets can open and close things (such as doors, boxes, bags, and folders). Find out if magnets are used this way in real life.

Group 2: How can magnets keep things together?

Plan: Using one magnet, test things that can be kept together (such as papers, books, bags, and clothing). Find out if magnets are used this way in real life.

Group 3: How are magnets used in machines or other technology?

Plan: Get on the Internet and find out more about uses of magnets. Call an expert who uses machines. Take apart old, broken machines and computers.

Group 4: How are magnets used in hobbies or crafts?

Plan: Visit a hobby or crafts store. Invite to class a parent who makes crafts. Try making a useful object out of magnets.

share their summaries with classmates and discuss what else they will need to do to answer the driving question.

In a project-based science classroom, teachers are more likely to structure the school day in the integrated manner discussed in this second example. The delivery of science content in this example is continuous and integrated across the other subject areas. Connections are made for students to show them how benchmark lessons fit with the driving question. For example, when students learn to graph, they understand that they need this skill in order to present information in their artifacts. When they learn about compasses, they know that they need this information to understand how some machines use magnets. Teachers who present science (and other subject areas) as separate entities run the risk that students won't see the relationships between knowledge and skills or transfer understanding and skills to new situations.

The Day's Schedule of Activities   Although planned, the daily schedule in an elementary project-based science classroom is flexible. In *some* middle schools organized around large blocks of time, the teacher has a great deal of flexibility, but in other middle schools, students switch classes every fifty minutes, and so the day is much less flexible. Regardless of the flexibility of school organizational structure, good teachers understand that *they* must be flexible, that some activities take more time or less time than anticipated, and that they must be willing to alter the day's schedule accordingly.

For example, the teacher may never get to the benchmark lesson on reading a compass on Monday because students' investigations take a different focus. These types of changes are expected and welcomed in a project environment. If it is necessary to teach the lesson on reading a compass, the teacher will introduce it on another day.

Because project-based science does not focus on correct answers, there are frequently multiple answers to a question. Therefore, lessons and activities evolve and flow with students' findings. Because learning is student directed, not all activities and lessons can be planned exactly as they will be executed. Imagine that students discover that magnets can be used to hold things (such as holding the lid of a can with a can opener) as well as close things (such as the door of a refrigerator). This discovery motivates students to invent a lunch box that can be opened and closed with a magnet. Although the hours needed to test this idea were not in the original plans, the teacher lets students complete the activity. It may even lead to a new benchmark lesson that she did not originally consider. For example, she may need to introduce a benchmark lesson on magnetic poles in magnets of different shapes—the poles of a bar magnet are on the ends, whereas the poles of a circular magnet are on opposite sides. Students may need this information if they opt to use a round magnet to open or close the lunch box.

Table 8.8 presents some key ideas to remember about structuring the school day. Activity 8.8 asks you to study a teacher's schedule and plans and observe how much they change.

ACTIVITY 8.8

Scheduling

MATERIALS NEEDED:
  ◆ pencil and paper or a tape-recorder
  ◆ one to three teachers to interview

A. Find a teacher to interview on a Monday of a week. Discuss with the teacher his or her lesson plans for the week. Interview the teacher again on Friday of the week. How did the teacher's schedule change? Why?

What implications does this have for teaching in a project-based environment?

B. If possible locate two more teachers—one who integrates science across the curriculum and one who teaches each subject area separately. How does the delivery of science (integrated versus separate) affect the schedule?

C. Record your findings in your portfolio.

TABLE 8.8   Structuring the School Day

Number of minutes allocated to subjects

◆ Preplan the number of minutes needed for a subject.
◆ Preplan the number of minutes a lesson will last.
◆ Have activities ready for situations in which too much time is left over.
◆ Become thoroughly aware of the curriculum so you know how to blend science throughout it.
◆ Don't worry about the exact number of minutes actually spent on a subject or lesson.
◆ Be concerned with meeting curriculum goals and lesson objectives.

Maintaining a Safe Classroom

Because students in a project-based science classroom are self-directed, they share a role in developing activities, locating resources, and conducting investigations. They frequently move about the room to collaborate with others, work on a computer, or engage in an activity. Often, different groups of students investigate different subquestions. All of this activity raises unique safety concerns.

In general, teachers need to be aware of school district policies on all safety-related issues. For example, does the school have a policy about having animals in the classroom or the use of chemicals in a science class? Is there a policy on administering first aid? Who is supposed to be notified in case of an accident or injury? How are field trips arranged, and what are the legal liabilities?

In this section, we will discuss several issues related to maintaining a safe classroom. These include working with animals and plants in the classroom; planning for safe use of equipment and materials; dealing with fire and glassware; planning safe field trips; and being prepared to administer first aid. At the end of the section is a checklist to assist you in planning for a safe classroom.

Animals and Plants in the Classroom   Many teachers like to have animals and plants in the classroom. Not only are living things motivating for students (they might lead to driving questions), but they are needed in some investigations. However, there are a number of considerations involved in bringing plants and animals into the classroom.

It is essential that animals be healthy and well cared for and that they not harm the students in the class by biting, scratching, or passing on a disease. The National Science Teachers Association handbook on safety in the elementary classroom (Dean, Dean, Gerlovich, & Spiglanin, 1993) suggests that several rules be adopted regarding animals in the classroom:

◆ Don't let students bring in live or deceased wild animals, snapping turtles, snakes, insects, or arachnids that might be carrying a disease.
◆ Make sure animals are housed properly: in clean and securely closed cages.
◆ Purchase animals from reputable stores or supply houses. Carolina Biological Supply Company (2700 York Road, Burlington, NC 27215; 1-800-334-5551;

carolina@carolina.com; http://www.carolina.com) is one of the most-used suppliers of live animals and specimens for science classes. Other suppliers can be found on the National Science Teachers Association Web page at http://www.nsta.org/scisupp/.

- If students bring personal pets to school as part of a class activity, make sure that the pets have proper housing during the day and that strangers don't handle them because they may become frightened and bite or scratch and because it may injure them.
- Don't let students pick up or touch unfamiliar animals—even if they are other students' pets.
- Don't allow students to tease or poke at an animal in a cage, even if their intention is only to wake up a sleeping animal and not to hurt it.
- Teach students how to properly pick up different animals. For example, a rabbit should be picked up by the scruff of the neck. Make sure students wear gloves when picking up most animals and always wash their hands after handling animals.
- Familiarize yourself with the necessary care and best way to handle the animals in your classroom. Check local libraries for books or call a local zoo or veterinarian for more information.

Some plants can be toxic (even fatal) to students. The National Science Teachers Association (Dean, Dean, Gerlovich, & Spiglanin, 1993) provides several guidelines for using plants safely in the classroom:

- Teach students not to put plants in their mouth.
- If students are handling plants, have them wash their hands after the investigation so that sap or juice doesn't remain on their skin and make sure they wash their hands before eating any food.
- Don't let students inhale smoke from any burning plant or pick any unknown flowers, seeds, or plants, because some fumes or toxins can be very dangerous. For example, poison sumac and poison oak

are poisonous to the skin, and foxglove or jimson weed are poisonous when eaten.

Equipment and Materials   Teachers should wear and require students to wear goggles to protect their eyes against impact or contact with liquids or fumes. Even simple activities such as burning a candle, working with a mild acid like vinegar, or melting sugar in a test tube have the potential to cause eye damage or irritation. Classrooms should have sets of safety goggles, and teachers need to teach students how to use them. Goggles should always be cleaned after each use, because eye diseases, such as conjunctivitis, are very contagious. Some activities involve blindfolding students. Once a blindfold has been used, it should not be used on another student.

Safety shields can protect students during demonstrations. For example, if you are conducting a benchmark lesson in which you demonstrate that hot air expands by heating a test tube with a cork in it, you should use a safety shield since the cork will pop out (and sometimes fly out) of the test tube.

Students in a project-based classroom are active participants in designing and carrying out investigations. This means that they may be getting out materials and supplies. Improperly stored materials are invitations for accidents. Make sure that the area where materials and supplies are stored has plenty of space, or limit the number of students allowed into the area. Make sure that the place where you store equipment and supplies has adequate shelving that is sturdy, deep enough so items don't easily fall off, and secured to a wall or floor so that it cannot tip over on students. Chemicals and glassware should be stored only on lower shelves so they are easy to get to. Keep supplies in small jars so that students can handle them easily. For example, rather than having students pour vinegar from a gallon jug, keep small dropper bottles of vinegar available for student use. Although the typical elementary classroom does not have many (if any) volatile liquids, some middle school or junior high classrooms have these items. A popular middle grade life science book on the market uses nitric acid in one of its protein activities. Do not store volatile items together, near heat sources, or near electricity, and keep these items in locked storage areas. Finally, make sure all items are labeled, and keep handy a quick reference on precautions, antidotes, and proper disposal.

Always be vigilant when students are using electricity. During one teacher's first year of teaching, students were investigating batteries and bulbs (using size D dry cells, bell wire, and flashlight bulbs). She asked the students to figure out a way to make the bulb brighter (by adding more batteries or using a different wattage flashlight bulb), and a student headed toward a wall outlet to plug in his little electrical setup. Fortunately, she caught the student before he got there and injured himself. Many elementary teachers let students connect too many batteries in a series circuit. The uninsulated wire in the overloaded circuit gets very hot, burning the students. Teach children how to use electrical devices. Teach them not to touch items (such as hot plates) right after they have been turned off, because they will usually still be hot. Teach them to unplug electrical objects by pulling on the plug rather than the wire. Avoid using electrical extension cords because they can be overloaded or students can easily trip over them in the classroom. Be very careful when using any small electrical device such as a hot plate, small motor, fish aquarium pump, or fan so that students' hands or clothing don't come in contact with a hot surface or fast-moving part.

Fire   Many elementary teachers do not let students use fire in the classroom, but some middle school and junior high schools use Bunsen burners, Sterno cans, matches, or other sources of flame. Teachers and students should know where fire alarms are positioned in a building and be aware of the quickest fire escape from the room. Accidental fires in a classroom often happen when clothing or hair come too close to an open flame. All classrooms should be equipped with fire extinguishers and fire blankets. There are different types of fire extinguishers (for electrical fire, flammable liquids, and so on), so most schools like to use multipurpose ABC fire extinguishers.

Glassware   Glassware presents particular problems in any classroom, but it is of great concern in an elementary classroom. Teachers need to think carefully about using glass jars, mirrors, thermometers, and prisms. Many teachers use glass only if it is absolutely necessary and a plastic alternative will not work. If glass is used, make sure that any sharp edges (such as on mirrors or prisms) are taped, painted, or ground smooth. If students are going to put glass tubing into a rubber or cork stopper, make sure that they use a lubricant and that they do not put the glass tubing into the palms of their hands to press into the stoppers (Dean, Dean, Gerlovich, & Spiglanin, 1993).

Field Trips   Field trips are valuable in a project-based environment, because they link the driving question and investigation to a broader community and the world outside of school. However, there are a number of precautions that should be taken when going on field trips. The National Science Teachers Association (Dean, Dean, Gerlovich, & Spiglanin, 1993) provides several tips:

◆ Don't take anything for granted on the trip.

◆ Bring along a second adult approved by the school administration.

◆ Obtain parent permission before taking students away from school.

◆ Alert parents about proper clothing or supplies needed for the trip. For example, ask students to wear long-sleeve clothing if they will be outside and could come in contact with ticks or be scratched by branches.

◆ Always bring along a first aid kit on a field trip in case something happens to a student while away from the school building. Many teachers also bring along cell phones in case they need to make an emergency phone call for help.

◆ Take special precautions for any field trip near a body of water, stream, or river. For example, become familiar with animals or plants near or in the water. Use a "buddy system" if students are actually in the water, and learn CPR.

◆ If taking a field trip to a factory, laboratory, or business, make sure that the trip is well supervised and that someone from the site conducts the field trip. On-site guides will be the most familiar with potential danger areas for students and can alert participants to situations in which more caution is needed.

First Aid First aid is meant to protect, not treat. The American National Red Cross is the best source of information for first aid procedures for staying calm, restoring breathing, stopping bleeding, and preventing shock, so we won't go into first aid procedures here. Become familiar with first aid procedures in case anything happens in the classroom.

Safe Lessons As a regular part of any lesson, teachers should think about potential safety precautions before beginning to teach. The checklist in Table 8.9 (modified from Dean, Dean, Gerlovich, & Spiglanin, 1993) summaries safety considerations and provides some guidelines for planning and teaching on a daily basis with safety in mind. Activity 8.9 will work you through a safety audit of a classroom.

MANAGEMENT STRATEGIES

Management strategies is the third area related to basic management concerns and challenges that we will discuss. In this section, we will focus on three stages of classroom management: before instruction, during instruction, and after instruction.

Before Instruction

In addition to establishing a positive classroom climate (discussed earlier in this chapter), there are several steps teachers need to take before starting any classroom lesson in order to ensure a smooth-running classroom. First, teachers must establish classroom norms about what is acceptable behavior. Second, they must establish an atmosphere that fosters "good" behavior. Third, they must set up agreements, or contracts, with students to define objectives, choices, and consequences of behavior. Fourth, they must anticipate problems before they happen.

Establishing Norms for Acceptable Student Behavior In order to establish acceptable student

behavior, many teachers begin a school year by setting general class rules and ground rules for behavior during different types of lessons (such as investigations, reading, or computer sessions). As discussed earlier in this chapter, an important question to ponder when setting rules is whether the teacher should determine acceptable classroom norms or whether the teacher should involve students in the development of those norms.

Kamii (1984, 1991) and Kamii, Clark, and Dominick (1994) argue that children need to invent ethical meanings. Katz (1984) suggests that getting children to comply with rules does not develop the primary goal of generating good children. What does is giving children choices and helping children learn for themselves in a caring classroom community. In other words, teachers need to move beyond simply enforcing rules. Kohn (1996) writes that it is far better to ask children to create rules—but even this strategy is not constructivist as students might come up with only the rules they think the teacher wants to hear or that they recall from previous years. He argues that it is better to get students

FIGURE 8.3
A well-managed classroom is planned and designed in advance.

TABLE 8.9   Planning Safe Lessons

Questions to ask regarding general safety concerns	Answers
1. Do you have a copy of the federal, state, and local regulations that relates to school safety as well as a copy of your school district's policies and procedures?	_____
2. Check your classroom. Are equipment and materials properly stored (in the right types of cabinets for chemicals, on sturdy shelving that won't tip over, and on deep shelving that items won't fall off of easily)?	_____
3. Are you familiar with possible hazards involved in using the equipment and materials in your room?	_____
4. Do you know your school's policies and procedures in case of accidents?	_____
5. At the start of each science activity, do you instruct students regarding potential hazards and precautions?	_____
6. Is the number of students working together on an experiment limited to a number that can safely perform the experiment without causing confusion and accidents?	_____
7. Do students have sufficient time to perform the experiments and clean up and properly store the equipment and materials after use?	_____
8. Do you instruct students not to taste or touch substances in the science classroom without first obtaining specific instructions from you?	_____
9. Are your students aware that all accidents or injuries—no matter how small—should be reported to you immediately?	_____
10. Do you instruct your students that it is unsafe to touch the face, mouth, eyes, and other parts of the body while they are working with plants, animals, or chemical substances and afterwards, until they have washed their hands and cleaned their nails?	_____
11. Does your classroom have safety goggles and a first aid kit? Do you know how to use these items? Do students use the safety goggles? Are the goggles cleaned and disinfected after each use?	_____
12. Are materials and supplies that students use stored in an area with plenty of space to avoid accidental collisions among students?	_____

Questions to ask regarding safe use of chemicals	Answers
1. Have you taught students that they must not mix chemicals "just to see what happens?"	_____
2. Have you taught students to never taste chemicals and to wash their hands after use?	_____
3. Do you forbid students from mixing acid and water?	_____
4. Do you keep combustible materials in a metal cabinet equipped with a lock?	_____
5. Do you store chemicals under separate lock in a cool, dry place but not in a refrigerator?	_____
6. Do you store only a minimum amount of chemicals in the classroom? Do you give students only small amounts of materials to work with (such as a dropper bottle of vinegar rather than a gallon jug)?	_____
7. Do you properly discard chemicals not used in a given period?	_____
8. Are all chemicals labeled?	_____
9. Do you keep handy a quick reference for precautions, antidotes, and proper disposal of all chemicals?	_____

Questions to ask regarding glassware	Answers
1. Do you use plastic instead of glass when possible?	_____
2. Do students know how to use glassware? (For example, do they know how to insert glass tubing into a rubber stopper and how to heat hard glass test tubes—not from the bottom but tipped slightly and not in the direction of another student?)	_____

Questions to ask regarding glassware *(continued)*	**Answers**
3. Are a whisk broom and dust pan available for sweeping up pieces of broken glass?	_____
4. Are students aware that they should not drink from glassware used for science experiments?	_____
5. Are thermometers for use in the classroom filled with alcohol, not mercury?	_____

Questions to ask regarding electricity	**Answers**
1. Are your students taught safety precautions for the use of electricity in all situations (not to touch an item recently turned off, not to pull out an electrical appliance using the cord, to keep fingers and clothing away from moving parts?	_____
2. Have you told students not to experiment with the electric current of home circuits?	_____
3. Are you allowed to use extension cords in your building? Are they in good condition and plugged into the nearest outlet (so they won't cause a short circuit)?	_____
4. Are students' hands dry when they touch electrical cords, switches, or appliances?	_____

Questions to ask regarding fire	**Answers**
1. Do you know your school's fire regulations and evacuation procedures and the location of and use of fire-fighting equipment?	_____
2. Does your room have an ABC fire extinguisher and a fire blanket? Do you know how to use them?	_____
3. What extra cautions do you take if dealing with fire? What special instructions do you give students?	_____

Questions to ask regarding plants and animals	**Answers**
1. Are the animals healthy, well cared for, and in a suitable habitat?	_____
2. Are your students aware that they are not allowed to bring live or deceased wild animals into the classroom?	_____
3. Do you buy animals only from reputable stores or supply houses?	_____
4. Do you instruct students not to pick up unfamiliar animals? Do they know not to poke at an animal in a cage?	_____
5. Do you and your students know how to properly care for the animal and how to pick it up?	_____
6. Are your students aware that they should never put a plant into their mouths?	_____
7. Do students wash their hands after touching plants and animals?	_____
8. Do you forbid students from inhaling smoke from a plant or picking up an unknown plant, flower, or seed?	_____

Questions to ask regarding field trips	**Answers**
1. Are you thoroughly familiar with a field trip location before you take students there?	_____
2. Do you have extra adult supervision for a trip?	_____
3. Are your field trips approved by the proper school administration?	_____
4. Do you secure written parent permission for taking students on a trip?	_____
5. Are the students aware of proper clothing or supplies needed for a trip?	_____
6. Do you have a first aid kit to take with you? Is a cellular telephone available to take with you?	_____
7. Do you have a "buddy system" set up for students?	_____
8. Do you have students' home phone numbers, medical records, and medications before leaving school?	

ACTIVITY 8.9

Conducting a Safety Audit

MATERIALS NEEDED:
- a copy of Table 8.9
- permission to conduct a safety audit of a classroom

A. Obtain permission from proper school personnel (such as the principal and teacher) to conduct a safety audit of a classroom.

B. Study the features of the classroom. Observe a science lesson.
C. Audit the school and classroom for the safety concerns listed in Table 8.9. What recommendations would you make to the teacher or school to improve safety?
D. Record your recommendations in your portfolio.

---

to solve problems and engage them in discussion about what they want their class to be like. Kohn writes, "The construction of meaning is an active process. It can't be done unless the learner has substantial power to make decisions. . . . If we are talking about learning to be a responsible, caring person, then the decisions include how to solve problems and get along with others" (p. 78).

Although the answer to the question of who should determine the rules, may, in part, be determined by the age level of the students, rules tend to be easier to enforce if students in the class helped create them. When students have some ownership over the classroom environment, they are invested in making it work. In addition, when students help generate rules, they understand them better because they put them in the language that they use and that has meaning for them. For example, a word like *vom*, while meaningless to the teacher, may be considered offensive by students and need to be put on the unacceptable language list.

To set general classroom rules, many teachers engage students in discussion about what their classroom should be like and what classroom rules might be established to make the classroom this way. Even very young students have experiences that help them accomplish this task. Frequently, students will come with rules such as "treat others with respect," "be fair to others," "no hitting," and "no cheating." Many teachers post these rules on a chart in a prominent place in the classroom.

Having students create classroom rules may sound easy, but it is not always. Children may not be used to making decisions about their behavior, and they may act out during the transition period. They might "test" you to see if you

are really going to let them have choices. There might be outright resistance. Some children might be silent and not attempt to solve classroom problems. Children may just "parrot" what they think you want to hear. To solve some of these transition problems, you can try several strategies:

- Try going slower; children may be overwhelmed with choices.

- Let students make some "bad" decisions and rules (as long as they are not emotionally or physically dangerous) and let them analyze and reflect on whether they are working. For example, if students say there is no reason to write their names on their papers, you might go along with this for a while. If students don't quickly decide to change this rule, then approach them to help you solve the problem of knowing who to give grades to for written work.

- If students refuse to participate, saying it is your job to make the rules, reassure them that you will still make some rules, but that you can make some rules together.

- Find out why students are silent when it comes to making rules. Are they shy? Do they feel safe? The reason will determine your approach.

- If students are only parroting answers, push them to defend the answers they give. Ask, "Why is it important?" "What does it mean?" "Does everyone agree?" (Kohn, 1996, pp. 96–97).

Although these general rules are important for any classroom, there are some ground rules specific to a project-based science classroom. These ground rules establish acceptable student behav-

TABLE 8.10   Activities and Related Ground Rules

Project-based activity	Questions to ponder	Resulting ground rules
Brainstorming ideas for driving questions	How can we brainstorm ideas without getting off track?	Keep to the topic.
	How can we brainstorm and not hinder good ideas?	Don't put down people's ideas.
	How can we value all students' ideas?	
Collaboration with others	How can we make sure all people participate?	Make sure everyone has a job to do in the group.
	How can we keep one person from taking over?	
	How can we make sure there aren't "loafers" in the group?	
	What voice level is acceptable?	
Critiquing each other's ideas	How can we make sure we don't insult someone?	Say good things about the project first.
	How can we nicely help someone make his or her project better?	
Investigations	How can we safely use science equipment?	Don't run with science equipment.
	How can we make sure we are exploring an idea fully?	
	How can we make sure all students help with the investigation?	
	Can we move around the classroom?	
	Can we get our own equipment or must the teacher get it for us?	
Working on the computer	How do we find only information that is related to our topic?	Let everyone in our group conduct one search on a topic.
	How do we use the computer safely?	
	How does everyone get a chance to use the computer?	
Demonstrations or guest speaker visits	How do we treat a guest speaker?	Don't talk when someone else is talking to the class.
	What is important to do during a demonstration?	
	How do we sit and listen respectfully?	
Field trips	How do we behave in public?	Make our community proud of kids at our school.
Making artifacts	How can we make sure that all students' ideas are used in the artifact?	Keep a list of each person's contribution or idea.
	What amount of noise is acceptable?	We should use talking voices.
Sharing artifacts	How do we give people new ideas without insulting them?	Say, "I like your idea, but did your group consider . . . ?

ior during various aspects of project activities. For example, teachers might want students to be quiet when they are reading, but lively when critiquing each other's ideas. Table 8.10 illustrates some aspects of project-based science instruction for which specific rules might be needed. You can use the table with students to establish ground rules. Many teachers find the table most helpful before the start of a specific activity.

The teacher in Scenario 2 at the beginning of this chapter established rules before taking students outdoors to play a game. Another important time for establishing ground rules is when students are brainstorming ideas for a driving question. Before brainstorming, the teacher draws three columns on the board: *Activity*, *Questions*, and *Ground rules*. Then the teacher might engage students in a discussion about the

---

ACTIVITY 8.10

Establishing Ground Rules

MATERIALS NEEDED:
- ◆ Table 8.10

A. Table 8.10 shows at least one ground rule that might be established during each phase of a project. Think about additional ground rules that might be established during each phase. List them in the third column.

B. Discuss your ideas with classmates or a practicing teacher. How did your ground rules differ from the ideas of others?

C. If possible, visit an elementary or middle grade classroom and discuss these ideas with students. What types of ground rules do students devise to answer the questions about project-based activities?

D. Record your findings in your portfolio.

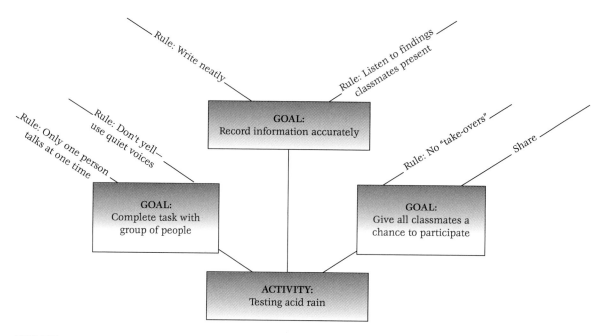

FIGURE 8.4
Behavior Tree Model

---

ground rules that need to be in place during the brainstorming activity. The resulting ground rules can be posted in the classroom and referred to at a later time.

Activity 8.10 will work you through the process of establishing ground rules.

Another useful technique for establishing acceptable student behavior is filling in a behavior tree. A **behavior tree** is a diagram in which the teacher and students establish the goals that need to be met during a specific activity and set ground rules that need to be followed to meet the goals. The behavior tree focuses students' at-

tention on behavior needed for a specific task or activity. The behavior tree in Figure 8.4 illustrates acceptable behavior during an acid rain activity. The teacher might say to the class, "Boys and girls, this afternoon we are going to be testing different samples of acid rain. You will be working in groups. What are some goals we have been working on as a class that might apply to group work during an investigation?" Students might respond, "Recording information accurately, completing the task, and giving everyone a chance to work." The teacher would record these three goals on the behavior tree, and students would generate the rules they believe applied to the desired goals.

Establishing an Atmosphere That Fosters "Good" Behavior

After classroom rules and ground rules for behavior during different situations have been set, an atmosphere that encourages the desired behaviors must be established. Helping students learn the required behaviors and norms often requires scaffolding. Also, many successful teachers encourage proper behavior by modeling it themselves. The teacher in Scenario 2 at the beginning of this chapter modeled for students how to come into the building quietly after being outdoors. Students are quick to notice when teachers say one thing but do another. For example, when a teacher sits in a corner grading papers while students are working on their investigations, as in Scenario 4 at the beginning of this chapter, the message to students is that the teacher is not interested in what they are doing. In addition, when teachers are grading papers, they cannot help students think through questions, design investigations, and find resources; facilitate collaboration among students; and help students develop artifacts. Some teachers give lectures about wearing goggles during investigations and fail to wear them themselves or insist that students be quiet when working but talk loudly with a colleague who walks by the room.

In addition to scaffolding learning about behavior and modeling classroom behaviors, teachers must reinforce good behavior. This reinforcement does not consist of tangible rewards like stickers, points for free time, or certificates to local fast-food restaurants. Kohn (1996) argues that tangible rewards only accomplish temporary compliance, and they do nothing to help a child become kind or caring. He says that rewards also warp the relationship between student and teacher, because it doesn't create a caring alliance based on warmth and respect. Successful reinforcement consists instead of praise and especially recognition. Students appreciate and respond well to the recognition of teachers, peers, and community members. A personalized note (that goes beyond a one-word comment like "good") by the teacher in a student's portfolio or a positive letter home to a student's parent(s) is very rewarding for most students. Having the results of a project published in the school or town newspaper, receiving a personal letter from a member of the community complimenting students' work, or comments from peers about how a student's ideas helped the group complete a project are all effective forms of recognition that reinforce positive behavior. So are simple comments from the teacher that indicate that she is noticing a student's efforts. It is very easy to say to a student, "I noticed that today you seemed really interested in the discussion," and comments like this go a long way. Remember that *all* students need to feel seen and appreciated.

Finally, a teacher can set an atmosphere for good behavior by focusing on what is positive rather than what is negative. An enthusiastic teacher who shows a positive interest in students is much more successful than the teacher who is constantly correcting students or who does not seem to care about them as people. For example, rather than reprimanding the student who is talking out of place, recognize the student who is working well (ignoring the other one). However, make sure the recognition is genuine and not contrived to make other students in the class jealous. A teacher can sincerely recognize a student for her unique idea or question, creative way of solving a problem, multifaceted conclusions to an investigation, or insightful way to display the results of a project.

Setting Up Contracts with Students

Some teachers find that using learning contracts effectively promotes self-responsibility. The teacher in Scenario 3 at the beginning of this chapter used a contract with his students. Learning contracts, a written agreement made between a teacher and members of a group, accomplishes several things. First, they force students to think about the expectations people have of them. They require them to delineate what type of project they will complete and what quality they expect to produce. Second, they outline specific ways students will meet objectives. Students can, for example, set parameters for work to be completed, artifacts to be created, or types of presentations to be given to the class. Third, contracts can also specify how projects will be evaluated. Will the teacher evaluate it? Will peers judge its quality? What will be evaluated?

Fourth, learning contracts can also establish procedures for group collaboration such as making decisions equitably, getting all members of the group involved, and coming to decisions in a fair manner.

Some essential features of contracts include, but are not limited to, the following:

- a description of the project (students list the driving question, the subquestions they are investigating, and the names of the students on their team);
- an outline of how students expect to accomplish tasks (students list what they will investigate, what materials they plan to obtain, who they intend to contact in the community, and what artifacts they expect to create); and
- an evaluation plan (students describe the quality of work they expect of themselves, how they want to be evaluated, such as with a rubric or with an interview by the teacher, and what aspects they want to be considered for assessment criteria, such as concepts learned and ability to collaborate together).

Figure 8.5 is an example contract that a group of fifth graders might complete for an acid rain project. Activity 8.11 will guide you through developing student contracts.

Anticipating Problems   Effective classroom teachers think about problems that might occur in their classroom, and they plan accordingly. In a project-based science classroom, teachers must consider the fact that different groups of students might be working on different tasks at the same time, compounding potential problems. In general, potential problems fall into several general categories:

- giving directions;
- materials and supplies;
- student behavior;
- timing;
- complexity of task; and
- sustaining interest over time.

Some teachers find it useful to think out potential problems using a *fish-bone model*. A fish-bone model is a diagram that lists tasks leading to a goal. On each "bone," teachers list possible problems. Figure 8.6 is a fish-bone model representing potential problems during four different tasks related to learning about acids and bases. Activity 8.12 works you through the creation of a fish-bone model.

During Instruction

We will discuss five factors to consider during instruction. These are the distributing of materials and supplies, making transitions, dealing with disturbances, handling multiple instances of the same activities, and handling multiple instances of different activities at the same time. On first sight, project-based science classrooms may seem chaotic. However, effective project-based classrooms are organized and efficient—and the reason is that the teachers have very clear management strategies for instruction.

Distributing Materials and Supplies   Whether it is the teacher or students who distribute materials and supplies in a science class, the distribution portion of a lesson is often the time when students misbehave or accidents occur. In part, this is because distribution represents downtime—a time when students are not actively participating in instruction or investigation. It is a time when students are simply waiting for something to happen, and so it often does. For this reason, it is important to distribute materials and supplies in an efficient manner to limit the amount of downtime between tasks. There are several efficient ways to distribute materials and supplies.

One way is to keep all materials and supplies in handy clear plastic boxes, plastic tubs, or zipper-closure bags that can be located quickly and easily passed around a table area to students.

Some teachers like to place all of the needed materials for an investigation or lesson in a single box or bag. For example, to investigate circuits (a benchmark lesson), students need a dry cell, wires, bulb holders, a flashlight bulb, and a dry cell holder. Rather than pass around five different boxes with these different items, the teacher could put one of each of the items into a zipper-closure bag before class and hand each table area one bag with all of the materials they would need for the lesson. This method is especially useful for young children with short attention spans who don't tolerate downtime well.

Names of team members: _____

Date: _____

Description of project:

We are trying to answer questions about acid rain. We are trying to find out if there is acid rain in our environment. Our group's driving question is "Can acid rain hurt plants in our neighborhood?"

How we're going to accomplish this project:

We are going to set up four geranium plants in pots. We are going to put all of them in the window in the room and give them the same amount of water. But to the water for one plant, we will add 1/2 teaspoon of vinegar. For the second plant, we will add 1 teaspoon of vinegar to the water, and for the third plant we will add 2 teaspoons of vinegar. The fourth plant will get plain water. We will measure the pH of the water with pieces of universal indicator paper that the teacher showed us how to use when we learned about acids and bases. We might call a nursery or a farmer to interview him or her about the effects of acid rain on plants.

Evaluation plan:

We will take photographs of our plants as they grow for 2 weeks. We will look up *acid rain* in the encyclopedia or on the Web to see what we can find out. We will measure the plants and see if they look healthy. The height and color of the plants will be recorded each day. The pictures, a graph of height versus time, and descriptions of how they look will be our artifacts. The teacher can grade this, but we will tell how well we think we did in our portfolio. We expect to get along with everyone in our group so we can answer this question.

Signatures: _____

FIGURE 8.5
Learning Contract

ACTIVITY 8.11

Making a Contract

MATERIALS NEEDED:
- a group of elementary or middle grade students

A. Visit an elementary or middle grade classroom and discuss the "essential features of a contract." From the discussion, develop a contract with the students. Find out if the students think the contract is fair. Would they sign it?
B. Based on this discussion, what features would you want to include in student contracts?
C. If you have the opportunity to teach, try implementing student contracts. Evaluate how successful they are in your classroom.
D. Record your contract ideas in your portfolio.

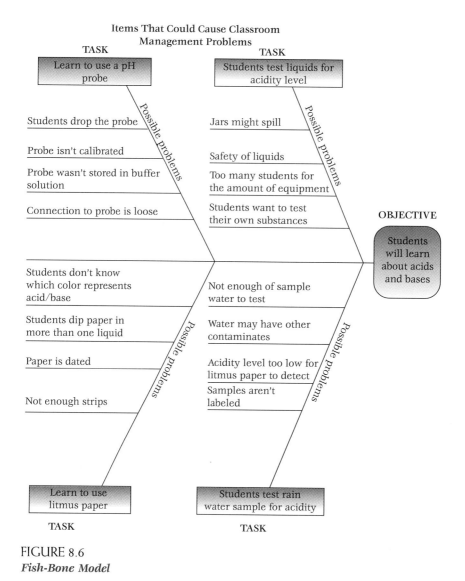

FIGURE 8.6
Fish-Bone Model

ACTIVITY 8.12

Anticipating Problems

MATERIALS NEEDED:
  ◆ Figure 8.6
  ◆ something to write with

A. Using the fish-bone diagram in Figure 8.6, determine what the teacher would need to do to avoid the potential problems.

B. Plan to teach a benchmark lesson. Complete a fish-bone diagram of the potential problems in the lesson.

C. How could the potential problems be resolved?

D. File your diagram in your portfolio.

It takes teachers a considerable amount of time to set up and organize materials in advance. Many teachers consider this part of their professional lives, and spend time gathering materials and setting up before school, during lunch, and after school. Other teachers solicit help from parents, grandparents, and retirees in the community, older students in the school, or students in the class who volunteer to be lab assistants.

Many teachers find that once students have materials and supplies in their possession, they are eager to begin the activity or investigation. At this point, it is usually very difficult to give directions to students. For this reason, it is most often a good idea to give clear and complete directions before materials are distributed for a benchmark lesson or other whole class activity.

In a project-based science classroom, students will frequently obtain their own supplies and materials because they are investigating different subquestions related to the driving question, and they are making different artifacts. For example, students using pillbugs to study ecosystems might investigate separate subquestions about the habitats of the bugs, the desired temperature preferred by the bugs, and the amount of light preferred by the bugs. Although these are related activities, they require different materials; bug cages, different soils, thermometers, sources of light, and light probes. For this reason, teachers in a project-based science classroom face some unique problems regarding distribution of materials and supplies. Students need to know where to obtain necessary supplies, and they need to have some parameters for doing this. Some teachers require students to submit to them lists of needed materials, materials that the teacher then gathers and distributes. Others teach students where materials and supplies are stored and allow them to get items for themselves. With this approach, it is important to make sure the supplies and materials are stored in an area that is safe for students. It is also important to teach students how to use materials. For example, students need to learn how to carry expensive microscopes and focus the lenses without scratching them.

Making Transitions Transitions are the few minutes that elapse between investigations, discussions, readings, and other activities. Transi-

tions, like distribution of materials, are points of departure for students. Teachers handle transitions in different ways but always try to limit the amount of time between activities. Some teachers like to establish a standing rule for transitions, such as requiring students to read silently or make entries in their journals during transitions. Some teachers like to make transitions fun and interesting. For instance, they might pose an interesting science question for students to ponder during this time. Some like to engage students in quick games or songs during transitions. Finally, teachers can engage students in discussions about what they think can be done during transitions; students may have good ideas for handling downtime.

Dealing with Disturbances Many potential disturbances are eliminated in a project-based environment because students are genuinely interested in what is happening. In addition, if there is a positive classroom climate, if there are established ground rules for behavior, if good behavior is modeled, and if downtime is minimized, the potential for disturbance is already lessened. Nevertheless, disturbances will still occur. For example, one group of students might be working at the computer while another group is conducting an investigation. These multiple instances of classroom activity create many situations where one group of students can disturb another group.

It is impossible within the scope of this book to discuss all potential disturbances and all possible teacher responses. However, there are several general strategies that are recommended in most cases that we can discuss.

First, it is usually best to *have students try to solve their own problems.* For example, when a disturbance occurs, you might ask the student involved to think about how he or she could solve the problem, or you might ask all the students in the class to come up with solutions. This technique fits with constructivist theories discussed earlier.

Second, *establish consequences* in advance for disturbances that are severe. Established consequences are *not* threats or punishments. Threats and punishments are usually only temporarily effective. They don't teach students to solve their problems, and they frequently cause more problems. Kohn (1996) argues that bribes and threats do three things: disrupt a lesson, warp the relationship between punisher and punished, and impede moral or ethical development. Threats and punishments teach children not to think about how the behavior affects others but rather about what might happen if they get caught. *Consequences,* on the other hand, are the predetermined outcomes of student choice. For example, if a student chooses to disrupt work in her group, she knows that the consequence is that she will have to take a time out. Consequences can be established when class rules are set, or if absolutely necessary, students can be informed of consequences by the teacher.

Third, *be consistent* in reacting to disturbances. Don't let students get away with a certain behavior sometimes but punish it on other instances. For example, if calling a classmate a bad name is considered inappropriate during science class, it should also be considered inappropriate on the playground.

Fourth, *be fair.* Some teachers treat girls less harshly than boys. For example, they might let girls talk in class but scold boys for doing the same thing. Similarly, teachers sometimes let more academically oriented students get away with behaviors that they would not tolerate from other students in the class. For example, they might let the brightest student in the class turn in a late paper but insist on deadlines for the other students. Students will be quick to spot unfair treatment, and perceiving that they are being treated unfairly may induce them to further misbehave.

For more information about classroom management and different viewpoints on discipline (sometimes conflicting viewpoints), consult these books, articles, and materials:

Albert, L. 1992. *An introduction to cooperative discipline.* Videotape. Circle Pines, Minn.: American Guidance Service.

Albert, L. 1989. *A teacher's guide to cooperative discipline: How to manage your classroom and promote self-esteem.* Circle Pines, Minn.: American Guidance Service.

Canter, L., and M. Canter. 1992. *Lee Canter's assertive discipline: Positive behavior management for today's classroom.* Santa Monica, Calif.: Lee Canter & Associates.

Child Development Project. 1996. *Ways we want our class to be: Class meetings that build commitment to kindness and learning.* Oakland, Calif.: Developmental Studies Center.

DeVries, R., and B. Zan. 1994. *Moral classrooms, moral children: Creating a constructivist atmosphere in early education.* New York: Teachers College Press.

Dreikurs, R., B. Grunwald, and F. C. Pepper. 1982. *Maintaining sanity in the classroom: Classroom management techniques,* 2d ed. New York: Harper-Collins.

Emmer, E. T., and C. M. Evertson. 1981. Synthesis of research on classroom management. *Educational Leadership,* Vol. 38, 342–47.

Evertson, C. M., E. T. Emmer, B. S. Clements, J. P. Sanford, and M. E. Worsham. 1984. *Classroom management for elementary teachers.* Englewood Cliffs, N.J.: Prentice Hall.

Kamii, C. 1991. Toward autonomy: The importance of critical thinking and choice making. *School Psychology Review* 20:382–88.

Kamii, C. 1984. Obedience is not enough. *Young children,* Vol. 39, 11–14.

Kohn, A. 1996. *Beyond discipline: From compliance to community.* Alexandria, Va.: Association for Supervision and Curriculum Development.

National Association for the Education of Young Children. 1986. *Helping children learn self-control: A guide to discipline.* Pamphlet. Washington, D.C.: Author.

Purkey, W. W., and D. B. Strahan. 1986. *Positive discipline: A pocketful of ideas.* Columbus, Ohio: National Middle School Association.

Handling Multiple Instances of the Same Activities

Even in project-based classrooms, teachers frequently facilitate the same activity for all students. This occurs frequently in a benchmark lesson on a concept or skill that all students will need to complete a project. The teacher described in Scenario 3 at the beginning of this chapter was handling multiple instances of the same activity to teach about parts per million. Several problems can occur when all students are participating in the same activity. Some students will finish earlier than others. Some students will "drop out."

The problem of early and late finishers can be caused by a diversity of abilities among students. More academically advanced or skilled students frequently finish activities much sooner than do their less academically labeled peers. Students with learning problems can have related behavioral problems. Gifted and talented students might become disruptive because they are unchallenged and bored. When there are differences among early and later finishers, it is a good idea to set classroom rules for finishing early, such as "Always take out a book to read silently when finished before others." Some teachers have students who finish early provide peer tutoring for classmates who are still struggling with an activity. Some teachers set up learning centers (locations in the room with enrichment activities) where students can go to work if they finish early. If learning centers are used, teachers need to be careful that the activities in these locations aren't more motivating than the primary classroom activity, or students may rush through their primary work to get to the enrichment activities.

"Dropping out" can become a problem when all students in the class are completing the same activity. Dropouts are students who lack interest in an activity or who fail to be motivated to complete it. Teachers need to monitor carefully students' interests and plan activities that are motivating. One way to monitor students' interests is to take time to talk with each student periodically. Ask questions to find out what the student is interested in, if he or she is challenged, frustrated, or bored. Another way is to have students keep dialogue journals (in which they write to each other or in which you and students correspond). These journals provide you with powerful insight into concerns students have about classroom activities.

Handling Multiple Instances of Different Activities at the Same Time The apparent chaos found in a project-based science class is compounded when there are different activities going on at the same time. Scenario 4 at the beginning of this chapter illustrates a classroom with multiple instances of different activities going on at the same time. In such situations, teachers must be able to orchestrate students working on different activities. They must be able to make different materials, supplies, and equipment available for different activities and keep different groups of students focused on the main project.

Having materials, supplies, and equipment available for different activities at the same time is no easy task. In fact, because of the evolving nature of projects, students don't even always know what they will need before the start of an investigation. To make this job easier, teach students how to get many of their own science supplies, materials, and equipment. In addition, rely on parent and community volunteers to help with materials distribution. Structure your lessons so that students submit supply lists to you before a break, lunch period, or classes taught by other teachers so that you will have time to gather materials.

To keep different groups of students focused on the project, a teacher must show students the relationships among their separate activities and with the driving question. Although one group of students may be on the computer looking up information about current weather conditions throughout the state and another group may be measuring current weather conditions outside the classroom, these two activities may be tied together by the driving question "How does weather affect our environment?" The activities are also related to each other since both are looking at current weather conditions. Students don't always see these connections, but knowing that everyone's work is connected can keep students focused and eliminate some of the management problems associated with working on different activities at the same time.

One way to emphasize this connection is to have students share ideas and discoveries with each other throughout a project. Groups can share their ongoing investigations with the whole class, or small groups can be paired to discuss their projects with each other. Another strategy is to have students draw Venn diagrams or complete charts like the one shown in Table 8.11.

After Instruction

Just because ground rules and procedures have been established in a classroom does not mean they will be followed. The teacher needs to continually reinforce classroom norms, revisit classroom norms, and evaluate progress *before, throughout,* and *after* the project. In addition, after instruction students and teachers should *reflect* on classroom norms, on the effectiveness of instruction, and on student behavior. The *National Science Education Standards* (NRC, 1996) promotes such reflective practices in science education: "Teachers of science engage in ongoing assessment of their teaching and of student learning. In doing this, teachers use student data, observations of teaching, and interactions with colleagues to reflect on and improve teaching practice" (p. 37). It adds, "They use

TABLE 8.11   Projects Are Linked

Group 1 activity	Group 2 activity	How it is related to the driving question "How does weather affect our environment?"
We're using the Web to find current weather conditions in Ohio.	We're taking the temperature outside of the school.	We're both trying to find out what the weather is right now.
We're doing an investigation to see if more molds grow in our environment when weather conditions are wet. We're growing mold in wet and dry conditions.	We're growing different grass seeds under different conditions (wet, dry, hot, and cold) to see if the weather will affect plants in our area.	We're both investigating how weather conditions affect the growth of things.

self-reflection and discussion with peers to understand more fully what is happening in the classroom and to explore strategies for improvement" (NRC, 1996, p. 42).

Reinforcing Classroom Norms   Teachers need to continually ask students to reflect on their objectives and encourage behaviors that help students meet these objectives. In a project-based environment, this is frequently accomplished by reminding students of the driving question they are trying to answer. This type of reminder focuses their attention on the purpose of their activities, and it can guide them in thinking about appropriate behaviors needed to accomplish their goals.

Teachers also need to reinforce established classroom rules. The teacher in Scenario 1 at the beginning of this chapter reminded students about classroom rules regarding talking when a reading assignment was given. Some teachers like to have students complete self-evaluation checklists or T-charts (like those discussed in Chapter 5) to assess at the end of a lesson whether they are following established classroom norms. Some teachers like to have debriefing sessions or class meetings in which students discuss their progress toward following classroom norms. Finally, some teachers like to send home "progress reports" or letters to report on students' behavior and progress in school.

Revisiting Classroom Norms   Classroom rules or norms are not established only once during a school year. Good teachers continually revisit and reexamine the established rules and norms. They have students analyze whether the rules make sense and if new rules should be made to replace those no longer appropriate. Not only does revisiting classroom norms limit problems

that might occur throughout the school year, it teaches students many of the problem solving skills that project-based science seeks to foster. Through this process, students learn to analyze whether rules are effective and solve the resulting problems if they are not working.

Evaluating Progress   One way to evaluate progress is to hold students accountable for their work. In a project-based environment, however, students must be accountable not only to the teacher, but also to one another. Each individual becomes accountable for his or her own learning, and the group is held accountable for learning and working well together. Therefore, we must examine two main aspects of accountability in a project-based science classroom—individual accountability and group accountability.

Individual Accountability   Individual accountability means that individuals in a group are responsible for their own learning, and the performance of each individual is assessed. Although there are many ways to evaluate students' progress (see Chapter 7), teachers make it clear to students that individual members of a group cannot coast along on the work of others and cannot disturb the learning of others. Each person must learn the assigned material with the support of the group. For example, while completing a project, all students in a group contribute to the creation of an artifact and to the group's presentation. However, students might keep journals or complete scoring rubrics to indicate their personal contributions to the project investigation, ideas, or artifacts. A rubric can also measure each person's collaborative skills such as accepting ideas from others, listening carefully to others, interacting constructively with others, and fol-

TABLE 8.12 How Did I Do?

Name: _____

Rate yourself on how well you think you collaborated with your teammates on this activity.

Criteria	5 Very well	4 Somewhat well	3 Somewhat	2 Somewhat poorly	1 Poorly
I accepted ideas from my classmates.	_____	_____	_____	_____	_____
I listened carefully to the people on my team.	_____	_____	_____	_____	_____
I provided constructive criticism to help my team.	_____	_____	_____	_____	_____
I followed the rules our class generated.	_____	_____	_____	_____	_____

TABLE 8.13 How Did Our Team Do?

Name: _____

Names of members on my team: _____

Rate how well you think you worked together on this activity.

Criteria	5 Very well	4 Somewhat well	3 Somewhat	2 Somewhat poorly	1 Poorly
Everyone participated.	_____	_____	_____	_____	_____
We solved problems without arguing.	_____	_____	_____	_____	_____
We talked in appropriate voices.	_____	_____	_____	_____	_____
We treated each other with respect.	_____	_____	_____	_____	_____
We stayed on task.	_____	_____	_____	_____	_____
We negotiated to solve problems.	_____	_____	_____	_____	_____

lowing classroom rules. Individual students might be required to pass a test on certain material, or each student might keep a portfolio to demonstrate his or her own personal progress toward mastering learning concepts. A sample rubric that students could use to evaluate their collaborative skills is pictured in Table 8.12.

Group Accountability We often think of accountability in terms of being able to demonstrate one's abilities to the teacher. In project-based classrooms, accountability also becomes the responsibility of the group. Group accountability most often falls into one of two types—collaboration and acquisition of certain knowledge or mastery of skills. In order for a group to demonstrate its ability to work well, many teachers have students complete questionnaires designed to ascertain whether interpersonal skills are being acquired and maintained, whether the classroom environment fosters sharing and respect, and whether students feel comfortable sharing and critiquing each other's work. Students can also complete a group scoring rubric that evaluates whether everyone participated, solved problems without arguing, talked in appropriate voices, treated one another with respect, stayed on tasks, and negotiated solutions. Another option is to assign to one student the task of evaluating with a rubric his or her group's collaborative skills. A sample group scoring rubric is shown in Table 8.13. The teacher may also assess the group's progress and have a conference with each team about its collaborative skill development.

To evaluate group members' acquisition of knowledge or mastery of skills, a teacher may have students ask one another questions about what they learned. Some teachers issue a final grade on a project based on a student's individual achievement and his or her accomplishment as part of a group. The grade could be the student's individual score plus bonus points from a

---

ACTIVITY 8.13

***Rethinking Your Views About Managing
a Project-Based Science Class***

MATERIALS NEEDED:
- a classroom to visit
- Activity 8.1

A. If possible, observe several elementary or middle grade classrooms. How would you characterize the climate, organization, and management of each? How does the classroom teacher view his or her classroom?

B. Has your view of a science classroom been reconceptualized since you completed Activity 8.1? If so, how? If not, why not?

C. Record your ideas in your journal.

---

group score. Teachers must decide what weights individual achievement and group accomplishment have in determining grades. Some teachers give all students in a group the same grade, the average of all students' work. Other teachers collect only one paper (sometimes randomly) from a group and assign the grade from that paper to all members of the group. Whatever method is used, it is important to establish assessment guidelines before the start of a project. Before a collaborative project is assigned, students should understand what weight will be given to individual and group progress. They should also understand how grades will be determined. If students recognize that collaboration is important and that they will not be harmed in the assessment process, there will be group cohesion and potential problems will be eliminated.

SUMMARY OF CHAPTER

This chapter introduced three key components of the basic management of a project-based science classroom: classroom climate, organization, and management strategies. In the classroom climate section, we considered a framework for establishing a positive classroom environment based on a constructivist model. Using a constructivist framework for classroom management, teachers try to have students participate fully in helping solve classroom problems and forming norms or ground rules. To build a positive classroom climate, the teacher serves as a role model who promotes a positive attitude toward science. The teacher develops affective factors such as curiosity about the world, excitement about science, enthusiasm to continue activities, and generates strong curriculum that is of interest to students. To develop a positive classroom climate in which students help solve problems, there must be a balanced relationship between the teacher and the students. Finally, a positive classroom climate is characterized as one in which all students—boys and girls, minorities and nonminorities—feel capable of learning science.

In the section on classroom organization, we discussed aspects of physical facilities, the structure of the school day, and safety. We considered specific strategies for managing a project environment.

In the section on management strategies, we focused on considerations before teaching such as establishing rules, using contracts, or anticipating problems; during instruction such as distributing materials, making transitions, dealing with disturbances, and working with multiple instances of activities; and after instruction such as reinforcing classroom norms, revisiting and reflecting upon norms, and evaluating progress.

Now that you have read this chapter, revisit your views on climate, organization, and management. In Activity 8.13, you will revisit your views in Activity 8.1.

REFERENCES

Ajzen, I., and M. Fishbein. 1980. *Understanding attitudes and predicting social behavior.* Englewood Cliffs, N.J.: Prentice Hall.

Baker, D. April, 1988. Teaching for gender differences. *Research matters to the science teacher.* Columbus, OH: National Association for Research in Science Teaching.

Bandura, A. 1986. *Social foundations of thought and action: A social cognitive theory.* Englewood Cliffs, N.J.: Prentice-Hall.

Barman, C. 1996. How do students really view science and scientists? *Science and Children,* Vol. 34, 30–33.

Bazler, J. A., and D. A. Simonis. 1992. Are women out of the picture? Sex discrimination in science texts. In *OPTIONS for girls: A door to the future,* ed. M. Wilson. Austin, Texas: Pro.Ed.

Boylan, C. R., D. M. Hill, A. R. Wallace, and A. E. Wheeler. 1992. Beyond stereotypes. *Science Education* 76 (5):465–76.

Brooks, J. G., and M. G. Brooks. 1993. *The case for constructivist classrooms.* Alexandria, Va.: Association for Supervision and Curriculum Development.

Campbell, P. 1996. http://www.tiac.net/users/ckas-soc/.

Campbell, P. 1994. http://www.tiac.net/users/ckas-soc/.

Dean, R., M. M. Dean, J. A. Gerlovich, and V. Spiglanin. 1993. *Safety in the elementary science classroom.* Washington D.C.: National Science Teachers Association.

Evertson, C. M., E. T. Emmer, B. S. Clements, J. P. Sanford, and M. E. Worsham. 1984. *Classroom management for elementary teachers.* Englewood Cliffs, N.J.: Prentice-Hall.

Guzzetti, B. J., and W. O. Williams. 1996. Gender, text, and discussion: Examining intellectual safety in the science classroom. *Journal of Research in Science Teaching,* 33:5–20.

Hardin, J., and C. J. Dede. 1992. Discrimination against women in science education: Even Frankenstein's monster was male. In *OPTIONS for girls: A door to the future,* ed. M. Wilson. Austin, Texas: Pro.Ed.

Huber, R. A., and G. M. Burton. 1995. What do students think scientists look like? *School Science and Mathematics* 95 (7):371–76.

Kahle, J., and M. Lakes. 1983. The myth of equality in science classrooms. *Journal of Research in Science Teaching* 20 (2):131–40.

Kamii, C. 1991. Toward autonomy: The importance of critical thinking and choice making. *School Psychology Review* 20:382–88.

Kamii, C. 1984. Obedience is not enough. *Young Children,* Vol. 39, 11–14.

Kamii, C., F. B. Clark, and A. Dominick. 1994. The six national goals: A road to disappointment. *Phi Delta Kappan,* Vol. 75, 672–77.

Katz, L. G. 1984. The professional early childhood teacher. *Young Children,* Vol. 39, 3–9.

Kohn, A. 1996. *Beyond discipline: From compliance to community.* Alexandria, Va.: Association for Supervision and Curriculum Development.

Mead, M., and R. Metraux. 1957. Image of the scientist among high school students. *Science* 126:387.

National Research Council. 1996. *National science education standards.* Washington, D.C.: National Academy of Sciences.

Nelson, B. H., I. R. Weiss, and J. Capper. 1990. *Science and mathematics education briefing book, volume II.* Chapel Hill, N.C.: Horizon Research, Inc.

Nelson, B. H., I. R. Weiss, and L. E. Conaway. 1992. *Science and mathematics education briefing book, volume III.* Chapel Hill, N.C.: Horizon Research, Inc.

Pajares, F. M. 1992. Teacher's beliefs and educational research: Cleaning up a messy construct. *Review of Educational Research* 62 (3):307–32.

Pollina, A. 1995. Gender balance: Lessons from girls in science and mathematics. *Educational Leadership* 53 (1):30–33.

Rampal, A. 1992. Images of science and scientists: A study of school teachers' views. I. Characteristics of scientists. *Science Education* 76 (4):415–36.

Rosser, S. V. 1990. *Female friendly science.* New York: Permagon Press.

Rutherford, F. J., and A. Ahlgren. 1990. *Science for all Americans.* New York: Oxford University Press.

Sadker, M., and D. Sadker. 1992. Sexism in the classroom: From grade school to graduate school. In *OPTIONS for girls: A door to the future,* ed. M. Wilson. Austin, Texas: Pro.Ed.

Sanders, J. 1994. *Lifting the barriers: 600 strategies that really work to increase girls' participation in science, mathematics, and computers.* Port Washington, N.Y.: Jo Sanders Publications.

Sumrall, W. J. 1995. Reasons for the perceived images of scientists by race and gender of students in grades 1–7. *School Science and Mathematics* 95 (2):83–90.

Taylor, P. C. S., B. J. Fraser, and L. R. White. March 1994. *A classroom environment questionnaire for science educators interested in the constructivist reform of school science.* Paper presented at the annual meeting of the National Association for Research in Science Teaching, Anaheim, Calif.

Third International Mathematics and Science Study. 1998. http://wwwcsteep.bc.edu/timss.

Tobias, R. 1992. *Nurturing at-risk youth in math and science: Curriculum and teaching considerations.* Bloomington, Ind.: National Educational Service.

Weiss, I. 1987. *1985–86 National survey of science and mathematics education.* Research Triangle Park, N.C.: Research Triangle Institute.

Weiss, I. 1978. *Report of the 1977 National Survey on Science, Mathematics, and Social Sciences.* Research Triangle Park, N.C.: Center for Educational Research and Evaluation, Research Triangle Institute.

Wilson, M. 1992. *OPTIONS for Girls: A Door to the Future,* Austin, Texas: Pro.Ed.

Chapter 9

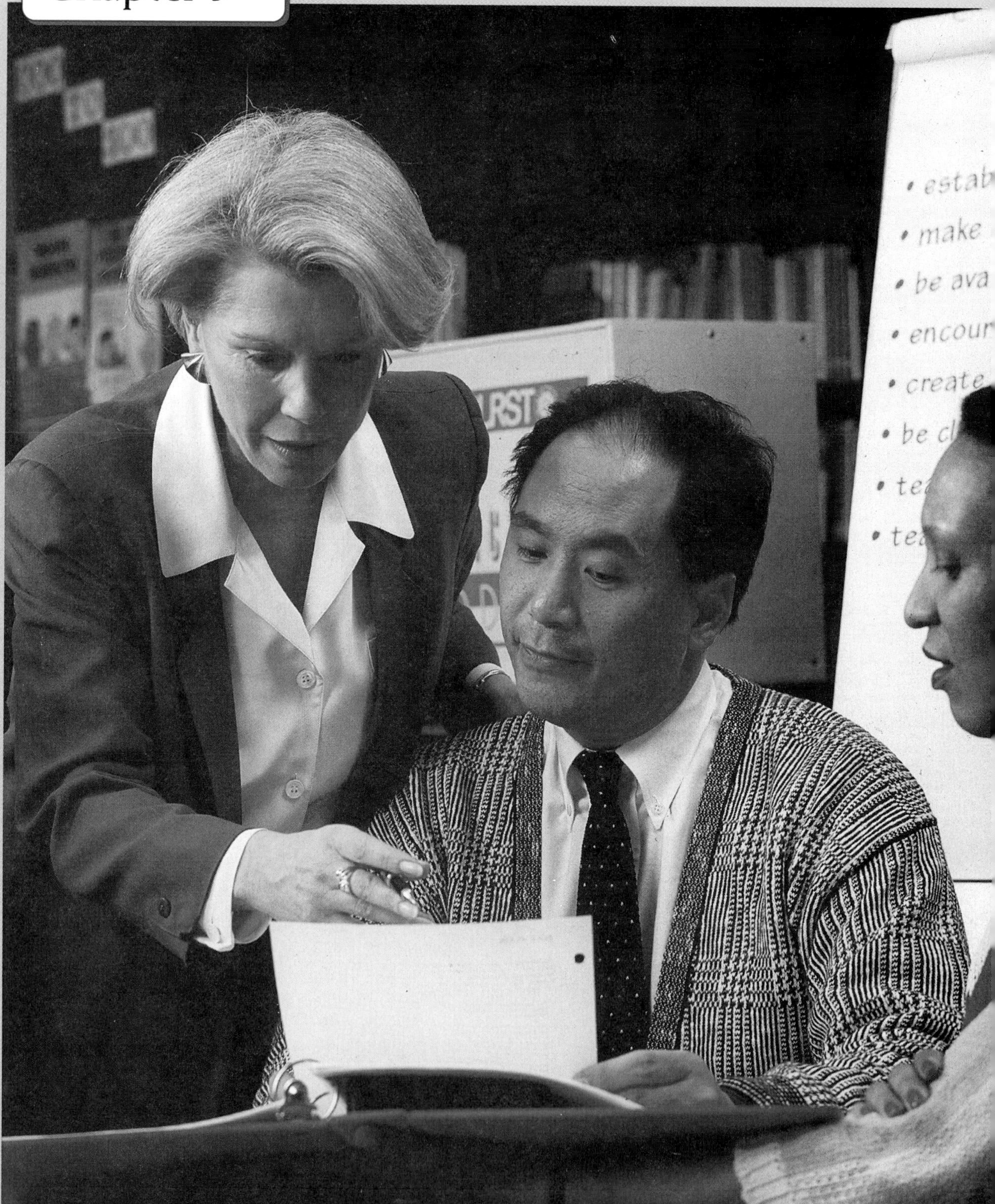

HOW DO I PLAN A PROJECT-BASED CURRICULUM?

INTRODUCTION

Teaching with a project-based science approach is rewarding and exciting, but it takes thought and time. How do you plan a project? How do you modify existing curriculum materials to fit a project approach? What resources are needed in a project environment? Where can you get help in finding resources? This chapter focuses on answering these types of questions and walks you through the process of planning a project-based curriculum using an insect project as an illustration of the process. We will discuss how to develop a project which includes deciding on concepts and objectives and developing a driving question, benchmark lessons, investigations, assessments, and a calendar of activities. Next we will discuss selecting and obtaining resources from a variety of sources including commercial suppliers, noncommercial suppliers, local stores, and community resources. Because a project-based curriculum is not limited to science, we will discuss how project-based science supports curriculum integration. We will consider concept mapping as a way to plan science integration with other subject areas. We'll begin by observing three teachers as they plan an insect project.

Planning the Curriculum

Imagine three teachers planning a unit on insects. Scattered in front of them is their district's curriculum framework, the textbook adopted by the school, the *National Science Education Standards* (NRC, 1996), and other curriculum resources.

"Well, our curriculum framework requires us to cover information about insects. I think we should cover this chapter in the spring when the insects reappear," says Mary.

Mike, looking at the district's curriculum framework, says, "Yeah. We could teach about metamorphosis, insect classification, and predator/prey relationships. Butterflies and other insects would be hatching in the spring."

Judy says, "To show metamorphosis, the kids could raise their own butterflies."

"No, we can just use this chapter. It has lots of nice photographs of butterfly metamorphosis," replies Mike. "If you really want, we could

go to the zoo's insect exhibit for the kids to see insects at different stages."

Judy says, "Well, how are we going to meet our inquiry objectives?"

Mary says, "Right. We have to worry about that."

Judy leans forward in her chair. "I've been learning about project-based science in this course I'm taking at the university, and I think we can cover many of our objectives using this approach. We just turn this insect chapter into an interesting driving question."

"But," asks Mary, "how can we do that?"

"Yeah, and what's a driving question?" Mike wants to know.

"Well, it is a question like 'What kinds of insects live in our neighborhood?' We could get kids interested in studying insects by taking them outside on a walk and looking for and collecting bugs. This way, kids could become really interested in the topic and learn lots about it."

"But aren't we supposed to use the school's adopted book? This textbook is what I think we are supposed to use," insists Mary.

"Sure. We could assign sections of the book for kids to read. And you're right; it has some nice pictures that kids could refer to. One of the things I learned in this course is that we need to cover basic science content through *benchmark lessons*. We could use this chapter to cover metamorphosis and animal classification."

Mike is worried. "But we have lots of other objectives to cover, and those objectives are going to be covered on the proficiency tests."

"Well, remember, like I said before, one of our objectives that is on the proficiency exam has to do with kids doing inquiry. By using a project approach, the kids could work together to investigate insects in the neighborhood. They can make posters, presentations, and maybe videos about insects. These things could demonstrate what the kids are learning. They can show that they know how to collect and analyze data, communicate information, and make conclusions. Those are objectives we're supposed to cover, too."

"Yeah, but what do we use for these investigations?" Mike is still feeling anxious.

Judy explains how project investigations work: "In a project approach, students are working on many different subquestions, so we can draw from lots of different resources. This STC kit on *The Life Cycle of Butterflies* (National Science Resources Center, 1992) is very good for teaching about metamorphosis. We can get butterfly eggs, raise caterpillars, and watch them grow into butterflies. This would make a great lesson to teach the objectives in our curriculum. The kids will also come up with some of their own ideas for the investigations in the project."

"Well, I think I'd like to try this. It sounds like a good way to teach these objectives," says Mary.

Mike says, "Well, I'm not sure."

Judy takes this as a green light: "Okay, let's start by mapping out our content and inquiry objectives. I think you'll see that we can also get in some math and language arts stuff, too."

DEVELOPING A PROJECT

As the scenario with Judy, Mike, and Mary illustrated, instructional planning is never an easy task, and planning project-based instruction is especially challenging. Teachers must do more than plan individual investigations, artifacts, and classroom activities; they must also interrelate these instructional components in such a way that they complement each other and build toward assessment goals. There are many different planning styles; we will examine one method for developing a project.

Deciding on Concepts and Curriculum Objectives

The decision to cover certain concepts and curriculum objectives at a particular grade level is usually not one that teachers make by themselves. Day-to-day lessons are usually guided by the need to cover basic concepts and curriculum objectives that a school district has for its students. At the national level, the *National Science Education Standards* were published in 1996 (NRC), and the American Association for the Advancement of Science established guidelines for school curriculum in *Benchmarks for Scientific Literacy* (AAAS) in 1993. Many school districts have adopted these ideas and formed curricula based on these sets of standards. Some states have established state-mandated curricula that spell out essential knowledge and skills. Therefore, although curriculum objectives may

vary from state to state or from school district to school district, you will find a great deal of similarity among concepts and objectives covered at most grade levels around the country. You may want to compare state and national guidelines using a computer program called *Curriculum Orchestrator* (Rose, London, Young, Mucci, & Jay, 1998) by MediaSeek Technologies, Inc.

What concepts do you hope students will learn by engaging in a particular project? To answer this question, start by creating a concept map of the major concepts to be learned. Concept mapping is described more thoroughly in Chapter 6. To help you with your brainstorming, consult your school's curriculum. State guidelines (if they exist) and national guidelines such as *The National Science Education Standards* (NRC, 1996) or *Benchmarks for Scientific Literacy* (AAAS, 1993) are helpful sources when you are building a list of concepts to be covered. Many teachers also like to look through textbooks. Once you have made a list of concepts, begin making a concept map. Link the concepts with linking words. You will notice that the teachers described in the opening scenario were using a variety of resources including the *National Science Education Standards* and their curriculum framework. They also started by creating a concept map.

Imagine that the grade level you teach is required by your state to learn about various concepts related to insects. This is a common standard in the primary grades. The *National Science Education Standards* (NRC, 1996) lists "life cycles of organisms" as a content standard for grades K–4. A concept map on insects might look like the one pictured in Figure 9.1.

After you have mapped the concepts, link them to the school's curriculum objectives. For example, the concept "life cycles" may be listed in a school's curriculum objectives as "Each fourth grade student will be able to draw the stages of the life cycle of a butterfly in correct sequence." Identifying concepts and matching them to curriculum objectives is actually a very iterative process. For example, you might just as easily ask yourself, "What concepts will students be learning if they explore this curriculum objective?" as "What curriculum objective will students match if they learn this concept?" Activity 9.1 will start you planning a project by having you select concepts and objectives.

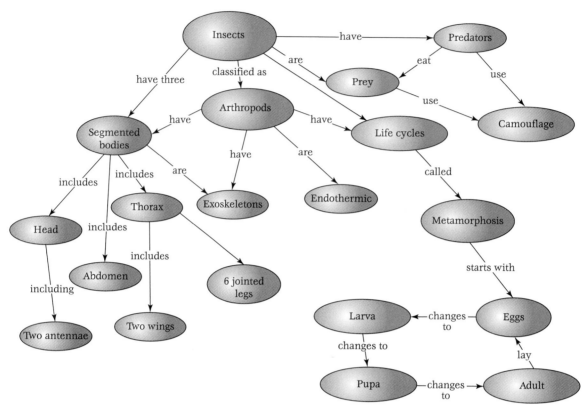

FIGURE 9.1
Insect concept map.

Developing the Driving Question

Often after identifying concepts and curriculum objectives, teachers brainstorm several driving questions that will allow students to explore the concepts selected. Sometimes, however, teach-

ers will brainstorm some driving questions before even starting the concept map.

Developing good driving questions is a challenge. Don't worry if a good question doesn't pop into your mind immediately. Driving questions can always be modified as project develop-

FIGURE 9.2
Teachers work together to create interesting driving questions.

ment progresses. As we discussed in Chapter 3, there are many sources for driving questions: personal experiences, students, hobbies and personal interests, the newspaper or television, other teachers, textbooks and other curriculum materials, and the World Wide Web.

Here are some initial examples of driving questions related to insects:

◆ What insects live on our playground? (The idea for this question came from a fellow teacher.)

◆ What are the names of common insects? (The idea for this question came from a commercial curriculum publisher.)

◆ How do insects grow and change? (The idea for this question came from a school's curriculum.)

◆ What insects did you see this morning on the way to school? (The idea for this question came from personal experiences.)

◆ Where do insects go in the winter? (The idea for this question came from a child.)

◆ Why are they spraying insecticide to kill gypsy moths? (The idea for this question came from a news story reported in the local paper.)

Of these possible driving questions, the best is most likely "What insects live on our playground?" This question meets all of the features of a good driving question (discussed in Chapter 3):

◆ **Feasibility.** Students can design and perform investigations about insects that live on the playground. For example, they can plot out a section of the playground to study the variety of insects that live on it.

◆ **Worth.** Students can learn science concepts related to the district's curriculum standards such as *metamorphosis, classification, predator and prey,* and *camouflage.*

◆ **Contextualization.** The question is a real-world question for students because it relates to their own physical environment—their playground.

◆ **Sustainability.** Students can learn about insects on the playground throughout the school year by studying subquestions like "Which insects are around in the fall?" "Where do they go in the winter?" and "Which reappear earliest in the spring?"

◆ **Meaning.** Insects are interesting and exciting to most children because they have strange defense mechanisms, use camouflage in fascinating ways, and have interesting life cycles.

Each of the other questions lacks fundamental features of a good driving question. For example, "What are the names of common insects?" is not sustainable over time. Students can learn the names of insects in a very short period of time, and then they will likely become bored. Learning the names of insects is also unlikely to be meaningful to most children. "How do insects grow and change?" is feasible—students can design and perform investigations to watch insects grow and change. However, the question may not be contextualized if it is unrelated to students' lives. Studying, for example, the growth of an insect students never see in their own environment might cause some children to lose interest in the topic. This question also can be subsumed as a subquestion under a

ACTIVITY 9.2

Turning Concepts and Curriculum Objectives into Driving Questions

MATERIALS NEEDED:
- the list of concepts and curriculum objectives generated in Activity 9.1

A. Take the list of concepts and curriculum objectives generated in Activity 9.1 and brainstorm several driving questions from it.

B. Share this list with a colleague or classmate to try to generate additional driving questions.

C. Evaluate each question for
- feasibility
- worth
- contextualization
- sustainability
- meaning

D. Select one driving question that you will develop into a project throughout the rest of this chapter. Write an argument about why you are selecting this question over others you brainstormed.

E. File the argument and the driving question in your portfolio.

broader driving question. "What insects did you see this morning on the way to school?" is contextualized, but it may not be worthwhile because important concepts in the curriculum are unlikely to be covered in a study of insects seen on the way to school one day. This question, too, can be subsumed under a broader driving question. "Where do insects go in the winter?" might seem sustainable since it covers a longer period of the year. However, the question may not be feasible, because students may not be able to design an investigation that they can conduct outdoors in the winter. Finally, "Why are they spraying insecticide to kill gypsy moths?" may be contextualized because it is related to students lives, but for safety reasons children should not be handling insecticide and, therefore, there is no investigation students can conduct related to the question. In Activity 9.2 you develop a driving question for your project.

Developing Benchmark Lessons

After teachers have identified concepts, curriculum objectives and a driving question, they might begin to develop benchmark lessons (sometimes teachers design an investigation before developing benchmark lessons). Remember that the role of benchmark lessons in project-based science is to help students learn difficult concepts, illustrate a laboratory technique, build new inquiry abilities, model thinking, or stimulate curiosity. The teachers described in the opening scenario were worried about covering important objectives, another reason to use a benchmark lesson.

Don't expect to develop benchmark lessons from scratch. Original ideas are a challenge. You might come up with some original ideas, but more likely you will modify activities that have already been developed. For our insect project, there are several good resources that we could use to develop benchmark lessons.

The FOSS *Insects* kit is valuable in teaching about the structure and life cycle of several different insects: mealworms, waxworms, milkweed bugs, silkworms, and butterflies (FOSS, 1993). The FOSS kit *Environments* has several lessons about insects. In one lesson, students investigate the environments (moisture and darkness) preferred by isopods and beetles. In another lesson, students investigate the level of salinity needed for brine shrimp to hatch (FOSS, 1993).

Another useful curriculum is the Science and Technology for Children (National Science Resources Center, 1992) curriculum *The Life Cycle of Butterflies.* Intended for second graders, this material can generate several benchmark lessons. Students raise painted lady butterflies to learn about metamorphosis; they use observation and recording skills to raise caterpillars and butterflies; they learn about caterpillars' basic needs of air, water, food, and shelter; and they learn about insect body parts and function.

The Ranger Rick series entitled *Incredible Insects* (Braus, 1989) is filled with interdisciplinary activities related to insect classification, metamorphosis, insect habitats, insect adaptations for survival, and the influence of insects on our lives. One activity that comes from *Incredible Insects* is a butterfly metamorphosis role-play.

The Lawrence Hall of Science GEMS series contains two useful books: *Hide a Butterfly* (Echols, 1993) and *Ladybugs* (Echols, 1993). *Hide a Butterfly,* designed for preschool through kindergarten, focuses on skills (observing, communicating, comparing, and matching), concepts (camouflage and predator/prey), and themes (systems and interactions, models and simulations, scale, structure, evolution, and diversity and unity). *Ladybugs,* which also focuses on skills, concepts, and themes covers body structure, life cycles, defense mechanisms, predatory/prey, and the environmental role of ladybugs.

Guest lecturers and field trips are also benchmark lesson sources. An entomologist from a local university could provide students with useful information and resources. A field trip to the zoo's insect exhibit would provide information and expose students to a variety of insects.

Children's literature is another rich resource for a benchmark lesson. The following books teach about insect metamorphosis and insect lore:

Livo, G. McGlathery, and N. J. Livo. 1995. *Of Bugs and Beasts.* Englewood, Colo.: Teacher Ideas Press.

Carle, E. 1969. *The Very Hungry Caterpillar.* New York: Philomel Books.

Ryder, J. 1989. *Where Butterflies Grow.* New York: Lodestar Books, E. P. Dutton.

Using these various resources, we can create a benchmark lesson for second graders. Our lesson will follow this structure introduced in Chapter 6 on benchmark lessons:

- **Learning objectives:** What do you hope to accomplish in the benchmark lesson? What concepts or inquiry skills will students develop? Will students develop background experiences for the project?
- **Relationship to the driving question:** How is the lesson related to the driving question of the project?
- **Materials needed:** What materials will you or the students need?
- **Instructional strategies:** What strategies or learning activities, demonstrations, or discussions will you use to help students reach the learning objectives?
- **Time required:** How much time will it take for you to complete the benchmark lesson?

- **Instructional sequence:** How will you proceed through this lesson?

  A. Introducing the lesson
  B. Representing the content
  C. Establish links to the driving question
  D. Evaluating learning

- **Cautions:** Are there any dangerous or hazardous components of the activities associated with the lesson? What precautions need to be taken?

Now here is the sample benchmark lesson:

- **Learning objectives:** Each student will understand that most insects change from egg to adult through a process called metamorphosis.

- **Relationship to the driving question:** The driving question "What insects live on our playground?" will be addressed through studying metamorphosis, because students may find different stages of insects on the playground at any given time (egg, larvae, pupa, or adult). In order to understand that these different stages are forms of the same insect, students must understand metamorphosis.

- **Materials needed:** Ryder, J. 1989. *Where Butterflies Grow.* New York: Lodestar Books, E. P. Dutton.

- **Instructional strategies:**

  A. reading a children's literature book
  B. role-playing butterfly metamorphosis
  C. drawing pictures for artifacts

- **Time required:** four to five days
- **Instructional sequence:**

  A. Introducing the lesson:
     1. Read Ryder, J. 1989. *Where Butterflies Grow.* New York: Lodestar Books, E. P. Dutton.
     2. Discuss what it might be like to change from a caterpillar to a butterfly.
     3. Discuss the stages that a butterfly goes through.
  B. Representing the content:
     1. Show students real butterfly eggs and an adult butterfly (if not available, show photographs of these stages).

   2. Ask the children if they know how
      the egg changes to a butterfly.
      Discuss the students' ideas.
   3. Have students role-play the stages of
      metamorphosis that a butterfly goes
      through. Ranger Rick's *Incredible
      Insects* has a good example of a play
      in which children can participate.

C. Establish links to the driving question:
   See if students can identify other insects
   on their playground that are simply in
   different stages of metamorphosis. For
   example, moths, ants, flies, and bees also
   go through complete metamorphosis.

D. Evaluating learning:
   1. Give students a set of photographs
      or drawings. Have them place them
      in the correct order of the
      metamorphosis.
   2. Have collaborative groups of students
      explain to others how their drawings
      illustrate complete metamorphosis.

◆ **Cautions:** Make sure students have a clear
   understanding of behavioral expectations
   during the role playing activity. Activity 9.3
   asks you to develop a benchmark lesson
   for your project.

Developing Investigations

Investigations allow students to plan and conduct
experiments that facilitate their construction of
partial solutions to important questions. As such,
investigations give students opportunities to
plan, make decisions, collect and analyze data,
draw conclusions, and present results. As you develop your investigations and classroom activities, link them to the questions and concepts.

After teaching about metamorphosis in a series of benchmark lessons, we might design a
class investigation based on the FOSS *Insects*
(Lawrence Hall of Science, 1993) curriculum and
the STC *The Life Cycle of Butterflies* unit (National
Science Resources Center, 1992). One option for
an investigation is to have student groups observe the development of a butterfly egg into an
adult butterfly. As with the benchmark lesson, to
plan this investigation we would have to think
about the learning objectives, the relationship to
the driving question, materials needed, instructional strategies, time required, the instructional
sequence, and cautions.

◆ **Learning objectives:**

   A. Each student will understand that most
     insects change from egg to adult
     through a process called *metamorphosis.*

   B. Each student will observe butterfly
     metamorphosis.

   C. Each student will record butterfly
     metamorphosis by drawing a picture
     and noting the date of each stage change.

◆ **Relationship to the driving question:** The
   driving question "What insects live on our
   playground?" will be addressed through
   studying metamorphosis, because students
   may find different stages of insects on the
   playground at any given time (egg, larvae,
   pupa, or adult). In order to understand that
   these different stages are forms of the
   same insect, students must understand
   metamorphosis.

◆ **Materials needed:**

   A. butterfly eggs (can be ordered from
     animal supply houses such as Carolina
     Biological)

ACTIVITY 9.4

Developing an Investigation

A. For the project topic you have chosen, identify several possible investigations that students could develop.

B. Design a lesson plan for conducting one of the investigations.

C. How does the investigation help students answer the driving question?

D. File your answer in your portfolio.

B. bug cages

C. drawing paper

D. drawing supplies (colored pencils, markers, or crayons)

E. magnifying glasses

F. caterpillar food supply (varies depending upon the stage the butterfly is in and the type of butterfly; for example, Monarch caterpillars eat Milkweed)

◆ **Instructional strategies:**

A. hands-on activity to raise butterflies

B. drawing pictures as artifacts

◆ **Time required:** four to six weeks

◆ **Instructional sequence:**

A. Have each group of students set up a bug cage with butterfly eggs and caterpillar food.

B. Each day, have students observe the butterfly's stage of metamorphosis using a magnifying glass.

C. Have students draw pictures of the stages and record the date. Have them keep these drawings in their science portfolios.

D. After students have observed and recorded the complete metamorphosis of the butterfly—egg, larvae (caterpillar), pupa (chrysalis), and adult (butterfly)—have them explain how their butterfly egg changed throughout the last several weeks.

E. Ask students how this investigation helps them answer the question "What insects live on our playground?" Remind them that when they found a caterpillar and a butterfly, that these were actually the same insect. To answer the driving question, they needed to understand that the caterpillar and adult were just in different stages.

◆ **Cautions:** Always have children wash their hands after touching insects being raised in the classroom. Bring only known species into the room (such as painted ladies, swallowtails, or monarchs).

After students complete the class investigation, we might want groups of students to ask their own questions and design their own investigations. For instance, one group might be interested in finding out what kinds of food that caterpillars eat. To answer this subquestion, students would need to plan and conduct an experiment. Students could observe other insects feeding on the playground, or they could research what insects eat. Then, they could place monarch caterpillars into different containers holding different foods such as milkweed, carrot tops, grass, and other leaves. Students could determine which foods the caterpillars ate the most by inspecting the leaves or by weighing the leaves before and after the caterpillars had eaten for a day. This investigation could be tied to important concepts of metamorphosis (what animals eat during various life cycle stages), and it would teach basic skills (observation, measurement, recording, and making conclusions). Other groups of students might be interested in the life cycle of other insects such as mealworms and waxworms. Through a series of investigations, these students could compare and contrast the life cycles of various insects. In Activity 9.4, you develop an investigation for your project.

Developing Assessments

Various assessments that are linked to classroom activities and investigations can be used to gain a complete view of student learning. In Chapter 7, we discussed many types of assessment strategies

ACTIVITY 9.5

Developing Assessments

A. For the project topic you have chosen, identify several possible assessments that could be used to measure student learning.

B. Design plans for carrying out one of the assessments. What would be included? How would it be evaluated?

C. How does the assessment help students show what they have learned about the driving question?

D. Record your assessment plans in your portfolio.

that teachers can use to measure student understanding. For our insect project, the following assessment strategies would be effective:

◆ **Discussion-based observations:** Discuss with students what they have noticed about the changes their butterflies are going through.

◆ **Anecdotal records:** Make a notation about which students seem to be having difficulty recording daily information about their insect's growth.

◆ **Checklists:** Check off which students have used a magnifying glass to observe insects up close.

◆ **Clinical interviews:** Talk with students about what they have noticed in their investigation about foods caterpillars eat.

◆ **Concept maps:** Have students develop maps to illustrate connections among concepts being studied in the insect project.

◆ **Performance-based assessment:** Have students design an investigation to explore life cycles of various insects.

◆ **Student writing samples:** Have students write stories about what it might feel like to be a butterfly.

◆ **Daily journals:** Have students make daily records of their observations of the life cycle of a butterfly and conclude what the pattern of cycles is for a butterfly.

◆ **Physical products:** Have students create models illustrating the life cycle of a butterfly.

◆ **Drawings:** Have students make daily drawings of each day in the life cycle of a butterfly.

◆ **Music:** Have students adapt songs to describe butterfly metamorphosis.

◆ **Videotapes:** Have students make videotapes explaining their investigation of the foods caterpillars eat and summarizing their findings.

◆ **Multimedia documents:** Have students create hypermedia documents illustrating the stages of butterfly growth including graphs and photographs of the changes a butterfly goes through.

Each of these assessment items can be embedded into instruction and can help teachers determine whether students have met science standards. For example, most of the aforementioned assessments could be used to show whether students know the K–4 AAAS benchmark on understanding life cycles. Many high-stakes assessments, such as state proficiency tests, require students to use higher level thinking and processing skills such as writing, analyzing data, and synthesizing information. For example, fourth graders in Ohio are expected to be able to "describe the duration and timing of a pattern given a repetitive pattern in nature" (OBE, 1994, p. 36). Students who can make daily records of observations of the life cycle of a butterfly, and conclude what the pattern of cycles is, have used important skills such as writing and synthesizing information that can be used on the fourth grade tests in Ohio. Activity 9.5 asks you to develop an assessment for your project.

Developing a Calendar of Activities

It is a good idea to develop calendars to guide the sequence of lessons and orchestrate the various components in a time frame. Some teach-

TABLE 9.1 Insect Project Calendar of Activities

Monday	Tuesday	Wednesday	Thursday	Friday
2 Introduce driving question "What insects live on our playground?" Read Ryder's story, *Where Butterflies Grow*.	3 Set up insect cages with butterfly eggs and record daily observation of butterflies.	4 Get on Web to find information on monarch butterflies. Record daily observation of butterflies.	5 Take field trip to playground to observe insects. Record daily observation of butterflies.	6 Read Carle's book, *The Very Hungry Caterpillar*. Record daily observation of butterflies. Take photographs or make drawings of insects on the playground in order to identify them.
9 Record daily observation of butterflies and weigh the gain in mass of the caterpillars. Research information about insects found on the playground.	10 Have students design investigations to help answer "What insects live on our playground?" Record daily observation of butterflies.	11 Set up student investigations. Record daily observation of butterflies.	12 Record daily observation of butterflies. Listen to guest speaker on pest control.	13 Record daily observation of butterflies. Take trip to insect exhibit at the zoo.
16 Record daily observation of butterflies. Role-play the stages the butterfly has gone through.	17 Record daily observation of butterflies. Work on investigations. Look on Web for more information about butterflies.	18 Record daily observation of butterflies. Listen to guest speaker—an entomologist from the local university.	19 Record daily observation of butterflies. Work on insect computer program. Use Web to find information related to groups' investigations.	20 Record daily observation of butterflies. Write a song to depict metamorphosis. Try to find insects in different life cycle stages on the playground.
23 Record daily observation of butterflies. Arrange drawings of butterfly stages in portfolio.	24 Record daily observation of butterflies. Revisit playground for additional observations.	25 Record daily observation of butterflies. Revisit playground for observations.	26 Record daily observation of butterflies. Prepare for hypermedia presentation (artifact).	27 Record daily observation of butterflies. Prepare for hypermedia presentation (artifact).
30 Record daily observation of butterflies. Prepare for hypermedia presentation.	31 Give presentation to parents.	1 Given presentation to parents.	2	3

ers like to use a concept map like the one generated earlier to organize the activities, because the hierarchy in the concept map helps define the sequence of concepts students need to learn in benchmark lessons. The calendar is an *estimate* of when each lesson will take place. It almost always gets changed during the course of implementation. Table 9.1 is a sample calendar of activities for our insect project. In Activity 9.6, you make a calendar for your project.

ACTIVITY 9.6

Developing a Calendar of Activities

MATERIALS NEEDED:
- ◆ a planning calendar

A. Using the ideas you have collected on your topic throughout this chapter, plan a calendar of activities for the project you are designing.
B. Put this calendar in your portfolio.

ACTIVITY 9.7

Revisiting Your Project Design

A. Go back through Activities 9.1 through 9.6. Think through ways that you might change your design. What new questions might arise as the project is being implemented?

B. What areas might you change if you could? How do you think such changes would improve your project?
C. Share your project design with a classmate or colleague. What new ideas does he or she have for you?
D. Put these ideas in your portfolio.

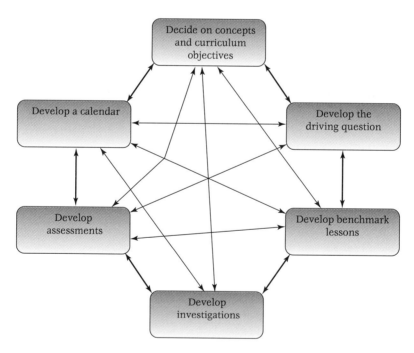

FIGURE 9.3
Process of developing a project.

Developing a Project

As mentioned, identifying concepts; designing driving questions, benchmark lessons, investigations, and assessments; and creating a calendar of activities is an iterative process. Investigations may lead to new questions that introduce other concepts. Figure 9.3 is a diagram that depicts the iterative process of project design. It shows one possible planning sequence: concepts, driving questions, benchmark lessons, investigations, assessments, and calendar of activities. Activity 9.7 asks you to revise the project you developed in Activities 9.1 through 9.6.

SELECTING AND OBTAINING RESOURCES

As illustrated in the planning sequences described earlier, teachers face many decisions as they design a project-based curriculum. Planning can be supported with a variety of printed and electronic resources such as textbooks, workbooks, kits of materials, slides, cassettes, transparencies, charts and maps, games, audiotapes, filmstrips, videotapes, television, computers, laser discs, CD-ROMs, and electronic notepads. Most communities also offer a wealth of resources through local businesses, organizations, zoos, and museums. Each type of resource is used for a different reason and has advantages and disadvantages. You might think of all the available resources as a tool kit for teaching. Several issues revolve around selecting and obtaining resources. In this section, we will discuss these issues.

Selecting Resources

Given the variety of resources available to a teacher, it is important to have criteria for selecting materials to use in a project-based science classroom. Several organizations have published guidelines for selecting resources that can help teachers make good judgments about materials (The National Science Resources Center; Tuomi, 1993; the National Association for the Education of Young Children; Bradekamp, 1987; the National Middle School Association, 1982; Alexander & George, 1981; Wiles & Bondi, 1981; and Barnes & Spector, 1989). Table 9.2 summarizes the common features of these recommendations.

The FOSS *Insects* curriculum meets almost all of the criteria for selecting resources for our insect project. For example, the FOSS unit on insects spans several months, giving students the opportunity to explore the topic in depth. Children work directly with concrete materials (insects such as mealworms, waxworms, and butterflies) to make their own observations and conclusions. They engage in inquiry to learn about the metamorphoses of various insects. Integration is incorporated in the form of suggested children's literature, writing assignments, and illustrations the children keep. Ongoing assessments occur throughout the unit—children keep observations of their insects, checklists that focus on process skills are included for the teacher to use, and alternative assessments (such as making models and drawing life cycles) are suggested. Although this unit does not use technology, it is an excellent example of a resource that stresses exploration and depth over coverage of information.

In Activity 9.8, you will select resources for the project you are developing throughout this chapter.

Obtaining Resources

Many types of resources are available to help teachers develop a project-based curriculum. A good classroom contains a mixture of inexpensive, everyday household materials as well as commercial and noncommercial materials, magazines, and books. Although there are numerous sources for obtaining materials, there are a few ideal places to start your search. In the following sections, we will discuss in more detail how to obtain a variety of resources, how to use the community as a resource, and how to use the Web to search for resources.

By exploring the Eisenhower National Clearinghouse for Mathematics and Science Education, you can identify both commercial and noncommercial resources. This clearinghouse, funded by the U.S. Department of Education, serves to improve access to mathematics and science resources for teachers, students, and parents. The Clearinghouse collects the most up-to-date materials and catalogs them. The materials can be accessed with a database in CD-ROM, in print format, or on the Web. The Clearinghouse is a free resource, and it can save you time. You can learn more about the Eisenhower National Clearinghouse for Mathematics and Science Education by writing to Eisenhower National Clearinghouse for Mathematics and Science Education, Area 200, Research Center, 1314 Kinnear Road, Columbus, OH 43212-1194, by calling 1-800-621-5785, or by visiting http://www.enc.org.

Commercial Suppliers   The National Science Teachers Association publishes an annual supplement to its journals entitled *NSTA Science Education Suppliers.* This publication is packed with information about commercial companies that sell

TABLE 9.2   Summary of Criteria for Selecting Resources

Criteria	Rating		
Allows children to explore a science topic in depth	Exceptional 1	Moderate 2	Poor 3
Presents the topic in a relevant manner to student's everyday lives	Exceptional 1	Moderate 2	Poor 3
Lets students engage in direct, purposeful experiences in which they can make their own observations and conclusions	Exceptional 1	Moderate 2	Poor 3
Allows children to work collaboratively	Exceptional 1	Moderate 2	Poor 3
Presents accurate information	Exceptional 1	Moderate 2	Poor 3
Actively engages students in their learning through experiences with concrete materials	Exceptional 1	Moderate 2	Poor 3
Promotes inquiry, problem solving, and critical thinking	Exceptional 1	Moderate 2	Poor 3
Uses technology as a tool to enhance learning	Exceptional 1	Moderate 2	Poor 3
Helps children learn how to learn (establishes a foundation for lifelong learning)	Exceptional 1	Moderate 2	Poor 3
Develops children's self-esteem, sense of competence, and positive feelings toward learning science	Exceptional 1	Moderate 2	Poor 3
Responds to children's individual differences in ability, development, and learning styles (the curricula are novel and varied, use a variety of instructional strategies)	Exceptional 1	Moderate 2	Poor 3
Integrates science across subject areas	Exceptional 1	Moderate 2	Poor 3
Engages children in discussions and conversation that challenge their thinking and help them construct understanding	Exceptional 1	Moderate 2	Poor 3
Stresses skills such as observing, measuring, hypothesizing, and predicting	Exceptional 1	Moderate 2	Poor 3
Uses portfolios, practical assessment, or other forms of alternative assessment	Exceptional 1	Moderate 2	Poor 3
Provides opportunities for physical movement	Exceptional 1	Moderate 2	Poor 3
Stresses exploration and depth over coverage of information	Exceptional 1	Moderate 2	Poor 3

ACTIVITY 9.8

Selecting Good Resources

MATERIALS NEEDED:

- ◆ Table 9.2

   A. Using the project topic that you have been developing throughout this chapter, find resources that you might use for lesson ideas for the project.

B. Using the criteria listed in Table 9.2, rate the quality of the resources.

C. Record your rating in your portfolio.

TABLE 9.3 Criteria for Using Noncommercial Resources

Criteria	Rating		
Furthers my objectives	Exceptional 1	Moderate 2	Poor 3
Is free from objectionable advertising, propaganda, or bias	Exceptional 1	Moderate 2	Poor 3
Is scientifically accurate	Exceptional 1	Moderate 2	Poor 3
Is interesting	Exceptional 1	Moderate 2	Poor 3
Is intellectually stimulating	Exceptional 1	Moderate 2	Poor 3
Is beneficial for children and classroom use	Exceptional 1	Moderate 2	Poor 3
Meets criteria for selecting resources (Table 9.2)	Exceptional 1	Moderate 2	Poor 3

equipment and supplies (such as microscopes, slides, dissecting kits, tuning forks, and hand generators), software (such as CD-ROMs, laser discs, and computer disk programs), media (such as maps, games, and kits), textbook programs (such as FOSS and STC), and tradebooks (such as children's literature). The publication includes addresses, telephone numbers, Web pages, and e-mail addresses of suppliers. It summarizes the type of equipment carried by each company and categorizes it in a number of ways such as by science subject and grade level. You can obtain this publication by either subscribing to the NSTA journals (*Science and Children, Science Scope,* or *Science Teacher*), contacting NSTA at The National Science Teachers Association, 1840 Wilson Boulevard, Arlington, VA 22201-3000, or browsing the supplement at http://www.nsta.org/scisupp/.

There is no shortage of ideas for teaching science. Teachers' resource books are packed with ideas for hands-on activities that make good benchmark lessons. Many include pages that can be duplicated for children. For example, teacher resource books such as *The Pillbug Project* (Burnett, 1992) can be purchased on-line at the National Science Teachers Association Web page (http//:www.nsta.org).

Noncommercial Suppliers Noncommercial suppliers include nonprofit groups such as the Audubon Society, businesses such as utility companies, and science parks such as Sea World. These types of suppliers frequently distribute free or inexpensive materials. Most of these materials are educationally sound and useful resources for the classroom. However, some business write materials for the purpose of conveying the value of their particular products or services. For example, a local utility company might publish free materials on the benefits of nuclear energy. Most of these materials are accurate, but you should beware of materials that present biased opinions. Table 9.3 shows criteria for evaluating free and inexpensive materials provided by noncommercial suppliers to your students.

Listed in Table 9.4 are some nationally recognized noncommercial suppliers. You may also want to contact local utility companies, fire departments, police departments, zoos, aquaria, botanical gardens, museums, departments of natural resources, environmental organizations, and businesses for science-related information and materials in your region. In Activity 9.9, you use the World Wide Web to find resources for the project you are developing.

Everyday Household Materials Everyday household materials such as cotton balls, cups, vinegar, and baking soda are used in numerous elementary and middle grade investigations and activities. Table 9.6 (at end of chapter) lists commonly used household materials and identifies places to locate these resources such as drug, hardware, grocery, pet, craft, and toy stores. For example, for our insect unit, food supplies and bug cages can be purchased at pet stores. Hardware stores have nylon screen and wood for building simple habitats. Grocery stores sell jars and food supplies that can be used for investigations on insects. Activity 9.10 asks you to identify local resources you could use in your project.

TABLE 9.4 National Noncommercial Suppliers	
Organization	**Resources provided**
National Wildlife Federation (http://www.nwf.org/nwf)	*Nature Scope* series of books *Ranger Rick* magazine *My Big Backyard* magazine
Project Wild (5430 Grosvenor Lane, Bethesda, MD 20814, 301-493-5447)	*Project WILD Aquatic* *Project Learning Tree*
NASA Spacelink (http://spacelink.msfc.nasa.gov/.index.html)	Slides, photographs, videotapes, lesson plans
Project WET (201 Culbertson Hall, Montana State University, Bozeman, MT 59717-0057, 406-994-5392)	*Project WET*
TERC (http://www.terc.edu/)	*Hands On!* magazine Papers Innovative projects

The Community as a Resource   Community resources provide valuable sites for field trips, sources of educational materials, and opportunities for experiences. Besides providing a change of pace, community resources show children how science is relevant to their daily lives. For example, for our insect project, a local public health official or nurse would be a good resource for talking about health hazards (such as Lyme disease) associated with insect bites. Science museums provide students with hands-on displays, interactive experiences, and special programs. Other community resources are local zoos, science centers, parks, hospitals, police stations, courts, radio stations, universities, and businesses. In the insect project, we could visit the zoo to see insects that are nonindigenous to our region.

The community can also be a wonderful network for providing teachers with free materials. Although schools usually provide teachers with a small budget for purchasing materials, many school budgets are very tight and teachers frequently need to identify creative alternatives for stocking their classrooms. Many schools have joined a trend toward collaborative alliances and partnerships with local businesses. These partnerships provide many advantages: Local businesses become engaged in education, businesses provide schools with

---

ACTIVITY 9.9

Finding Resources Using the Web

MATERIALS NEEDED:

♦ access to the Web

A. Use the URLs provided in Table 9.4 to find resources and ideas for the project you are developing in this chapter.

B. Conduct a search on the Web using a search engine such as Yahoo or Webcrawler to find additional resources and ideas for your project.

C. File these resources, ideas, and URLs in your portfolio.

ACTIVITY 9.10

Identifying Resources in Local Stores

MATERIALS NEEDED:

♦ local stores to visit

A. Visit a local drug, hardware, grocery, pet, craft, and toy store to identify possible resources that could be used in your project.

B. Keep track of items you could use and their costs.

C. List them in your portfolio.

needed supplies and materials, and students see the relevance of what they are learning to local businesses. If your school does not have a partnership with local businesses, you might want to consider asking local businesses for donations. Many teachers do this by writing simple letters. A personal follow-up in the form of a telephone call or visit can often secure a donation. Check to make sure your school district's policies allow you to seek donations. Figure 9.4 shows a sample letter requesting donations from businesses.

INTEGRATED CURRICULUM

Curriculum integration has become popular among educators. However, even at the elementary level, it is common for students to move from subject to subject and learn topics in a fragmented, disconnected fashion that bears little resemblance to real life. This frequently leads students to be overloaded with information that they view as boring and as having little relevance to their lives. It seems

September 3, 1999

Dear Local Grocery Store Owner:

     I am a fifth grade teacher at Kenwood Elementary School, and I am very interested in improving the science skills of my students. As a member of our community and a business leader, you are, I am sure, also concerned about the quality of our students' science education. Most science activities in the elementary grades require only simple household items. However, with limited financial resources at our school, we cannot purchase these items. I am asking that you consider donating to our school the items listed below. These materials will be used in a series of lessons to teach students about insects.

    10 aluminum pans
     5 lbs. of flour
       rolls of netting
    10 plastic jars
    10 sets of mixing spoons
    10 measuring cups
     2 bags of potting soil
     1 bag of cornmeal
     5 flashlights
  100 Styrofoam cups

I will call you in a week to see if you are interested in meeting about this donation. Thank you for you interest in our students' educational needs.

Sincerely,

Teacher's Name

FIGURE 9.4
Letter requesting donations from local businesses.

FIGURE 9.5
Integration helps students see how science relates to real world contexts.

only logical that subject areas should not be separated in schools, because they are not separated in the world. Paul DeHart Hurd (1991) in an article entitled "Why We Must Transform Science" wrote,

> Science today is characterized by some 25,000 to 30,000 research fields. Findings from these fields are reported in 70,000 journals, 29,000 of which are new since 1978. Traditional disciplines have been hybridized into such new research areas as biochemistry, biophysics, geochemistry, and genetic engineering. . . . These changes in the way modern science is organized have yet to be reflected in science courses. There is little recognition that in recent years the boundaries between the various natural sciences have become more and more blurred and major concepts more unified.

Hurd stresses the need for greater integration of school subjects and the integration of science with social issues, technology, and other school subjects.

Consistent with Hurd's recommendations, most national reform efforts currently stress the

need to integrate the curriculum (National Council of Teachers of Mathematics, 1989; National Research Council, 1996; International Reading Association, 1996; National Council of Teachers of English, 1996; and National Council of Social Studies, 1994). Integration is a major focus in such science reform initiatives as *Science for All Americans* (Rutherford & Ahlgren, 1990) and *The National Science Education Standards* (NRC, 1996). Curriculum integration is also stressed by the National Association for the Education of Young Children (NAEYC), an organization that specializes in instructional practices appropriate for the education of the young child, and the National Middle School Association (NMSA), an association that focuses on young and early adolescents.

Before we continue with discussing ideas about integrating school subject areas, think about your beliefs about curriculum integration with the help of Activity of 9.11.

The Definition of Integration

Sometimes educators use the terms *integrated, interdisciplinary,* and *thematic* synonymously. Lederman and Niess (1997) define *integrated* as a blending of subject areas such that the separate parts are not discernible. They use the metaphor of tomato soup; you cannot discern the tomatoes in the soup. They define *interdisciplinary* as a mixture of subjects connected but still identifiable. The metaphor they use is chicken noodle soup; it's a soup but you can still recognize the broth, chicken, and noodles. Similarly, Jacobs (1989) defines *interdisciplinary* as "a knowledge view and curriculum approach that consciously applies methodology and language from more than one discipline to examine a central theme, issue, problem, topic, or experience." Finally, Lederman and Niess (1997) define *thematic* as a unifying topic or subject transcending traditional subject boundaries. For purposes of this book, we use the word *integrated* to define the crossing of subject matter boundaries.

Beane (1995) suggests that curriculum integration, like project-based science, begins with "problems, issues, and concerns posed by life itself" (p. 616). Integrated curriculum, according to Beane (1996), has four characteristics: (1) it is

---

ACTIVITY 9.11

Investigating Your Beliefs about Curriculum Integration

MATERIALS NEEDED:
- an elementary or middle grade science textbook
- pencil and paper

A. Examine a fourth grade science textbook for a selected topic. A traditional textbook will usually contain topics such as the human body, electricity, magnetism, sound, light, animals, plants, machines, the earth's crust, volcanoes, earthquakes, and the solar system.

B. Form a team with four other classmates and assign yourselves the roles of particular subject matter specialists (science teacher, mathematics teacher, social studies teacher, language/reading teacher, and art teacher). Take the topic selected and together design a set of integrated lesson ideas for teaching the topic.

C. After you have finished planning, individually critique the lessons using the following criteria. This should establish what you personally believe about integrated

planning. Then, have your group critique the lesson ideas using the same criteria. Make sure your group comes to a consensus.

1. What prior knowledge and experiences do students need before engaging in integrated lessons?
2. Will important content and inquiry objectives be met? If not, what is missing? Explain.
3. If a teacher teaches this way for the entire school year, will there be important topics that are not covered? Standards that are not met?
4. Are the learning objectives watered-down or less meaningful in these lessons? Explain.
5. Should the topic stay as it is in the textbook (taught separately by subject matter)? Why or why not?
6. Is curriculum integration beneficial? Why or why not?
7. Do you know enough about each subject area to teach this way? Explain.

D. Put your ideas in your portfolio.

---

organized around problems and issues that have personal and social significance in the real world, (2) it uses pertinent knowledge in the context of topic without regard for subject lines, (3) it is used to study current problems rather than for a test or grade level outcome, and (4) it emphasizes projects and activities with real application of knowledge and problem solving. Interestingly, Hopkins (1937, as cited in Beane, 1996) defined *integration* similarly—as cooperatively planned, problem-centered, and integrated knowledge. These definitions of curriculum *integration* are consistent with our view of project-based learning as crossing curricular subject areas.

How Project-Based Science Supports Curriculum Integration

Project-based science supports curriculum integration because its key features (driving questions, student engagement in investigations, communities of learners collaborating together, use of technology, and creation of artifacts) are all congruent with curriculum integration. As students answer driving questions, they develop deeper understandings because they make connections among the central concepts of a variety of subject areas. Driving questions are contextualized; they are anchored in the lives of learners and deal with important, real-world issues. Real-world questions are not separated into different subject areas.

Integration builds understanding of concepts. When science topics involve people, as they usually do, social studies concepts such as economics, politics, culture, and history come into play. Teachers can use children's literature of all types (realistic fiction, historical fiction, fantasy, plays, newspapers, science fiction, traditional or classical literature, poetry, trade books, and biographies) to teach about science topics. Many science investigations make use of the arts: painting, sketching, drawing, collages, sculpture, drama, role-playing, pantomime, charades, skits, movies, puppets and improvisation, musical, songs, instruments, and jingles. Integrating mathematics into science allows students to use computation, measurement, ratios and proportion, graphing, and geometry in their investigations. For example, students studying the question "Where does all the garbage go?" will study science concepts such as decomposition and pollution. However, the question does not fit neatly into the school subject of science. The question flows over to social studies because it involves laws, regulations, ethics, value judgments, and decisions. Mathematics comes into play when the shear amount of garbage is mathematically extrapolated for every human on earth over the next few years at present rates. Language, reading, and communication are used to find information, debate issues, discuss possible solutions to our garbage problem, and communicate findings.

When students engage in investigations in project-based science, they use many skills that cross the curriculum. For example, they ask questions, look for relationships, organize procedures, consider multiple factors, take notes, use reference materials, record data, summarize information, interpret data, formulate conclusions, and communicate results. These skills are also used in other subject areas such as mathematics, language arts, and social studies.

Project-based science emphasizes communities of learners collaborating together. Such collaboration allows students to integrate understandings from a variety of careers and subject areas. For example, students investigating the topic of insects might interact with an entomologist from a local university to learn about biological research on insects, cultural norms regarding insects, and mathematical models associated with insect population control.

Use of technology is an integral component of project-based science. Technology is rarely separated along subject area lines. Software programs frequently include digital photographs, sound, and music, for example. Many provide students with opportunities to read and write. Some include mathematics concepts and social studies concepts. For example, a popular software program called *Great Ocean Rescue* (Tom Synder Productions, 1992, 1994) integrates the sciences and tackles social issues related to oceans such as pollution and coral reef destruc-

tion. The Web is not separated into subject areas; topics are organized as they are in the real-world around themes. For example, if you were to conduct a search on acid rain, you would uncover a host of subjects: coal mining, air pollution laws, industrial regulations, sulfur in coal, and mutations in frogs.

As students create artifacts, they use all types of knowledge and skills from other subject areas such as music, art, mathematics, and language arts. Students might develop posters on an issue or make models from recycled materials. They might write songs, write reports of their results, or give oral presentations. Students might mix written work, sound, video, and graphics in hypermedia artifacts.

A Word of Warning

Lonning and DeFranco (1997) argue that integration can be justified only when connecting subjects enhances the understanding of them. In other words, teachers should not force integration for the sake of integration. Driving questions in project-based science should be feasible (students should be able to design and perform investigations to answer the questions), worthwhile (they should contain rich content, relate to what scientists and professionals really do, and be able to be broken down into smaller questions), contextualized (they should be real world, nontrivial, and important), meaningful (they should be interesting and exciting to learners), and sustainable (students should be able to pursue detailed answers to them over time). These types of questions will allow you to integrate curriculum in a meaningful way.

Another way to judge the worth of curriculum integration is to use the rubric in Table 9.5 which lists standards of the *National Science Education Standards* (NRC, 1996), the National Council for the Social Studies (NCSS, 1994), the National Council of Teachers of English/International Reading Association (1996), and the National Council of Teachers of Mathematics (1989).

Example of Curriculum Integration

If students are investigating the question "What kinds of insects live in our neighborhood?" there are many opportunities for them to integrate

---

TABLE 9.5 Rubric for Evaluating Integrated Curriculum*

Project Topic: _____

Rating scale   4 = strong   3 = adequate   2 = weak   1 = no evidence

National Standards in Science are followed (for grades 5–8):

4 3 2 1   ◆ The activities support unifying concepts and processes (systems, order, and organization; evidence, models, and explanation; constancy, change, and measurement; evolution and equilibrium; and form and function).

4 3 2 1   ◆ The activities support scientific inquiry (abilities to do scientific inquiry and understand scientific inquiry).

4 3 2 1   ◆ Activities develop understanding in physical science (properties and changes of properties in matter; motions and forces; and transfer of energy), life science (structure and function in living systems; reproduction and heredity; regulation and behavior; populations and ecosystems; diversity and adaptations of organisms), and/or earth-space science (structure of the earth system; earth's history; and earth in the solar system).

4 3 2 1   ◆ Activities connect science with technology (students have understandings about science and technology, and they have abilities of technological design).

4 3 2 1   ◆ Science is presented as it relates to personal and societal perspectives (personal health; populations, resources, and environments; natural hazards; risks and benefits; and science and technology in society).

4 3 2 1   ◆ The history and nature of science are presented to students (science as a human endeavor, nature of science, and history of science).

National Standards in Mathematics are followed:

4 3 2 1   ◆ The activities support mathematical communications.

4 3 2 1   ◆ The activities support mathematical connections.

4 3 2 1   ◆ The activities support mathematical problem solving.

4 3 2 1   ◆ The activities support mathematical reasoning.

National Standards in Language Arts/Reading are followed:

4 3 2 1   ◆ Students have opportunities to read a variety of print and nonprint materials.

4 3 2 1   ◆ Students are able to write for a variety of purposes.

4 3 2 1   ◆ Students are able to adjust their spoken language for a variety of audiences.

4 3 2 1   ◆ Students use the language arts—reading, writing, listening, and speaking—to nurture their learning through research.

National Standards in Social Studies are followed:

4 3 2 1   ◆ The activities provide for the study of culture and cultural diversity.

4 3 2 1   ◆ The activities provide for the study of time, continuity, and change.

4 3 2 1   ◆ The activities provide for the study of people, places, and environments.

4 3 2 1   ◆ The activities provide for the study of individual development and identity.

4 3 2 1   ◆ The activities provide for the study of individuals, groups, and institutions.

4 3 2 1   ◆ The activities provide for the study of power, authority, and governance.

4 3 2 1   ◆ The activities provide for the study of production, distribution, and consumption.

4 3 2 1   ◆ The activities provide for the study of science, technology, and society.

4 3 2 1   ◆ The activities provide for the study of global connections.

4 3 2 1   ◆ The activities provide for the study of civic ideas and practices.

Lessons include connections across the curriculum:

4 3 2 1   ◆ The lessons integrate science, mathematics, social studies, and/or language arts.

4 3 2 1   ◆ The learning of concepts and skills is enhanced because of the connections made across the curriculum.

4 3 2 1   ◆ The unit allows students to see one subject from the viewpoint of another subject (multiple perspectives).

* This rubric is modified from various professional standards (NRC, 1996; NCSS, 1994; NCTE-IRA, 1996; & NCTM, 1989). It was used in an Eisenhower Professional Development Grant entitled PRISM-CLASS (Project for Integrating Science and Mathematics Curriculum with Language Arts and Social Studies) at the University of Toledo.

the curriculum. In science, students can study camouflage, metamorphosis, classification, body structure, and predator/prey relationships.

Mathematics can come into play in several ways. Students might investigate the area of an insect's territory. They might graph the number of insects found in different areas of the playground or graph the weight of the insects during different stages of development. They might use ratio and proportion to contrast the weight of an ant with the mass it can carry. Students might calculate the length of tunnels that ants build. They might explore the geometric shapes found in nature's insect populations or find the average number of days it takes for insects to complete metamorphosis.

Social studies are involved when students learn about the historical impact of insects (such as locusts) and the research and development of insecticides to limit insect populations. Students might study the cultural behaviors (such as eating insects) of people in other countries.

Language arts are involved when students write reports, communicate findings, give each other feedback, and read and discuss insect-related stories. What follows are some stories that could be used in an insect project science-language arts activity:

Livo, L. J., G. McGlathery, and N. J. Livo. 1995. *Of Bugs and Beasts*. Englewood, Colo.: Teacher Ideas Press.

Carle, E. 1969. *The Very Hungry Caterpillar*. New York: Philomel Books.

Ryder, J. 1989. *Where Butterflies Grow*. New York: Lodestar Books, E. P. Dutton.

Concept Mapping to Plan Integrated Projects

In Chapter 8, we discussed the idea of integrating various disciplines and how it impacts the structure of a school day. In Chapter 6, we explored the use of concept mapping in planning a lesson. Earlier in this chapter, we again discussed concept maps as a way to identify and organize important concepts in a project. Concept mapping can also be used to organize the integration of a project across the curriculum. A teacher in a *self-contained classroom* (with one group of students all day) can use concept mapping to develop lessons across subject areas. Teachers in *departmentalized* (separated by subject area) schools can plan together to integrate a theme or topic across their disciplines. Frequently, intermediate and middle schools (usually grades 4–8) purposely place teachers in teams so that they can plan integrated lessons together. Regardless of how you plan integrated lessons, you will find that the approach provides an exciting way to teach science that is consistent with current reform efforts in science education. Figure 9.6 is a sample concept map for the integration of science with language arts, reading, mathematics, and social studies in our insect project. Activity 9.12 asks you to integrate the project you have developed with other disciplines.

SUMMARY OF CHAPTER

Planning is a critical aspect of developing a project environment. This chapter focused on several steps that teachers typically take to plan a project-based curriculum. Throughout the chapter we developed an insect project. First, we selected concepts and curriculum objectives. We used local, state, and national standards to help us identify the concepts and curriculum objectives. We used concept mapping to organize the concepts.

Next, we discussed ways that teachers can develop a driving question, benchmark lessons, investigations, assessments, and a calendar of activities. Because the process for developing a project is iterative, we considered a model in which these steps operate as a back-and-forth process.

Resources are important in any project. We examined some ways to locate commercial, noncommercial, household, and community resources.

A project-based environment naturally supports curriculum integration. We discussed the reasons for this support. Once again, we used concept mapping as a planning tool for integrating the curriculum.

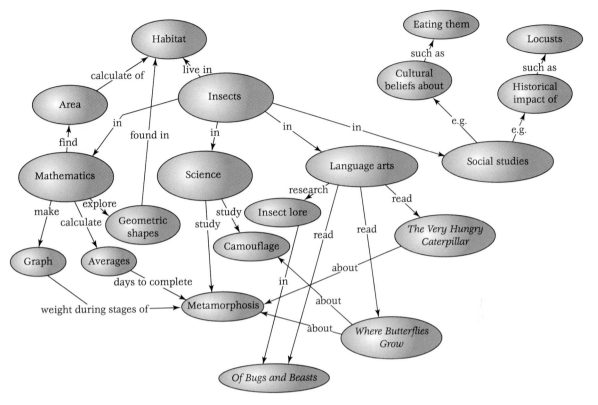

FIGURE 9.6
Concept map for science integration.

ACTIVITY 9.12

Developing Integrated Curriculum

MATERIALS NEEDED:
- the National Council of Teachers of Mathematics (1989) standards
- the National Research Center (1996) science standards
- the International Reading Association (1996) standards
- the National Council of Teachers of English (1996) standards
- the National Council of Social Studies (1992) standards

A. Using the project you have been developing throughout this chapter, compare and contrast the science concepts and skills that need to be covered with important content in the NCTM, NRC, IRA, NCTE, and NCSS standards.

B. What reading, language arts, mathematics, and social studies content might be covered in this project?

C. To the concept map you developed earlier add integrated reading, language arts, social studies, and mathematics content. You might also add art, music, and drama content to your map.

D. Outline several lesson ideas that can be integrated with mathematics, social studies, reading, and language arts.

E. File your revised concept map and lesson ideas in your portfolio.

TABLE 9.6   Resources for Materials Needed in an Elementary or Middle Grades Science Classroom

				Source				
Item	Drug-store	Hardware store	Grocery store	Commercial supplier	Non-commercial supplier	Pet store	Craft store	Toy store
Alcohol—rubbing	X		X	X				
Aluminum foil			X	X				
Aluminum pans		X	X	X			X	
Ammonia		X	X	X				
Aquariums/fish supplies			X	X		X		
Baking soda			X	X				
Balances—pan				X				
Balances/scales				X				
Balances—triple beam				X				
Ball and ring heating apparatus				X				
Ball bearings		X		X			X	
Balloons	X		X	X			X	X
Battery clips				X				
Bell wire		X		X				
Benedict's solution				X				
Bimetal strip heating apparatus					X			
Bleach			X	X				
Bones—sets of animals				X				
Bulb holders (small)				X				
Bulbs—flashlight size	X	X	X	X				
Bulbs—household size		X		X			X	
Bulb socket holders				X				
Candles	X		X	X			X	
Cellophane			X	X			X	
Cheesecloth	X	X	X	X			X	
Clothespins		X	X	X			X	
Compass		X		X				
Construction paper			X	X		X	X	
Convex and concave lenses				X				
Copper wire		X		X				
Corks		X		X			X	
Cornstarch			X	X				
Cotton balls	X		X	X			X	
Cotton swabs	X		X	X			X	
Cover slips for microscope slides				X				
Cups			X	X			X	
Diffraction gratings				X				
Dissecting kits and trays				X				
Dropping bottles				X				X
Dry cells (1.5 volt)		X	X	X				
Dry cells (12 volt)		X	X	X				
Electrical switches		X		X				
Electric motors		X		X				
Electronic scale				X				
Elmer's glue		X	X	X			X	
Eyedroppers	X		X	X				
Eye wash				X				
Feathers				X			X	
Filter paper			X	X				
Fire blanket				X	X			
Fire box				X	X			
Fishing line		X		X				
Fishing weights		X		X				

TABLE 9.6 Resources for Materials Needed in an Elementary or Middle Grades Science Classroom—*Continued*

				Source				
Item	Drug-store	Hardware store	Grocery store	Commercial supplier	Non-commercial supplier	Pet store	Craft store	Toy store
Flashlights		X	X	X				
Flour			X					
Food coloring			X	X				
Forceps				X				
Friction boards				X				
Fuses		X		X				
Gear kits				X				
Genecon hand generators				X				
Glassware				X	X			
Glue		X	X	X			X	
Goggles				X				
Graduated cylinders				X				
Gravel		X		X			X	
Hole punchers			X	X				
Hot plates		X		X				
Ice cream salt			X	X				
Incandescent lightbulbs	X	X	X	X				
Ink			X	X				
Iodine	X		X	X				
Iron filings				X				
Lab glassware drying rack				X				
Lamp sockets—household size		X	X	X				
Large poster paper				X			X	
Magnets—bar				X				
Magnets—circle				X				
Magnets—horseshoe				X				
Magnets—marble				X				
Magnet wire				X				
Magnifying lenses		X		X				
Marbles				X				X
Markers			X	X			X	
Masking tape			X	X			X	
Matches		X	X	X				
Metal rods—brass, copper, aluminum		X		X				
Meter sticks				X				
Microscopes				X				
Microscope—stereoscope				X				
Microscope slides—blank				X				
Microscope slides—prepared				X				
Mirrors (convex and concave)				X				
Mirrors (plane)		X		X			X	
Modeling clay				X			X	X
Motors				X				
Nails		X		X				
Netting		X		X			X	
Newsprint				X			X	
Owl pellets				X	X			
Paper clips				X			X	
Paper cups			X	X				
Paraffin			X	X			X	
Pencils			X	X			X	
Petri dishes				X				
Petroleum jelly	X		X	X				

TABLE 9.6   Resources for Materials Needed in an Elementary or Middle Grades Science Classroom—*Continued*

				Source				
Item	Drug-store	Hardware store	Grocery store	Commercial supplier	Non-commercial supplier	Pet store	Craft store	Toy store
Ping-Pong balls				X				X
Pipe cleaners				X			X	
Plastic aquariums with lids				X		X		
Plastic gloves		X	X	X				
Plaster of paris		X		X			X	
Plastic spoons			X	X				
Plastic storage tubs		X	X	X				
Poster board				X			X	
Potting soil		X		X				
Prism				X				
Pulleys		X		X				
Razor blades		X	X	X			X	
Rubberbands		X	X	X			X	
Rubber cement			X	X			X	
Rubber stoppers		X		X				
Rubber tubing		X		X				
Rulers		X	X	X				
Salt			X	X				
Sandpaper		X		X			X	
Scissors		X	X	X			X	
Soap—bar and liquid dish			X	X				
Spatulas			X	X				
Sponges	X	X	X	X			X	
Spoons—plastic and silverware			X	X				
Spring scales				X				
Steel wool		X		X				
Sterno can		X	X	X				
Stopwatch		X		X				
Storage bags (various sizes)		X	X	X				
Strainers			X	X				
Straws			X	X				
Straws—clear			X	X			X	
String		X		X			X	
Styrofoam cups		X	X	X				
Sugar			X	X				
Sulfur				X				
Surface boards (sandpaper, rubber, etc.)				X				
Tape—clear, 1″ wide			X	X		X		
Test tube holders				X				
Test tube racks				X				
Test tubes				X	X			
Thermometers		X		X				
Thread				X			X	
Toothpicks			X	X				
Tuning forks				X				
Vegetable oil				X				
Vinegar			X	X				
Wax			X	X				
Wax paper			X	X				
Weather instruments				X	X			
Wire—copper (insulated)		X		X				
Wire—copper (uninsulated)		X		X				
Wire—electrical, variety of gauges		X		X				

REFERENCES

Alexander, W. M., and P. S. George. 1981. *The exemplary middle school.* New York: Holt, Rinehart and Winston.

American Association for the Advancement of Science. 1993. *Benchmarks for science literacy.* New York: Oxford University Press.

Barnes, M. B., T. J. Shaw, and B. S. Spector. 1989. *How science is learned by adolescents and young adults.* Dubuque, Iowa: Kendall/Hunt.

Beane, J. 1996. On the shoulders of giants! The case for curriculum integration. *Middle School Journal* 28:6–11.

Beane, J. 1995. Curriculum integration and the disciplines of knowledge. *Phi Delta Kappan* 76:616–22.

Bradekamp, S. 1987. *Developmentally appropriate practice in early childhood programs serving children from birth through age 8.* Washington, D.C.: National Association for the Education of Young Children.

Braus, J., ed. 1989. *Ranger Rick's nature scope: Incredible insects.* Washington, D.C.: National Wildlife Federation.

Burnett, R. 1992. *The pillbug project: A guide to investigation.* Washington, D.C.: National Science Teachers Association.

Echols, J. C. 1993. *Ladybugs.* Berkeley, Calif.: Lawrence Hall of Science.

Echols, J. C. 1986. *Hide a butterfly.* Berkeley, Calif.: Lawrence Hall of Science.

Hurd, P. D. 1991. Why we must transform science education. *Educational Leadership* 49 (2):33–35.

Jacobs, H. H. J. 1989. *Interdisciplinary curriculum: Design and implementation.* Alexandria, Va.: Association for Supervision and Curriculum Development.

Lawrence Hall of Science. 1993. *Full option science system (FOSS).* Chicago, Ill.: Encyclopedia Britannica Educational Corporation.

Lederman, N. G., and M. L. Niess. 1997. Integrated, interdisciplinary, or thematic instruction? Is this a question or is it questionable semantics? *School Science and Mathematics* 97 (2):57–58.

Lonning, R. A., and T. C. DeFranco. 1997. Integration of science and mathematics: A theoretical model. *School Science and Mathematics* 97 (4):212–15.

National Council for the Social Studies. 1994. *Curriculum standards for social studies.* Washington, D.C.: Author.

National Council of Teachers of English/International Reading Association, (IRA) 1996; Standards for English Language Arts. Newark, DE: Author.

National Council of Teachers of Mathematics. 1989. *Curriculum and evaluation standards for school mathematics.* Reston, Va.: National Council of Teachers of Mathematics.

National Middle School Association. 1982. *This we believe.* Columbus, Ohio: Author.

National Research Council. 1996. *National science education standards.* Washington, D.C.: National Academy Press.

National Science Resources Center. 1994. *STC: Science and technology for children.* Washington, D.C.: National Academy of Sciences.

National Science Resources Center. 1992. *The life cycle of butterflies.* Burlington, N.C.: Carolina Biological.

Ohio Board of Education. 1994. *Science: Ohio's model competency-based program.* Columbus, Ohio: Author.

Rose, C., D. London, D. Young, G. Mucci, and M. Jay. 1998. *Curriculum orchestrator.* Bellingham, Wash.: MediaSeek Technologies, Inc.

Rutherford, J., and A. Ahlgren. 1989. *Science for all Americans: Project 2061.* New York: Oxford University Press.

Tom Snyder Productions. 1992, 1994. *The great ocean rescue.* Watertown, Mass.: Author.

Tuomi, J. Fall, 1993. *Effective materials for science instruction. NSRC Newsletter.* Washington, D.C.: National Science Resources Center.

Wiles, J., and J. Bondi. 1981. *The essential middle school.* Columbus, Ohio: Merrill.

WHAT ARE THE NEXT STEPS?

INTRODUCTION

What challenges will you face when you first implement project-based science? What are the benefits of project-based science? How will you improve your science teaching? What did you learn as you read this book? This chapter summarizes features of project-based science and some of the benefits of this approach. Project-based science also presents challenges, so we will discuss ways to overcome a number of them. Since one way to overcome challenges is to continue your professional growth, we will examine some strategies for becoming a professional teacher who is a lifelong learner. The chapter concludes with an analysis of the portfolio you have kept as you have read this book. This will help you reflect on your beliefs and analyze what you learned.

SUMMARY OF PROJECT-BASED SCIENCE

Although teaching science to young students is a complex task, it is also very rewarding. As we have described, one of the most rewarding ways to teach science is a method known as *project-based science.* This approach engages young learners in exploring important and meaningful questions through a process of investigation and collaboration. Students ask questions, make predictions, design investigations, collect and analyze data, make products, and share ideas. As they explore, students learn fundamental science concepts and principles that they apply to their daily lives. Project-based science is an approach that can help all students, regardless of culture, race, or gender, engage in science learning.

As we have discussed throughout this book, project-based science has several fundamental features. The **driving question** serves to organize and drive instructional tasks and activities. Driving questions are meaningful and important to learners, and they are one vehicle for contextualizing the learning of science. As such, driving questions are critical to initiating, implementing, and sustaining inquiry. Driving questions need to be feasible, worthwhile, contextualized, meaningful, and sustainable.

To answer driving questions, students engage in **investigations.** The process of carrying out an investigation is known as the **investigation web.** Children need to be supported in the process of doing investigations. They find solutions to questions by messing about with ideas, asking and refining questions, finding information, planning and designing, building apparatus, collecting data, analyzing data, making conclusions, and communicating findings.

As we discussed, learning occurs in a social context and children can learn from more knowledgeable others, including peers, than they could on their own. Project-based science involves students, teachers, and members of a community collaborating to investigate questions. **Collaboration** involves sharing ideas to find resolutions to questions. Collaboration helps to build learning communities in which students express ideas, debate the viability of evidence, and come to a resolution on ideas, concepts, and theories.

Technology, when used as a tool, can support science teaching and learning. In a project-based science environment, students can use technology to investigate, develop artifacts or products, collaborate, and access information. Students use technology to access current data on the Web, expand interaction and collaboration with others via networks (such as e-mail), use tools to gather data (such as temperature and pH probes), employ graphing and visualization tools to analyze data, and produce multimedia products.

Assessment is a critical component of teaching and learning. In a project environment, students create various **artifacts,** or products, that address the driving question and show what they have learned. Often, teachers have students share their artifacts with other class members, teachers, parents, and members of the community. In project environments, students can create a range of artifacts, from posters to multimedia documents.

Another critical component of teaching and learning, especially in a project-based classroom, is **scaffolding.** This is a process in which a more knowledgeable individual provides support to other learners. We modeled scaffolding by providing numerous diagrams, figures, and tables to give you suggestions on how to support children in project-based science.

Because children frequently lack the knowledge or skills required to investigate a question for any length of time, the teacher needs to introduce **benchmark lessons.** Benchmark lessons are teacher-directed classroom activities that present concepts, principles, or skills necessary for students to understand the work of a project. Benchmark lessons may include demonstrations, discussions, role-play, presentations of information, concept mapping, field trips, and the use of literature. Benchmark lessons help students learn difficult concepts, illustrate laboratory techniques, build new inquiry abilities, model thinking, and stimulate curiosity.

Managing a project-based science classroom creates many unique challenges. To be successful, a teacher needs to create a learning environment of trust and self-responsibility. Establishing a positive learning environment is essential to the success of project-based teaching. Fortunately, a variety of management skills can be used to help create this positive learning environment. For example, teachers can set expectations for acceptable student behavior, distribute materials and supplies in a manner that reduces classroom disruptions, and keep students accountable to classroom norms.

Finally, planning is key to the success of any curriculum. In planning, teachers must decide on concepts and curriculum objectives and carry out steps to develop a project (develop a driving question, present benchmark lessons, lead investigations, conduct assessments, and generate a calendar of activities). Teachers need to be cognizant of criteria for selecting and obtaining good resources for a project environment. Resources need to be relevant to students' daily lives, worthwhile, and actively engage students in inquiry. Planning for integration across the curriculum is also important so that students see connections between science and other subject areas.

BENEFITS OF PROJECT-BASED SCIENCE

Teaching is hard work. Nevertheless, you will find many benefits from running a project-based classroom.

First, because your students are pursuing solutions to important and meaningful questions, you too will find the work interesting and motivating. Your teaching will vary each year since you will be exploring new projects with each new group of students. Even within a project, students are exploring several subquestions, making daily lessons novel and varied. Finally, because students are interested in and excited about the questions they are investigating, you will find teaching a pleasurable experience.

Often, as your students pursue answers to questions, they explore interesting content. A second benefit of teaching in a project-based manner is that you continually learn new ideas about how the world works. This makes you a lifelong learner.

A third benefit of project-based science is that classroom management is facilitated. Because students are interested and motivated, discipline problems are minimized. This doesn't mean that you don't need good classroom management skills. As we discussed in Chapter 8, good classroom management is essential. However, when students are interested and their minds are active, they are less likely to cause discipline problems. The best way to manage classrooms is to keep children intellectually engaged in the work.

A fourth benefit of teaching in a project-based classroom is that your teaching and student learning will match the reform efforts in science

FIGURE 10.1
Even at a very young age, children in a project-based science classroom learn to work together.

ACTIVITY 10.1

Benefits of Project-Based Science

MATERIALS NEEDED:
* pencil and paper

A. Of the eight benefits of project-based science listed, which are the most important to you. Why?

B. What additional benefits do you see for project-based teaching?

C. Share your ideas with a classmate. How are your ideas similar or different?

D. Record your ideas in your portfolio.

---

education including *The National Science Education Standards* (National Research Council, 1996), *Project 2061: Science for All Americans* (Rutherford & Ahlgren, 1989), *Benchmarks for Science Literacy* (AAAS, 1993), and the National Science Teachers Association recommendations for elementary science (NSTA, 1991). For example, the National Research Council (1996) argues that "there needs to be new emphasis placed on inquiry-based learning focusing on having students develop a deep understanding of science embedded in the everyday world." Many states have structured their objectives and high stakes tests to correspond with these national standards. For example, many state tests now ask students to make conclusions from data, write responses to situations, and demonstrate skills on performance-based components.

A fifth benefit is that, through engaging in project-based science, learners develop deep, integrated understanding of content and process. Learners build meaningful relationships with and connections between ideas that they can use to understand their world. Students also learn the process of science, which can be used to solve problems in a variety of contexts. For example, students can apply the ability to ask good questions, plan and design investigations, and make conclusions to everyday problems.

A sixth benefit of project-based science is that students learn to work together to solve problems. In order to be successful in the real world, students need to know how to work with people from different backgrounds. Collaborative skills such as being able to listen to others, debate ideas respectfully, and share ideas are abilities that can be used in many contexts at all ages. Moreover, these are important abilities that employers seek in order to create a productive workforce.

A seventh benefit is that project-based science promotes responsibility and independent learning. As students come up with their questions and design investigations, they learn to take responsibility for their own learning. In an investigation, students learn to find information from a variety of different sources, follow through on data collection procedures, and take responsibility for gathering necessary materials. Teachers also encourage students to engage in self-evaluation strategies, such as assessing progress in their portfolios, which encourages reflection and self-improvement. Collaboration encourages both group and individual accountability.

An eighth benefit of project-based science is that it is sensitive to the needs of a diverse group of students. Project-based science meets the needs of male and female students of varied cultures, races, and academic abilities by focusing on issues and questions important in their lives. Because project-based science actively engages students in different types of tasks, it meets the varied learning needs of many different students. Multidimensional assessment techniques allow students to demonstrate their understandings in a variety of formats, formats that work for them. Collaboration teaches students to work together despite their differences—in fact, project-based science puts these differences to work. In Activity 10.1 you will further explore the benefits of project-based science.

CHALLENGES

Often, elementary and middle school teachers face a number of challenges when implementing project-based science for the first time. In previous chapters, we discussed some challenges of implementing project-based science and some strategies for dealing with these challenges. For example, obtaining resources is a challenge. Some of the strategies for dealing with this challenge are to use free and inexpensive materials such as 2-liter soda bottles and to find a local company or university that is willing to donate equipment. Another challenge is to get students to debate ideas. One strategy for dealing with this challenge is to build collaborative skills such as trust-building and communication. Conflict management strategies are also helpful.

Additional challenges not addressed in this book might confront you. For example, sometimes you may feel that your science background is not strong enough and you might feel uncomfortable with the subject matter involved. You may feel uncomfortable helping your students carry out an investigation if you have never carried one out yourself. Although these are critical issues, there are a number of positive steps that can be taken to overcome these situations. Next we will discuss a number of challenges—teachers' content knowledge and knowledge of the process of science, limited student experience, lack of time, and real or perceived external pressures. We will consider a number of recommendations for meeting these challenges. However, don't expect to meet all potential challenges your first year of teaching in a project environment. Teaching is lifelong learning. Even after twenty years of teaching, you will still wrestle with how to improve many aspects of your teaching, each year showing more improvement. Any ideas we consider here are just a start. You will need to continue your professional development throughout your career. For this reason, we will also discuss strategies for continuing professional development.

Teacher Discomfort with Content Knowledge

Numerous reports claim that teachers' lack of content knowledge limits the teaching of science at the K–8 level (Weiss, 1978, 1987). Certainly, teachers need to understand what they are teaching, and feeling uncomfortable with content is a major reason that science is cut out of the curriculum. Although you might feel a little shaky during your first attempts to teach science, as we all did, there are ways to increase your science knowledge and increase your comfort level with science.

First, scientific knowledge expands daily. Neither you nor anyone can know everything. The authors of this book have on many occasions had the experience of students asking questions to which the authors did not know the answers. It is okay to answer, "I don't know," and then to model how to find the answer. Showing your students that you are interested in learning more and how to learn is more important than demonstrating that you know everything. Demonstrate to students how you can use reference books, the Web, and local experts to find answers to questions.

Second, like your students, use each project to learn more about a science topic and about engaging in the process of science. If you take this approach, you will gradually become more comfortable with science content. This gradual, "learn as you go" approach is less intimidating than trying to learn a great deal of new information at one time.

Third, develop the habit of reading science magazines and books. Reading is a wonderful way to learn. Magazines such as *Science Scope* and *Science and Children,* published by the National Science Teachers Association, and *Nature Scope,* published by the National Wildlife Federation, are excellent, nonthreatening choices. Often, the articles in them give additional sources of reading materials. Also, develop your own personal library of books. For instance, *The PillBug Project* by Robin Burnett will give you some good background knowledge of pillbugs as well as a sense of how to carry out investigations. Finally, the National Science Foundation distributes a number of books that you will find valuable both for your learning and your classroom teaching. Table 10.1 gives the addresses of several professional organizations that publish journals.

Fourth, attending science classes, workshops, and local, regional, and national science conferences will help you learn new science content. Local school districts, a local university, a local environmental group, or a state organization may offer some workshops. You will find these types of classes and conferences extremely valuable; you will not only get new ideas for teaching and learn some science, but also meet

TABLE 10.1   Professional Science Education Organizations

Name of organization	Mailing address	E-mail address	Focus
National Science Teachers Association	1840 Wilson Blvd. Arlington, VA 22201-3000 703-243-7100	http://www.nsta.org	Science education at all ages
School Science and Mathematics Association	Department of Curriculum and Foundations Bloomsburg University 400 East Second Street Bloomsburg, PA 17815-1301	http://www.ssma.org	Science and mathematics education; integration of science and mathematics
AIMS Education Foundation	1595 S. Chestnut Ave. Fresno, CA 93702 209-255-4094 Fax: 209-255-6396	http://www.aimsedu.org	Activities for integration of science and mathematics at the elementary level
American Association of Physics Teachers	AAPT Membership Dept. One Physics Ellipse College Park, MD 20740 Fax: 301-209-0845	http://www.aapt.org	Physical science teaching and learning
Chemical Educational Foundation	1525 Wilson Blvd. Suite 750 Arlington, VA 22209 703-527-6223 Fax: 703-527-7747	http://www.chemed.org	Chemistry education
National Association of Biology Teachers	11250 Roger Bacon Drive 19 Reston, VA 20190-5202 703-471-1134 800-406-0775 Fax: 703-435-5582	http://www.nabt.org	Biology teaching and learning
Geological Society of America	P.O. Box 9140 Boulder, CO 80301-9140 303-447-2020 Fax: 303-447-1133	http://www.geosociety.org	Geology and geology education
National Association for Research in Science Teaching	Executive Secretary 1929 Kenny Road Room 200E The Ohio State University Columbus, OH 43210	http://science.coe.uwf.edu/ NARST/NARST.html	Research in science teaching and learning

others who are as interested as you are in improving teaching and learning. (We will discuss more thoroughly how to join professional organizations in the section on professional development.) Once you join a professional development organization, you will receive in the mail information about workshops and conferences.

Fifth, community members and parents can be guest speakers who provide science content expertise. You and your students can learn valuable science knowledge when guest speakers come to your class. For example, if your class is carrying out a project on water quality and some of your students want to perform chemical tests that you don't understand, there is likely to be a parent or other community member who would be very willing to volunteer time to talk with your class and help with a demonstration.

Sixth, the World Wide Web is a valuable source of science information. Although you might have to do a little digging, you will find that the Web is filled with a number of very useful pages that help you and your students learn content. For instance, the Great Lakes Information Network (http://www.great-lakes.net/) provides a wealth of information about the Great Lakes region and its economy, environment, tourism, news, events, and weather. Volcano World (http://volcano.und.nodak.edu/) contains all the information you could want about all aspects of volcanoes. You can even send a question to a volcanologist via the Web site. Finally, The National Science Foundation (http://www.nsf.gov) offers many on-line documents with up-to-date science information.

Teacher Discomfort with the Process of Science

Many of us have performed cookbook activities, following steps to complete science-related tasks, but these are not investigations. Unfortunately, few of us have had experiences conducting investigations. Like content knowledge, lack of experience and understanding of how to carry out investigations can inhibit your ability and willingness to help students engage in the process of investigation. The best way to learn how to carry out an investigation is to do it—ask questions, make observations, manipulate variables, and analyze data. If you take an active role in your students' projects, you will soon develop a level of comfort. Similar to activities in everyday life, like baking a cake, you don't become good at it unless you do it.

Belonging to professional organizations also will help you become comfortable with the process of science. At conferences, speakers present sessions that focus on inquiry. These presentations can help you learn how to support students in the process of investigations. Further, at conferences expert teachers frequently model inquiry activities they use with their own students, and you may be able to talk with these teachers after such sessions.

Another very valuable mechanism to improve your teaching is observation of an expert teacher carrying out an investigation with his or her class. Notice how a knowledgeable teacher supports students in the process of inquiry. Discuss the lesson with the teacher after class to learn the reasons behind the approach.

It is perhaps more important to invite an expert teacher in to observe and critique your teaching. This will be difficult to do at first. We all are hesitant to invite others to critique us, but commentary from an experienced teacher can be very valuable. If you can establish a long-term, mentor arrangement with an expert teacher, you will profit even more. Another way

to get feedback on your teaching is to videotape it. You can show the videotape to a colleague or critique it yourself. How are you supporting students? In what ways are you promoting understanding of science?

The Web also provides opportunities for teachers and students to learn more about the process of science. For example, the Center for Highly Interactive Computing in Education (http://hi-ce.eecs.umich.edu) provides information about projects that students in the Ann Arbor and Detroit areas are investigating. Lab-Net (http://www.netlab.org:8888/) allows students, teachers, and professionals to interact in a virtual environment to gain information about scientific investigations. Resources like these can help you learn more about the process of science and help you build confidence-building relationships with others who are conducting investigations.

Finally, field trips and internships in science settings can help you learn about the process of science as it is actually carried out in the real world. Field trips to governmental and commercial research laboratories, local university science laboratories, and medical hospitals can provide valuable insight into the process of science. Sometimes these institutions offer summer paid or volunteer internships in the laboratories.

Limited Student Experience

Carrying out an investigation is difficult cognitive work. You are challenging your students with such activities. Many students see the purpose of school as learning content knowledge. As students advance through grade levels, they become more regimented in their learning. Many develop good strategies for memorizing information, and they may resist new ways of learning that require them to think in more cognitively challenging ways. Although memorizing is an important learning strategy, finding information, analyzing data, making plans, carrying out investigations, developing concept maps, and making products that synthesize understanding cannot be done through memorization.

Children will sometimes ask, "Why can't we just read from the book?" or "Why can't we just answer the questions at the end of the chapter?" These children have likely learned strategies that require very little effort: They read from

FIGURE 10.2
Children play on a structure they created as part of a class project on simple machines.

the book, look for reading cues (such as bold-print words, topic sentences, or summary sentences), and easily identify the answers to questions at the end of the chapter. Although reading for information is a central component of project-based science, it can be easier for some students to find answers at the end of a chapter than develop a design for an investigation.

You can take several positive measures to overcome this resistance to learning in a more active manner. First, make your expectations clear to your class. Stress to children that, although they may have done activities differently in other years, this is the way your classroom works.

Second, explain to children that they are working the way scientists work. Scientists find information, ask questions, analyze data, and collaborate with others. Explain that just reading and finding answers distorts what science is all about. Science is about inquiry, and that is what students will do in your class. Interactions

with scientists in the community will reinforce this spirit of inquiry.

Third, point out to your students how the work they are doing in class helps find solutions to real problems and issues. Most children, especially pre- and young adolescents, have a strong desire to engage in meaningful activities.

Fourth, encourage students to take risks to ask questions and plan designs, even if they don't work. Young inquirers will go down a number of wrong paths, as do real scientists, and students need to know this.

Lack of Time

Having students learn science through inquiry takes time. There is no way around this. It will take your time and it will take classroom time. We are interested in creating useful science knowledge, knowledge that students will retain, and investigations and projects, as time-consuming as they are, foster such knowledge. The *National Science Education Standards* (NRC, 1996, p. 219) suggest that time is a major resource that must be allotted in the school day. A few suggestions for finding time in the day to teach science is described below.

Often there are downtimes during an investigation—while the plants are growing, material is decomposing, or metal is rusting. Science teachers should use these downtimes productively, slipping benchmark lessons into them. For example, while plants are growing, the class could be learning how to take measurements of plant growth using rules or calipers. These downtimes are also periods in which elementary teachers can teach lessons in other subject areas.

Another way to make maximal use of time is to integrate the curriculum. In Chapter 9, we discussed how project-based science supports curriculum integration. Curriculum integration can be a time-saving device, because it allows many academic objectives to be reached at once. For example, curriculum integration would blend the following objectives into a project designed to answer "Where does all of our garbage go?": (1) students will be able to discern why people make laws (in social studies, students could learn why recycling laws were created in their state); (2) students will be able to discern fact from opinion (in reading, students could debate whether it is a fact or an opinion that recycling should be mandatory in your city); and (3) students will be able to find the volume of a container (in mathematics, students can calculate the amount of garbage that fills a trash dumpster outside of the school building during a week's time). Coordinating subject areas to save time is also suggested in the *National Science Education Standards* (NRC, 1996, p. 214).

One common complaint is how time-consuming it is to set up investigations and clean up after them. Don't deny your students the opportunity to learn through inquiry because of these problems. One solution is to assign class jobs. Some teachers have students help pass out materials at the beginning of class, and they save five minutes or so at the end of every class session by having the entire class help clean up. Teachers of young elementary students frequently rely on the help of volunteer parents or older students in the school.

Another technique that has worked for many schools is block scheduling (creating longer class periods of time such as ninety-minute blocks instead of forty-five–minute segments) or flexible scheduling, which creates extended time periods for students to work on the projects. Since much class time is devoted to setting up and cleaning up project work, longer work periods save the time of setting up and cleaning up for numerous shorter periods. In an elementary school where you teach several subjects, it will be easier for you to build in extended periods of time to work on projects.

At the middle school level, where subject matter classes are forty-five to fifty-five minutes long, it is harder to accomplish this. You might take a proactive approach, as some teachers have, to lead efforts to shift your school to a block schedule. In block scheduling, classes meet for double periods for two or three days each. If your students move from class to class as a group, which is common in middle schools, you might also arrange to trade classes with a teacher who teaches in the time slot before or after you so that you can have a longer period of time for a science investigation.

Real or Perceived External Pressures

Because project-based science is built around meaningful, hands-on science investigations

that extend over time, it can create tension between breadth (superficial coverage of many topics and objectives) and depth (extensive coverage of a few topics). Meaningful, in-depth learning of limited but question-relevant content is preferable to superficial surveys of a wide body of content, which is the approach of most science survey texts. Doing science is more important than being exposed to a wide body of meaningless science content that is frequently forgotten. This position is supported by the Third International Mathematics and Science Study (TIMSS, 1997, 1998) which suggests that students would learn more if the curriculum covered fewer topics in a more in-depth manner. Engaging learners in investigations is now strongly supported by a number of prominent national organizations like the National Research Council (1996) and the American Association for the Advancement of Science (1993). These organizations have taken strong "less is more" stances and advocate sustained, project-oriented science teaching. A number of local school districts and state education agencies are becoming more sensitive to these new ideas in education and are beginning to stress cognitive strategies, such as planning and analyzing data, on state examinations.

Unfortunately, curriculum in the United States has, for many years, taken the breadth approach, and it has only been in the last few years that educators have been moving toward covering fewer subjects in a school year. As a result, many principals, parents, and school board members are more familiar with learning science the old way, reading about numerous topics in a textbook, than they are with learning a few science topics in-depth through long-term inquiry. This difference in viewpoint can cause problems for a teacher trying to implement a project-based approach.

Parents, administrators, colleagues, and even the janitor may question what you are doing. This is only natural, since you are doing something new. To counteract this questioning, take positive steps.

First, gain the support of administrators and colleagues. Talk to your principal and administrators about how you plan to do science, and explain the project-based science approach. You might share a copy of the *National Education Standards* (NRC, 1996) with them to show them how this approach is supported in national reform

ACTIVITY 10.2

Your Challenges

MATERIALS NEEDED:
+ paper and pencil

A. Of the challenges listed, which one is the most critical for you to overcome? Why?

B. What other challenges do you think you experience as you implement project-based science?

C. How might you resolve these challenges?

D. Work with a few colleagues. What are their suggestions for resolving these challenges?

E. File these ideas in your portfolio.

efforts. Extend an open invitation to your principal to visit your class. Share with your colleagues your methods of teaching science, and invite them into your classroom as well.

Second, hold a science open house to inform parents and members of the community of your science practices. Create a school or class newsletter that includes information about your science class, write information sheets to parents about specific projects students are working on, and extend open invitations to parents to visit your class. Some teachers have even videotaped their teaching and shared it with parents to illustrate how the approach motivates students to learn and how the teaching objectives match state-mandated tests or curriculum standards. You could also lend a copy of *Every Child a Scientist: Achieving Literacy for All* to parents. This is a useful resource for parents, showing them how they can help implement science standards. It is available from the National Research Council and can be ordered by calling 1-800-624-6242 or 202-334-3313, or it can be ordered on-line at http://www.nap.edu/bookstore. Teachers who have used these techniques have found them to be very successful.

Third, you need to inform people in your school community of your teaching approach and educate them about the importance of in-depth coverage of topics through long-term inquiry. Several resources can help you educate others about your position. First, the *National Science Education Standards* (NRC, 1996) support project-based science. This book can be ordered from the National Academy Press, 2101 Constitution Ave., NW, Box 285, Washington, DC, 1-800-624-6242 or 202-334-3313. Information about the *National Science Education Standards* can also be found on-line at http://www.nap.edu. Other excellent resources that can be used to educate others about effective science teaching are the National Science Teach-

ers Association position papers. Position papers are available on a number of topics such as the use of computers, elementary science, multicultural science education, research in science education, and parent involvement in science education. These position papers are available on-line at http://www.nsta.org. The National Eisenhower Clearinghouse (http://www.enc.org/) contains a wealth of information including interesting articles, standards frameworks, findings from educational research, and information about reform efforts. Finally, the National Association for Research in Science Teaching (NARST) publishes a series of pamphlets entitled *What Research Says to the Science Teacher* that can be obtained by writing to NARST, Executive Secretary, 1929 Kenny Road, Room 200E, The Ohio State University, Columbus, OH 43210. These papers provide useful information about a variety of topics such as gender equity in science, inquiry, and constructivism. Activity 10.2 asks you to further explore each of these challenges.

CONTINUING YOUR PROFESSIONAL GROWTH

Teaching presents challenges, but it also gives rewards. Perhaps one of the best rewards is becoming part of a community that cares about the learning of children. As a teacher, you will need to continue your professional growth by joining professional organizations, attending conferences, subscribing to journals, and getting information from the World Wide Web.

Joining Professional Organizations

Joining professional organizations is essential to being a professional, because it is one of the best ways to continue your development as a teacher. Joining national, state, and local organizations will allow you to build connections with other teachers who may have many of the same questions and issues that you do. These organizations, through their publications, conferences, newsletters, and Web sites, are also sources of information on content and instruction. They can also inform you about national policy and upcoming events.

At the national level, join the National Science Teachers Association (NSTA), which focuses on teaching science to children at all levels. Many states have science education organizations affiliated with NSTA. You can find out about them by contacting NSTA. State Departments of Education employ science consultants who are good sources of information about professional organizations in your state. If you live in a large urban area, there may be local science teacher organizations that you can join. If your school district has a curriculum director, this person should be knowledgeable about local organizations. Principals and other school administrators are also helpful sources of information. Table 10.1 lists national organizations you may want to join.

Attending Conferences

Membership in professional organizations like those listed in Table 10.1 will give you opportunities to attend their conferences. Conferences are exciting because they connect you with other educators. In the process, you get to learn about what others are doing in their teaching. You can also see presentations by nationally known scientists and educators. At most conferences, you can attend the exhibit hall where you can see some of the newest commercially available materials. Free materials are often distributed at these conferences. As you become comfortable in your own teaching, you might want to share some of your project ideas with others by presenting at professional conferences yourself. Many teachers find it more comfortable to first present at local or state conferences to gain more experience and confidence.

Subscribing to Publications

Many professional organizations also have associated publications. For example, NSTA has a number of important publications including *Science and Children* (for elementary teachers) and *Science Scope* (for middle grade teachers). These publications are filled with articles written by educators, science teaching ideas, information about science education reform, reviews of curriculum materials and software, and conference information. State and local organizations usually publish newsletters with helpful teaching hints and important local information. Table 10.2 lists the publications associated with each organization.

Using the World Wide Web

As we have discussed throughout this book, the World Wide Web can be used as a source of both content and instructional resources. It also can serve as a source of professional development, because it is filled with numerous sites that can give you helpful information regarding various education topics. For example, the National Eisenhower Clearinghouse contains information about science and mathematics reform, research findings in education, and curriculum materials. Table 10.3 lists the Web addresses of several organizations that can provide you with information that will help you continue your professional development.

INQUIRY INTO YOUR TEACHING

One of the best ways to improve your teaching is to reflect on and to engage in inquiry about your own teaching. In this book, you have often been asked to reflect on your beliefs and past experiences. You can continue to use **reflection** throughout your professional career to improve your teaching. This book has also stressed the importance of inquiry to learn about the world. You can use a form of inquiry, called **action research,** to learn about your own teaching.

Reflection can be defined as a voluntary effort to share and critique ideas about teaching, assess one's teaching and students' learning, formulate aims and goals about the curriculum through collaboration, and take responsibility for actions and the consequences of actions (Baird, 1992; Barnes, 1992; Putnam & Grant, 1992). The *National Science Education Standards* (NRC, 1996) promotes reflective practices in science education: "Teachers

TABLE 10.2   Professional Publications

Name of organization	Mailing address	E-mail address	Title of journal
The National Science Teachers Association	1840 Wilson Blvd. Arlington, VA 22201-3000 703-243-7100	http://www.nsta.org	*Science and Children* *Science Scope* *Science Teacher*
School Science and Mathematics Association	Department of Curriculum and Foundations Bloomsburg University 400 East Second Street Bloomsburg, PA 17815-1301 Fax: 717-389-3615	http://www.ssma.org	*School Science and Mathematics*
National Association for the Education of Young Children	1509 16th Street, NW Washington, DC 20036	http://www.naeyc.org	*Young Children*
National Middle School Association	2600 Corporate Exchange Dr., 370 Columbus, OH 43231 1-800-528-NMSA	http://www.nmsa.org	*Middle School Journal* *Middle Ground*
Association for Supervision and Curriculum Development	1250 N. Pitt Street Alexandria, VA 22314-1453 1-800-933-ASCD Fax: 703-299-8631	http://www.ascd.org	*Educational Leadership*
Phi Delta Kappa	408 N. Union P.O. Box 789 Bloomington, IN 47402	http://www.pdkintl.org/kappan/kappan/htm	*Kappan*

TABLE 10.3   Useful Science Professional Development WWW Addresses

Name	E-mail address	Focus
The National Science Teachers Association	http://www.nsta.org	Science teaching and learning at all ages
National Eisenhower Clearinghouse	http://www.enc.org	Information about science and mathematics education
The National Science Foundation	http://www.nsf.gov	Science research and funding
National Center for Educational Statistics	http://nces.ed.gov/timss/	Findings from the Third International Science and Mathematics Study
The American Association for the Advancement of Science	http://www.aaas.org	Advancement of Science; publisher of *Science for All Americans* and *Benchmarks for Scientific Literacy*
National Academy of Science	http://www.nas.edu http://www.nap.edu	Advice on scientific issues; author of the *National Science Education Standards*

of science engage in ongoing assessment of their teaching and of student learning. In doing this, teachers use student data, observations of teaching, and interactions with colleagues to reflect on and improve teaching practice" (p. 37).

Action research, like the inquiry process described, involves asking questions, making plans, carrying out the plans, and analyzing and making use of what was learned. The process is similar to the investigation web described in Chapter 5. The main difference is that action research is not for the purpose of generating findings to share with others but to generate information to put into practice in your own teaching. For example, a teacher might want to investigate whether collaborative learning increases motivation among students in her class. She would make a plan to answer this question, carry out an investigation, and analyze whether collaboration changed motivation levels. Dick Arends (1994) in his book, *Learning to Teach*, provides great detail about inquiry into and reflection on one's own teaching.

The following strategies are part of reflection and action research:

- **Keep a journal.** Keeping a journal and taking notes of what works and doesn't work is one form of action research. For example, you might want to keep notes on the types of driving questions that students seem to find meaningful. What types of questions do children seem to be interested in?

- **Videotape your teaching.** Another way you can examine your own teaching is to videotape your teaching. Many people dislike seeing themselves on videotape, but videotaping your teaching and then analyzing the tape is an excellent way of improving your teaching. Like athletes who watch videotapes of themselves constantly to learn how they can maximize their performance, teachers can maximize their teaching by analyzing videotapes of their teaching. Keeping a record also can show how you change over time.

- **Collaborate with colleagues.** Colleagues can be excellent sources of help for reflection and action research. They can serve as mentors who can provide helpful suggestions to improve your teaching, and they can be good role models. Visiting the classrooms of others can provide you with new ideas and practical suggestions for improving your teaching. Letting others critique your teaching by visiting your classroom or watching you on videotape can provide you with valuable insight, insight that you might not have on your own.

- **Have students fill out questionnaires.** Many teachers ask their students to fill out questionnaires about their teaching. These questionnaires can be simple open-ended statements like, "The thing I liked most about this lesson was . . ." or "One thing I would change about this project is . . . ." Questionnaires can also be simple scales: "The acid rain project was 1 (excellent), 2 (good), 3 (satisfactory), 4 (bad)." Teachers of younger students oftentimes use "smile faces" on their questionnaires—students circle a picture of a smile, a neutral face, or a frowning face next to pictures or statements like, "Using growing plants, a magnifying glass, and recording our results."

Looking back at what we have done can also lead to improvements in teaching. In Activity 10.3, you will reexamine some of your initial ideas about teaching and learning.

In Activity 10.4, you will examine the items you put in your portfolio to help you summarize what you learned as you read this book.

SUMMARY OF CHAPTER

This book has presented a new approach to teaching elementary and middle school science, an approach called *project-based science*. We started this last chapter by reviewing the key features of project-based science and considering some of the benefits of this approach. This approach can present a number of challenges for the teacher. Some teachers are not comfortable with the science content knowledge necessary to carry out projects. Some do not know how to conduct an investigation with students. Time is always a problem in teaching, but it can be a bigger problem for teachers who are trying to carry out long-term investigations. Finally, because using a project-based

ACTIVITY 10.3

Revisiting Initial Ideas in Your Portfolio

MATERIALS NEEDED:
- your portfolio

A. In Activity 1.5, you identified your science teaching goals. Have these goals changed since you completed this activity? How so?

B. Examine your response to Activity 1.4. How have your beliefs about why children should learn science changed since the beginning of this book?

C. Throughout this book, you have encountered a number of ideas about teaching science to children. Examine your beliefs now about these ideas.
- What are your beliefs about the role of investigations now? How have they changed since before you read the book?
- What are your views on collaboration? Have they changed? How? What will you do differently in your classroom in the future?

- What were your views about covering basic science content and skills before reading this book? Have they changed? How will this affect your teaching?
- What were your views about assessment before reading this book? Have your views changed? How will this affect your teaching in the future?
- What were your beliefs about classroom management before reading this book? Have they changed? How so? How will they affect your teaching in the future?
- What did you think about curriculum integration prior to reading this book? Explain your beliefs now. How will your teaching be affected?

D. How has this book informed your teaching practices? What will you try to change? What will you keep about your current teaching?

E. Record your thoughts in your portfolio.

ACTIVITY 10.4

Reexamining Your Portfolio

MATERIALS NEEDED:
- your portfolio

A. Go back to Activity 1.7. Have your top three or four driving questions about teaching elementary or middle grade science been answered by this book? How so? What questions remain unanswered? How might you resolve them?

B. Go back to Activity 7.9. What items have you included in your portfolio? Why have you included these specific artifacts? How do they show what you have learned?

approach may be new to parents, colleagues, administrators, and community members, this approach may be met with resistance. These real or perceived pressures can affect a teacher who is trying to implement this new teaching approach.

In this chapter, we discussed these challenges and ways to overcome them. One way to become a better teacher who can implement a project approach is to continue your professional development. We discussed several ways to do this: join professional organizations, attend conferences, read professional publications, and access information on the Web. Finally, we examined the notion of inquiry into your teaching and reexamined your portfolio.

We hope you will continue to grow as a teacher, and we wish you luck as you begin using a project approach in your teaching.

REFERENCES

American Association for the Advancement of Science. 1993. *Benchmarks for science literacy.* New York: Oxford University Press.

Arends, R. 1994. *Learning to teach.* New York: McGraw-Hill, Inc.

Baird, J. R. 1992. Collaborative reflection, systematic inquiry, better teaching. In *Teachers and Teaching from Classroom to Reflection,* ed. T. Russell and H. Munby. Bristol, Penn.: The Falmer Press.

Barnes, D. 1992. The significance of teachers' frames for teaching. In *Teachers and Teaching from Classroom to Reflection,* ed. T. Russell and H. Munby. Bristol, Penn.: The Falmer Press.

National Research Council. 1996. *National science education standards.* Washington, D.C.: National Academy of Sciences.

National Science Teachers Association. 1991. An NSTA position statement: Elementary school science. Washington, D.C.: Author. http://www.nsta.org/.

Putnam, J., and S. S. Grant. 1992. Reflective practice in the multiple perspective program at Michigan State University. In *Reflective Teacher Education Cases and Critiques,* ed. L. Valli. New York: State University of New York Press.

Rutherford, J., and A. Ahlgren. 1989. *Science for all Americans: Project 2061.* New York: Oxford University Press.

Third International Mathematics and Science Study. 1998. http://nces.ed.gov/TIMSS/.

Third International Mathematics and Science Study. 1997. http://nces.ed.gov/TIMSS/.

Weiss, I. 1987. *1985–86 national survey of science and mathematics education.* Research Triangle Park, N.C.: Research Triangle Institute.

Weiss, I. 1978. *Report of the 1977 national survey on science, mathematics, and social sciences.* Research Triangle Park, N.C.: Center for Educational Research and Evaluation, Research Triangle Institute.

CREDITS

Photos

Photo Research by Kim Moss

Chapter 1: *Opener:* Barbara Rios/Photo Researchers, Inc.; *Figure 1.1:* © Will & Deni McIntyre/Photo Researchers Inc.; *Figure 1.2:* © Richard Nowitz/Photo Researchers.

Chapter 2: *Opener:* © Hale Zucker/Stock Boston; *Figure 2.4:* © Gabe Palmer/Stock Market; *Figure 2.6:* © Ed Bock/Stock Market.

Chapter 3: *Opener:* © Bob Kramer/Stock Boston; *Figure 3.1:* © Bill Bachman/Photo Researchers, Inc.; *Figure 3.3:* © Erika Stone/Photo Researchers, Inc.

Chapter 4: *Opener:* © Will & Deni McIntyre/Photo Researchers Inc.; *Figure 4.3:* © Richard T. Nowitz/Photo Researchers, Inc.; *Figure 4.11:* © Elizabeth Crews/Stock Boston.

Chapter 5: *Opener:* © Elizabeth Crews/Stock Boston; *Figure 5.1:* © Richard Hutchings/Photo Researchers, Inc.; *Figure 5.4:* © Barbara Rios/Photo Researchers, Inc.

Chapter 6: *Opener:* © Richard Hutchings/Photo Researchers, Inc.; *Figure 6.3:* © Elizabeth Crews/Stock Boston; *Figure 6.5:* © Ulrike Welsch/Photo Researchers, Inc.

Chapter 7: *Opener:* © Elizabeth Crews/Stock Boston; *Figure 7.1:* © Elizabeth Crews/Stock Boston; *Figure 7.4:* © Michael A. Dwyer/Stock Boston.

Chapter 8: *Opener:* © Bohdam Krynewych/Stock Boston; *Figures 8.1 & 8.3:* © Elizabeth Crews/Stock Boston.

Chapter 9: *Opener:* © Richard Hutchings/Photo Researchers, Inc.; *Figure 9.2:* © Will & Deni McIntyre/Photo Researchers Inc.; *Figure 9.6:* © Anestis Diakopoulos/Stock Boston.

Chapter 10: *Opener:* © Lawrence Migdale/Photo Researchers, Inc.; *Figure 10.1:* © Jean-Claude Lejune/Stock Boston; *Figure 10.2:* © Spencer Grant/Photo Researchers, Inc.

Line Art and Text

Chapter 1: *Table 1.1:* Reprinted with permission from *Benchmarks for Science Literacy,* © 1993 The American Association for the Advancement of Science. New York: The Oxford Press.

Chapter 2: *Figure 2.3:* Talsma, V. L. (1998). Student's Scientific Understandings in a Project-Based Science Classroom. Doctoral Dissertation, University of Michigan, Ann Arbor, MI; *Figure 2.5:* Figure from AUDIO-VISUAL METHODS IN TEACHING, Third Edition by Edgar Dale, copyright © 1969 by Holt, Rinehart and Winston, reproduced by permission of the publisher.

Chapter 4: *p. 102:* Reprinted with permission from Ann Novak; *Figure 4.12:* Reprinted with permission from Jonathan Ellis and Alex McEachern.

Chapter 6: *Figure 6.4:* Adapted with permission from BSCS, 1992.

Chapter 7: *p. 225:* Reprinted with permission from Jodi Haney and Andrew Lumpe.

Chapter 8: *p. 258:* Reprinted with permission from SCIENCE, vol. 126, p. 387. 1957 American Association for the Advancement of Science. *Table 8.9:* "Planning Safe Lessons" from Dean, R., Dean, M. M., Gerlovich, J. A., & Spiglanin, V. (1993). Safety in the elementary science classroom. Washington, DC: National Science Teachers Association.

Chapter 9: *Table 9.6, various sections:* Reprinted with permission from the National Council of Teachers of Mathematics; Reprinted with permission from the National Council of Teachers of English; Reprinted from *Expectation of Excellence: Curriculum Standards for Social Studies* with permission from the National Council of Social Studies; Reprinted with permission of the National Academy Press.

INDEX

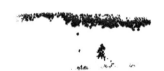